VICTORIAN POETS.

AMS PRESS
NEW YORK

VICTORIAN

POETS

REVISED, AND EXTENDED, BY A SUPPLEMENTARY
CHAPTER, TO THE FIFTIETH YEAR OF THE
PERIOD UNDER REVIEW

BY

EDMUND CLARENCE STEDMAN

AUTHOR OF " POETS OF AMERICA "

BOSTON AND NEW YORK
HOUGHTON, MIFFLIN AND COMPANY
The Riverside Press, Cambridge
1903

Library of Congress Cataloging in Publication Data

Stedman, Edmund Clarence, 1833-1908.
  Victorian poets.

    Reprint of the 1903 ed.
    CONTENTS: The period.--Walter Savage Landor.--Thomas
Hood. Matthew Arnold. Bryan Waller Procter.--[etc.]
    1. English poetry--19th century--History and criti-
cism. I. Title.
PR591.S8 1972   821'.8'09   78-148307
ISBN 0-404-06237-7

Reprinted from the edition of 1903, Boston and New York
First AMS edition published in 1972
Manufactured in the United States of America

AMS PRESS INC.
NEW YORK, N. Y.   10003

PREFACE TO THE THIRTEENTH EDITION.

(1887.)

———

THE origin of the book now presented in an enlarged form is given in the Preface to the edition of 1875. While it was an outgrowth, as stated, of a few essays each relating to a single personage, its main value, from the ultimate point of view, consisted first in the statement of what appear to me the true canons of imaginative art, as applied to the office of the poet ; again, in studies of the creative temperament derived from sympathetic examination of its possessors; and finally, in a record of the progress of song during a noteworthy period, and of phases reflecting the thought, passion, ideality, of the specified country and age.

Chapters VII and VIII, in which miscellaneous groups were considered, though written as an afterthought, and not possessing the artistic unity of other chapters, proved especially serviceable in the last-named capacity. My gain in comprehension of the general drift was greater than any fancied loss through deviation from an eclectic literary standard. They completed, moreover, the annals of the period, and gave my book a practical if secondary value as a work of reference.

Whether its early welcome at home and abroad, and the favor still vouchsafed to it, have been due to the quality of my argument, or to the need of such a record, or to both together, it is in view of this encouragement, and of the changes incident to the close of the typical Victorian epoch, that I add the supplemental matter which extends our survey to the present year.

This seems the more expedient, because in a later treatise, *Poets of America*, I have applied the same method of criticism, with similar objects in view, to the poets and poetry of my own land. The rise of true poetry here was singularly coincident with that of the Victorian school in Great Britain, and my home-survey applies to the fifty years now ending with the celebration of Her Majesty's prolonged reign. The *Victorian Poets*, as enlarged, and its companion-volume thus proffer a general view of the poetry of our English tongue for the last half-century. The supplement itself, beyond that portion devoted to the afterwork of veteran leaders, is necessarily compressed and inclusive : in other words, is written upon the plan of Chapters VII and VIII, to discover current tendencies and the outlook, and to enhance the reference-value of the entire work.

After a lapse of time which enables me to examine my original chapters almost as if they were the production of another hand, it would be strange if I did not observe certain portions that would be written differently, with later and perhaps riper judgment, if I were to write them now.

I see that frequent attention was paid to matters of art and form. Technical structure is of special interest to the young artist or critic. There was a marked and fascinating advance in rhythmical variety and finish during the early influence of Tennyson. I do not regret its discussion, since throughout the book persistent stress is also laid upon the higher offices of art as the expression of the soul, and its barrenness without simplicity, earnestness, native impulse, and imaginative power. The American treatise, less occupied with technical criticism, and examining its topic in connection with the formation of national sentiment, enabled me to finish all I desired to say concerning poetry. These books are hopefully addressed to those who will read the two together, and each of them not in fragments but as a whole.

As to the brief opinions with respect to younger singers, I think that a good deal of what was said has been justified, and in a few cases notably, by their subsequent careers. Examining the more elaborate reviews of other poets, I wish to amend in some degree my early criticism.

With the comments upon Landor, Hood, Mrs. Browning, Tennyson, Rossetti, Morris, and Swinburne, I have no serious disagreement. What is said of the last-named four, in the new text, is in keeping with what was first said, and illustrated by an account of their recent works.

I confess, however, that the prominence given to Procter seems hardly in accord with the just perspective of a synthetic view. It grew out of the writer's distaste for two characteristics of latter-day verse : on the one

hand, the doubt and sadness of that which is the most intellectual ; on the other, the artificial tone of that offered
by many younger poets, in whom the one thing needful
seemed to be the spontaneity so natural to " Barry Cornwall."

While I thought the first of these characteristics too excessive in the poetry of Arnold, the cultured master of his
school, I paid full tribute to the majesty of his epic verse.
But I was unjust in a scant appreciation of what is after
all his most ideal trait, and his surest warrant as a poet.
For this fault I now make reparation in the supplement.

One or two errors of fact have been corrected in the
original chapter on Browning, our most suggestive figure
at the close of a period which Tennyson dominated in its
prime. My feeling with respect to some of this profound
writer's idiosyncrasies is still unchanged. Yet in view of
my extended recognition of his matchless insight and resources, — and conscious of my own respect for the genius
and personality of one to whose works I was guided in
youth by kindred that knew and honored him, — it is hard
for me to understand that even his uncompromising wor-
shippers can discover between the lines of my criticism
traces of hostility. The chapter, however, is defective in
one important respect. Drawing a sharp distinction between the histrionic, objective method of the early dramatists and that of Browning, I did not at once follow it with
an incisive statement of the qualities in which his power
and effectiveness consist. A praiseworthy reader — by
which, as before, I mean one who accepts an essay in its

entirety, and does not hang his approval or disapproval upon a single point — can find these qualities plainly set forth in the comments upon Dramatic Lyrics, Men and Women, Pippa Passes, etc. But that there may be no doubt, and to make up for possible shortcomings, I have referred in the supplement at some length to the specific originality and nature of this poet's dramatic genius.

Beyond these modifications, I have none with which in this place to trouble the reader, — deprecating, as I do, finical changes in prose or poetry once given to the public, and choosing to let a treatise that has been so leniently judged stand in most respects as it was originally written.

A revision and extension has been made of dates, etc., in the marginal notes, and some pains taken to insure correctness. The new Analytical Index covers both divisions of the book. My thanks are again due to friends, especially to Messrs. R. H. Stoddard, R. W. Gilder, Brander Matthews, George R. Bishop, — and to Mr. William T. Peoples, of the N. Y. Mercantile Library, — for the use of various books which were not already upon my shelves, and which my London agents were unable to procure.

E. C. S.

New York, July, 1887.

TO

GEORGE RIPLEY, LL.D.,

WHOSE JUDGMENT, LEARNING, AND PROFESSIONAL DEVOTION
HAVE CONTRIBUTED TO THE

ADVANCEMENT OF CRITICISM,

AND FURNISHED AN ENVIABLE EXAMPLE TO MEN
OF LETTERS,

𝕿𝖍𝖎𝖘 𝖁𝖔𝖑𝖚𝖒𝖊 𝖎𝖘 𝕴𝖓𝖘𝖈𝖗𝖎𝖇𝖊𝖉.

PREFACE TO THE FIRST EDITION.

(1875.)

———◆———

THE contents of this volume chiefly relate to the design announced at the beginning of the introductory chapter, but I will prefix a brief statement of its scope, and of the principles that underlie its judgment. Although presented as a book of literary and biographical criticism, it also may be termed an historical review of the course of British poetry during the present reign, — if not a minute, at least a compact and logical, survey of the authors· and works that mainly demand attention. Having made a study of the poets who rank as leaders of the recent British choir, a sense of proportion induced me to enlarge the result, and to use it as the basis of a guide-book to the metrical literature of the time and country in which those poets have flourished. It seemed to me that, by including a sketch of minor groups and schools, and giving a connection to the whole, I might offer a work that would have practical value for uses of record and reference, in addition to whatever qualities, as an essay in philosophical criticism, it should be found to possess.

To this end Chapters VII. and VIII. were written ; side-notes have been affixed throughout the volume, and an analytical index prepared of the whole. There is much dispute among the best authorities with respect to literary and biographical dates, and a few matters of this sort remain open to doubt ; but in many instances, where the persons concerned are still living, I have been successful in obtaining the requisite information at first hand.

A reference to the notes and index will show what seems to my own mind, after the completion of these essays, their most conspicuous feature. So many and various qualities are displayed by the poets under review that, in writing of their works and lives, I have expressed incidentally such ideas concerning the aim and constituents of Poetry as I have gathered during my acquaintance with the historic body of English verse. Often, moreover, a leading author affords an illustration of some special phase of the poetic art and life. The case of Browning, for example, at once excites discussion as to the nature of poetic expression ; that of Mrs. Browning involves a study of the poetic temperament, its joys and sorrows, its growth, ripeness, and decline. Hood's life was that of a working man of letters ; in Tennyson's productions we observe every aspect of poetry as an art, and the best average representation of the modern time ; while Landor not only affords another study of temperament, but shows the benefits and dangers of culture, of amateurship, and of intellectual versatility as opposed to special gift. In Arnold we find a passion of the intellect, in Procter the pure lyrical faculty, in Buchanan the force and weakness of transcendentalism, in Swinburne the infinite variety of melodious numbers, and the farthest extreme of rhythm and diction reached at this stage of metrical art. Horne, Bailey, Lytton, Morris, and Rossetti are each suggestive of important and varying elements which make up the general quality of recent imaginative song. The different forms of poetry — reflective, idyllic, lyric, and dramatic — successively or in combination pass under review, for the modern era has been no less composite than refined. If not so eminent for poetic vigor as the impetuous Georgian revival which preceded it, nor characterized by dramatic greatness like that of the early and renowned Elizabethan age, it is in its own way as remarkable as either of those historic times, and on the score of complex and technical achievement full of real significance to the lyric artist and the connoisseur.

In pursuing the general subject by an examination of the foremost poets, I have tried to convey a just idea of the career and genius of each, so that any portrait, taken by itself, might seem complete, and distinct from its fellows. In certain cases we are required to observe temperament, — in others, extended lyrical achievements or unusual traits of voice and execution. If my criticism seems more technical than is usual in a work of this kind, it is due, I think, to the fact that the technical refinement of the period has been so marked as to demand full recognition and analysis It is seldom that an earnest reviewer, whether lay or professional, can escape wholly the charge of dogmatism. Doubtless every reader will discover points that neither accord with his judgment, nor seem to him fairly taken ; yet I trust that there will be few who will not elsewhere find reason to consider my work something better than labor thrown away.   After all, a critic speaks only for himself, and his opinion must be taken for what it is worth, — as being always open to the broader criticism of those to whom it is submitted.

The chapter on the relations of Tennyson and Theocritus, though somewhat in the nature of an excursus, relates to a matter which seems to me of more significance than the obligations of the modern idyllist to the ancient, — namely, the singular likeness of the Victorian period to the Alexandrian, manifest in both external conditions and poetic results.

Let me now say that this book is not the fulfilment of a deliberate plan, but that a peculiar train of thought and incident has led to its completion.   There are times when a writer pauses to consider the work produced by his associates, and the influences by which this has been enlarged or injured.   Reviewing the course of American poetry, since it may be said to have had a pathway of its own, I have tried to note the special restrictions and special advantages by which it has been affected.   Our men of true poetic genius, although they have produced charming verse of an emotional, lyrical, or descriptive kind, have seemed indisposed or unable to compose many sustained

and important works. At first I designed to write of the
difficulties which they have experienced, consciously or
unconsciously, — some of these pertaining to the youth of
the country, and to the fact that, as in the growth of a
sister-art, landscape-painting usually must precede the rise
of a true figure-school. I might touch upon the lack of
inspiring theme and historic halo, of dramatic contrast
and material, and of a public that can appreciate the
structure, no less than the sweetness and quality, of a noble
poem. With various exceptions, there has been a want
of just criticism ; and even now a defect with many of
the poets themselves is a cloudy understanding of their
true mission and of what poetry really is. Beyond the
charm of freshness, no great success in verse is attainable
without that judicial knowledge of the poet's art which
is the equivalent of what is indispensable to the painter,
the sculptor, and the musician, in their respective departments.

But with regard to the causes of the success and failure
of our own poets I easily perceived that some of the most
important were not special, but general : belonging to the
period, and equally affecting the verse of the motherland.
This led me to make a study of a few British poets : first
of one, Landor, whose metrical work did not seem, upon
the whole, a full expression of his unusual genius ; then
of others, notably Tennyson, who more obviously represent
the diverse elements of their time. In order to formulate
my own ideas of poetry and criticism, it seemed to me

that I could more freely and graciously begin by choosing a foreign paradigm than by entering upon the home-field, and that none could be so good for this purpose as the poetry of Great Britain, — there being none so comprehensive, and none with which myself and my readers are more familiar. Affection, reverence, national feeling, or some less worthy emotion, may be thought to prevent an American from writing without prejudice of Bryant, Longfellow, Whittier, Lowell, and the rest; doubtless there are considerations which sometimes render British journalists disinclined to review Tennyson and Browning with that indifferent spirit which characterizes their judgment of eminent American poets. Lastly, upon a survey of the last forty years, I saw that what I term the Victorian period is nearly at an end, and that no consecutive and synthetic examination of its schools and leaders had yet been made. This led me to go on and to complete the present work.

It follows that these essays are not written upon a theory. The author has no theory of poetry, and no particular school to uphold. I favor a generous eclecticism, or universalism, in Art, enjoying what is good, and believing that, as in Nature, the question is not whether this or that kind be the more excellent, but whether a work is excellent of its kind. Certain qualities, however, distinguish what is fine and lasting. The principles upon which I rely may be out of fashion just now, and not readily accepted. They are founded, nevertheless, in the Miltonic canon of poetry, from which simplicity no more can be excluded than sensuousness and passion. The spirit of criticism is intellectual; that of poetry (although our curiously reasoning generation often has forgotten it) is normally the offspring of emotion, — secondly, it may be, of thought. I find that the qualities upon which I have laid most stress, and which at once have opened the way to commendation, are simplicity and freshness, in work of all kinds; and, as the basis of persistent growth, and of greatness in a masterpiece, simplicity and spontaneity, refined by art, exalted by imagination, and sustained by intellectual power. Simplicity does not imply poverty of thought, — there is a strong simplicity belonging to an intellectual age; a clearness of thought and diction, natural to true poets, — whose genius is apt to be in direct ratio with their possession of this faculty, and inversely as their tendency to cloudiness, confusion of imagery, obscurity, or "hardness" of style. It may almost be said that everything really great is marked by simplicity. The poet's office is to reveal plainly the most delicate phases of wisdom, passion, and beauty. Even in the world of the ideal we must have clear imagination and language: the more life-like the dream, the longer it will be remembered.

The traits, therefore, which I have deprecated earnestly are in the first place obscurity and hardness, and these either natural, — implying defective voice and insight, or affected, — implying conceit and poor judgment; and sec-

ondly that excess of elaborate ornament, which places
decoration above construction, until the sense of originality is lost — if, indeed, it ever has existed. Both obscurity and super-ornamentation are used insensibly to
disguise the lack of imagination, just as a weak and
florid singer hides with trills and flourishes his inability
to strike a simple, pure note, or to change without a slid-
ing scale.

But among true poets of the recent schools some have
gone to the other extreme, putting the thought too far
above the art, and have neglected melody and finish altogether, as if despising accomplishments now so widely
diffused. This also is a fault common in an advanced
period, especially in one eminent for speculative and metaphysical research. I have not overlooked this heresy,
although steadfastly opposing meretricious efforts to attract
notice by grotesque, fantastic, and other artificial means.
If such methods prevail in an over-ripe country they should
not in our own, and I point to them as errors which
American poetry, as it gathers strength, should be able
easily to avoid. And thus seeing how poorly charlatanism
and effrontery can make up for patient, humble endeavor
and experience in art, we must discern and revere, on the
other hand, those gifts of inspiration which endow the
born poet, and without which no amount of toil and learning can insure the favor of the Muses. As to the latter
requirements, the instinct of the world, that would not
recognize Bulwer and still pays tribute to Burns, is almost

unerring ; as to the former, it often is for a while deceived ; so I have found occasion to write of dilettanteism, lack of apprenticeship, and of the assumption of those who would clutch the laurel "with a single bound." Finally, the intellectual activity of our time constantly demands a reviewer's notice ; and passion, rare in an idyllic period, must be sought out and welcomed at every visible turn.

The spirit of the following chapters has now been indicated. I have made few quotations, depending on the reader's means of acquaintance with the poetry of his time. In treating the abstract portion of my subject, where some generalization has seemed requisite, I have tried to state my meaning in brief and open terms. Much originality is not claimed for either manner or thought. My effort simply has been to illustrate, through analysis of the careers of various poets, what already is widely understood among philosophical critics. No single sketch has been colored to suit the author's ideas, but each poet has been judged upon his own merits ; yet I think the general effect to be as stated.

I trust that it may not prove a wholly thankless office, since it certainly is not one frequently undertaken, to write a purely critical volume, exclusively devoted to the literature of another land. Criticism, like science, latterly has found a more interested public than of old. The catholic reviewer will not shut his eyes to the value of new modes, but even that conventional criticism, which holds to accepted canons, has its use as a counterpoise to license and bewilderment. As to the choice of field :—while I would not reassert in behalf of any verdict, least of all in behalf of my own, that "a foreign nation is a kind cf contemporaneous posterity," it yet may be true that from this distance a reviewer can advantageously observe the general aspect of British poetry, whatever minor details may escape his eye.

In concluding this work, I wish to acknowledge my obligations to friends who have assisted me in its revision :— to Professor Roswell D. Hitchcock, D. D., for valuable hints concerning recent hymnology ; to Mr. Richard H. Stoddard, for access to his choice collection of English verse ; to Messrs. William J. Linton and George P. Philes, for important data relating to the recent minor poets ; and especially to Mr. Robert U. Johnson, of New York, and Mr. Henry H. Clark, of Cambridge, for careful and unstinted aid, at a time when, from prolonged illness, it was impossible for me to verify the statistical portion of my volume, or even to revise the proof-sheets as they came from the press.

E. C. S.

New York, July, 1875.

CONTENTS.

———◆———

VICTORIAN POETS.

VICTORIAN POETS.

———•———

CHAPTER I.

THE PERIOD.

I.

THE main purpose of this book is to examine the lives and productions of such British poets as have gained reputation within the last forty years. Incidentally, I hope to derive from the body of their verse, — so various in form and thought, — and from the record of their different experiences, correct ideas in respect to the aim and province of the art of Poetry, and not a few striking illustrations of the poetic life. *Design of the present work.*

In reviewing the works and careers of these singers, especially of the large number that may be classed as minor poets, we naturally shall be reminded of a process to which M. Taine has made emphatic reference in a history of previous English literature, and in his analysis of the one poet selected by him to represent the quality of recent song. This process is the insensible moulding of an author's life, genius, manner of expression, by the conditions of race, circumstance, and period, in which he is seen to be involved. *Taine's theory: that an author is governed by his period.*

But on the other hand, and chiefly in our recognition of the few master-spirits whose names, by common and just agreement, hold the first places upon the list under review, we shall observe with equal certainty that great *Genius, however, is, largely independent of place or time.*

poets overcome all restrictions, create their own styles, and even may determine the lyrical character of a period, or indicate that of one which is to succeed them.

Illustration of the former statement;

Among authors of less repute we therefore shall find more than one rare and attractive poet hampered by lack of fortune and opportunity, or by a failure to harmonize his genius with the spirit of his time. For example, several persons having the true dramatic feeling arose, but cannot be said to have flourished, during or just before the early portion of the era, and were overborne by the reflective, idyllic fashion which then began to prevail in English verse. These isolated singers — Taylor, Darley, Beddoes, Horne, and others like them — never exhibited the full measure of their natural gifts. The time was out of keeping; and why? Because it

and of the exceptions which confirm and modify it.

followed the lead, and listened to the more courageous voices of still greater poets, who introduced and kept in vogue a mode of feeling and expression to which the dramatic method is wholly antagonistic. These suc-

Cp. " Poets of America " : pp. 3, 12.

cessful leaders, no less sensitive than their rivals to the feeble and affected mood which poetry then had assumed, and equally familiar with the choicest models of every age and literature, were more wise in selecting the ground upon which the expression of their own genius and the tendencies of the period could be brought together. They persisted in their art, gathered new audiences, and fulfilled the mission for which they were endowed with voice, imagination, and the poet's creative desire. This surer instinct, this energy and success, this utterance lifted above opposing voices, are what have distinguished poets like Tennyson, the Brownings, Rossetti, Swinburne, from less fortunate aspirants whose memory is cherished tenderly by our united guild, but who failed to reach the popular heart or to make a significant impression upon the literature of their own time.

It is an open question, however, whether a poet need be conscious of the existence and bearing of the laws and conditions under which he produces his work. It may be a curb and detriment to his genius that he should trouble himself about them in the least. But this rests upon the character of his intellect and includes a further question of the effects of culture. Just here there is a difference between poetry and the cognate arts of expression, since the former has somewhat less to do with material processes and effects. The freedom of the minor sculptor's, painter's, or composer's genius is not checked, while its scope and precision are increased, by knowledge of the rules of his calling, and of their application in different regions and times. But in the case of the minor poet, excessive culture, and wide acquaintance with methods and masterpieces, often destroy spontaneity. They shut in the voice upon itself, and overpower and bewilder the singer, who forgets to utter his native, characteristic melody, awed by the chorus and symphony of the world's great songs. Full-throated, happy minstrels, like Béranger or Burns, need no knowledge of thoroughbass and the historical range of composition. Their expression is the carol of the child, the warble of the skylark scattering music at his own sweet will. Nevertheless, there is no strong imagination without vigorous intellect, and to its penetrative and reasoning faculty there comes a time when the laws which it has instinctively followed must be apparent ; and, later still, it cannot blind itself to the favoring or adverse influences of period and place. Should these forces be

Diverse effects of culture upon spontaneity.

Cp. " Poets of America": pp. 109, 135, 320, 342.

restrictive, their baffling effect will teach the poet to recognize and deplore them, and to endeavor, though with wind and tide against him, to make his progress noble and enduring.

In regard to the province of the critic there can, however, be no question. It is at once seen to be twofold. He must recognize and broadly observe the local, temporal, and generic conditions under which poetry is composed, or fail to render adequate judgment upon the genius of the composer. Yet there always are cases in which poetry fairly rises above the idealism of its day. The philosophical critic, then, in estimating the importance of an epoch, also must pay full consideration to the messages that it has received from poets of the higher rank, and must take into account the sovereign nature of a gift so independent and spontaneous that from ancient times men have united in looking upon it as a form of inspiration.

Cp. " Poets of America" : pp. 26, 223.

Aspects of the time under review.

As we trace the course of British poetry, — from a point somewhat earlier than the beginning of the present reign, down to the close of the third quarter of our century, — we observe that at the outset of this period the sentiment of the Byronic school had degenerated into sentimentalism, while for its passion there had been substituted the calm of reverie and introspective thought. Two kinds of verse were marked by growing excellence. The first was that of an art-school, taking its models from old English poetry and from the delicate classicism of Landor and Keats ; the second was of a didactic, yet elevated nature, and had the imaginative strain of Wordsworth for its loftiest exemplar. We see these two combining in that idyllic method which, upon the whole, has distinguished the recent time, and has maintained an atmosphere unfavorable to the revival of high passion and dramatic power. Nevertheless, and lastly, we observe that a new dramatic and lyric school has arisen under this adverse influence and brought its methods into vogue, obtaining the favor of a new generation, and therewith rounding to completion the poetic cycle which I have undertaken to review.

The evolution of the art-school, partly from classicism, partly from a renewal of early and natural English feeling, may be illustrated by a study of the life and relics of Landor: first, because Landor, while an intellectual poet, was among the most perfect of those who have excelled in the expression of objective beauty; again, because, although contemporary with Keats, his career was prolonged into the second half of our era, and thus was a portion of its origin, progress, and maturity. Throughout this time, as in other eras, various phases of metrical art have been displayed by authors who have maintained their independence of the dominant mode. Mrs. Browning wins our attention, as the first of woman-poets, endowed with the rarest order of that subjective faculty which is the special attribute of feminine genius. Hood, Arnold, and Procter may be selected as prominent representatives of the several kinds of feeling and rhythmical utterance that are noticeable in their verse. Elsewhere, as we look around, we soon begin to discover the influence of the eminent founder and master of the composite school. The method of Tennyson may be termed composite or idyllic: the former, as a process that embraces every variety of rhythm and technical effect; the latter, as essentially descriptive, and resorting to external portraiture instead of to those means by which characters are made unconsciously to depict themselves. Other-

Names which illustrate successive poetic phases.

Outline of a proposed critical survey.

wise, it is suggestive rather than plain-spoken, and greatly relies upon surrounding accessories for the fuller conveyance of its subtle thought. After some comparison of the laureate with the father of Greek idyllic verse, — pointing out, meanwhile, the significant likeness between the Alexandrian and Victorian eras, — I shall give attention to a number of those minor poets, from whose diverse yet blended rays we can most readily derive a general estimate of the time and its poetic tendency. These may be partially assorted in groups depending upon specific feeling or style ; but doubtless many single lights will be found scattered between such constellations, and each shining with his separate lustre and position. Finally, in recounting the growth of the new dramatic and romantic schools, under the leadership of Browning and Rossetti, we shall find their characteristics united in the verse of Swinburne, — in some respects the most notable of the poets who now, in the prime of their creative faculties, strive to maintain the historic beauty and eminence of England's song.

The conditions of the period.

Before entering upon a citation of the poets themselves, I wish to make what reference may be needful to the conditions of the period. Let us see wherein it has been marked by transition, how far it has been critical and didactic, to what extent poetical and creative. A moment's reflection will convince us that it has witnessed a change in the conditions bearing upon art, as important and radical as those changes, more quickly recognized, that have affected the whole tone of social order and philosophic thought. Our rhythmical expression originated in phenomenal language and imagery, an inheritance from the past ; modern poetry has struggled painfully, even heroically, to cast this off and adjust itself to a new revelation of the truth of things. The struggle is not yet ended, but continues, — and will continue, until the relations between imagination and knowledge shall be fairly harmonized upon a basis that will inure to the common glory of these twin servitors of every beautiful art.

II.

IT follows that, in any discussion of the recent era, *Modern* the scientific movement which has engrossed men's *iconoclasm.* thoughts, and so radically affected their spiritual and material lives, assumes an importance equal to that of all other forces combined. The time has been marked by a stress of scientific iconoclasm. Its bearing upon theology was long since perceived, and the so-called conflict of Science with Religion is now at full height. Its bearing upon poetry, through antagonism to the traditional basis of poetic diction, imagery, and thought, has been less distinctly stated. The stress has been vaguely felt by the poets themselves, but they are not given to formulating their sensations in the polemical manner of those trained logicians, the churchmen, — and the attitude of the latter has so occupied our regard that few have paused to consider the real cause of the technical excellence and spiritual barrenness common in the modern arts of letters and design. Yet it is impossible, when we once set about it, to *The rela-* look over the field of late English verse, and not, to *tions be-* *tween Poetry* see a question of the relations between Poetry and *and Science.* Science pressing for consideration at every turn and outpost.

Scientific iconoclasm is here mentioned simply as an existing force : not as one to be deplored, for I have

faith that it will in the end lead to new and fairer
manifestations of the immortal Muse. However irre-
pressible the conflict between accepted theologies and
the spirit of investigation, however numerous the traditions of faith that yield to the advances of knowledge,
No inherent there is no such inherent antagonism between science
antagonism. and poetry. In fact, the new light of truth is no more
at war with religious aspiration than with poetic feeling, but in either case with the ancient fables and
follies of expression which these sentiments respectively have cherished. A sense of this hostility has
oppressed, I say, the singers clinging to forms of
beauty, which long remain the dearest, because loved
the first. Their early instinct of resistance is manifest
in the following sonnet by a poet who saw only the
beginning of the new dispensation : —

An early   " Science ! true daughter of old Time thou art,
sonnet by   Who alterest all things with thy peering eyes.
E. A. Poe.   Why preyest thou thus upon the poet's heart,
                     Vulture, whose wings are dull realities ?
                 How should he love thee ? or how deem thee wise,
                 Who wouldst not leave him in his wandering
                     To seek for treasure in the jewelled skies,
                 Albeit he soared with an undaunted wing ?
                 Hast thou not dragged Diana from her car,
                     And driven the Hamadryad from the wood
                 To seek a shelter in some happier star ?
                     Hast thou not torn the Naiad from her flood,
                 The Elfin from the green grass, and from me
                 The summer dream beneath the tamarind-tree ? "

Had this youth lived to the present hour, he would
begin, I think, to discern that Poetry herself is struggling to be free from the old and to enter upon the
new, to cast off a weight of precedent and phenomenal imagery and avail herself of the more profound

suggestion and more resplendent beauty of discovered truth ; and he would not forbid her to light the flames of her imagination at the torch which Science carries with a strong and forward-beckoning hand.

While, therefore, there can be no irreconcilable warfare between poetry and science, we discover that a temporary struggle is under way, and has seriously embarrassed the poets of the era. Let us observe the operation of this contest, or, rather, of this enforced transition to the method of the future. *A temporary conflict.*

There are two ways of regarding natural objects : first, as they appear to the bodily eye and to the normal, untutored imagination ; second, as we know they actually are, — having sought out the truth of their phenomena, the laws which underlie their beauty or repulsiveness. The former, purely empirical, hitherto has been the simple and poetic function of art ; the latter is that of reason, scientifically and radically informed. The one is Homeric, the other Baconian. Up to Coleridge's time, therefore, his definition of poetry, that it is the antithesis of science, though not complete, was true as far as it extended. Let us see how the ideals of an imaginative, primitive race, differ from those of the children of knowledge, who make up our later generations. *The poetic and rational methods examined and compared.*

The most familiar example will be found the best. Look at the antique spirit as partially revived by a painter of the seventeenth century. The Aurora fresco in the Rospigliosi palace expresses the manner in which it once was perfectly natural to observe the perpetual, splendid phenomena of breaking day. Sunrise was the instant presence of joyous, effulgent deity. A pagan saw the morning as Guido has painted it. The Sun-God in very truth was urging on his fiery- *1. The poetic, or phenomenal mode.*

1 *

footed steeds. The clouds were his pathway; the early morning Hour was scattering in advance flowers of infinite prismatic hues, and her blooming, radiant sisters were floating in air around Apollo's chariot; the earth was roseate with celestial light; the blue sea laughed beyond. Swiftly ascending Heaven's archway the retinue swept on; all was real, exuberant life and gladness; the gods were thus in waiting upon humanity, and men were the progeny of the gods. The elements of the Hellenic idealism, so often cited, are

The antique spirit. readily understood. It appeared in the blithesome imagery of a race that felt the pulses of youth, with no dogmas of the past to thicken its current and few analytical speculations to perturb it. Youth, health, and simplicity of life brought men to accept and inform after their own longings the outward phenomena of natural things. Heaven lies about us in our infancy. I refer to the antique feeling (as I might to that of the pastoral Hebraic age), not as to the exponent of a period superior to our own, or comparable with it in knowledge, comfort, grasp of all that enhances the average of human welfare, but as that of a poetical era, charged with what has ever, until now, made the excellence of such times, — an era when gifted poets would find themselves in an atmosphere favoring the production of elevated poetry, and of poetry especially among the forms of art, since this has seemed more independent of aid from material science than the rest.

The mediæval spirit. But there are other types of the poetical age. Pass from the simple and harmonious ideals of classicism to the romantic Gothic era, whose genius was conglomerate of old and new, and the myths of many ages and countries, but still fancy-free, or subject only to a pretended science as crude and wanton as the

fancy itself; whose imagination was excited by chival-
rous codes of honor, brave achievement, and the recurrent chances and marvels of new discovery. Such, for
example, the Elizabethan period of our own literature;
such the great Italian period from which it drew its
forms. There was a certain largeness of mechanical
achievement, and a mass of theological inquiry, in the
time of Dante, Boccaccio, and Petrarch, and in that
of Tasso and Ariosto, but all subject to the influence
of superstition and romance. The world was only
half discovered; men's fancy was constantly on the
alert; nothing commonplace held the mind; even
the lives and ventures of merchants had a wealth of
mystery, strangeness, and speculation about them,
which might well make an Antonio and a Sebastian
the personages of Shakespeare's and Fletcher's plays.
Each part of the globe was a phantasmal or fairy land
to the inhabitants of other parts. A traveller was a
marked man. Somewhere in Asia was the Great Khan;
later, in America, were cities of Manoa paved with
gold. Nothing was extraordinary, or, rather, everything
was so. The people fed on the material of poetry,
and wove laurel-wreaths for those who made their
song.

Our own time, so eminently scientific, so devoted to *The modern*
investigation of universal truth, has found such wonders *spirit.*
in the laws of force and matter, that the poetic bearing
of their phenomena has seemed of transient worth;
enjoyment and excitation of the intellect through the
acquisition of knowledge are valued more and more.
Thinkers become unduly impressed with the relative
unimportance of man and his conceptions. Our first
knowledge of the amazing revelations of astronomy —
which I take as a most impressive type of the cognate

sciences — tends. to repress self-assertion, and to make one content with accepting quietly his little share of life and action. In earlier eras of this kind, discovery and invention occupied men's minds until, fully satiated, they longed for mental rest and a return to a play of heart and fancy. Too much wisdom seemed folly indeed; dance and song and pastoral romance resumed their sway; the harpers harped anew, and from the truer life and knowledge scientifically gained broke forth new blossoms of poetic art. But our own period has no exact prototype. It is advanced in civilization; but the time of Pericles, though also exhibiting a modern refinement, was one of scientific ignorance. There was, as we have seen, a mediæval spirit of scientific inquiry, but almost wholly guided by superstition. Even nature's laws were compelled to bow to church fanaticism; experiments were looked upon with distrust, or conducted in secrecy; and poetry, at least in respect to its cherished language and ideals, had no occasion to take alarm.

The realistic tendencies of the present time. But in the nineteenth century, science, freedom of thought, refinement, and material progress have moved along together. The modern student often has been so narrowed by his investigations as to be more unjust to the poet than the latter was of old to the philosopher. Art has seemed mere pastime and amusement, as once it seemed the devil's frippery and seduction to the ascetic soul of the Puritan, aglow with the gloomy or rapturous mysteries of his theology. Also by the multitude whom the practical results of science at last have thoroughly won over, — and who now are impelled by more than Roman ambition to girdle the earth with engineering and conquer the elements themselves, — neither the songsters nor the metaphysicians, but the physical investigators and men of action, are held to be the world's great men. The De Lesseps, Fields, Barings, and Vanderbilts, no less than Lyell, Darwin, and Agassiz, wear the bay-leaves of to-day. Religion and theology, also, are subjected to analysis and the universal tests, and at last the divine and the poet, traditionally at loggerheads, have a common bond of suffering, — a union of toleration or half-disguised contempt. Eating together at the side-tables, neither is adequately consoled by reflecting that the other is no more to be envied than himself. The poet's hold upon the youthful mind and sentimental popular emotion has also measurably relaxed ; for a learned professor, who has spoken of poetic expression as "sensual caterwauling," and possibly regards the gratification of the æsthetic perceptions as of little worth, grossly underrated his position when he said that, "at present, education is almost entirely devoted to the cultivation of the power of expression and of the sense of literary beauty." The truth is that our school-girls and spinsters wander down the lanes with Darwin, Huxley, and Spencer under their arms ; or if they carry Tennyson, Longfellow, and Morris, read them in the light of spectrum analysis, or test them by the economics of Mill and Bain. The very tendency of modern poetry to wreak its thoughts upon expression, of which Huxley so complains, naturally follows the iconoclastic overthrow of its cherished ideals, confining it to skilful utilization of the laws of form and melody. Ay, even the poets, with their intensely sympathetic natures, have caught the spirit of the age, and pronounce the verdict against themselves. One of them envies his early comrade, who forsook art to follow learning, and thus in age addresses him : —

Theology.

Huxley on "Scientific Education": "Appletons' Journal," Aug. 14, 1869.

*Whittier's
dedication of
"Miriam"
to President
Barnard.*

" Alike we loved
The muses' haunts, and all our fancies moved
To measures of old song.   How since that day
Our feet have parted from the path that lay
So fair before us !   Rich, from life-long search
Of truth, within thy Academic porch
Thou sittest now, lord of a realm of fact,
Thy servitors the sciences exact ;
Still listening, with thy hand on Nature's keys,
To hear the Samian's spheral harmonies
And rhythm of law. . . . .

.   .   .   .   .

And if perchance too late I linger where
The flowers have ceased to blow, and trees are bare,
Thou, wiser in thy choice, will scarcely blame
The friend who shields his folly with thy name."

*Surrender
of the poets.*

The more intellectual will confess to you that they weary less of a new essay by Proctor or Tyndall than of the latest admirable poem ; that, overpowered in the brilliant presence of scientific discovery, their own conceptions seem less dazzling.   A thirst for more facts grows upon them ; they throw aside their lyres and renew the fascinating study, forgetful that the inspiration of Plato, Shakespeare, and other poets of old, often foreshadowed the glory of these revelations, and neglecting to chant in turn the transcendent possibilities of eras yet to come.   Science, the modern Circe, beguiles them from their voyage to the Hesperides, and transforms them into her voiceless devotees.

Every period, however original and creative, has a transitional aspect in its relation to the years before and after.   In scientific iconoclasm, then, we have the most important of the symptoms which mark the recent era as a transition period, and presently shall observe features in the structure and composition of its poetry which justify us in thus ranking it.   The Victorian

poets have flourished in an equatorial region of common-sense and demonstrable knowledge. Thought has
outlived its childhood, yet has not reached a growth
from which experience and reason lead to visions
more radiant than the early intuitions. The zone of
youthful fancy, excited by unquestioning acceptance
of outward phenomena, is now well passed; the zone
of cultured imagination is still beyond us. At present,
skepticism, analysis, scientific conquest, realism, scornful unrest. Apollo has left the heavens. The modern
child knows more than the sage of antiquity.

To us the Sun is a material, flaming orb, around
which revolves this dark, inferior planet, obedient to
central and centrifugal forces. We know that no celestial flowers bestrew his apparent pathway; that all this
iridescence is but the refraction of white light through
the mists of the upper skies. Let me in advance dis-
avow regret for the present, or desire to recall the
past : I simply recognize a condition which was inevitable and in the order of growth to better things.
" Much of what we call sublime," said Landor, " is
only the residue of infancy, and the worst of it." I
cannot disbelieve the words of a latter-day writer, that,
" so far from being unfriendly to the poetic imagination, science will breathe into it a higher exaltation."
In my chapter on Tennyson I shall have occasion to
cite the language of Wordsworth, who, with prophetic
vision, depicted an era when the poet and the man
of science shall find their missions harmonious and
united. But the change is none the less severe, and
the period has been indeed trying for the votaries of
song. True, that already, in our glimmerings of the
source and motion of the " offspring of Heaven first-
born," in our partial knowledge of the meaning of

*2. The ra-
tional, or
scientific
mode.*

*Words-
worth's
Preface to
the second
edition of
his poems.*

appearances, we can use this meaning for the language and basis of poetical works ; but recent poets have had to contend with the fact that, while men are instructed out of the early phenomenal faith, their recognition of scientific truth has not yet become that *second nature* which can replace it. The poet of to-day, burdened with his new wisdom, represents the contemporary treatment when he says, —

> " There sinks the nebulous star we call the Sun,
> If that hypothesis of theirs be sound " ;

but it is by a prosaic effort that he recalls a fact at variance with the impression of his own childhood, subduing his fancy to his judgment and to the spirit of the time. Let myths go by, and it still remains that every child is a natural Ptolemaist, who must be educated to the Copernican system, and his untutored notions generally are as far from the truth with regard to other physical phenomena.

Embarrass-ment of the idealists. The characteristics of the middle portion of the nineteenth century have been so perplexing, that it is but natural the elder generation among us should exclaim, " Where is it now, the glory and the dream ? " While other arts must change and change, the pure office of poetry is ever to idealize and prophesy of the unknown ; and its lovers, forgetting that Nature is limitless in her works and transitions, mourn that — so much having been discovered, robbed of its glamour, and reduced to prosaic fact — the poet's ancient office is at last put by. Let them take fresh heart, recalling the Master's avowal that Nature's " book of secrecy " is infinite ; let them note what spiritual and material spheres are yet untrod ; rejoicing over the past rather than hopeless of future achievement, let them examine

with me the disenchanting process which has made
their own time a turbulent, unrestful interval of transition from that which was to that which shall be ; a
time when, more than his perpetual wont, the poet
looks " before and after, and pines for what is not."

As in chemical physics, first sublimation, then crys-
tallization, then the sure and firm-set earth beneath
our feet; so in human progress, first the ethereal fantasy of the poet, then discovery by experience and
induction, bringing us to what is deemed scientific,
prosaic knowledge of objects and their laws.   Thus in
the earlier periods, when poets composed empirically,
the rarest minds welcomed and honored their productions in the same spirit.   But now, if they work in this
way, as many are still fain, it must be for the tender
heart of women and the delight of youths, since the
fitter audience of thinkers, the most elevated and
eager spirits, no longer find sustenance in such empty
magician's food.   With regard to the so il of men and
things, they still give rein to fancy and empiricism,
for that is still unknown.   Hence the new phases of
psychical poetry, which formerly repelled the healthy-
minded by its morbid cast.   But touching material phenomena they no longer accept, even for its beauty, the
language of myth and tradition ; they *know* better ; the
glory may remain, but verily the dream has passed
away.

Progress, and its law.

A skeptical period may call forth heroic elements of
self-devotion ; criticism is endured and even courted,
and the vulnerable point of an inherited faith is surely
found.   Earnest minds sadly but manfully give up their
ancestral traditions, and refuse to seek repose in any
creed that cannot undergo the extreme test.   But an
age of distrust, however stoical and brave, rarely has

Features of an investi- gating pe- riod.

*Skepticism
unfriendly
to creative
art. Cp.
" Poets of
Amer-
ica " : p.
128.*
been favorable to high and creative art. Great productions usually have been adjusted to the formulas
of some national or world-wide faith, and its common
atmosphere pervades them. The Iliad is subject to
the Hellenic mythology, whose gods and heroes are
its projectors and sustainers. The Divine Comedy,
Paradise Lost, the most imaginative poems, the greatest dramas, — each, as it comes to mind, seems, like
the most renowned and glorious paintings, to have
been the product of an age of faith, however sharply
minor sects may have contended within the limits of
the general belief. The want of such a belief often
has led to undue realism, or to inertness on the part
of the best intellects, and in many other ways has
checked the creative impulse, the joyous ardor of the
visionary and poet.

*The real
and the
ideal.*
To make another statement of the old position of
art in relation to knowledge, we may say that until a
recent date the imagination, paradoxical as it may
seem, has been most heightened and sustained by the
contemplation of natural objects, *rather as they seem to
be* than as we know they are. For to the pure and
absorbed spirit it is the ideal only that seems real ;
as a lover adores the image and simulacrum of his
mistress, pictured to his inner consciousness, more than
the very self and substance of her being. Thus Keats,
the English apprentice, surrounded himself with all
Olympus's hierarchy, and breathed the freshness of
Thessalian forest-winds. But for an instance of perfect substitution of the seeming for the true, commend
me to the passion and rhapsody of Heine, who on the
last days of his outdoor life, blind to the loving sympathy of the actual men and women around him, falls
smitten and helpless at the feet of the Venus of Milo,

his loved ideal beauty, sees her looking upon him with
divine pity and yearning, and hears her words, spoken
only for his ear, " Dost thou not see that I have no
arms, and therefore cannot help thee?" The knowledge of unreality was present to his reason, but the
high poetic soul disdained it, and received such consolation as only poets know. So also Blake, that
sublime visionary, tells us : " I assert for myself that
I do not behold the outward creation, and that to me
it is hindrance and not action. 'What!' it will be
questioned, 'when the sun rises, do you not see a
disk of fire, somewhat like a guinea?' 'O no, no! I
see an innumerable company of the heavenly host,
crying, " Holy, holy, holy, is the Lord God Almighty!"
I question not my corporeal eye, any more than I
would question a window concerning a sight. I look
through it, and not with it.'"

There are passages in modern poetry that seem to
forebode the approaching harmony of Poetry and Science ; the essays of Tyndall and Spencer are, the
question of form left out, poems in themselves ; and
there are both philosophers and poets who feel that
no absolute antagonism can exist between them. Dr.
Adolphe Wurtz, in a paper before the French Association, declared that the mission of science is to struggle
against the unknown, while in letters it is enough to
give an expression, and in art a body, to the conceptions of the mind or the beauties of nature. To this
we may add that science kindles the imagination with
the new conceptions and new beauties which it has
wrested from the unknown, and thus becomes the
ally of poetry. The latter, in turn, is often the herald
of science, through what is termed the intuition of the
poet. Whether by means of some occult revelation,

*Approaching har-
mony of
Poetry and
Science.*

*Address on
" The Pro-
gress of
Chemistry,"
at Lille,
Aug. 20,
1874.*

Cp. " Poets of America": pp. 153-155, 262.

or by a feminine process of quick reasoning that approaches instinct, or, again, by his subtile power to " see into the life of things," the poet foretokens the discoveries of the man of science in the material world and concerning the laws of mind and being. A modern philosopher goes back to Lucretius for the basis of the latest theory of matter. Before the general acknowledgment of the vibratory transmission of light, and of the doctrine of the correlation of forces, Goethe made Mephistopheles avow that

Goethe.

> " Light, howe'er it weaves,
> Still, fettered, unto bodies cleaves :
> It flows from bodies, bodies beautifies ;
> By bodies is its course impeded."

Beddoes.

In " Death's Jest-Book," that weird tragedy composed by a poet who preceded Darwin, we find the idea of evolution carried to its full extreme : —

> " I have a bit of *Fiat* in my soul,
> And can myself create my little world.
> Had I been born a four-legged child, methinks
> I might have found the steps from dog to man,
> And crept into his nature."

The speaker then hints at the development of mind from inert matter, through the crystal, through the organic plant, and so on through successive grades of animal life culminating with the intellectual man. Even then he adds, —

> " Have patience but a little, and keep still,
> I'll find means, by and by, of flying higher."

Beddoes, it is true, was a learned investigator, and so was Goethe. But such poets, observing the merest germs of scientific discovery, foresee their ultimate possibilities, and thus suggest and anticipate the empirical confirmation of their truth. Finally, the poet must always have a separate and independent *The poet in* province, for the spirit of Nature is best revealed by *undisturbed possession of* an expression of her phenomena and not by analysis of *one domain.* her processes. Visible beauty exalts our emotions far more than a dissection of the wondrous and intricate system beneath it. The sight of a star or of a flower, or the story of a single noble action, touches our humanity more nearly than the greatest discovery or invention, and does the soul more good.

Poetry will not be able to fully avail herself of the *A complete* aid of Science, until her votaries shall cease to be *understanding not yet* dazed by the possession of a new sense. Our horizon *possible.* is now so extended that a thousand novel and sublime objects confuse us : we still have to become wonted to *Cp. " Poets* their aspects, proportions, distances, and relations to *of America ": pp.* one another. We are placed suddenly, as it were, in a *26, 27.* foreign world, whose spiritual significance is but dimly understood. At last a clearer vision and riper faith will come to us, and with them a fresh inspiration, expressing itself in new symbols, new imagery and beauty, suggested by the fuller truth. Awaiting this, it is our present office to see in what manner the quality of the intervening period has been impressed upon the living pages of its written song.

III.

WHILE in one sense the recent era, and with more *The recent* point than usual, may be called a transition period, it *period both transitiona* s found to possess, in no less degree than eras that *and crea-* have witnessed smaller changes, a character and his-*tive.* tory of its own. Such a period may be negative, or composite, in the value of its art-productions. The dreary interval between the times of Milton and Cowper was of the former non-creative type. An eclipse of imagination prevailed and seemed to chill and benumb the poets. They tried to plod along in the well-worn paths, but, like men with bandaged eyes, went astray without perceiving it. Substituting pedantry for emotion, and still harping on the old myths, they reduced them to vapid, artificial unreality, not having the faculty of reviving their beauty by new forms of expression. Of the art to conceal art none save a few like Collins and Goldsmith had the slightest instinct or control. As for passion, that was completely extinct. At last the soul of a later generation demanded the return to natural beauty, and the heart clamored for pulsation and utterance: Cowper, Burns, Wordsworth, Byron, and their great contemporaries, arose, and with them a genuine creative literature, of which the poetry strove to express the spirit of nature and the emotions of the heart, — subtile, essential elements, in which no amount of scientific environment could limit the poet's restless explorations.

The period transitional in thought and feeling;

Our recent transition period ensued, but, in its composite aspect, how different from that to which I have referred! The change which has been going on during this time pertains to imaginative thought and feeling; the specific excellence which characterizes its poetry is that of form and structure. In technical finish and variety the period has been so advanced that an examination of it should prove most instructive to lovers of the arts. For this reason, much of the criticism in the following pages will be more technical than is common in a work of this scope; nor can it be otherwise, and adequately recognize the distinctive eminence of the time. The poets have been generously endowed at birth, and who shall say that they have

creative, chiefly in style and form. Cp. " Poets of America" : pp. 459, 460.

not fulfilled their mission to the attainable extent? When not creative, their genius has been eclectic and refining. Doubtless the time has displayed the inva- *A critical* riable characteristics of such periods. In fact, there *and schol-* *arly period.* never were more outlets to the imagination, serving to distract public attention from the efforts of the poets, than are afforded in this age of prose-romance and journalism. It has been a learned and scholarly period ; writers have busied themselves with enjoying and annotating the great works of the past ; criticism has predominated, — but how exact and catholic! How searching the tests by which tradition and authority have been tried ; how high the standard of excellence in art ; how intolerant the healthy spirit of the last thirty years toward cant and melodramatic affectation ; how vigorous the crusade against sham ! In all this we discern the remaining features which, though less radical in their importance than the scientific revolu- tion, have marked the Victorian period as one of tran- sition, and as composite in the thought and structure of its poetic art.

Besides the restrictions to which the poets have been *Other re-* subjected by the triumphs of the journalists and novel- *strictions to* *ideality.* writers, their enthusiasm also is checked by the mod- ern dislike of emotional outgivings and display. This aversion naturally results from the peace, security, and ultra-comfortableness of the English people. It has been a time of repose and luxury, a felicitous Satur- nian era, when all rare things that poets dream of are close at hand. Fulfilment has stilled the voice of prophecy. We see disease averted, life prolonged and *Modern* increasing in average duration, the masses clothed and *comfort and* *refinement.* housed, vice punished, virtue rewarded, the landscape beautiful with the handiwork of culture and thrift.

Restraint.

Granted : but in most countries advanced to the front of modern refinement, the dominant spirit has been antagonistic to the production of great and lasting poetry, — and of this above other arts. For it is the passion of song that makes it lofty and enduring, and the snows of Hecla have overlaid human passion in English common life during most of the Victorian age. I am not deploring the so-called materialism of our century, 'for this may be more heroic and beneficial to mankind than the idealism of the past. Nevertheless, and without magnifying the poet's office, it is fair to assume that, although a poetical era may not be best for the contemporary world, it is well for a poet to be born in such an era, and not ill for literature that he was so born.

Breeding.

Having thus gone beyond the zone of idealism and the morning halo of impulsive deed and speech, we have reached the noonday of common-sense, breeding, facts as they are. Men do not mouth it in the grand manner, for the world has no patience to hear them, and deems them stagey or affected. Human emotions are the same, but modern training tones us

Impassibility.

down to that impassibility wherein the thoroughbred Christian woman has been said to rival the Indian squaw ; madmen are not, as of old, thought to be inspired ; eccentricity bores us ; and poets, who should be prophets, are loath to boldly dare and differ. Men's hearts beat on forever, but Thackeray's Englishmen are ashamed to acknowledge it at their meetings and partings. The Platonists taught that the body should be despised ; we quietly ignore the heart and soul. The time is off-hand, chaffy, and must be taken in its mood.

Remark by Grant White.

A point was very fairly made by "Shakespeare's Scholar," in his essay on "The Play of the Period," that the latter days have been unfavorable to strong dramatic verse, the highest form of poetry, and the surest mark of a true poetical era. The modern English have not been devoted to intense heroic feeling: whether above or below it, who shall say? — but certainly not within it. The novel is their drama; true, but chiefly the photographic novel of conventional life; others have obtained a hearing slowly, by accident, or by sheer force of genius. They subject their tears to analysis, but do not care for tragic rage; avoiding high excitements as carefully as Septimius Felton in his effort to perpetuate life, they distribute their passion in a hundred petty emotions, and rather than be exalted are content with the usufruct of the five external wits. Domestic peace and comfort have resulted in absence of enthusiasm, and the rise and prolongation of an idyllic school in art. Adventure is the English amusement, not a mode of action; but the converse of this was true in the days of Raleigh, Drake, Sidney, and Richard Grenville. Not that England is wholly utilitarian, "domestic, student, sensualist," as has been charged, but she has well defined and studied the science of society. All this the Victorian poets have had to contend with as poets, or adapt themselves to as clever artists, and, above all, as men of their time.

Lastly, however, we find that the structural, artistic phases of modern English poetry, in scorn of the stilted conventionalism of the eighteenth century, have been of the most composite range, variety, and perfection. Of course the natural forms were long since discovered, but lyrists have learned that combinations are endless, so that new styles, if not new orders, are constantly brought out. In the ultra-critical spirit of the time, they enhance the strength and beauty of their meas-

The novel.

Cp. " Poets of America": p. 463.

Great advance in poetry as an art.

2

ures by every feasible process, and the careful adaptation of form to theme. This is an excellence not
to be underestimated; for if, as Huxley asserts, "expression is not valuable for its own sake," it is at least
the wedded body of inspiration, employing the poet's
keenest sensibilities, and lending such value to thought
as the cutting of a diamond adds to the rugged stone.
Never was the technique of poetry so well understood
as since the time of Keats and the rise of Tennyson
and his school. The *best* models are selected by the
song-writers, the tale-tellers, the preachers in verse;
and a neophyte of to-day would disdain the triteness
and crudeness of the master-workmen of fifty years ago.

Its modern range and perfection. The greater number, instead of restricting themselves
to a specialty, range over and include all departments
of their art, and are lyrists, balladists, and idyllists by
turn, achieving excellence in every direction except the
dramatic, which indeed but few venture upon. Modern
poetry, in short, has been as composite as modern
architecture; and if, as in the case of the latter, grotesque and tawdry combinations abound, there also are
many strong and graceful structures, which excel those
of former periods in richness and harmony of adornment. The rhythm of every dainty lyrical inspiration
which heralded the morning of English minstrelsy has
been caught and adapted by 'the song-writers, all of
whom, from Barry Cornwall and Hood to Kingsley
and Jean Ingelow, have new arrangements and effects
of their own. The extreme of word-music and word-
painting has been attained, together with a peculiar
condensation in imagery and thought; so that, whereas
the poets of the last era, for all their strength of wing,
occupied whole passages with a single image, their
more refined successors discover its essential quality

(somewhat as chemists embody the active principle of a plant in the crystalline salt), and express it by a single adjective or epithet. If "the light that gilds" our recent English poetry be "the light of sunset," it is indeed beautiful with all prismatic hues, and its lustres are often as attractive in themselves as for the truth and beauty which they serve to illumine.

So far as progress is a change from the simple to the complex, from the homogeneous to the heterogeneous, we may hold that an advance is making in English art. But a period of transition is also one of doubt and turbulence; one whose characteristics it is especially requisite to bear in mind, in order to obtain a true appreciation of the leading poets who represent it. For we must consider an artist's good or ill fortune, *Tendency of art to reflect its own time.* his struggles and temptations, his aids and encouragements; remembering that the most important art of any period is that which most nearly illustrates its manners, thoughts, and emotions in imaginative language or form. Through his sensitive organization the poet is exquisitely affected by the spirit of his time; and, to render his work of future moment, seeks to reflect that spirit, or confines himself to expression of the spiritual experiences common to all ages and all mankind. Mr. Emerson, in his search for the underlying principle of things, finds it a defect even in *Emerson: Essay "The Poet."* Homer and Milton, that their works are clogged with restrictions of times, personages, and places. Yet these are the world's great names; it has no greater. The potent allegory of their poems comes nearer to us than the abstract Shastras. Their personages and places are but the media through which the Protean forms of nature are set forth. The statement of unmixed thought and beauty has not been the splendor of the

masters. And while it is true that nature and history
are the poet's workshop, and all material his property,
the studies and reproductions of foreign or antique
models, except as practice-work, are of less value than
what he can show or say of his own time.

Hence it is of the highest importance to the poet
that he should live in a sympathetic, or co-operative, if
not heroic period. In studying the minor poets, we
see with especial clearness the adverse influences of a
transition era, composite though it be. A likeness of
manner and language is common to the Elizabethan
writers, various as were their themes and natural gifts.
The same is apparent in the Cromwellian period with
regard to Marvell, Shirley, and their contemporaries.

Adverse in-
fluence of
the recent
era upon the
minor poets.

But now, as if in despair of finding new themes to suit
their respective talents, yet driven on to expression,
we discern the Victorian poets, — one copying the refrains and legendary feeling of illuminated missals and
black-letter lays ; another recasting the most enchanting and famous romances of Christendom in delicious
language and measures caught from Chaucer himself ;
others adopting the quaint religious manner of Herbert and Vaughan ; a host essaying new and conscientious presentations of the undying beauty of Greek
mythologic lore. We see them dallying with sweet

Cp. " Poets
of Amer-
ica " : pp.
458–461.

sense and sound, until our taste for melody and color
is more than surfeited. The language which Henry
Taylor applied to the poets of a former generation
seems even more appropriate with respect to these
artists. They, too, are characterized " by a profusion
of imagery, by force and beauty of language, and by
a versification peculiarly easy and adroit. . . . . But
from this undoubted indulgence in the mere luxuries
of poetry, has there not ensued a want of adequate ap-

preciation for its intellectual and immortal part? . . . .
They wanted, in the first place, subject-matter. A feeling came more easily to them than a reflection, and
an image was always at hand when a thought was not
forthcoming." It is but just to say that the recent
poets are not so wanting in reflection as in themes
and essential purpose. These defects many have
striven to hide by excessive finish and ornamentation.
Conscious of this, a few, with a spasmodic effort to
be original, break away in disdain of all art, palming
off a "saucy roughness" for strength, and coarseness
for vigor ; and even this return to chaos wins the
favor of many who, from very sickness of over-refine-
ment, pass to the other extreme, and welcome the
meaner work for a time because it is a change. The
effect of novelty gives every fashion a temporary
hold ; but the calmer vision looks above and along
the succession of modes, and seeks what is in itself
ennobling ; and every disguise of dilettanteism, aristocratic or democratic, whether it struts in the rags
of Autolycus, or steals the robe of Prospero and apes
his majestic mien, must ultimately fall away. In the
search for a worthy theme, more than one of the poets
to whom I refer has, by a *tour de force*, allied himself to
some heroic mission of the day. On the other hand,
honest agitators have been moved, by passionate zeal
for their several causes, to outbursts of rhythmical
expression. In most cases the lyrics of either class
have been rhetorical and eloquent rather than truly
poetical. Finally, in the wide diffusion of a partial
culture, the Victorian period has been noteworthy for
the multitudes of its tolerable poets. It has been a
time of English minnesingers, hosts of them chanting
" the old eternal song."

See the Preface to "Philip Van Artevelde," London, 1834.

Two forms of dilettante-ism.

Triumph of the greater poets over their restrictions.
But the poets of such a period are like a collection of trout in water that has become stagnant or turbid. The graceful smaller fry, unconscious that the real difficulty is in the atmosphere about them, one after another yield to it and lose their color, flavor, and elastic life. But the few noble masters of the pool adapt themselves to the new condition, or resist it altogether, and abide till the disorder of the waters

Landor.
is assuaged. Reviewing the poetic genius of the closing era, we find one strong spirit maintaining an independent beauty and vigor through successive generations, composing the rarest prose and poetry with slight regard to temporal mode or hearing, — a man neither of nor for an age, — who has but lately passed

Tennyson.
away. Another, of a different cast, the acknowledged master of the composite school, has reflected his own period by adapting his poems to its landscape, manners, and speculation, with such union of strength and varied elegance as even English literature has seldom

Mrs. Browning.
displayed. We find a woman — an inspired singer, if there ever was one — all fire and air, her song and soul alike devoted to liberty, aspiration, and ethereal love.

Browning.
A poet, her masculine complement, whose name is rich with the added glory of her renown, represents the antiquity of his race by study of mediæval themes, and exhibits to the modern lover, noble, statesman, thinker, priest, their prototypes in ages long gone by ; he constantly exalts passion above reason, while reasoning himself, withal, in the too curious fashion of the present day ; again, he is the exponent of what dramatic spirit is still left to England, — that of psychological analysis, which turns the human heart inside out, judging it not from outward action, in the manner of the early, simply objective masters of the stage.

Youngest and latest, we find a phenomenal genius, | *Swinburne.*
the extreme product of the time, carrying its artistic and spiritual features to that excess which foretokens exhaustion ; possessed of unprecedented control over the rhythm and assonance of English poetry ; in the purpose and structure of his early verse to be studied as a force of expression carried to its furthest limits, but in his mature, dramatic work exhibiting signs of a reaction or transformation which surely is even now at hand.

For that the years of transition are near an end, | *A new dispensation.*
and that, in England and America, a creative poetic literature, adapted to the new order of thought and the new aspirations of humanity, will speedily grow into form, I believe to be evident wherever our common tongue is the language of imaginative expression. The idyllic philosophy in which Wordsworth took refuge from the cant and melodrama of his predecessors has fulfilled its immediate mission ; the art which was born with Keats, and found its perfect work in Tennyson, already seems faultily faultless and over-refined. A craving for more dramatic, sponta- | *The dramatic instinct revived.*
neous utterance is prevalent with the new generation. There is an instinct that to interpret the hearts and souls of men and women is the poet's highest function ; a disposition to throw aside precedents, — to study life, dialect, and feeling, as our painters study landscape, out of doors and at first hand. Considered as the floating land-drift of a new possession, even careless and faulty work after this method is | *British taste subordinate to love of novelty.*
eagerly received ; although in England, so surfeited of the past and filled with vague desire, the faculty to discriminate between the richer and poorer fabric seems blunted and sensational ; experimental novel-

ties are set above the most admirable compositions
in a manner already familiar ; just as an uncouth carv-
ing or piece of foreign lacquer-work is more prized
than an exquisite specimen of domestic art, because it
is strange and breathes some unknown, spicy fragrance
of a new-found clime. The transition period, doubt-
The future. less, will be prolonged by the ceaseless progress of
the scientific revolution, occupying men's imaginations
and constantly readjusting the basis of language and
illustration. Erelong some new Lucretius may come
to reinterpret the nature of things, confirming many
of the ancient prophecies, and substituting for the
wonder of the remainder the still more wondrous tes-
timony of the lens, the laboratory, and the millennial
rocks. The old men of the Jewish captivity wept with
a loud voice when they saw the foundations of the
new temple, because its glory in their eyes, in comparison with that builded by Solomon, was as nothing ;
but the prophet assured them that the Desire of all
nations should come, and that the glory of the latter
house should be greater than of the former. But I do
not endeavor to anticipate the future of English song.
It may be lowlier or loftier than now, but certainly
it will show a change, and my faith in the reality
of progress is broad enough to include the field of
poetic art.

CHAPTER II.

WALTER SAVAGE LANDOR.

I.

LISTENING to the concert of modern song, a critical ear detects the notes of one voice which possesses a distinct quality and is always at its owner's command. Landor was never mastered by his period, though still in harmony with it; in short, he was not a discordant, but an independent, singer. He was the pioneer of the late English school; and among recent poets, though far from being the greatest in achievement, was the most self-reliant, the most versatile, and one of the most imaginative. In the enjoyment of his varied writings, we are chiefly impressed by their constant exhibition of mental prowess, and everywhere confronted with an eager and incomparable *intellect*.

Last of all to captivate the judgment of the laity, and somewhat lacking, it may be, in sympathetic quality of tone, Landor is, first of all, a poet for poets, of clear vision and assured utterance throughout the Victorian Year. His station resembles that of a bulkhead defending the sea-wall of some lasting structure, — a mole or pier, built out from tuneful, grove-shaded Arcadian shores. He stretches far into the channel along which the tides of literary fashion have ebbed and flowed. Other poets, leading or following the changeful current, often appear to leave him behind; but

Landor a pioneer of the recent school.

A poet for poets.

Intellectual and self-reliant.

2 *　　　　　　　　C

often find themselves again where he looms, unchanged
and dauntless, wearing a lighted beacon at his head.

*Born in
Warwick,
Jan. 30,
1775.*

Why, among Victorian poets, do I first mention this
one, — who was born under George III.; who bandied epithets with Byron, was the life-long friend of
Southey, — the contemporary, likewise, in their prime,
of Wordsworth, Scott, and Coleridge ; in whose maturity occurred the swift and shining transits of Keats

*His pro-
longed
career.*

and Shelley, like the flights of shooting-stars ; whose
most imposing poem was given to the world at a
date earlier than the first consulate of Napoleon ;
who lived, from the times of Warton and Pye, to see
three successive laureates renew the freshness of England's faded coronal, while he sang aloof and took
no care? Because, more truly than another declared
of himself, he stood among these, but not of them ;
greater or less, but different, and with the difference
of a time then yet to follow. His style, thought, and

*His method
Victorian.*

versatility were Victorian rather than.Georgian ; they
are now seen to belong to that school of which Tennyson is by eminence the representative. So far as his
manner was anything save his own, it was that of
recent years; let us say, instead, that the popular
method constantly approached Landor's until the epoch
of his death, — and he died but even now, when it
is on the point of yielding to something, we know not
what. He not only lived to see the reflection and
naturalism of Wordsworth produce fatigue, but to the
borders of a reaction from that finesse and technical
perfection which succeeded. His influence scarcely
yet has grown to reputation, by communication from
the select few to the receptive many, though he has
always stood, unwittingly, at the head of a normal
school, teaching the teachers. Passages are easily

traceable where his art, at least, has been followed by poets who themselves have each a host of imitators. He may not have been the cause of certain phenomena; they may have sprung from the tendency of the age, — if so, he was the first to catch the tendency. Despite his appreciation of the antique, his genius found daily excitants in new discovery, action, and thought; he never reached that senility to which earlier modes and generations seem the better, but was first to welcome progress, and thoroughly up with the times. The larger portion of his work saw print long after Tennyson began to compose, and his epic, tragedies, and miscellaneous poems were not brought together, in a single volume, until 1837, — a date within five years of the laureate's first collective edition. Hence, while it is hard to confine him to a single period, he is a tall and reverend landmark of the one under review; and the day has come for measuring him as a poet of that time, whatever he may have been in any other. Nor is he to be observed as an eccentric and curious spectacle, but as a distinguished figure among the best. As an artist he was, like a maple, swift of development, but strong to hold it as an elm or oak; while many poets have done their best work under thirty, and ten years after have been old or dead, the very noontide of Landor's faculties *Landor's* was later than his fiftieth year. We could not regard *retention of* *creative* him as a tyro, had he died, like Keats, at twenty-five, *power.* nor as a jaded old man, dying, as he did, at ninety; for he was as conservative in youth as he ever grew to be, and as fiery and forward-looking in age as in youth. He attained the summit early, and moved along an elevated plateau, forbearing as he grew older to descend the further side, and at death flung off

somewhere into the ether, still facing the daybreak
and worshipped by many rising stars.

Sustained equality.

Were it not for this poet's sustained equality with
himself, we should be unable here to write of his career of seventy years, filled with literary recreations,
each the companion of its predecessor, and all his
own.   Otherwise, in considering his works, we should
have to review the history of that period, — as one
who writes, for example, the life of Voltaire, must
write the history of the eighteenth century.   Landor's
volumes not only touch upon the whole procession of
those seventy years, with keen intuitive treatment of
their important events, but go further, and almost

Intellectual range.

cover the range of human action and thought.   In this
respect I find no such man of our time.   A writer
of dialogues, he subjects affairs to the scrutiny of a
modern journalist; but his newspaper has every age
for its date of issue, and the history of the world
supplies it with local incident.

What is there in the air of Warwickshire to breed
such men?   For he was born by Shakespeare's stream,
and verily inhaled something of the master's spirit at
his birth.   Once, in the flush of conscious power, he
sang of himself, —

> "I drank of Avon too, a dangerous draught,
>   That roused within the feverish thirst of song."

Lowell has said of him, that, "excepting Shakespeare, no other writer has furnished us with so many
delicate aphorisms of human nature"; and we may

Univer-sality.

add that he is also noticeable for universality of contemplation and the objective treatment of stately
themes.   In literature, his range is unequalled by that
of Coleridge, who was so opulent and suggestive; in

philosophy, history, and art, Goethe is not wiser or more imaginative, though often more calm and great; in learning, the department of science excepted, no writer since Milton has been more thoroughly equipped. We place Landor, who was greater, even, as a prose-writer, among the foremost poets, because it was the poet within the man that made him great; his poetry belongs to a high order of that art, while his prose, though strictly prosaic in form, — he was too fine an artist to have it otherwise, — is more imaginative than other men's verses. Radically a poet, he ranks among the best essayists of his time; and he shares this distinction in common with Milton, Coleridge, Emerson, and other poets, in various eras, who have been intellectual students and thinkers. None but sentimentalists and dilettanti confuse their prose and verse, — tricking out the former with a cheap gloss of rhetoric, or the false and effeminate jingle of a bastard rhythm.

Prose and verse. Cp. " Poets of America " : pp. 327, 373.

I have hinted, already, that his works are deficient in that broad human sympathy through which Shakespeare has found his way to the highest and lowest understandings, — just as the cloud seems to one a temple, to another a continent, to the child a fairy-palace, but is dazzling and glorious to all. Landor belonged, in spite of himself, to the Parnassian aristocracy; was, as has been said, a poet for poets, and one who personally impressed the finest organizations. Consider the names of those who, having met him and known his works, perceived in him something great and worshipful. His nearest friends or admirers were Southey, Wordsworth, Hunt, Milnes, Armitage Brown; the philosophers, Emerson and Carlyle; such men of letters as Charles Lamb, Hazlitt, Forster, Julius and Francis Hare; the bluff old philologist, Samuel Parr;

His work addressed to noble minds.

the fair and discerning Blessington; Napier, the soldier and historian; Elizabeth and Robert Browning, the most subtile and extreme of poets, and, in the sunrise of his life, the youngest, Algernon Swinburne; among the rest, note Dickens, who found so much that was rare and undaunted in the man: — I am almost persuaded to withdraw my reservation! True, Landor lived long: in seventy years one makes and loses many votaries and friends; but such an artist, who, whether as poet or man, could win and retain the affection and admiration, despite his thousand caprices, of so many delicate natures, varying among themselves in temperament and opinion, must indeed possess a many-sided greatness. Nor is the definition of sympathetic quality restricted to that which touches the popular heart. There are persons who might read without emotion much of Dickens's sentiment and humor, yet would feel every fibre respond to the exquisite beauty of Landor's "Pericles and Aspasia"; — persons whom only the purest idealism can strongly affect. But this is human also. Shall not the wise, as well as the witless, have their poets? There is an idea current that art is natural only when it appeals to the masses, or awakens the simple, untutored emotions of humble life. In truth, the greater should include the less; the finer, if need be, the coarse; the composer of a symphony has, we trust, melody enough at his command. Stage presentation has done much to popularize Shakespeare; his plays, moreover, are relished for their stories, as "Pilgrim's Progress" and "Gulliver's Travels" are devoured by children without a thought of the theology of the one or the measureless satire of the other. Landor's work has no such vantage-ground, and much of it is "caviare to the general"; but he is

The law of sympathy.

none the less human, in that he is the poet's poet, the artist's artist, the delight of high, heroic souls.

When nineteen years old, in 1795, he printed his first book, — a rhymed satire upon the Oxford dons, — and his muse never left him till he died in 1864, lacking four months only of his ninetieth birthday. Seventy years of literary life, of which the noteworthy portion may be reckoned from the appearance of "Gebir" in 1798, to that of the later series of the "Hellenics" in 1847 : since, although compositions dating the very year of his death exhibit no falling off, and his faculty was vigorous to the end, he produced no important work subsequent to the one last mentioned. His collections of later poems and essays are of a miscellaneous or fragmentary sort, and, though abounding in beautiful and characteristic material, exhibit many trifles which add nothing to his fame. In reviewing his career, let us first look at his poetry, which contains the key to his genius and aspirations.

His earliest verses, like those of Shelley and Byron, have a stilted, academic flavor, and, though witty enough, were instigated by youthful conceit and abhorrence of conventional authority. They were followed by a red-hot political satire, in the metre and diction of Pope. Thus far, nothing remarkable for a boy of nineteen : merely an illustration of the law that "nearly all young poets . . . . write old." [1] The great poetic revival had

His first book: "The Poems of W. S. L." 1795.

"A Moral Epistle to Earl Stanhope."

---

[1] Not having a copy of Landor's first book, I have taken the description, given in the side-note, from Forster's biography, but am informed by Mr. Swinburne that *Poems, English and Latin*, is the correct title. My correspondent adds : "It contains a good deal besides satire, though that is perhaps its best part. The Epistle to Lord Stanhope, which I have also, *is*, I think, something remarkable for a boy of nineteen, — singularly polished and vigorous."

"Gebir,"
1798.

not begun. Burns was still almost unknown ; Cowper very faintly heard ; fledglings tried their wings in the direction of Pope, Warton, and Gray. The art of verse, the creation of beauty for its own sake or for that of imaginative expression, at first took small hold upon Landor. Considering the era, it is wonderful how soon the converse of this was true. Three years to a young man are more than three times three in after-life ; but never was there a swifter stride made than from Landor's prentice-work to *Gebir*, which displayed his royal poetic genius in full robes. Where now be his politics and polemics? Henceforth his verse, for the most part, is wedded to pure beauty, and prose becomes the vehicle of his critical or controversial thought. In "Gebir," art, treatment, imagination, are everything ; argument very little ; the story is of a remote, Oriental nature, a cord upon which he strings his extraordinary language, imagery, and versification. The structure is noble in the main, though chargeable, like Tennyson's earlier poetry, with vagueness here and there ; the diction is majestic and sonorous, and its progress is specially marked by sudden, almost random, outbursts of lofty song. I do not hesitate to say that this epic, as poetry, and as a marvelous production for the period and for Landor's twenty-two years, stands next to that renowned and unrivaled torso, composed so long afterward, the "Hyperion" of John Keats. It was the prototype of our modern formation, cropping out a great distance in advance. To every young poet who has yet his art to learn, I would say — do not overlook "Gebir," this strangely modern poem, which, though seventy-five years old, has so much of Tennyson's finish, of Arnold's objectivity, and the romance of Morris and Keats. Forster, Landor's biographer,

says that it is now unknown. When was it ever known?
The first edition had little sale; a sumptuous later
issue, including the Latin translation "Gebirus," had
still less. But the poets found it out; it was the
envy of Byron; the despair of Southey, who could
appreciate, if he could not create; the bosom-com-
panion of Shelley, to the last; nor can I doubt that,
directly and indirectly, it had much to do with the
inception and development of the Victorian School.

In recalling Landor's writings, prose and verse, I
make no specific allusion to the minor pieces which
he composed from time to time, careless about their
reception, easily satisfied with the expression of his
latest mood. A catalogue of them, extending from the
beginning to the middle of our century, lies before
me: *The Phocæans*, an unfinished epic; *The Charitable
Dowager*, a comedy that never saw the light; various
Icelandic poems, all save one of which are wisely
omitted from his collected works; epigrams, letters,
critiques, and what not; often mere Sibylline leaves,
— sometimes put forth in obscurest pamphlet-form,
sometimes elaborate with revision and costly with the
utmost resources of the press; making little mark at
the time, but all idiosyncratic, Landorian, though closer
scrutiny of them need not detain us here. His literary life was like the firmament, whose darkest openings
are interspersed with scattered stars, but only the
luminous, superior constellations herewith invite our
regard. His first dramatic effort, made after a stormy
and ill-regulated experience of fifteen years, was the
gloomy but magnificent tragedy of *Count Julian.*
Like Shelley's "Cenci," Byron's "Manfred," and Coleridge's adaptation of "Wallenstein," it is a dramatic
poem rather than a stage-drama of the available kind.

*Miscellane-
ous produc-
tions.*

*Dramatic
work.*

*"Count Ju-
lian,"* 1812.

Compared with kindred productions of the time, however, it stands like the "Prometheus" among classic
plays; and as an exposition of dramatic force, a conception of the highest manhood in the most heroic
and mournful attitude, — as a presentment of impassioned language, pathetic sentiment, and stern resolve,
— it is an impressive and undying poem.   Landor's
career must be measured by Olympiads or lustra, not
by years; he was thirty-five when he took this fearless
dramatic flight, and then, save for occasional fragmentary scenes, his special faculty remained unused until
he was nearly sixty-five, in 1839–40, at which date
he composed and published his *Trilogy.*   The three
plays thus grouped — "Andrea of Hungary," "Gio-
vanna of Naples," and "Fra Rupert" — are, excepting the one previously mentioned, the only extended
dramatic poems which he has left us.   Though rarely
so imaginative and statuesque as "Count Julian," they
are better adapted in action, and show no decline of
power.   Between the one and the others occurred the
marvellous prose period of Landor's career, by which
he first became generally known and upon which so
largely rests his fame.   From 1824 to 1837, — these
thirteen years embrace the interval during which was
written the most comprehensive and delightful prose
in the English tongue, upon whose every page is
stamped the patent of the author as a sage and poet.

*The "Tril-
ogy,"
1839–40.*

One is more nearly drawn to Landor — with the
affection which all lovers of beauty, pure and simple,
feel for the poet — by the *Hellenics* than by any
other portion of his metrical work.   The volume bearing that name was written when he was well past the
Scriptural limit of life, at the age of seventy-two, and
published in 1847.   It consisted of translations from

*The "Hel-
lenics,"
1847.*

his own *Idyllia Heroica :* Latin poems (many of them composed and printed forty years earlier) which were finally collected and revised for publication in a little volume, *Poemata et Inscriptiones,* which appeared, I think, in 1846. Of Landor's aptitude and passion for writing in Latin verse I shall speak hereafter. His sin in this respect (if it be a sin),[1] is amply expiated by the surpassing beauty of " Corythus," the " Last of Ulysses," and other translations from the " Idyllia." Still more exquisite, if possible, are the fifteen idyls, also called Hellenics, which previously had been collected in the standard octavo edition of his works, edited by Julius Hare and John Forster, and printed in 1846. During the past thirty years a taste for experimenting with classical themes has seized upon many a British poet, and numberless fine studies have been the result, from the " Œnone " and " Tithonus " of the laureate to more extended pieces, — like the "Andromeda " of Kingsley, and Swinburne's " Atalanta in Calydon." But to Landor, from his youth, the antique loveliness was a familiar atmosphere, in which he dwelt and had his being with a contentment so natural that he scarcely perceived it was not common to others, or thought to avail himself of it in the way of metrical art. Finding that people could not, or would not, read the " Idyllia," he was led to translate them into English verse ; and of all the classical pieces in our language, his own, taken as a whole, are the most varied, natural, simple, least affected with foreign forms : —

> " Sweet, sweet, sweet, O Pan !
> Piercing sweet by the river."

"Poemata et Inscriptiones."

---

[1] See remarks upon Swinburne's Greek and Latin verse, etc., in Chapter XI. of this book.

Generally they are idyllic, and after the Sicilian school. Now and then some Homeric epithets appear; as where he speaks of "full fifty slant-browed, kingly-hearted swine," — but such examples are uncommon. For the most part the Greek manner and feeling are veritably *translated.* "The Hamadryad" is universally known, — possessed of delicious melody and pathos which commend it to the multitude: I am not sure that any other ancient story, so tranquilly and beautifully told, is in our treasury of English song. The overture to the first of the "Hellenics" suggests the charm and purpose of them all: —

"Who will away to Athens with me? who
Loves choral songs and maidens crowned with flowers,
Unenvious? mount the pinnace; hoist the sail."

That splendid apostrophe to liberty, the fifteenth of the first series, beginning,

"We are what suns and winds and waters make us;
The mountains are our sponsors, and the rills
Fashion and win their nursling with their smiles,"

recalls the Hellenic spirit from its grave, and brings these antique creations within the range of modern thought and sympathy. In fine, it must be acknowledged that for tender grace, sunlight, healthfulness, these idyls are fresh beyond comparison, the inspiration of immortal youth. Never have withered hands more bravely swept the lyre.

Landor a faultless and spontaneous artist.

Landor, as I have said, was noticeable among recent poets as an artist, and the earliest to revive the partially forgotten elegance of English verse. Whoever considers the metrical product of our era must constantly bear in mind the stress laid upon the technics of the poet's calling. No shiftlessness has been tol-

erated, and Landor was the first to honor his work
with all the finish that a delicate ear and faultless
touch could bestow upon it. But in observing the
perfection of the "Hellenics," for example, you discern at a glance that it is only what was natural to
him and reached by the first intention; that he falsified the distich with reference to easy writing and
hard reading, and composed admirably at first draught.
By way of contrast, one sees that much of the famous
poetry of the day has been carved with pains, "laborious, orient ivory, sphere in sphere." The morning
grandeur of "Count Julian" and "Gebir," and the
latter-day grace of Landor's idyls and lyrics, came to
their author as he went along. A poor workman
blames his tools; but he was so truly an artist and
poet, that he took the nearest instrument which suggested itself, and wrought out his conceptions to his
own satisfaction, — somewhat too careless, it must be
owned, whether others relished them or not. At
certain times, from the accident of study and early
training, his thoughts ran as freely in Latin numbers
as in English; and, without considering the utter
uselessness of such labor, he persisted in writing
Latin verses, to the alternate amusement and indignation of his friends; always quite at ease in either
language, strong, melodious, and full of humor, —
"strength's rich superfluity." The famous shell-pas-
sage in "Gebir" was written first in Latin, and more
musically than its translation. Compare the latter
with the counterpart in Wordsworth's "Excursion,"
and determine, — not which of the two poets had the
profounder nature, — but which was Apollo's darling
and the more attractively endowed. Landor's blank *His blank*
verse, the test of an English singer, is like nothing *verse.*

before it; but that of Tennyson and his followers resembles it, by adoption and development. Like the best pentameter of the present day, it is akin to Milton's; affected, like his, by classical influence, but rather of the Greek than the Latin; more closely assimilated to the genius of our tongue and with fewer inversions; terse, yet fluent, assonant, harmonious. Grace and nobility are its prominent characteristics.

Lyrical affluence.

Landor's affluence embarrassed him. He had nothing costive in his nature, — disdained the tricks of smaller men, and could not spend days upon a sonnet; it must come at once, and perfect, or not at all. He was a Fortunatus, and, because the ten pieces of gold were always by him, delayed to bring together a store of poetry for his own renown. This was one secret of his leaving so few extended compositions; other reasons will be named hereafter; meantime it is certain that he never hoarded and fondled his quatrains, and that there was no waste, the supply being infinite. The minor lyrics, epigrams, fragments, — thrown off during his capricious life, in which every mood was indulged to the full and every lot experienced, — are numberless; sometimes frivolous enough, biting and spleenful, yet bearing the mark of a delicate hand; often, like "Rose Aylmer," possessed of an ethereal pathos, a dying fall, upon which poets have lived for weeks and which haunt the soul forever. Ideality belonged to Landor throughout life; for seventy years he reminds one of the girl in the fairy-tale, who could not speak without dropping pearls and diamonds. A volume might be made of the lyrical gems with which even his prose writings are interspersed. He had an aptitude for the largest and smallest work, the true Shakespearian range ; and could make anything in poetry, from the posy of a ring to the chronicle of its most heroic wearer.

While Landor's art is thus varied and original, his strongest hold — the natural bent of his imagination — lay, as I have suggested, in the direction of the drama. This he himself felt and often expressed ; yet his dramatic works are only enough to show what things he might have accomplished, under the favorable conditions of a sympathetic age. Few modern poets have done much more. Procter, Taylor, Beddoes, Browning, — his dramatic compeers can almost be numbered on the fingers of one hand. I am not speaking of the playwrights. Had he written many dramas, doubtless they would have been of the Elizabethan style : objective rather than subjective ; their personages distinct in manner, language, and action, though not brought under the close psychological analysis which is a feature of our modern school. We have substituted the novel for the drama, yet, were Shakespeare now alive, he might write novels — and he might not. Possibly, like Landor, he would be repelled by the mummery of the plot, which in the novel must be so much more minutely developed than in a succession of stage-scenes. Landor might have constructed a grand historical romance, or a respectable novel, but he never attempted either. Had the stage demanded and recompensed the labor of the best minds, he would have written plays, doing even the "business" well ; for he had the intellect and faculty, and touched nothing without adorning it. As it was, the plot seemed, in his view, given up to charlatans and hacks ; he had small patience with it, because, not writing in regular course for the theatre,

Dramatic faculty.

the framework of a drama did not come from him spontaneously.   His tragedies already named, and various fragments, — "Ippolito di Este," "Ines de Castro," "The Cenci," and "Cleopatra," — are to be regarded as dramatic studies, and are replete with evidences of inspiration and tragic power.   Sometimes a passage like this, from "Fra Rupert," has the strength and fire of Webster, in "The Duchess of Malfi" : —

> "*Stephen.*   Worst of it all
> Is the queen's death.
>   *Maximin.*   The queen's ?
>   *Stephen.*   They stifled her
> With her own pillow.
>   *Maximin.*   Who says that ?
>   *Stephen.*   The man
> Runs wild who did it, through the streets, and howls it,
> Then imitates her voice, and softly sobs,
> '*Lay me in Santa Chiara.*' "

We say that Landor was an independent singer, but once more the inevitable law obtains.   He was *His restric-* restricted by his period, which afforded him neither *tions.* poetical themes most suited to his intellect, nor the method of expression in which he could attain a full development.   He had little outside stimulus to frequent work.   In his youth the serial market was limited to *The Gentleman's Magazine* and the pretentious quarterly reviews.   His early poems did not sell : they were in advance of the contemporary demand. In poetry, let us confess that he fell short of his own standard, — never so well defined as in "The Pentameron" : "Amplitude of dimensions is requisite to constitute the greatness of a poet, besides his symmetry of form and his richness of decoration. . . . . We may write little things well, and accumulate one

upon another; but never will any justly be called a
great poet, unless he has treated a great subject wor-
thily. . . . . A throne is not built of bird's-nests, nor
do a thousand reeds make a trumpet." The one
great want of many a master-mind oppressed him, —
lack of theme. Better fitted to study things at a dis- *Lack of theme.*
tance, always an idealist and dreaming of some large
achievement, Landor, with his imaginative force un-
met by any commensurate task, wandered like "blind
Orion, hungry for the morn." Or, like that other
hapless giant, he groped right and left, but needed
a guide to direct his strong arms to the pillars, that
he might bow himself indeed and put forth all his
powers.

How great these were the world had never known, *Greatness as a writer of English prose.*
were it not for that interlude of prose composition
which occupied a portion of the years between his
early and later work. From youth his letters, often
essays and reviews in themselves, to his selectest
intellectual companions, exhibit him as a splendid
artist in prose and a learned and accurate thinker.
He had been drinking the wine of life, reading, reflecting, studying "cities of men . . . . and climates,
councils, governments," at Tours, Como, Pisa, Florence, Bath; and, at the age of forty-five or forty-six,
with every faculty matured, he became suddenly aware
of the fitness of written dialogue as the vehicle of
his conceptions, and for the exercise of that dramatic tendency which had thus far found no practi-
cable outlet. Forster has pointed out that this form
of literature was suited alike to his strength, dogmatism, and variety of mood. The idea, once conceived,
was realized with his usual impetuosity. It swelled
and swelled, drawing up the thought and observation

of a lifetime; in two years the first and second books
of *Imaginary Conversations* were given to the world,
and in four more, six volumes in all had been completed. For the first time the English people were
dazzled and affected by this author's genius; the
books were a success; and all citizens of the republic
of letters discovered, what a few choice spirits had
known before, that Landor was their peer and master.

It is needless to eulogize the series of "Imaginary
Conversations,"—to which the poet kept adding, as
the fancy seized him, until the year of his decease,
within the memory of us all. They have passed into
literature, and their influence and charm are undying.
They are an encyclopædia, a panoramic museum, a
perpetual drama, a changeful world of fancy, character, and action. Their learning covers languages,
histories, inventions; their thought discerns and an-
alyzes literature, art, poetry, philosophy, manners, life,
government, religion,— everything to which human
faculties have applied themselves, which eye has seen,
ear has heard, or the heart of man conceived. Their
personages are as noble as those of Sophocles, as
sage and famous as Plutarch's, as varied as those of
Shakespeare himself: comprising poets, wits, orators,
soldiers, statesmen, monarchs, fair women and brave
men. Through them all, among them all, breathes the
spirit of Landor, and above them waves his compelling wand. Where his subjectivity becomes apparent,
it is in a serene and elevated mood; for he is traversing the realm of the ideal, his better angel rules the
hour, and the man is transfigured in the magician and
poet.

Paulo majora canamus. From the exhaustless resources of Landor's imagination, he was furthermore

enabled to construct a trinity of prose-poems, not fragmentary episodes or dialogues, but round and perfect compositions, — each of them finished and artistic in the extreme degree. The *Citation of Shakespeare*, the *Pentameron*, and *Pericles and Aspasia* depict England, Italy, and Greece at their renowned and characteristic periods: the greenwood and castle-halls of England, the villas and cloisters of Italy, the sky and marbles of ancient Greece; the pedantry and poetry of the first, the mysticism of the second, the deathless grace and passion of Athens at her prime. Of "The Citation and Examination of William Shakespeare, etc., etc., Touching Deer-Stealing," I can but repeat what Charles Lamb said, and all that need here be said of it, — that only two men could have written it, he who wrote it, and the man it was written on. It can only be judged by reading, for there is nothing resembling it in any tongue. "The Pentameron" (of Boccaccio and Petrarca) was the last in date of these unique conceptions, and the favorite of Hunt, Crabb Robinson, Disraeli; a mediæval reproduction, the tone of which — while always in keeping with itself — is so different from that of the "Citation," that one would think it done by another hand, if any other hand were capable of doing it. Even to those who differ with its estimation of Dante, its learning, fidelity, and picturesqueness seem admirable beyond comparison. The highest luxury of a sensitive, cultured mind is the perusal of a work like this. Mrs. Browning found some of its pages too delicious to turn over. Yet this study had been preceded by the "Pericles and Aspasia," which, as an exhibition of intellectual beauty, may be termed the masterpiece of Landor's whole career.

A trinity of prose-poems.

"Citation of Shakespeare," 1834.

"The Pentameron," 1837.

"Pericles and Aspa- sia," 1836.

Critics are not wanting who maintain "Pericles and Aspasia" to be the purest creation of sustained art in English prose. It is absolutely devoid of such affectations as mark the romances and treatises of Sidney, Browne, and many famous writers of the early and middle periods; and to "The Vicar of Wakefield," and other classics of a time nearer our own, it bears the relation of a drama to an eclogue, or that of a symphony to some sweet and favorite air. What flawless English! what vivid scenery and movement! Composed without a reference-book, it is accurate in scholarship, free from inconsistencies as Becker's "Charicles"; nevertheless, the action is modern, as that of every golden era must appear; the personages, whether indicated lightly or at full length, are living human beings before our eyes. As all sculpture is included in the Apollo Belvedere, so all Greek life, sunshine, air, sentiment, contribute to these eloquent epistles. A rare imagination is required for such a work. While comparable with nothing but itself, it leaves behind it the flavor of some "Midsummer Night's Dream" or "Winter's Tale," maugre the unreality and anachronisms. Landor's dainty madrigals are scattered throughout, coming in like bird-songs upon the sprightly or philosophical Athenian converse: here we find "Artemidora" and "Aglaë"; here, too, is the splendid fragment of "Agamemnon." How vividly Alcibiades, Anaxagoras, Socrates, Pericles, Aspasia, appear before us: the noonday grace and glory, the indoor banquet and intellectual feast! We exclaim, not only: What rulers! what poets and heroes! but — What children of light! what laurelled heads! what lovers — what passionate hearts! How modern, how intense, how human! what beauty, what delicacy, what fire! We penetrate the love of high-bred men and women: nobles by nature and rank;—surely finer subjects for realistic treatment than the boor and the drudge. Where both are equally natural, I would rather contemplate a horse or a falcon, than the newt and the toad. Thus far, I am sure, one may carry the law of aristocracy in art. The people of this book are brave, wise, and beautiful, or at least fitly adapted: some unhappy,—others, under whatsoever misfortune, enraptured, because loving and beloved. Never were women more tenderly depicted. Aspasia, with all her love of glory, confesses: "You men often talk of glorious death, of death met bravely for your country; I too have been warmed by the bright idea in oratory and poetry: but ah! my dear Pericles! I would rather read it on an ancient tomb than a recent one." Again, in the midst of their splendor and luxury, she exclaims: "When the war is over, as surely it must be in another year, let us sail among the islands Ægean and be as young as ever!" Just before the death of Pericles by the plague, amid thickening calamities, they write tragedies and study letters and art. All is heroic and natural: they turn from grand achievements to the delights of intellect and affection. Where is another picture so elevating as this? Fame, power, luxury, are forgotten in the sympathy and glorious communion of kindred souls. Where is one so fitted to reconcile us with death, — the end of all such communings, — the common lot, from which even these beautiful ideals are not exempt? Ay, their deaths, in the midst of so much that made life peerless and worth living, follow each other in pathetic, yet not inharmonious succession, like the silvery chimings of a timepiece at the close of a summer's day.

Cp. " Poets of America " : p. 430.

Aristocratism in art.

"Pericles and Aspasia" is a Greek temple, with frieze and architrave complete. If it be not Athens, it is what we love to think Athens must have been, in the glory of Pericles' last days. It is a thing of beauty for all places and people ; for the deep-read man of thought and experience, for the dreamy youth or maiden in the farthest Western wilds. The form is that of prose, simple and translucent, yet it is a poem from beginning to end. I would test the fabric of a person's temper by his appreciation of such a book. If only one work of an author were given as a companion, many would select this : not alone for its wisdom, eloquence, and beauty, but for its pathos and affection. You can read it again and again, and ever most delightfully. The "Citation" and the "Pentameron" must be studied with the scholar's anointed eyes, and are sealed to the multitude ; but "Pericles and Aspasia" is clear as noonday, a book for thinkers, — but a book for lovers also, and should be as immortal as the currents which flow between young hearts.

II.

Study of Landor's personal history.

THERE has been much confusion of Landor's personal history with his writings, and an inclination to judge the latter by the former. The benison of Time enables us, after the lapse of years, to discriminate between the two ; while the punishment of a misgoverned career is that it hinders even the man of genius from being justified during his lifetime. However, before further consideration of Landor's works, — that we may see what bearing the one had on the other, and with this intention solely, — let us observe the man himself.

We need not rehearse the story of his prolonged, adventurous life. It was what might be expected of such a character, and to speak of the one is to infer the other. Frea's address to her liege, in Arnold's " Balder Dead," occurs to me as I think of the hoary poet. " Odin, thou Whirlwind," he was, forsooth: tempestuous, swift of will ; an egotist without vanity, but equally without reason ; impatient of fools and upstarts ; so intellectually proud, that he suspected lesser minds of lowering him to their own level, when they honestly admired his works ; scornful, yet credulous ; careless of his enemies, too often suspicious of his friends ; a law unto himself, even to the extreme fulfilment of his most erratic impulse ; enamored of liberty, yet not seldom confounding it with license ; loving the beautiful with his whole soul, but satisfied no less with the conscious power of creating than with its exercise. Such was Landor, though quite transfigured, I say, when absorbed in the process of his art. Every inspired artist has a double existence: his " life is twofold," and the nobler one is that by which he should be judged. *His paradoxical temperament.*

And yet, our poet's temperament was so extraordinary that it is no less a study than his productions. He was wayward, unrestful, full-veined, impetuous to the very end. Nothing but positive inability restrained him from gratifying a single passion or caprice. His nature was so buoyant that, like the Faun, he forgot both pain and pleasure, and had few stings of sorrow or regret to guard him from fresh woes and errors. As he learned nothing from experience, his life was one perpetual series of escapades, — of absurd perplexities at Rugby, Oxford, Llanthony, and in foreign lands. Even in art he often seemed like a wind-harp, *Extraordinary disposition and career.*

responding to every breath that stirred his being: a
superb voice executing voluntaries and improvisations,
but disinclined to synthetic utterance. He lacked that
guiding force which is gained only by the wisest discipline, the most beneficent influences in youth : — under
such influences this grand character might have been
strong and perfect, but his fortunes served to lessen
the completeness of his genius. The author's traditional restrictions were wanting in Landor's case. He
stood first in the entail of a liberal estate, and self-
control was never imposed upon him. One great gift
denied to him was the suspicion of his own mortality.
It has been rightly said that he and his brothers
came of a race of giants. His physical health and
Physical   strength were so absolute, that no fear of the short-
gifts.   ness of life was present to stimulate his ambition. He
needed, like the imperator, some faithful slave to whis-
per in his ear, Remember that thou too art mortal!
His tendencies never were evil, but in their violence
illustrated Fourier's theory of the reverse action of
the noblest passions. More than all else, it was this
lack of self-restraint that made the infinite difference
between himself and the great master to whose univer-
sality of genius his own was most akin.

Had Landor been poor, had he felt some thorn in
the flesh — but he was more handicapped at the outset with wealth and health than Wordsworth with
poverty or Hood with want and disease. Born a
patrician, his caste was assured, and his actions were
of that defiant, democratic kind, upon which snobs
and parvenus dare not venture. He scattered his
wealth as he chose, and would not let his station
restrict him from the experiences of the poor. The
audacious conceptions of novelists were realized in

his case. It was impossible to make him a conventional respecter of persons and temporal things. If ever a man looked through and through clothes and titles, Landor did; and as for property, — it seemed to him *impedimenta* and perishable stuff. Yet he loved luxury, and was uncomfortable when deprived of it. Determined, first of all, to *live his life,* to enjoy and develop every gift and passion, he touched life at more points than do most men of letters. Possibly he had not the self-denial of those exalted devotees, who eat, marry, and live for art alone. The lust of the flesh, the lust of the eye, and the pride of life were strong within him. Here he resembled Byron and Alfieri, — to whom he was otherwise related, except that his heart was too warm and light for the vulgar misanthropy of the first, and his blood too clean and healthful for the grosser passions of either. *No respecter of persons.*

Trouble bore lightly enough upon a man who so readily forgot the actual world, that we find him writing Latin idyls just after his first flight from his wife, or turning an epigram when his estate was ruined forever. Inconstant upon the slightest cause, he yet was faithful to certain life-long friends, and, if one suffered never so little for his sake, was ready to yield life or fortune in return. Such was his feeling toward Robert Landor, Forster, Southey, Browning, and the great novelist who drew that genial caricature by which his likeness is even now most widely known. Dickens, who of all men was least fit to pronounce judgment upon Landor's work, and cared the least to do it, was of all most fit to estimate his strength and weakness, his grim and gentle aspects. In " Boythorn " we hear his laugh rising higher, peal on peal; we almost see his leonine face and lifted brow, the *Buoyancy of temperament.*

Dickens's portrait of him in "Bleak House."

3*

strong upper lip, the clear gray eye, and ineffably
sweet and winsome smile. We listen to his thousand
superlatives of affection, compliment, or wrath, and
know them to be the safety-valves of a nature over-
charged with " the hate of hate, the scorn of scorn,
the love of love " ; of a poet and hero in the extreme,
who only needed the self-training that with years
should bring the philosophic mind.

His prose writings measurably reflect 'his temperament, though he is at special pains to disclaim it.
His minor epigrams and lyrics go still further in this
direction, and were the means of working off his sur-
plus energy of humor, sympathy, or dislike. The moment he regarded men and things *objectively*, he was
the wisest of his kind ; and some fine instinct mostly
kept him objective in his poetry, while his personality
expended itself in acts and conversation. If he seldom did " a wise thing," he as seldom wrote " a foolish one." Entering upon his volumes, we are in the
domain of the pure serene ; and his glorious faculties
of scholarship and song compensate us for that of
which his nature had too little and that of which it
wantoned in excess.

Amateur-
ship to be
distrusted.

Many texts could be found in Landor's career for
an essay upon amateurship in literature or art. As a
rule, distrust the quality of that product which is not
the result of legitimate professional labor. Art must
be followed *as a means of subsistence* to render its creations worthy, to give them a human element. Poetry
is an unsubstantial worldly support ; but true poets
have frequently secluded themselves, like Milton, Cowper, and Wordsworth, so that their simple wants were

Art as a
means of
subsistence.

supplied ; or, plunging into life, have still made labor
with the pen — writing for the stage or the press — a

means of living, enjoying the pleasure which comes from being in harness and from duty squarely performed. They plume themselves — *et ego in Arcadia* — upon sharing not only the transports, but the drudgery of the literary guild. Generally, I say, distrust writers who come not in by the strait gate, but clamber over the wall of amateurship. Literary men, who have had both genius and a competence, have so felt this that they have insisted upon the uttermost farthing for their work, thus maintaining, though at the expense of a reputation for avarice, the dignity of the profession, and legitimizing their own connection with it. This Landor was never able to do: his writing either was *His work unremunerative.* not remunerative, because not open to popular sympathy, or unsympathetic because not remunerative; 'at all events, the two conditions went together. He began to write for the love of it, and was always, perforce, an amateur rather than a member of the guild. As he grew older, he would have valued a hundred pounds earned by his pen more than a thousand received from his estate; but although he estimated properly the value of his work, and, thinking others would do the same, was always appropriating in advance hypothetical earnings to philanthropic ends, he never gained a year's subsistence by literature; and such of his works as were not printed at his own expense, with the exception of the first two volumes of " Imaginary Conversations," entailed losses upon the firms venturing their publication.

But amateurship in Landor's case, enforced or *Landor not a dilettant.* chosen, did not become dilettanteism; on the contrary, it made him finely independent and original. His own boast was that he was a " creature who imitated nobody and whom nobody imitated; the man who walked through the crowd of poets and prose-men, and never was touched by any one's skirts." This haughty self-gratulation we cannot allow. No human being ever was independent, in this sense. Landor in his youth imitated Pope, and afterwards made beneficial study of Milton before reaching a manner of his own. Pindar, Theocritus, and Catullus, among the ancients, he read so closely that he could not but feel the influence of their styles. Yet he might justly claim that he had no part in the mere fashion of the day, and that he wrote and thought independent of those with whom he was on the most intimate and coadmiring terms. He often shed tears in the passion of his work, and his finest conceptions were the most spontaneous, — for his instinct with regard to beauty and the canons of literary taste had the precision of law itself. His poetic qualities, like his acquirements, were of the rare and genuine kind.

His love of nature.

He had a thorough sympathy with nature and a love for outdoor life. His biographer, while careful to de-tail the quarrels and imbroglios into which his temper betrayed him along the course of years, gives us only brief and fitful. glimpses of his better and prevailing mood. Happily, Forster avails himself of Landor's letters to fill out his bulky volume, and hence cannot wholly conceal the striking poetic qualities of the man. Landor knew and loved the sky, the woods, and the waters; a day's journey was but an enjoyable walk for him; and he passed half his time roaming over the hills, facing the breeze, and composing in the open air. It was only, in fact, when quite alone that he could be silent enough to work. For trees he had a reverential passion. Read his Conversation with Pallavicini; and examine that episode in his life,

when he bought and tried to perfect the Welsh estate,
and would have grown a forest of half a million trees,
but for his own impracticability and the boorishness
of the country churls about him. Unlike many reflective poets, however, he never permits landscape
to distract the attention in his figure-pieces, but with
masterly art introduces it sufficiently to relieve and
give effect to their dramatic purpose. That he is
often tempted to do otherwise he confesses in a letter
to Southey, and adds: "I am fortunate, for I never
compose a single verse within 'doors, except in bed
sometimes. I do not know what the satirists would
say if they knew that most of my verses spring from
a gate-post or a mole-hill." Trees, flowers, every
growing thing was sacred to him, and informed with
happy life. It was his wish and way

> "To let all flowers live freely, and all die,
>   Whene'er their Genius bids their souls depart,
>   Among their kindred in their native place.
>   I never pluck the rose; the violet's head
>   Hath shaken with my breath upon its bank,
>   And not reproached me; the ever-sacred cup
>   Of the pure lily hath between my hands
>   Felt safe, unsoiled, nor lost one grain of gold."

His affection for dogs and other dumb creatures, *Affection*
like his understanding of them, is no less instinctive *for animals.*
and sincere. Of all the Louis Quatorze rhymesters
he tolerates La Fontaine only, "for I never see an
animal," he writes, "unless it be a parrot or a mon-
key or a pug-dog or a serpent, that I do not converse
with it either openly or secretly."

In the dialogue to which I have referred he pro-
tests against the senseless imitation of Grecian architecture in the cold climate of our North, — and this

reminds me of Landor's classicism and its relation to the value of his work. In Latin composition he excelled any contemporary, and was only equalled by Milton and a few others of the past. Latin, as I have shown, was at times the language of his thoughts, and, as he wrote for expression only, he loved to use it for his verse. Greek was less at his command, but he could always recall it by a fortnight's study, and his taste and feeling were rather Athenian than Roman. Undoubtedly, as judicious friends constantly were assuring him, he threw away precious labor in composing Latin epigrams, satires, and idyls; yet his English style, like that of other famous masters, acquired a peculiar strength and nobleness from the influence of his classical diversions. He has not escaped the charge of valuing only what is old, and holding the antique fashion to be more excellent than that of his own period. Americans are sufficiently familiar with this conceit of shallow critics and self-made men; yet the finest scholars I have known have been the most fervent patriots, the most advanced thinkers, the most vigorous lovers and frequenters of our forests, mountains, and lakes. With regard to Landor, never was a prejudice so misapplied. He was essentially modern and radical, looking to the future rather than to the past, and was among the first to welcome and appreciate Tennyson, the Brownings, Margaret Fuller, Kossuth, and other poets and enthusiasts of the time. He was called an old pagan; while in truth his boast was just, not only that he " walked up to the ancients and talked with them familiarly," but that he " never took a drop of wine or crust of bread in their houses." There was, to be sure, something of the

Epicurean in the zest with which he made the most
of life, and his nearness to nature may seem pagan
to those whose idealism is that of the desk and closet
only. "It is hard," he says of gunning, "to take.
what we cannot give ; and life is a pleasant thing, at
least to birds. No doubt the young ones say tender
things one to another, and even the old ones do not
dream of death."

Landor's appetite for knowledge was insatiable, wor- *His knowledge.*
thy of the era, and his acquisitions were immense. He
gathered up facts insensibly and retained everything
that he observed or read. Of history he was a close
and universal student. As he possessed no books of
reference, it is not surprising that his memory was
occasionally at fault. De Quincey said that his learning was *sometimes* defective,—but this was high praise
from De Quincey,—and of his genius, that he always
rose with his subject, and dilated, "like Satan, into
Teneriffe or Atlas when he saw before him an an-
tagonist worthy of his powers." Landor is not so
generous to himself, but affirms, "I am a horrible
compounder of historical facts. . . . . I have usually
one history that I have read, another that I have
invented." In his "Imaginary Conversations" the
invented history, like that of Shakespeare's, seems to
me its own excuse for being. The philosophies of
every age are no less at his tongue's end, and subject to his wise discrimination. With unsubstantial
metaphysics he has small patience, and believes that
"we are upon earth to learn what can be learnt upon
earth, and not to speculate upon what never can be."
Politics he is discussing constantly, but has too broad
and social a foothold to satisfy a partisan. Whatsoever things are just and pure, these he supports ;

*His republi-
canism.*

above all, his love of liberty is intense as Shelley's,
Mazzini's, or Garibaldi's, and often as unreasoning.
Always on the side of the poor and oppressed, he indirectly approves even regicide, but is so tender of
heart that he would not really harm a fly. His individuality was strong throughout, and he was able to
maintain no prolonged allegiance to party, church, or
state; nay, not even to obey when he undertook obedience,—for, although he was at munificent expense in a
personal attempt to aid the Spanish patriots, and received an officer's commission from the Junta, he took
offence almost at the outset, and threw up his command
after a brief skirmishing experience on the frontier.
He admired our own country for its form of government, but seemed to think Washington and Franklin its
only heroic characters. If there was an exception to
his general knowledge, it was with regard to America:
like other Englishmen of his time, he had no adequate comprehension of men and things on this side
of the Atlantic. Could he have visited us in his
wanderings, the clear American skies, the free atmosphere, and the vitality of our institutions would have
rejoiced his spirit, and might have rendered him more
tolerant of certain national and individual traits which,
although we trust they are but for a season, served at
a distance to excite his irritation and disdain.

*Critical
powers.*

For criticism Landor had a determined bent, which
displays itself in his essays, talk, and correspondence.
The critical and creative natures are rarely united in
one person. The greatest poets have left only their
own works behind them, too occupied or too indifferent to record their judgment of their contemporaries.
But Landor lived in a critical age, and so acute was
his sense of the fitness of things, that it impelled him

to estimate and comment upon every literary production that came under his observation. In the warmth of his heart, he was too apt to eulogize the efforts of his personal friends; but, otherwise considered, his writings are full of criticism than which there is nothing truer, subtler, or more comprehensive in the English tongue. He had, furthermore, a passion for scholarly notes and minute verbal emendation. In the former direction his scholia upon the classical texts are full of learning and beauty; but when he essayed philology, — of which he had little knowledge, in the modern sense, — and attempted to regulate the orthography of our language, the result was something lamentable. His vagaries of this sort, I need scarcely add, were persisted in to the exclusion of greater things, and partly, no doubt, because they seemed objectionable to others and positively hindered his career.

While the literary consciousness and thoroughly genuine art of Landor's poetry are recognized by all of his own profession, much of it, like certain still-life painting, is chiefly valuable for technical beauty, and admired by the poet rather than by the popular critic. As one might say of Jeremy Taylor, that it was impossible, even by chance, that he could write profane or libidinous doctrine, so it seemed impossible for Landor, even in feeble and ill-advised moments, to compose anything that was trite or inartistic. The touch of the master, the quality of the poet, is dominant over all. His voice was sweet, and he could not speak unmusically, though in a rage. His daintiest trifles show this: they are found at random, like precious stones, sometimes broken and incomplete, but every one — so far as it goes — pure in color and absolutely without flaw. A slight object served him for a text, and in

Technical excellence.

E

honor of a woman who pleased him, but who seemed far enough beneath him to ordinary eyes, he composed eighty-five lyrics that might have beguiled Diana.

Poetic extravagance.

In discoursing upon elevated themes he was seized with that divine extravagance which possessed the bards of old ; and, in verse addressed to persons whom he loved or detested, he took the manner of his favorite classical lyrists, and in every instance went to the extreme of gallant compliment or withering scorn. His determination to have freedom from restraint, at all hazards and any cost, exhibits itself in his poetry and prose. Here he found a liberty, an independence of other rules than his own judgment or caprice, which he could not enjoy in daily life, — although in conduct, as in letters, he was so obstreperous and unpleasant an opponent that few cared to set themselves in his way. I repeat that, for all his great powers, he was a royal Bohemian in art, as throughout life, and never in poetry composed the ample work which he himself asserted is requisite to establish the greatness of a poet ; yet, in a more barren period, one fourth as much as he accomplished sufficed for the reputation of Goldsmith, Collins, or Gray.

His fame.

With regard to the fame of Landor it may be said, that, while he has not reached a rank which emboldens any publisher to issue a complete edition of his varied and extensive writings,[1] — and even his poems, alone, are not brought together and sold with Byron,

---

[1] At present, the best collection of Landor's works is that made in 1846 (2 vols. 8vo), of such as he himself then deemed worthy of preservation. A new edition has lately been printed. It contains the *Imaginary Conversations, Citation of Shakespeare, Pentameron, Pericles and Aspasia, Gebir,* the first series of *Hellenics,* and most of the author's dramatic and lyric poems which pre-

Longfellow, Tennyson, and other public favorites, — it is certain, nevertheless, that he has long emerged from that condition in which De Quincey designated him as a man of great genius who might lay claim to a reputation on the basis of *not* being read. He has gained a hearing from a fit audience, though few, which will have its successors through many generations. To me his fame seems more secure than that of some of his popular contemporaries. If Landor himself had any feeling upon the subject, it was that time would yield him justice. No one could do better without applause, worked less for it, counted less upon it; yet when it came to him he was delighted in a simple way. It pleased him by its novelty, and often he pronounced it critical — because it *was* applause — and overestimated the bestower: that is, he knew the verdict of his few admirers was correct, and by it gauged their general understanding. He challenged his critics with a perfect consciousness of his own excellence in art; yet only asserted his rights when they were denied him. In all his books there is no whit of cowardice or whining. Nothing could make them morbid and jaundiced, for it was chiefly as an author that he had a religion and conscience, and was capable of self-denial.

His attitude toward applause.

Landor's prolonged discouragements, however, made him contemptuous of putting out his strength before people who did not properly measure him, and he felt all the loneliness of a man superior to his time.

ceded its date of compilation. The later *Hellenics, Last Fruit off an Old Tree, Heroic Idyls, Scenes for a Study,* etc., can only be procured in separate volumes and pamphlets and, in bookseller's diction, are fast becoming "rare." — January, 1875: a complete edition of Landor, in six volumes, is now announced for early publication by a London house.

Desire for appreciation. In youth he once or twice betrayed a yearning for appreciation. How nobly and tenderly he expressed it! "I confess to you, if even foolish men had read 'Gebir,' I should have continued to write poetry; there is something of summer in the hum of insects." And again: "The *popularis aura*, though we are ashamed or unable to analyze it, is requisite for the health and growth of genius. Had 'Gebir' been a worse poem, but with more admirers, and I had once filled my sails, I should have made many and perhaps more prosperous voyages. There is almost as much vanity in disdaining the opinion of the world as in pursuing it."

He did not disdain it, but reconciled himself with what heart he might to its absence. In later years he asserted: "I shall have as many readers as I desire to have in other times than ours. I shall dine late; but the dining-room will be well lighted, the guests few and select." Southey buried himself in work, when galled by his failure to touch the popular heart; Landor, in life and action, and in healthful Nature's haunts. The "Imaginary Conversations" were, to a certain degree, a popular success, — at least, were generally known and read by cultured Englishmen; and for some years their author heartily enjoyed the measure of reputation which he then, for the first time, received. It was during this sunlit period that he addressed a noble ode to Joseph Ablett, containing these impulsive lines: —

> "I never courted friends or Fame;
> She pouted at me long, at last she came,
> And threw her arms around my neck and said,
> 'Take what hath been for years delayed,
> And fear not that the leaves will fall
> One hour the earlier from thy coronal.'"

Threescore years and ten are the natural term of *Threescore*
life, yet we find Landor at that point just leaving *years and ten.*
the meridian of his strength and splendor.   When
seventy-one, he saw his English writings collected
under Forster's supervision, and his renown would
have been no less if he had then sung his *nunc di-*
mittis and composed no longer.   Yet we could not
spare that most poetical volume which appeared near
the close of the ensuing year.   At a dash, he made
and printed the English version of his Latin Idyls,—
written half a lifetime before.   We already have
classed the "Cupid and Pan," "Dryope," "The Children of Venus," with their companion-pieces, as a
portion of his choicest work.   Five years afterward
he gathered up *The Last Fruit off an Old Tree*, and *"The Last*
meant therewith to end his literary labors.   To this *Fruit off an Old Tree,"*
volume was prefaced the "Dying Speech of an Old *1853.*
Philosopher," — and who but Landor could have written the faultless and pathetic quatrain?

> "I strove with none, for none was worth my strife;
>   Nature I loved, and, next to Nature, Art;
> I warmed both hands before the fire of life;
>   It sinks, and I am ready to depart."

Our author's prose never was more characteristic
than in this book, which contained some modern dialogues, much literary and political disquisition, and
the delightful critical papers upon Theocritus and
Catullus.   The poetry consisted of lyrics and epistles,
with a stirring dramatic fragment, — "The Cenci."
Many a time thereafter the poet turned his face to
the wall, but could not die: the gods were unkind,
and would not send Iris to clip the sacred lock.   He
was compelled to live on till nothing but his voice
was left him; yet, living, he could not be without

" Dry Sticks Fagoted," 1858.

expression.　In 1857 – 58 came a sorrowful affair at Bath, where the old man was enveloped in a swarm of flies and stopped to battle with them ; engaged at eighty-two in a quixotic warfare with people immeasurably beneath him, and sending forth epigrams, like some worn-out, crazy warrior toying with the bow-and-arrows of his childhood.　I am thankful to forget all this, when reading the classical dialogues printed

" Heroic Idyls," 1863.

in his eighty-ninth year, under the title of *Heroic Idyls*.　Still more lately were composed the poetical scenes and dialogues given in the closing pages of his biography.[1]

Deaf, lame, and blind, as Landor was, — *qualis artifex periit!*　The letters, poems, and criticisms of his last three years of life are full of thought and excellence.　The love of song stayed by him ; he was a poet above all, and, like all true poets, young in feeling to the last, and fond of bringing youth and beauty around him.　We owe to one enthusi-

Kate Field.

astic girl, in whom both these graces were united, a striking picture of the old minstrel with his foam-white, patriarchal beard, his leonine visage, and head not unlike that of Michael Angelo's " Moses " ; and it was to the fresh and eager mind of such a listener, with his own æsthetic sensibilities for the time well pleased, that he offered priceless fragments of wit

---

[1] Besides additions, in English, to the "Imaginary Conversations," Landor wrote, in Italian, a dialogue entitled *Savonarola e il Priore di San Marco*. It appeared in 1860, but was speedily suppressed through Church influence, and the edition remained on his hands in sheets. The author's old prejudice against Plato breaks out in this pamphlet, quaintly and incongruously, but Mr. Swinburne justly says of the production that "it is a noble 'last fruit' of the Italian branch of that mighty tree."

and courtesy, and expounded the simply perfect canons of his verse. The finest thing we know of Swinburne's life is his pilgrimage to Italy and unselfish reverence at the feet of the incomparable artist, the unconquerable freeman, to whom he

> "Came as one whose thoughts half linger,
>   Half run before;
> The youngest to the oldest singer
>   That England bore."

To some who then for the first time knew Landor, and who were not endowed with the refined perceptions of these young enthusiasts, the foibles of his latter days obscured his genius; to us, at this distance, they seem only the tremors of the dying lion. When, at the age of eighty-nine years and nine months, he breathed his last at Florence, it was indeed like the death of some monarch of the forest, — most untamed when powerless, away from the region which gave him birth and the air which fostered his scornful yet heroic spirit.

A. C. Swinburne.

W. S. L. died in Florence, Sept. 17, 1864.

CHAPTER III.

THOMAS HOOD.—MATTHEW ARNOLD.—BRYAN WALLER PROCTER.

I.

I BRING together the foregoing names of poets, whose works very clearly reflect certain phases of English life and literature. It would be difficult to select three more unlike one another in genius, motive, and the results of their devotion to art, or any three whose relations to their period can be defined so justly by a process of contrast and comparison. *Comparative criticism.* This process is objectionable when we are testing the success of an author in the fulfilment of his own artistic purpose; it has its use, nevertheless, in a general survey of the poetry of any given time.

Here are the poet of sympathy, the poet of cultured intellect, and the born vocalist of lyric song. The first is thoroughly democratic in his expression of the mirth and tragedy of common life. The second equally represents his era, with its excess of culture, subtile intellectuality, poverty of theme, reliance upon the beauty and wisdom of the past. His sympathies may be no less acute, but the popular instinct has deemed them loyal to his own class; his humanity takes little note of individuals, but regards social and psychological problems in the abstract; as for his genius, it is critical rather than creative. The

Comparative criticism.

Three poets.

last of this trinity is delightful for the troubadour quality of his minstrelsy: a dramatist and song-writer, loving poetry for itself, possessing what the musician would call a genuine "voice," and giving blithe, unstudied utterance to his tuneful impulses. Hood is the poet of the crowd; Arnold, of the closet; Procter, of the open air: — all are purely English, and belong to the England of a very recent day.

II.

EXAMINING the work of these minor, yet representative poets, we find that of Thomas Hood so attractive and familiar, that in his case the former qualification seems a distinction by no wide remove from the best of his contemporaries. He had a portion of almost every gift belonging to a true poet, and but for restricted health and fortune would have maintained a higher standard. His sympathetic instinct was especially tender and alert; he was the poet of the heart, and sound at heart himself, — the poet of humane sentiment, clarified by a living spring of humor, which kept it from any taint of sentimentalism. To read his pages is to laugh and weep by turns; to take on human charity; to regard the earth mournfully, yet be thankful, as he was, for what sunshine falls upon it, and to accept manfully, as he did, each one's condition, however toilsome and suffering, under the changeless law that impels and governs all. Even his artistic weaknesses (and he had no other) were frolicsome and endearing. Much of his verse was the poetry of the beautiful, in a direction opposite to that of the metaphysical kind. His humor — not his jaded humor, the pack-horse of daily task-work, but

Thomas Hood: born in London, May, 1799.

4

his humor at its best, which so lightened his pack of
ills and sorrows, and made all England know him —
was the merriment of hamlets and hostels around the
skirts of Parnassus, where not the gods, but Earth's
common children, hold their gala-days within the
shadow. Lastly, his severer lyrical faculty was musical and sweet: its product is as refined as the most
exacting need require, and keeps more uniformly than
other modern poetry to the idiomatic measures of
English song.

His youth. Hood failed in a youthful effort to master the
drudgery of a commercial desk. He then attempted
to practise the art of engraving, but found it ruin-
ous to his health. It served to develop a pleasant
knack of sketching, which was similar in quality and
after-use to Thackeray's gift in that line, and came
as readily to its owner. At last he easily drifted into
the life of a working man of letters, and figured
creditably, both as humorist and as poet, before the
commencement of the present British reign. Yet that
portion of his verse which is engrafted upon literature as distinctively his own was not composed, it
will be seen, until within the years immediately preceding his death. He thus occupies a niche in the
arcade along which our vision at present is directed.

His youthful career, in fact, belongs to that interval when people were beginning to shake off the
influence of Byron and his compeers, and to ask for
something new. It is noticeable that the works of
Keats, Shelley, and Coleridge separated themselves
from the *débris*, and greatly affected the rising generation of poets, inciting a reaction, from the passionate
unrestraint of the romantic school, to the fastidious
art of which Keats was the rarest and most intuitive

master. The change was accelerated by such men as Leigh Hunt, — then at his poetic meridian, and a clear, though somewhat gentle, signal-light between the future and the past. Hood's early and serious poems are of the artistic sort, evincing his adherence to the new method, and an eager study of Shakespeare and other Elizabethan models.

At various times between 1821 and 1830 were composed such pieces as " Hero and Leander," — in the manner of " Venus and Adonis " ; " The Two Swans," " The Two Peacocks of Bedfont," and " The Plea of the Midsummer Fairies," — carefully written after the fashion of Spenser and his teachers ; " Lycus, the Centaur " ; numberless fine sonnets ; and a few lyrics, among which the ballad of " Fair Ines " certainly is without a peer. Much of this verse exhibits Hood's persistent defect, — a failing from which he never wholly recovered, and which was due to excess of nervous imagination, — that of overloading a poem with as much verbal and scenic detail as the theme and structure could be made to bear. Otherwise it is very charming : such work as then commended itself to poets, and which the modern public has been taught to recognize. " Lycus, the Centaur," for instance, reads like a production of the latest school ; and Hood's children, in their " Memorials " of the poet, justly term " The Plea of the Midsummer Fairies " a " most artistic poem," which " has latterly been more fairly appreciated in spite of its antiquated style." But his own public took little interest in these fanciful compositions of Hood's younger muse, however clearly they reveal the artist side of his nature, his delicate taste, command of rhythm, and devotion to his ideal. These traits were more acceptable in his

Hood's early poems. 1821 - 30.

Lyrical ballads.

shorter lyrics of that period, many of which were delicious, and beyond his own power to excel in later years. His ballads — contributed to the magazines and annuals, then in vogue, with which he was connected — are full of grace, simplicity, pathos, and spirit. All must acknowledge, with Poe, that " Fair Ines " is perfect of its kind. Take this exquisite ballad, and others, written at various dates throughout his life, — " It was not in the Winter," " Sigh on, sad Heart," " She's up and gone, the graceless Girl," " What can an old Man do but die ? " " The Death-Bed," " I Remember, I Remember," " Ruth," " Farewell, Life ! " ; take also the more imaginative odes to be found in his collected works, — such as those " To Melancholy " and " To the Moon " ; take these lyrical poems, and give them, after some consideration of present verse-making, a careful reading anew. They are here cited as his lyrical conceptions, not as work in what afterward proved to be his special field, and we shortly may dismiss this portion of our theme. I call these songs and ballads, poetry : poetry of the lasting sort, native to the English tongue, and attractive to successive generations. I believe that some of them will be read when many years have passed away ; that they will be picked out and treasured by future compilers, as we now select and delight in the songs of Jonson, Suckling, Herrick, and other noble kinsmen. Place them in contrast with efforts of the verbal school, — all sound and color, conveying no precise sentiment, vivified by no motive sweet with feeling or easeful with unstudied rhythm. Of a truth, much of this elaborate modern verse is but the curious fashion of a moment, and as the flower of grass : " the grass withereth, and the flower thereof falleth away."

The verbal school.

Although Hood took little recognition by the delicate poems which were the children nearest their
begetter's heart, he at once gained the favor of his
countrymen through that ready humor which formed
so large a portion of his birthright.   He had versatility, and his measures, however lacking in strength
of imagination, exhibit humane and dramatic elements
which we miss in those of his greatest contemporary.
His fantastic image, though topped with the cap and
bells, may well be garlanded with rue, and placed,
like Garrick's, between the Muses of Comedy and
Tragedy.   He had the veritable gift of Humor, —
that which makes us weep, yet smile through our
tears.   But how this faculty was overworked! and
how his verse was thinned and degraded, to suit the
caprice of a rude public, by that treacherous facility
which it seemed beyond his power rightly to control!

Hood's *Odes and Addresses*, his comic diversions in
The London Magazine, and the pronounced success of
Whims and Oddities (1826), gave him notoriety as a
fun-maker, and doomed him either to starve, or to
grimace for the national amusement during the twenty
after-years of his toiling, pathetic life.   The British
always will have their Samson, out of the prison-
house, to make them sport.   Tickle the ribs of those
spleen-devoured idlers or workers, in London and a
score of dingy cities; dispel for a moment the insular melancholy; and you may command the pence
of the poor, and the patronage, if you choose, of the
rich and titled.   But at what a sacrifice!   The mask
of more than one Merryman has hidden a death's-
head; his path has slanted to the tomb, though
strewn with tinsel and taffeta roses, and garish with
all the cressets of the circus-ring.   Whatever Hood

Hood's humor.

Cp. " *Poets of Amer-ica* ": *pp.* 258–260, 321.

A jester by profession.

might essay, the public was stolidly expecting a quip or a jest. These were kindly given, though often poor as the health and fortunes of the jester; and it is no marvel that, under the prolonged draughts of *Hood's Own* and the *Comic Annuals,* the beery mirth ran swipes. Even then it was just as eagerly received, for the popular sense of wit is none too nice, and the British commons retain their honest youthfulness, coarse of appetite, pleased with a rattle, tickled with a straw.

His poorer verse and prose.

There is no more sorrowful display of metrical literature — a tribute extorted from the poet who wrote for a living — than the bulk of his comic verses brought together in the volumes of Hood's remains. It was a sin and a shame to preserve it, but there it lies, with all its wretched puns and nonsense of the vanished past, a warning to every succeeding writer! To it might be added countless pages of equally valueless and trivial prose. Yet what clever work the man could do! In extravaganzas like "The Tale of a Trumpet" his sudden laughter flashes into wit; and there are half-pensive, half-mirthful lyrics, such as "A Retrospective Review," and the "Lament for the Decline of Chivalry," thrown off no less for his own than for the public enjoyment, of which the humor is natural and refined: not that of our day, to be sure, but to be estimated with the author's nationality and time. The "Ode to Rae Wilson, Esquire," though long and loosely written, is an honest, healthful satire, that would have delighted Robert Burns.

Comic poetry.

In one sense the term "comic poetry" is a misnomer. A poem often is just so much the less a poem by the amount it contains of puns, sarcasm, "broad grins," and other munitions of the satirist or *farceur.*

Yet the touch of the poet's wand glorifies the lightest, commonest object, and consecrates everything that is human to the magician's use. There is an imaginative mirth, no less than an imaginative wrath or passion, and with this element Hood's most important satirical poem is charged throughout. The " Golden Legend " of " Miss Kilmansegg and her Precious Leg," as a sustained piece of metrical humor, is absolutely unique. The flexible metre takes the reader with it, from the first line to the last, and this is no small achievement. The poem is utterly unhampered, yet quite in keeping; the satire faithful and searching; the narrative an audacious, fanciful story; the final tragedy as grotesque as that of a Flemish Dance of Death. At first the poet revels in his apotheosis of gold, the subject and motive of the poem : the yellow, cruel, pompous metal. lines the floor, walls, and ceiling of his structure ; it oozes, molten, from every break and crevice ; the personages are clothed in it ; threads of gold bind the rushing couplets together. What a picture of rich, auriferous, vulgar London life ! Passages of grim pathos are scattered here and there, as by Thackeray in the prose satires of " Catherine " and " Barry Lyndon." When the murdered Countess's " spark, called vital," has departed, — when in the morning,

"Miss Kilmansegg."

> "Her Leg, the Golden Leg, was gone,
> And the ' Golden Bowl was broken,' " —

then comes the " Moral " of the jester's tale : —

> "Gold! Gold! Gold! Gold!
> Bright and yellow, hard and cold,
> Molten, graven, hammered, and rolled ;
> Heavy to get, and light to hold ;

> Hoarded, bartered, bought, and sold,
> Stolen, borrowed, squandered, doled :
> Spurned by the young, but hugged by the old
> To the very verge of the churchyard mould ;
> Price of many a crime untold ;
> Gold ! Gold ! Gold ! Gold !
> Good or bad a thousand-fold !
> How widely its agencies vary —
> To save — to ruin — to curse — to bless —
> As even its minted coins express,
> Now stamped with the image of Good Queen Bess,
> And now of a Bloody Mary."

The legend of the hapless Kilmansegg is known to every reader. Who can forget her auspicious pedigree, her birth, christening, and childhood, her accident, her precious leg, her fancy-ball, her marriage *à la mode*, followed in swift succession by the Hogarthian pictures of her misery and death? The poem is full of rollicking, unhampered fancy ; long as it is, the movement is so rapid that it almost seems to have been written at a heat, — at least, can easily be read at a sitting. Though not without those absurd lapses which constantly irritate us in the perusal of Hood's lighter pieces, it is the most lusty and characteristic of them all. Standing at the front of its author's facetious verse, it renders him the leading poet-humorist of his generation ; and, in a critical review of any generation, the elements of mirth and satire cannot be overlooked. Of course, we are now *Thackeray and Hood.* considering a time when the genius of Thackeray scarcely had made itself felt and known. The grave-and-gay ballads of the novelist were but the overflow of his masterful nature ; yet so bounteous was that overflow, so compounded of all parts which go to the making of a Shakespearean mind, that, brief and without pretension as Thackeray's trifles are, more than one of them — for wit, grace, fancy, and other poetic constituents — is worth whole pages of the doggerel by which Hood earned his bread. What the latter did professionally the former executed with the airy lightness of a cavalier trying his sword-blade.

Contrasting the taste revealed in Hood's lyrics with the paltriness of his comic jingles, it would seem that his deterioration might be due to the constant necessity for labor which poverty imposed upon him, and to the fact that his labor was in the department of journalism. Only the most unremitting toil could support him as a magazine-writer; he gained the ear of the public not so much by humor as by drollery, and joke he must, be the sallies wise or otherwise, or the fire would go out on the hearth-stone, and the wolf enter at the door. In his day it was the laughter inspired by the actual presence of the comedian, upon the stage, that, in the nature of things, was measured at its worth and paid for. A few hundred pounds to the year were all that England gave the weary penman who could send a smile wreathing from Land's End to John o' Groat's.

If a poet, or aspiring author, must labor for the daily subsistence of a family, it is well for his art that he should follow some other calling than journalism; for I can testify that after the day's work is over, — when the brain is exhausted and vagrant, and the lungs pant for air, and body and soul cry out for recreation, — the intellect has done enough, and there is neither strength nor passion left for imaginative composition. I have known a writer who deliberately left the editorial profession, for which he was adapted both by taste and vocation, and took up a pursuit

Poverty unfriendly to the Muse.

Cp. " Poets of America": p. 268.

Authorship and journalism.

4*   F

*Cp. " Poets
of Amer-
ica " : pp.
75, 108,
233, 417.*

which bore no relation to letters; hoping that authorship would proffer him thenceforth the freshness of
variety, that upon occasion of loss or trouble it might
be his solace and recompense, and that, with a less
jaded brain, what writing he could accomplish would
be of a more enduring kind. It is so true, however,
that one nail drives out another! As an editor, this
person was unable to do anything beyond his newspaper work; as a business-man, with not the soundest
health, and with his heart, of course, not fully in his
occupation, he found himself neither at ease in his
means, nor able to gain sturdier hours for literature
than vigorous journalist-authors filch from recreation
and sleep. Fortunate in every way is the æsthetic
writer who has sufficient income to support him altogether, or, at least, when added to the stipend earned
by first-class work, to enable him to follow art without
harassment. For want of such a resource, poets, with
their delicate temperaments, may struggle along from
year to year, composing at intervals which other men
devote to social enjoyment, rarely doing their best;
possibly with masterpieces stifled in their brains till
the creative period is ended; misjudged by those
whom they most respect, and vexed with thoughts of
what they *could* perform, if sacred common duties
were not so incumbent upon them.

*Hood a
journalist-
poet.*

Nevertheless, if Hood's life had been one of scholastic ease, in all likelihood he would not have written that for which his name is cherished. He was
eminently a *journalist-poet*, and must be observed in
that capacity. Continuous editorial labor, beginning
in 1821 with his post upon *The London Magazine*,
and including his management of *The Comic Annual*,
Hood's Own, The New Monthly, and, lastly, *Hood's*

Magazine, — established but little more than a year before his death, — this journalistic experience, doubtless, gave him closer knowledge of the wants and emotions of the masses, and especially of the populace in London's murky streets. Even his facetious poems depict the throng upon the walks. The sweep, the laborer, the sailor, the tradesman, even the dumb beasts that render service or companionship, appeal to his kindly or mirthful sensibilities and figure in his rhymes. Thus he was, also, *London's poet*, the nursling of the city which gave him birth, and now holds sacred his resting-place in her cemetery of Kensal Green. Like the gentle Elia, whom he resembled in other ways, he loved " the sweet security of streets," and well, indeed, he knew them. None but such as he could rightly speak for their wanderers and poor.
London's Poet.

The rich philanthropist or aristocratic author may honestly give his service to the lower classes, and endeavor by contact with them to enter into their feelings, yet it is almost impossible, unless nurtured yourself at the withered bosom of our Lady of Poverty, to read the language of her patient foster-children. The relation of almoner and beneficiary still exists, a sure though indefinable barrier. Hood was not exclusively a poet of the people, like Elliott or Béranger, but one who interpreted the popular heart, being himself a sufferer, and living from hand to mouth by ill-requited toil. If his culture divided him somewhat from the poor, he all the more endured a lack of that free confession which is the privilege of those than whom he was no richer. The genteel poor must hide their wounds, even from one another. Hood solaced his own trials by a plea for those " whom he saw suffer." A man of kindred genius,
Fellowship of the poor.

the most potent of the band of humanitarian writers, who, in his time, sought to effect reform by means of imaginative art, also understood the poor, but chiefly through the memory of his own youthful experiences. In after years the witchery of prose-romance *Hood and Dickens.* brought to Charles Dickens a competence that Hood never could hope to acquire. Most men of robust physical vigor, who have known privation, yield to luxury when they achieve success, and Dickens was no exception; but his heart was with the multitude, he never was quite at home in stately mansions, and, though accused of snobbery in other forms, would admit no one's claim to patronize him by virtue of either rank or fortune.

Similarity of their methods. We readily perceive that Hood's modes of feeling resembled those which intensify the prose of Dickens, though he made no approach to the latter in reputation and affluent power. Could Dickens have written verse, — an art in which his experiments were, for the most part, utter failures, — it would have been marked by wit and pathos like Hood's, and by graphic, Doresque effects, that have grown to be called melodramatic, and that give a weird strength to "The Dream of Eugene Aram," "The Haunted House," and to several passages in the death-scene of "Miss Kilmansegg." Hood has nearly equalled Dickens in the analysis of a murderer's spectral conscience: —

> "But Guilt was my grim Chamberlain
>   That lighted me to bed;
> And drew my midnight curtains round,
>   With fingers bloody red!
>
>   .   .   .   .
>
> "Merrily rose the lark, and shook
>   The dew-drop from its wing;

> But I never mark'd its morning flight,
> I never heard it sing:
> For I was stooping once again
> Under the horrid thing."

The old Hall in "The Haunted House" is a counterpart to the shadowy grand-staircase in the Ded-
lock Mansion, or to Mr. Tulkinghorn's chamber, —
where the Roman points through loneliness and
gloom to the dead body upon the floor. This poem
is elaborate with that detail which, so painful and
over-prolonged, gives force to many of Dickens's
descriptive interludes, — such as, for instance, the
opening chapter of "Bleak House." The poet and *Alike in melodra-*
the novelist were fellow-workers in a melodramatic *matic feel-*
period, and there is something of stage effect in the *ing.*
marked passages of either. Take an example from
"Miss Kilmansegg": —

> "As she went with her taper up the stair,
>   How little her swollen eye was aware
>   That the Shadow which followed was double!
>   Or, when she closed her chamber door,
>   It was shutting out, and forevermore,
>   The world, — and its worldly trouble.
>
>   .   .   .   .
>
> "And when she quench'd the taper's light,
>   How little she thought, as the smoke took flight,
>   That her day was done, — and merged in a night
>   Of dreams and duration uncertain, —
>   Or, along with her own,
>   That a Hand of Bone
>   Was closing mortality's curtain!"

In extravagance, also, Dickens and Hood resembled *Other re-*
each other, and it seems perfectly natural that the *semblances.*
fantasies of both should be illustrated by the same
Cruikshank or Phiz. Both, also, give us pleasant

glimpses of England's greensward and hedge-rows, yet the special walk and study of each were in the streets and alleys of London; together they breathed the same burdened, whispering, emotional atmosphere of the monster town. They were of the circle which Jerrold drew around him, the London group of humane satirists and poets. Theirs was no amateur or closet work, but the flower of zeal and fellow-craft, which binds the workmen's hearts together, and makes art at once an industry, a heroism, and a vitalizing faith.

His most famous lyrics.   Our digression at length has brought us to the special group of lyrics upon which Hood's fame indubitably rests. The manner of what I call his proper style had been indicated long before, in such pieces as "The Elm-Tree" and "The Dream of Eugene Aram," of which the former is too prolonged, a still-life painting, barren of human elements, — and the latter, as has been seen, a remarkable ballad, approaching Coleridge's "Rime of the Ancient Mariner" in conception and form. In Hood's case the intellectual flames shone more brightly as his physical heat went out; in the very shadow of death he was doing his best, with a hand that returned to the pure ideals of his youth, and a heart that gained increase of gentleness and compassion as its throbs timed more rapidly the brief remainder of his earthly sojourn. In his final year, while editor of *Hood's Magazine,* a journal to which he literally gave his life, he composed three of the touching lyrics to which I refer: "The Lay of the Laborer," "The Lady's Dream," and "The Bridge of Sighs." The memorable "Song of the Shirt" was written a few months earlier, having appeared anonymously in the preceding Christmas

number of *Punch.* With regard to this poem the
instinct of the author's devoted wife, who constituted
his first public, was prophetic when she said : " Now,
mind, Hood, mark my words, this will tell wonderfully ! It is one of the best things you ever did ! "
No other lyric ever was written that at once laid such
hold upon the finest emotions of people of every class
or nationality, throughout the whole reading or listening world, — for it drew tears from the eyes of princes,
and was chanted to rude music by ballad-mongers in
the wretchedest streets.

The judgment of the people has rightly estimated
the two last-named poems above their companion-
pieces. They are the unequalled presentment of their
respective themes, the expressed blood and agony of
" London's heart." " The Song of the Shirt " was
the impulsive work of an evening, and open to some
technical criticism. But who so cold as to criticise
it ? Consider the place, the occasion, the despair of
thousands of working-women at that time, and was
ever more inspired and thrilling sermon preached by
a dying poet ? With like sacredness of feeling, and
superior melody, " The Bridge of Sighs " is a still more
admirable poem. It is felicitously wrought in a metre
before almost unused, and which few will henceforth
have the temerity to borrow : " Who henceforth shall
sing to thy pipe, O thrice-lamented ! who set mouth to
thy reeds ? " The tragedy of its stanzas lies at the
core of our modern life. The woes of London, the
mystery of London Bridge, the spirit of the materials
used by Dickens or by Ainsworth in a score of turbid
romances, — all these are concentrated in this precious lyric, as if by chemic process in the hollow of a
ring. It is the sublimation of charity and forgiveness,

" The Song of the Shirt."

" The Bridge of Sighs."

the compassion of the Gospel itself; the theme is here touched once and forever; other poets who have essayed it, with few exceptions, have smirched their fingers, and soiled or crushed the shell they picked from the mud, in their very effort to redeem it from pollution. The dramatic sorrow which attends the lot of womanhood in the festering city reaches its ultimate expression in "The Bridge of Sighs" and "The Song of the Shirt." They were the twin prayers which the suffering poet sent up from his death-bed, and, methinks, should serve as an expiation for the errors of his simple life.

General character- istics.

Our brief summary of the experience and work of Thomas Hood has shown that his more careful poetry is marked by natural melody, simplicity, and directness of language, and is noticeable rather for sweetness than imaginative fire. There are no strained and affected cadences in his songs. Their diction is so clear that the expression of the thought has no resisting medium, — a high excellence in ballad-verse. With respect to their sentiment, all must admire the absolute health of Hood's poetry written during years of prostration and disease. He warbled cheering and trustful music, either as a foil to personal distress, — which would have been quite too much to bear, had he encountered its echo in his own voice, — or else through a manly resolve that, come what might, he would have nothing to do with the poetry of despair. The man's humor, also, buoyed him up, and thus was its own exceeding great reward.

"Memorials of T. H.": by his daughter, Mrs. Brod- erip, 1860.

How prolonged his worldly trials were, — what were the privations and constant apprehensions of the little group beneath his swaying roof-tree, — something of this is told in the *Memorials* compiled by his

daughter, and annotated by his son, — the Tom Hood
of our day: an imperfect and disarranged biography,
yet one which few can read without emotion. Ill
health lessened his power to work, and kept him
poor, and poverty in turn reacted disastrously upon
his health. With all his reputation he was a literary
hack, whose income varied as the amount of writing
he could execute in a certain time. To such a man,
however, the devotion of his family, and the love of
Jane Reynolds, — his heroic, accomplished wife, a
woman in every way fit to be the companion of an
artist and poet, — were abundant compensation for
his patient struggle in their behalf. To the last mo-
ment, propped up in bed, bleeding from the lungs, *The poet's distress and heroism.*
almost in the agony of death, he labored equally in a
serious or sportive vein; but while thousands were
relishing his productions, they gave no delight to the
anxious circle at home. One passage in the Memorials tells the whole sad story: " His own family
never enjoyed his quaint and humorous fancies, for
they were all associated with memories of illness and
anxiety. Although Hood's *Comic Annual*, as he himself used to remark with pleasure, was in every home
seized upon, and almost worn out by the handling
of little fingers, his own children did not enjoy it till
the lapse of many years had mercifully softened down
some of the sad recollections connected with it."

The sorrow and anguish of the closing hours were
not without their alleviation. His last letter was written to Sir Robert Peel, in gratitude for the pension
conferred on Mrs. Hood. When it was known that
he lay dying, public and private sympathy, for which *Sympathy of the English people.*
he cared so greatly, comforted him in unnumbered
ways. His friends, neighbors, brother-authors, read-

ers, and admirers, throughout the kingdom, alike profoundly touched, gave him words of consolation as
well as practical aid.   A new generation has arisen

*T. H. died
in London,
May 3, 1845.*

since his death at the age of forty-six, but it is pleasant to remember the eagerness and generosity with
which, seven years afterward, the English people contributed to erect the beautiful monument that stands
above his grave.   The rich gave their guineas; the
poor artisans and laborers, the needlewomen and
dress-makers, in hosts, their shillings and pence.   Beneath the image of the poet, which rests upon the
structure, are sculptured the words which he himself,
with a still unsatisfied yearning for the affection of
his fellow-beings, — and a beautiful perception of the
act for which it long should be rendered to his memory, — devised for the inscription: " He sang THE
SONG OF THE SHIRT."

III.

*Matthew
Arnold:
born in
Laleham,
Dec. 24,
1822.*

FROM the grave of Hood we pass to observe a living writer, in some respects his antipode, who deals
with precisely those elements of modern life which
the former had least at heart.   It is true that Matthew Arnold, whose first volume was issued in 1848,
had little reputation as a poet until some years after
Hood's decease; but up to that time English verse
was not marked by its present extreme variety, nor
had the so-called school of culture obtained a foothold.   Arnold's circumstances have been more favorable than Hood's, and in youth his mental discipline
was thorough; yet the humorist was the truer poet,
although three fourths of his productions never should
have been written, and although there scarcely is a

line of Arnold's which is not richly worth preserving. It may be said of Hood that he was naturally a better poet than circumstances permitted him to prove himself; of Arnold, that through culture and good fortune he has achieved greater poetical successes than one should expect from his native gifts. His verse often is the result, not of "the first intention," but of determination and judgment; yet his taste is so cultivated, and his mind so clear, that, between the two, he has o'erleapt the bounds of nature, and almost falsified the adage that a poet is born, not made.

Arnold and Hood.

Certainly he is an illustrious example of the power of training and the human will. Lacking the ease of the lyrist, the boon of a melodious voice, he has, by a *tour de force*, composed poems which show little deficiency of either gift, — has won reputation, and impressed himself upon his age, as the apostle of culture, spiritual freedom, and classical restraint.

There is a passion of the voice and a passion of the brain. If Arnold, as a singer, lacks spontaneity, his intellectual processes, on the contrary, are spontaneous, and sometimes rise to a loftiness which no mere lyrist, without unusual mental faculty, can ever attain. His head not only predominates, but exalts his somewhat languid heart. A poet once sang of a woman, —

A poet of the intellect.

　　　"Affections are as thoughts to her,"

but thought with Arnold is poetical as affection, and in a measure supplies its place. He has an intellectual love for the good, beautiful, or true, but imparts to us a vague impression that, like a certain American statesman, he cares less for man in the concrete than for man in the abstract, — a not unusual phenomenon among æsthetic reformers. While admiring his delineations of Heine, the De Guérins, Joubert, and other far-away saints or heroes, we feel that he possibly may overlook some pilgrim at his roadside-door. Such is the effect of his writings, at this distance, and it is by his works that an artist chiefly should be judged.

Wanting in lyrical flow.

Through the whole course of Arnold's verse one searches in vain for a blithe, musical, gay, or serious off-hand poem : such, for example, as Thackeray's "Bouillabaisse," Allingham's "Mary Donnelly," Hood's "I Remember, I Remember," or Kingsley's "The Sands o' Dee." Yet he can be very nobly lyrical in certain uneven measures depending upon *tone*, and which, like "Philomela," express an ecstatic sensibility : —

> "Hark ! ah, the nightingale !
>   The tawny-throated !
>   Hark ! from that moonlit cedar what a burst !
>   What triumph ! hark — what pain !
>
>   .   .   .   .   .
>
>   "Listen, Eugenia —
>   How thick the bursts come crowding through the leaves !
>   Again — thou hearest !
>   Eternal Passion !
>   Eternal Pain ! "

Arnold's poetic theory.

In other poems, which reveal his saddest or profoundest intellectual moods, he is subjective and refutes his own theory. For his work claims to be produced upon a theory, — that of epic or classical objectivity, well and characteristically set forth in the preface to his edition of 1854. Possibly this was written shortly after the completion of some purely objective poem, like "Sohrab and Rustum," and the theory deduced from the performance. An

objective method is well suited to a man of large
or subtile intellect and educated tastes, who is
deficient in the minor sympathies. Through it he
can allow his imagination full play, and give a
pleasure to readers without affecting that feminine
instinct which really is not a constituent of his
poetic mould.

Arnold has little quality or lightness of touch. His *His limita-*
hand is stiff, his voice rough by nature, yet both are *tions.*
refined by practice and thorough study of the best
models. His shorter metres, used as the framework
of songs and lyrics, rarely are successful ; but through
youthful familiarity with the Greek choruses he has
caught something of their irregular beauty. " The
Strayed Reveller " has much of this unfettered charm.
Arnold is restricted in the range of his affections ; but
that he is one of those who can love very loyally the
few with whom they do enter into sympathy, through
consonance of traits or experiences, is shown in the
emotional poems entitled " Faded Leaves " and " Indifference," and in later pieces, which display more
lyrical fluency, " Calais Sands " and " Dover Beach."
A prosaic manner injures many of his lyrics : at least,
he does not seem clearly to distinguish between the
functions of poetry and of prose. He is more at ease *His blank-*
in long, stately, and swelling measures, whose graver *verse.*
movement accords with a serious and elevated purpose. Judged as works of art, " Sohrab and Rustum "
and " Balder Dead " really are majestic poems. Their
blank-verse, while independent of Tennyson's, is the
result, like that of the " Morte d'Arthur," of its
author's Homeric studies ; is somewhat too slow in
Balder Dead, and fails of the antique simplicity, but *" Balder*
is terse, elegant, and always in " the grand manner." *Dead."*

Upon the whole, this is a remarkable production ; it stands at the front of all experiments in a field remote as the northern heavens and almost as glacial and clear. Fifty lines, which describe the burning of Balder's ship, — his funeral pyre, — have an imaginative grandeur rarely excelled in the " Idyls of the King." Such work is what lay beyond Hood's power even to attempt ; and shows the larger mould of Arnold's intellect. A first-class genius would display the varying endowments of them both.

"Sohrab and Rustum."

Sohrab and Rustum is a still finer poem, because more human, and more complete in itself. The verse is not so devoid of epic swiftness. The powerful conception of the relations between the two chieftains, and the slaying of the son by the father, are tragical and heroic. The descriptive passage at the close, for diction and breadth of tone, would do honor to any living poet : —

> " But the majestic river floated on,
>   Out of the mist and hum of that low land,
>   Into the frosty starlight, and there moved,
>   Rejoicing, through the hushed Chorasmian waste
>   Under the solitary moon : he flowed
>   Right for the Polar Star, past Orgunjè,
>   Brimming, and bright, and large : then sands begin
>   To hem his watery march, and dam his streams,
>   And split his currents ; that for many a league
>   The shorn and parcelled Oxus strains along
>   Through beds of sand and matted rushy isles, —
>   Oxus, forgetting the bright speed he had
>   In his high mountain cradle in Pamere,
>   A foiled circuitous wanderer : — till at last
>   The longed-for dash of waves is heard, and wide
>   His luminous home of waters opens, bright
>   And tranquil, from whose floor the new-bathed stars
>   Emerge, and shine upon the Aral Sea."

" Tristram and Iseult," an obscure, monotonous variation upon a well-worn theme, is far inferior to *Objective*
either of the foregoing episodes. " The Sick King *themes.*
in Bokhara " and " Mycerinus " are better works, but
Arnold's narrative poems, and the " Empedocles on
Etna," — his classical drama, — are *studies*, in an age
which he deems uncreative, of as many forms of early
art, and successively undertaken in default of con-
genial latter-day themes. Their author, a poet and
scholar, offers, as an escape from certain heresies,
and as a substitute for poetry of the natural kind, a
recurrence to antique or mediæval thought and forms.
However well executed, is this a genuine addition to
literature? I have elsewhere said that finished reproductions cannot be accepted in lieu of a nation's
spontaneous song.

Arnold thus explains his own position : " In the *Preface to*
sincere endeavor to learn and practise, amid the *edition of*
bewildering confusion of our times, what is sound *1854.*
and true in poetical art, I seemed to myself to find
the only sure guidance, the only solid footing, among
the ancients. They, at any rate, knew what they
wanted in Art, and we do not. It is this uncertainty which is disheartening, and not hostile criticism." This is frank and noteworthy language, but
does not the writer protest too much? Are not his
sadness and doubt an unconscious confession of
his own special restrictions, — restrictions other than
those which, as he perceives, belong to England in
her weary age, or those which, in a period of transition from the phenomenal to the scientific, are common to the whole literary world? Were he a greater
poet, or even a small, sweet singer, would he stop to
reason so curiously? Rather would he chant and

chant away, to ease his quivering heartstrings of some impassioned strain.

We cannot accept his implication that he was born too late, since by this very reflection of the unrest and bewilderment of our time he holds his representative position in the present survey. The generation listens with interest to a thinker of his speculative cast. He is the pensive, doubting Hamlet of modern verse, saying of himself: " *Dii me terrent, et Jupiter hostis !* Two kinds of *dilettanti*, says Goethe, there are in poetry: he who neglects the indispensable mechanical part, and thinks he has done enough if he shows spirituality and feeling; and he who seeks to arrive at poetry by mere mechanism, in which he can acquire an artisan's readiness, and is without soul and matter. And he adds, that the first does the most harm to Art, and the last to himself." Quite as frankly Arnold goes on to enroll himself among *dilettanti* of the latter class. These he places, inasmuch as they prefer Art to themselves, before those who, with less reverence, exhibit merely spirituality and feeling. Here, let me say, he is unjust to himself, for much of his verse combines beautiful and conscientious workmanship with the purest sentiment, and has nothing of dilettanteism about it. This often is where he forsakes his own theory, and writes subjectively. " The Buried Life," " A Summer Night," and a few other pieces in the same key, are to me the most poetical of his efforts, because they are the outpourings of his own heart, and show of what exalted tenderness and ideality he is capable. A note of ineffable sadness still arises through them all. A childlike disciple of Wordsworth, he is not, like his master, a law and comfort to himself; a worshipper of Goethe, he at-

His mental structure and attitude.

Cp. " Poets of America" : pp. 339-341.

tributes, with unwitting egotism, his inability to vie
with the sage of Weimar, not to a deficiency in his
own nature, but to the distraction of the age : —

> " But we, brought forth and reared in hours
>   Of change, alarm, surprise, —
> What shelter to grow ripe is ours?
>   What leisure to grow wise ?

> .   .   .   .   .

> " Too fast we live, too much are tried,
>   Too harassed, to attain
> Wordsworth's sweet calm, or Goethe's wide
>   And luminous view to gain."

Arnold falters upon the march, conscious of a mission
too weighty for him to bear, — that of spiritualizing
what he deems an era of unparalleléd materialism.
The age is dull and mean, he cries,

> " The time is out of joint ; O, cursed spite !
>   That ever I was born to set it right."

And as Hamlet, in action, was inferior to lesser personages around him, he thus yields to introspection,
while protesting against it, and falls behind the bard
of a fresher inspiration, or more propitious time.   In
all this we discern the burden of a thoughtful man,
who in vain longs to create some masterpiece of art,
and whose yearning and self-esteem make him loath
to acknowledge his limitations, even to himself.

In certain poems, breathing the spirit of the tired
scholar's query, — " What is the use ? " he betrays a
suspicion that knowledge is not of itself a joy, and
an envy of the untaught, healthy children of the wild.
Extremes meet, and this is but the old reaction from
over-culture ; the desire of the wrestler for new strength
from Mother Earth.   " The Youth of Nature," " The
Youth of Man," and " The Future," are the fruit of

Reaction from over-culture.

5   G

these doubts and longings, and, at times, half sick of bondage, he is almost persuaded to be a wanderer and freeman. "The Scholar Gipsy" is a highly poetical composition, full of idyllic grace, and equally subtile in the beauty of its topic and thought. The poet,

Clough and Arnold.

and his poet-friend, Arthur Hugh Clough, in their wanderings around Oxford, realize that the life of the vagrant "scholar poor" was finer than their own : —

> "For early didst thou leave the world, with powers
>   Fresh, undiverted to the world without,
>   Firm to their mark, not spent on other things :
>   Free from the sick fatigue, the languid doubt,
>   Which much to have tried, in much been baffled, brings.
>   O Life, unlike to ours ! "

In after years Clough himself broke away somewhat from the trammels which these lines deplore. Arnold says of him, in "Thyrsis,"

> "It irked him to be here, — he could not rest.
>   He loved each simple joy the country yields,
>   He loved his mates ; but yet he could not keep,
>   For that a shadow lowered on the fields.
>
> .   .   .   .   .
>
> He went ! "

But even Clough made no such approach as our own Thoreau to the natural freedom of which he was by spells enamored. And who can affirm that Thoreau truly found the secret of content ? Was not his ideal, even as he seemed to clutch it, as far as ever from his grasp ?

"Thyrsis."

"Thyrsis," Arnold's more recent idyl, — "a monody to commemorate the author's friend," — is the exquisite complement of "The Scholar Gipsy." It is another, and one of the best, of the successful English imitations of Bion and Moschus ; among which " Lycidas " is the most famous, though some question whether Swinburne, in his " *Ave atque Vale,*" has not surpassed them all. Before the appearance of the last-named elegy, I wrote of " Thyrsis " that it was noticeable for exhibiting the precise amount of aid which classicism can render to the modern poet. As a threnode, nothing comparable to it had then appeared since the " Adonais " of Shelley. If not its author's farewell to verse, it has been his latest poem of any note ; and, like " The Scholar Gipsy," probably exhibits the highest reach of melody, vigor, and imagination, which it is within his power to show us.

That the bent of Arnold's faculty lies in the direction rather of criticism and argument than of imaginative literature, is evident from the increase of his prose-work in volume and significance. Some of the most perfect criticism ever written is to be found in his essays, of which that " On Translating Homer " will serve for an example. He carries easily in prose those problems of religion, discovery, and æsthetics which so retard his verse ; is thoroughly at home in polemic discussion, and a most keen and resolute opponent to all who heretically gainsay him. The critical faculty is not of itself incompatible with imaginative and creative power. We are indebted for lasting æsthetic canons to great poets of various eras. Even the fragmentary comments and marginalia of Goethe, Byron, Landor, Coleridge, etc., are full of point and suggestion. For one, I believe that, as able lawyers are the best judges of a lawyer's powers and attainments, so the painters, sculptors, musicians, and poets are most competent to decide upon the merits of works in their respective departments of art, —

Prose-writings.

The critical faculty in poets. Cp. " Poets of America": pp. 326-338.

though not always, being human, openly honest and
unprejudiced. Doubtless many lawyers will assent to
the first portion of this statement, and scout the
remainder. But, at all events, poets, like other men,
are wont to become more thoughtful as they grow
older, and I do not see that the work of the masters
has suffered for it. Arnold, however, is so much
greater as a writer of critical prose than as a poet,
that people have learned where to look for his genius,
and where for his talent and sensibility.

His essays are illuminated by his poetic imagination, and he thus becomes a better prose-writer than
a mere didactician ever could be. In fine, we may
regard Matthew Arnold's poetry as an instance of what
elevated verse, in this period, can be written, with
comparatively little spontaneity, by a man whose vigorous intellect is etherealized by culture and deliberately creates for itself an atmosphere of " sweetness
and light."

IV.

Bryan Wal-
ler Procter:
born in
Wiltshire,
Nov. 21,
1787.

A WIDE leap, indeed, from Matthew Arnold to
" Barry Cornwall," — under which familiar and musical lyronym **Bryan Waller Procter** has had more
singers of his songs than students of his graver
pages. No lack of spontaneity here! Freedom is
the life and soul of his delicious melodies, composed
during thraldom to the most prosaic work, yet tuneful as the carols of a lark upon the wing. It is hard
to think of Procter as a lawyer, who used to chant
to himself in a London omnibus, on his daily jour-
neys to and from the city. He is a natural vocalist,
wete it not for whom we might almost affirm that

song-making, the sweetest feature of England's most poetical period, is a lost art, or, at least, suspended during the present reign. There never was a time when little poems were more abundant, or more carefully finished, but a lyric may be exquisite and yet not possess the attributes of a successful song.

I can recall a multitude of such productions, each well worth a place in any lyrical " treasury "; among them, some that are graceful, touching, refined to perfection ; yet all addressed as much to the eye as to the ear, — to be read with tone and feeling, it may be, but not really demanding to be sung. The special quality of the song is that, however carelessly fashioned, it seems alive with the energy of music; the voice of its stanzas has a constant tendency to break into singing, as a bird, running swiftly, breaks into flying, half unawares. You at once associate true songs with music, and if no tunes have been set to them, they haunt the mind and " beat time to nothing " in the brain. The spirit of melody goes hunting for them, just as a dancing-air seeks and enters the feet of all within its circuit. Procter's lays have this vocal quality, and are of the genuine kind. To freedom and melody he adds more refinement than any song-writer of his time, and has a double right to his station in the group under review.

His stanzaic poems have, in fact, the rare merit of uniting the grace and imagery of the lyric to the music and fashion of song. It is well to look at this conjunction. The poet Stoddard, in a preface to his selection of English Madrigals, pronounces the lyric to be " a purer, as it certainly was an earlier, manifestation of the element which underlies the song," and says that " there are no songs, modernly speak-

Special quality of the song.

" Melodies and Madrigals," New York, 1866.

ing, in Shakespeare and the Elizabethan dramatists,
but lyrics in abundance." His distinction between a
lyric and a song is that the one is "a simple, unstudied expression of thought, sentiment, or passion;
the other its expression according to the mode of
the day." Unquestionably the abundant songs of
the eighteenth century, and those, even, of the generation when Moore was at his prime, are greatly inferior as poetry to the lyrics of the early dramatists.
Yet, were not the latter songs as well, save that the
Barry Corn- mode of their day was more delicate, ethereal, fine,
wall a lyrist
and true and strong? It seems to me that such of the early
song-writer. lyrics as were written to music possess thereby the
greater charm. And the songs of Barry Cornwall,
beyond those of any other modern, have an excellence of "mode" which renders them akin to the
melodies of Shakespeare, Marlowe, Jonson, Heywood,
Fletcher, and to the choicer treasures of Davison,
and of the composers, Byrd, Wilbye, and Weelkes.
They are, at once, delightful to poets and dear to
the singing commonalty. I refer, of course, to their
pervading character. It may be that none are so absolutely flawless as the Bugle-Song of Tennyson. The
melody and dying fall of that lyric are almost without comparison this side of Amiens' ditties in "As
You Like It" and Ariel's in "The Tempest." But
how few there are of Procter's numerous songs which
stand lower than the nearest place beneath it! Many
of them excel it in swiftness, zest, outdoor quality,
and would be more often trolled along the mountain-
side, upon the ocean, or under the greenwood-tree.

The fountain of Procter's melody has not so long
been sealed as to exclude him from our synod of the
later poets, although — how strange it seems! — he

was the schoolfellow of Byron at Harrow, and won popular successes when he was the friend and associate of Hunt, Lamb, and Keats. Born ten years earlier than Hood, he was before the public in time to act the prophet, and in the dedication of "The Genealogists" predicted the humorist's later fame. He dates back in years, not in literature, almost as far as Landor, and like him was among the foremost *A pioneer.* to discern the new spirit of poetry and to assist in giving it form. In a preface to his "Dramatic Scenes" he tells us: "The object that I had in view, when I wrote these scenes, was to try the effect of a more natural style than that which has for a long time prevailed in our dramatic literature. I have endeavored to mingle poetical imagery with natural emotion." Like Landor, also, he performed some of his best work at dates well toward the middle of this century; in fact, it is upon songs given to the public during the fourth and fifth decades that his influence and fame depend. This has led me to consider him among recent poets, rather than in his youthful attitude as the pupil of Leigh Hunt.

Hunt's poetic mission (taken apart from his career *James* as a radical) was of note between 1815 and 1830, and *Henry* was that of a propagandist. Without much originality, *Leigh* he was a poet of sweetness, fluency, and sensibility, *Hunt.* *1784–1859.* who became filled with the art-spirit of Keats and his masters, and both by precept and example was a potent force in its dissemination. Beyond the position attained as a shining light of what was derisively called "The Cockney School," Leigh Hunt made little progress. He lived, it is true, until 1859, — a writer of dainty verse and most delightful prose, beloved by the reading world, and viewed with a queer mixture of pity, reverence, and affection, by his younger brethren of the craft. Procter's early studies were influenced by Keats and Hunt, to whose work he was attracted by affinity with the methods of their Elizabethan models, as opposed to those of Byron and Scott. His nature, also, was too robust — and too æsthetic — to acquire any taste for the metaphysical processes of Wordsworth, which were ultimately to shape the mind, even as Keats begat the body, of the idyllic Victorian School. The fact that Procter's genius was essentially dramatic finally gave him a position independent of Keats, and, against external restrictions, drew him in advance of Hunt, who — whatever he may have been as critic and essayist — was in some respects the lesser poet. Nevertheless, those restrictions compelled Procter, as Landor was compelled, to forego the work at which he would have been greatest, and to exercise his gift only in a fragmentary or lyrical manner. He found the period, between the outlets of expression afforded by the newspaper and the novel, unsuited to the reception of objectively dramatic verse, though well enough disposed toward that of an introspective kind. In short, Procter at this time was — as Miss Hillard has felicitously entitled his early friend, Thomas Lovell Beddoes — a "strayed singer," — an Elizabethan who had wandered into the nineteenth century. His organization included an element of practical common-sense, which led him to adapt himself, as far as possible, to circumstances, and, forbearing a renewal of sustained and lonely explorations, to vent his natural impulses in the "short swallow-flights of song" to which he owes his reputation. The love of minstrelsy is perpetual. Barry Cornwall, the songwriter, has found a place among his people, and

Procter's dramatic genius.

developed to the rarest excellence at least one faculty
of his poetic gift.

But we have, first, to consider him as a pupil of
the renaissance : a poet of what may be termed the
interregnum between Byron and Tennyson, — for the
Byronic passion is absolutely banished from the idyllic
strains of Tennyson and his followers, who, nevertheless, betray the influences of Wordsworth and Keats
in wedded · force.   Procter's early writings were embraced in three successive volumes of *Dramatic Scenes,*
etc., which appeared in 1819 – 21, and met with a
friendly reception.   Some of the plays were headed
by quotations from Massinger, Webster, and such
dramatists, and otherwise indicated the author's choice
of models.   His verse, though uneven, was occasionally poetical and strong.   There is breadth of handling in these lines from " The Way to Conquer " : —

His early writings, 1819-21.

> " The winds
> Moan and make music through its halls, and there
> The mountain-loving eagle builds his home.
> But all 's a waste : for miles and miles around
> There 's not a cot."

An extract from a poem entitled " Flowers " has the
beauty of favorite passages in " The Winter's Tale "
and " A Midsummer-Night's Dream," — the flavor and
picturesque detail of Shakespeare's blossomy descriptions : —

> " There the rose unveils
> Her breast of beauty, and each delicate bud
> O' the season comes in turn to bloom and perish.
> But first of all the violet, with an eye
> Blue as the midnight heavens, the frail snowdrop,
> Born of the breath of Winter, and on his brow
> Fixed like a pale and solitary star ;

5 *

The languid hyacinth, and wild primrose,
And daisy trodden down like modesty ;
The foxglove, in whose drooping bells the be
Makes her sweet music ; the narcissus (named
From him who died for love) ; the tangled woodbine,
Lilacs, and flowering limes, and scented thorns,
And some from whom voluptuous winds of June
Catch their perfumings."

Influence upon other poets.

It may be noted that Procter's early verse had an effect upon poets who have since obtained distinction, and who improved on the hints afforded them. Two of the pieces in the first and second volumes, " A Vision " and " Portraits," contain the germs of Tennyson's " Dream of Fair Women," and of his best-known classical poem. The " Lines to —— " and " Lines on the Death of a Friend " bear a striking resemblance in metre, rhythm, and technical " effects," to those wild and musical lyrics written long afterward by Edgar A. Poe, " The Sleeper " and " The City in the Sea." In several of his metrical tales, Procter, no less than Keats and Hunt, went to that Italian source which, since the days of Chaucer, has been a fountain-spring of romance for the poet's use. His " Sicilian Story " is an inferior study upon the theme of Keats's " Isabella " ; and some of his other themes from Boccaccio have been handled by later poets, — the story of " Love Cured by Kindness," by Mrs. Lewes, and that of " The Falcon," by our own Longfellow. Among his dramatic sketches, " The Way to Conquer," " The Return of Mark Antony," and especially " Julian the Apostate," have admirable scenes ; their verse displays simplicity, passion, sensuousness ; one derives from them the feeling that their author might have been a vigorous. dramatic poet in a more suitable era. As it was, he stood in the front rank of his contemporaries, not only as one of the brilliant writers for *The London Magazine*, but respected by practical judges who cater for the public taste. His stage tragedy, *Mirandola*, was brought out at the Covent Garden theatre, apparently with suc- cess. Macready, Charles Kemble, and Miss Foote figured in the cast. It is an acting drama, with a plot resembling that of Byron's "Parisina." A volume of two years' later date exhibits less progress in con- structive power. It contained "The Flood of Thes- saly," "The Girl of Provence," "The Letter of Boc- caccio," "The Fall of Saturn," etc., — poems which show greater finish, but little originality, and more of the influence of Hunt and Keats. Throughout the five books under review, the blank-verse, some- times effective, as in "Marcelia," is often jagged and diffuse. The classical studies are not equal to those of the poet's last-named associate. In Procter's lyrical verses, however, we now begin to see the groundwork of his later eminence as a writer of Eng- lish songs.

Among the sweetest of these melodies was "Golden- tressed Adelaide," a ditty warbled for the gentle child whose after-career was to be a dream-life of poesy and saintliness, ending all too early, and bearing to his own the relation of a song within a song. I give the opening stanza : —

"Miran- dola," 1821.

Adelaide Anne Procter.

> "Sing, I pray, a little song,
>   Mother dear !
> Neither sad, nor very long :
> It is for a little maid,
> Golden-tressed Adelaide !
> Therefore let it suit a merry, merry ear,
>   Mother dear ! "

The poet had married, it is seen, and other children blessed his tranquil home, where life glided away as he himself desired, gently : —

> " As we sometimes glide,
> Through a quiet dream! "

The most perfect lyric ever addressed by a poet to his wife is the little song, known, through Neukomm's melody, in so many homes : —

> " How many summers, love,
> Have I been thine ? "

The final stanza is exquisite : —

> " Ah ! — with what thankless heart
> I mourn and sing !
> Look, where our children start,
> Like sudden Spring !
> With tongues all sweet and low,
> Like a pleasant rhyme,
> They tell how much I owe
> To thee and Time ! "

After Procter's marriage his muse was silent for a while ; partly, no doubt, from a growing conviction that no mission was then open to a dramatic poet ; partly, from the necessity for close professional work, under the domestic obligations he had assumed. What was lost to art was gained in the happiness of the artist's home ; and if he escaped the discipline of learning in suffering what he taught in song, I, for one, do not regret this enviable exception to a very bitter rule.

The Muse cannot be wholly banished, even by the strong felicity of wedded love. She enters again and again, and will not be denied. Barry Cornwall's voice

came back to him, after a moulting period; and
although he wrote no plays, he exercised it in that
portion of dramatic composition which, like music in
every-day life, is used as a relief and beguilement, —
the utterance of expressive song.

Dramatic poetry, embracing in completeness every
department of verse, seems to reach a peculiar excellence in its lyrical interludes. Procter says that "the
songs which occur in dramas are generally more natural than those which proceed from the author in
person," and gives some reasons therefor. My own
belief is that the dramatic and lyrical faculties are
correlative, a lyric being a dramatic and musical outburst of thought, passion, sorrow, or delight; and
never was there a more dramatic song-writer than is
Barry Cornwall. His *English Songs* appeared at a
time when, — setting aside the folk-minstrelsy of Scotland and Ireland, — the production of genuine lyrics
for music was, as we have seen, almost a lost art.
He declared of it, however, "The spring will return!" and was the fulfiller of his own prediction.
By the agreement of musicians and poets, his songs,
whether as melodies or lyrics, approach perfection,
and thousands of sweet voices have paid tribute to
their beauty, unconscious of the honeyed lips from
which it sprung. Mr. Stoddard — than whom there
is no higher authority with respect to English lyrical
poetry — judges Procter to be its "most consummate
master of modern days": in fact, he questions
"whether all the early English poets ever produced
so many and such beautiful songs as Barry Cornwall," and says that "a selection of their best would
be found inferior as a whole to the one hundred and
seventy-two little songs in Mr. Procter's volume, —

*The dra-
matic and
lyrical fac-
ulties re-
lated.*

Procter's "English Songs," 1832.

narrower in range, less abundant in measures, and infinitely less pure as expressions of love."

There are many who would demur to this comparative estimate, and for whom the starry Elizabethan lyrics still shine peerless, yet they too are charmed by the spirit, alternately tender and blithesome, of Procter's songs; by their unconscious grace, changeful as the artless and unexpected attitudes of a fair girl; by their absolute musical quality and comprehensive range. They include all poetic feelings, from sweetest melancholy to "glad animal joy." Some heartstring answers to each, for each is the fine expression of an emotion; nor is the emotion simulated for the song's sake. Now, how different in this respect are Barry Cornwall's melodies from the still-life lyrics, addressing themselves to the eye, of many recent poets! How assured in their audible loveliness! Sometimes fresh with the sprayey breeze of ocean, and echoing the innumerous laughter of waves that tumble round the singer's isle : —

> "The sea! the sea! the open sea!
> The blue, the fresh, the ever free!
> Without a mark, without a bound,
> It runneth the earth's wide regions round;
> It plays with the clouds; it mocks the skies;
> Or like a cradled creature lies.
>
> .   .   .   .   .
>
> "I never was on the dull, tame shore,
> But I loved the great sea more and more,
> And backwards flew to her billowy breast,
> Like a bird that seeketh its mother's nest;
> And a mother she *was* and *is* to me;
> For I was born on the open sea!"

It is a human soul that wanders with "The Stormy

Petrel," dips its pinions in the brine, and has the liberty of Prospero's tricksy spirit, "be't to fly, to swim, to dive " : —

> " A thousand miles from land are we,
> Tossing about on the roaring sea ;
> From billow to bounding billow cast,
> Like fleecy snow on the stormy blast:
>
> .   .   .   .   .
>
> Up and down ! Up and down !
> From the base of the wave to the billow's crown,
> And amidst the flashing and feathery foam
> The Stormy Petrel finds a home ! "

The zest and movements of these and a few kindred melodies have brought them into special favor. Their virile, barytone quality is dominant in the superb " Hunting Song," with its refrain awakening the lusty morn : — *Fresh and buoyant music.*

> " Now, thorough the copse, where the fox is found,
> And over the stream, at a mighty bound,
> And over the high lands, and over the low,
> O'er furrows, o'er meadows, the hunters go !
> Away ! — as a hawk flies full at its prey,
> So flieth the hunter, away, — away !
> From the burst at the cover till set of sun,
> When the red fox dies, and — the day is done !
> *Hark, hark ! — What sound on the wind is borne?*
> *'Tis the conquering voice of the hunter's horn.*
> *The horn, — the horn !*
> *The merry, bold voice of the hunter's horn.*"

Procter's convivial glees are the choruses of robust and gallant banqueters, and would stifle in the throat of a sensual debauchee. The Vine Song, —

> " Sing ! — Who sings
> To her who weareth a hundred rings ? " —

has the buoyancy of Wolfe's favorite, " How stands the Glass around ? " Among the rest, " Drink, and fill the Night with Mirth ! " and " King Death " are notable, the first for its Anacreontic lightness, and the last for a touch of the grim revelry which so fascinates us in " Don Giovanni," and reflects a perfectly natural though grotesque element of our complex mould.

Lyrical variety.

In one of the many editions of Barry Cornwall's lyrical poems I find two hundred and forty songs, of surprising range and variety: songs of the chase, the forest, and the sea ; lullabies, nocturnes, greetings, and farewells ; songs of mirth and sorrow ; few martial lays, but many which breathe of love in stanzas that are equally fervent, melodious, and pure. Some have a rare and subtile delicacy, so characteristic of this poet as at once to mark their authorship. Such is the melody, commencing

> " Sit down, sad soul, and count
> The moments flying " ;

such, also, " A Petition to Time " ; and such the lyric, entitled " Life," the beautiful dirge, " Peace ! what can Tears avail ? " and " The Poet's Song to his Wife," — already quoted. Another class of songs, to which earlier reference has been made, mostly composed in a major key, may fairly be compared with the work of other poets. Bayard Taylor's early lyrics, " The Mariners " and " Wind at Sea," have the same clear, healthy ring, and his " Bedouin Song," in fine poetic quality, is not excelled by any similar effort of the British lyrist. Again, without knowing the author, we might assume that Emerson had traced the royal lines descriptive of " The Blood Horse " : —

> "Gamarra is a dainty steed,
>   Strong, black, and of a noble breed,
>   Full of fire, and full of bone,
>   With all his line of fathers known;
>   Fine his nose, his nostrils thin,
>   But blown abroad by the pride within!
>   His mane is like a river flowing,
>   And his eyes like embers glowing
>   In the darkness of the night,
>   And his pace as swift as light."

More than other poets, Barry Cornwall tempts the writer to linger on the path of criticism and make selection of the jewels scattered here and there. Like the man in the enchanted cavern, one cannot refrain from picking up a ruby or an emerald, though forbidden by the compact made. The later chips from Procter's dramatic workshop are superior to his early blank-verse in wisdom, strength, and beauty. It is a pity, that, after all, they are but "Dramatic Fragments," and not passages taken from complete and heroic plays. Bryan Waller Procter, restricted from the production of such masterworks, at least did what he could. For some years before his recent death the world listened in vain for the voice of this sweet singer. He lingered to an extreme old age: a white-haired, silent minstrel, into whose secluded mind the reproach would have fallen unheeded, had the rosy-cheeked boys, whom Heine pictures, sprung around him, placed the shattered harp in his trembling hand, and said, laughing, "Thou indolent, gray-headed old man, sing us again songs of the dreams of thy youth!"

"Dramatic Fragments."

B. W. P. died in London, Oct. 4, 1874.

H

CHAPTER IV.

ELIZABETH BARRETT BROWNING.

I.

THERE are some poets whom we picture to ourselves as surrounded with aureolas; who are clothed in so pure an atmosphere that when we speak of them, — though with a critical purpose and in this exacting age, — our language must express that tender fealty which sanctity and exaltation compel from all mankind. We are not sure of our judgment: ordinary tests fail us; the pearl is a pearl, though discolored; fire is fire, though shrouded in vapor, or tinged with murky hues. We do not see clearly, for often our eyes are blinded with tears; — we love, we cherish, we revere.

A spiritual temperament. The memory and career of Elizabeth Barrett Browning appear to us like some beautiful ideal. Nothing is earthly, though all is human; a spirit is passing before our eyes, yet of like passions with ourselves, and encased in a frame so delicate that every fibre is alive with feeling and tremulous with radiant thought. Her genius certainly may be compared to those sensitive, palpitating flames, which harmonically rise and fall in response to every sound-vibration near them. Her whole being was rhythmic, and, in a time when art is largely valued for itself alone, her utterances were the expression of her inmost soul.

I have said that while the composite period has exhibited many phases of poetic art, it is not difficult, with respect to each of them taken singly, to find some former epoch more distinguished. The Elizabethan age surpassed it in dramatic creation, and in those madrigals and canzonets which — to transpose Mendelssohn's fancy — are music without harping ; the Protectorate developed more epic grandeur, — the Georgian era, more romantic sentiment and strength of wing. Recent progress has been phenomenal, chiefly, in variety, finish, average excellence of work. To this there is one exception. The Victorian era, with its wider range of opportunities for women, has been illumined by the career of the greatest female poet that England has produced, — nor only England, but the whole territory of the English language ; more than this, the most inspired woman, so far as known, of all who have composed in ancient or modern tongues, or flourished in any land or time.

Former periods more eminent in special quality,

but the Victorian has produced the greatest of woman-poets.

What have we of Sappho, beyond a few exquisite fragments, a disputed story, the broken strings of a remote and traditional island-lyre? Yet, from Sappho down, including the poetry of Southern and Northern Europe and the whole melodious greensward of English song, the remains of what woman are left to us, which in quantity and inspiration compete with those of Mrs. Browning? What poet of her own sex, except Sappho, did she herself find worthy a place among the forty immortals grouped in the hemicycle of her own " Vision of Poets "? Take the volume of her collected writings, — with so much that we might omit, with so many weaknesses and faults, — and what riches it contains! How different, too, from other recent work, thoroughly her own, eminently that of a woman, — a Christian sibyl, priestess of the melody, heroism, and religion of the modern world !

II.

Her years of unmar- ried life.

WHAT is the story of her maidenhood? Not only of those early years which, no matter how long we continue, are said to make up the greater portion of our life; but also of an unwedded period which lasted to that ominous year, the thirty-seventh, which has ended the song of other poets at a date when her own — so far as the world heard her — had but just begun. How grew our Psyche in her chrysalid state? For she was like the insect that weaves itself a shroud, yet by some inward force, after a season, is impelled to break through its covering, and come out a winged tiger-moth, emblem of spirituality in its birth, and of passion in the splendor of its tawny dyes.

Elizabeth Barrett Barrett: born at Hope End, near Led- bury, 1809.

Elizabeth Barrett Barrett was born of wealthy parents, in 1809, and began her literary efforts almost contemporaneously with Tennyson. Apparently, — for the world has not yet received the inner history of a life, which, after all, was so purely intellectual that only herself could have revealed it to us, — apparently, I say, she was the idol of her kindred ; and especially of a father who wondered at her genius and encouraged the projects of her eager youth.

"An Essay on Mind, with Other Poems," 1826.

Otherwise, although she was a rhymer at the age of ten, how could she have published, in her seventeenth year, her didactic Essay, composed in heroics after the method of Pope? Apparently, too, she had a mind of that fine northern type which hungers after learning for its own sake, and to which the study of books or nature is an instinctive and insatiable de-

sire. If Mrs. Browning left no formal record of her
youth, the spirit of it is indicated so plainly in " Aurora Leigh," that we scarcely need the letter : —

> " Books, books, books!
> I had found the secret of a garret-room
> Piled high with cases in my father's name ;
>
> .　　.　　.　　.　　.
>
> The first book first. And how I felt it beat
> Under my pillow, in the morning's dark,
> An hour before the sun would let me read !
> My books !
> 　　At last, because the time was ripe,
> I chanced upon the poets."

Doubtless this sleepless child was one to whom her
actual surroundings, even if observed, seemed less
real than the sights in dreamland and cloudland re- *Influence of*
vealed to her by simply opening the magical covers *reading on the imagi-*
of a printed book. An imaginative girl sometimes *nation.*
becomes so entranced with the ideal world as to
quite forego the billing and cooing which attend upon
the springtime of womanhood. Such natures often
awake to the knowledge that they have missed something : love was everywhere around them, but their
eyes were fixed upon the stars, and they perceived it
not. This abnormal growth is perilous, and to the
feebler class of dreamers, who have poetic sensibility
without true constructive power, insures blight, loneliness, premature decay. For the born artist, such
experiences in youth not only are inevitable, but are
the training which shapes them for their after work.
The fittest survive the test.

Miss Barrett's early feasts were of an omnivorous
kind, the best school-regimen for genius : —

"I read books bad and good — some bad and good
    At once : .   .   .   .
        .   .   .   .   And being dashed
    From error on to error, every turn
    Still brought me nearer to the central truth."

*Unconscious
training
of genius.
Cp. " Poets
of Amer-
ica": p.
307.*

A gifted mind in youth has an unconsciousness of evil, and an affinity for the beautiful and true, which enable it, when given the freedom of a library, to assimilate what is suited to its needs. Fact and fiction are inwardly digested, and in maturer years the logical faculty involuntarily assorts and distributes them. Aurora reads her books,

" Without considering whether they were fit
    To do me good. Mark, there. We get no good
    By being ungenerous, even to a book,
    And calculating profits . . so much help
    By so much reading. It is rather when
    We gloriously forget ourselves and plunge
    Soul-forward, headlong, into a book's profound, *
    Impassioned for its beauty and salt of truth —
    'T is then we get the right good from a book."

Much of this reading was of that grave character to which court-maidens of Roger Ascham's time were wonted, for her juvenile " Essay on Mind " evinced a knowledge of Plato, Bacon, and others of the world's great thinkers : I do not say familiarity with them ; scholars know what that word means, and how loosely such terms are bandied. She gained that general conception of each, similar to what we learn of a man upon first acquaintance, and often not far wrong.

*Her classi-
cal studies.*

With time and occasion afterward came the more disciplinary process of her education. Fortunate influences, possibly those of her father, — if we may still follow " Aurora Leigh," — guided her in the direction of studies as refining as they were severe. She read Latin and Greek. Now, it is noteworthy that a girl's intellect is more adroit in acquirement, not only of the languages, but of pure mathematics, than that of the average boy. Any one trained at the desks of a New England high-school is aware of this. In later years the woman very likely will stop acquiring, while the man still plods along and grows in breadth and accuracy. Miss Barrett became a loving student of Greek, and we shall see that it greatly influenced her literary progress.

Among her maturer friends was the sweetly gentle and learned Hugh Stuart Boyd, to whom in his blindness she read the Attic dramatists, and under whose guidance she explored a remarkably wide field of Grecian philosophy and song. What more beautiful subject for a modern painter than the girl Elizabeth, — "that slight, delicate figure, with a shower of dark curls falling on each side of a most expressive face, large tender eyes richly fringed by dark eyelashes, and a smile like a sunbeam," — than this ethereal creature seated at the feet of the blind old scholar, her face aglow with the rhapsody of the sonorous drama, from which she read of Œdipus, until

Hugh Stuart Boyd. 1782–1848.

Her portrait in Miss Mitford's "Recollections of a Literary Life."

> "the reader's voice dropped lower
> When the poet called him BLIND!"

Here was the daughter that Milton should have had! An oft-quoted stanza from her own "Wine of Cyprus," addressed to her master in after years, may be taken for the legend of the picture: —

> "And I think of those long mornings,
> Which my Thought goes far to seek,
> When, betwixt the folio's turnings,
> Solemn flowed the rhythmic Greek.

> Past the pane the mountain spreading,
> Swept the sheep-bell's tinkling noise,
> While a girlish voice was reading,
> Somewhat low for *ai*'s and *oi*'s."

Aside from repeated indications in her other writing, this graceful poem shows the liberal extent of her delightful classical explorations.   Homer, Pindar, Anacreon, — " Æschylus, the thunderous," " Sophocles, the royal," " Euripides, the human," " Plato, the divine one," — Theocritus, Bion, — not only among the immortal pagans did Miss Barrett follow hand in hand with Boyd, but attended him upon his favorite excursions to those " noble Christian bishops " — Chrysostom, Basil, Nazianzen — " who mouthed grandly the last Greek."

Beneficent effect of culture.
Cp. " Poets of America": pp. 109, 135.

What other woman and poet of recent times has passed through such a novitiate, in the academic groves and at the fountain-heads of poetry and thought?   I dwell upon Miss Barrett's culture, because I am convinced that it had much to do with her preeminence among female poets.   Many a past generation has produced its songsters of her sex, whose voices were stifled for want of atmosphere and training.   An auspicious era gave her an advantage over predecessors like Joanna Baillie, and her culture placed her immeasurably above Miss Landon, Mrs. Hemans, and others who flourished at the outset of her own career.   Lady Barnard, the Baroness Nairn, Mrs. Norton, — women like these have written beautiful lyrics ; but here is one, equally feminine, yet with strength beyond them all, lifting herself to the height of sustained imagination.   George Sand, Charlotte Brontë, and Mrs. Lewes have been her only compeers, but of these the first — at least in form, and the two latter both in form and by instinct, have been writers of prose, before whom the poet takes precedence, by inherited and defensible prerogative.

It was a piece of good fortune that Miss Barrett's technical study of roots, inflections, and what not was elementary and incidental. She and her companion read Greek for the music and wisdom of a literature which, as nations ripen and grow old, still holds its own, — an exponent of pure beauty and the universal mind. The result would furnish a potent example for those who hold, with Professor Tayler Lewis, that the classical tongues should be studied chiefly for the sake of their literature. She was not a scholar, in the grammarian's sense; but broke the shell of a language for the meat which it contained. Hence her reading was so varied as to make her the most powerful ally of the classicists among popular authors. Her poetical instinct for meanings was equal to Shelley's; — as for Keats, he created a Greece and an Olympus of his own.

Her scholarship liberal, but not pedantic.

Her first venture of significance was in the field of translation. *Prometheus Bound, and Miscellaneous Poems*, was published in her twenty-fourth year. The poems were equally noticeable for faults and excellences, of which we have yet to speak. The translation was at that time a unique effort for a young lady, and good practice; but abounded in grotesque peculiarities, and in fidelity did not approach the modern standard. In riper years she freed it from her early mannerism, and recast it in the shape now left to us, "in expiation," she said, "of a sin of my youth, with the sincerest application of my mature mind." This later version of a most sublime tragedy is more poetical than any other of equal correctness, and has the

"Prometheus Bound, and Miscellaneous Poems," 1833.

6

fire and vigor of a master-hand. No one has succeeded better than its author in capturing with rhymed
measures the wilful rushing melody of the tragic
chorus. Her other translations were executed for her
own pleasure, and it rarely was her pleasure to be
exactly faithful to her text. She was honest enough
to call them what they are ; and we must own that
her " Paraphrases on " Theocritus, Homer, Apuleius,
etc., are enjoyable poems in themselves, preserving
the spirit of their originals, yet graceful with that
freedom of which Shelley's " Hymn to Mercury " is
the most winsome English exemplar since Chapman's
time.

Our poet was always healthful and at ease wherever her classicism suggested the motive of her own
song. "The Dead Pan" is an instance of her peculiar utilization of Greek tradition, and in other
pieces her antique touches are frequent. Late in life,
when unquestionably failing, — her eyes growing dim
and her poetic force abated, — amid a peal of verses,
that sound to me like sweet bells jangled, there is no
clearer strain than that of " A Musical Instrument."
For a moment, indeed, as she sang a melody of the
pastoral god, her

> " sun on the hill forgot to die,
> And the lilies revived, and the dragon-fly
> Came back to dream on the river."

Her classi-
cism distinct
from Lan-
dor's.

A distinction between Landor's workmanship and
that of Mrs. Browning was, that the former rarely
used his classicism allegorically as a vehicle for modern sentiment ; the latter, who did not write and think
as a Greek, goes to the antique for illustration of her
own faith and conceptions.

Of Miss Barrett's life we now catch glimpses through the kindly eyes of Miss Mitford, who became her near friend in 1836. She had entered upon a less secluded period, and probably the four years which followed the appearance of her " Prometheus " were as happy as any of her maidenhood. But, always fragile, in 1837 she broke a blood-vessel of the lungs ; and after a lingering convalescence was again prostrated in 1839 by the death of her favorite brother, — drowned in her sight off the bar of Torquay. Months elapsed before she could be removed to her father's house, there to enter upon that absolute cloister-life which continued for nearly seven years. It was the life of a couch-ridden invalid, restricted to a large but darkened chamber, and forbidden all society but that of a few dear friends. I think of her, however, in that classic room as of one shut up in some belvedere, where, by means of a camera, the outer world is reflected upon the table at your breast. For she returned to her books as a diversion from her thoughts, and with an eagerness that her physicians could not restrict. Miss Mitford says that she was now " reading almost every book worth reading in almost every language, and giving herself, heart and soul, to that poetry of which she seemed born to be the priestess." The creative faculty reasserted itself ; the moon will draw the sea despite the storms and darkness that brood between.

Prolonged illness and seclusion.

In 1838 she published *The Seraphim and other Poems ;* in another year, *The Romaunt of the Page*, a volume of ballads entitled from the one which bears that name. In 1842 she contributed to the London *Athenæum* some Essays on the Greek-Christian and English Poets, — the only specimens of her prose left

" The Seraphim," 1838.

" The Romaunt of the Page," 1839.

Critical prose-writings, 1842.

First collective edition of her poems, 1844.

Her early style.

Disadvantages of over-culture.

Shelley.

Her ballads.

to us, — enthusiastic, not closely written, but showing unusual attainments and critical perception. In 1844 — her thirty-fifth year — she found strength for the collection of her writings in their first complete edition, which opened with "A Drama of Exile." These volumes, comprising the bulk of her works during her maiden period, furnish the material and occasion for some remarks upon her characteristics as an English poet.

Her style, from the beginning, was strikingly original, uneven to an extreme degree, equally remarkable for defects and beauties, of which the former gradually lessened and the latter grew more admirable as she advanced in years and experience. The disadvantages, no less than the advantages, of her education, were apparent at the outset. She could not fail to be affected by various master-minds, and when she had outgrown one influence was drawn within another, and so tossed about from world to world. "The Seraphim," a diffuse, mystical passion-play, was an echo of the Æschylean drama. Its meaning was scarcely clear even to the author; the rhythm is wild and discordant; neither music nor meaning is thoroughly beaten out. I have mentioned Shelley as one with whom she was akin, — is it that Shelley, dithyrambic as a votary of Cybele, was the most sexless, as he was the most spiritual, of poets? There are singers who spurn the earth, yet scarcely rise to the heavens; they utter a melodious, errant strain that loses itself in a murmur, we know not how. Miss Barrett's early verse was strangely combined of this semi-musical delirium and obscurity, with an attempt at the Greek dramatic form. Her ballads, on the other hand, were a reflection of her English studies;

and, as being more English and human, were a vast poetic advance upon "The Seraphim." Evidently, in these varied experiments, she was conscious of power, and strove to exercise it, yet with no direct purpose, and half doubtful of her themes. When, therefore, as in certain of these lyrics, she got hold of a rare story or suggestion, she made an artistic poem; all are stamped with her sign-manual, and one or two are as lovely as anything on which her fame will rest.

My own youthful acquaintance with her works be- *"Rhyme of the Duchess May."* gan, for example, with the "Rhyme of the Duchess May." It was different from any romance-ballad I had read, and was to me a magic casement opening on "faerylands forlorn"; and even now I think, as I thought then, that the sweetness and power of scenery and language, the delicious metre, the refrain of the passing bell, the feeling and action, are highly poetical and have an indescribable charm. The blemishes of this lyric are few: it is nicely adjusted to the proper degree of quaintness; the overture and epilogue are exquisitely done, and the tone is maintained throughout, — an unusual feat for Mrs. Browning. I have never forgotten a pleasure which so contrasted with the barren sentiment of a plain New England life, and here fulfil my obligation to lay a flower of gratitude upon her grave. Yes, indeed: all she needed was a theme to evoke her rich imaginings, and I wish she had more frequently ceased from introspection and composed other ballads like that of the "Duchess May."

Of her minor lyrics during this period, — "Isobel's *Minor lyrics.* Child," "The Romaunt of the Page," "The Lay of the Brown Rosary," "The Poet's Vow," etc., — few are so good as the example just cited; but each is quite removed from commonplace, and, with its contrasts of strength and weakness, entirely characteristic of its author.

Her diction.   The effect of Miss Barrett's secluded life was visible in her diction, which was acquired from books rather than by intercourse with the living world ; and from books of all periods, so that she seemed unconscious that certain words were obsolete, or repellent even to cultured and tasteful people. Reviewers who accused her of affectation were partly correct ; yet many uncouth phrases and forgotten words seemed to her no less available than common forms obtained from the same sources. By this she gained a richer structure ; just as Kossuth, learning our language from books, had a more copious vocabulary than many English orators. But she lost credit for good sense, and certainly at one time had no sure judgment in the use of terms. Since she explored the French, Spanish, and Italian classics as eagerly as those of her own tongue, perhaps the wonder is that her diction was

Lack of taste.   not even more fantastical. Her *taste* never seemed quite developed, but through life subordinate to her

Nobility of feeling.   excess of feeling. So noble, however, was the latter quality, that the critics gave her poetry their attention, and endeavored to correct its faults of style. For a time she showed a lack of the genuine artist's reverence, and not without egotism followed her wilful

Grossly defective art.   way. The difficulty with her obsolete words was that they were introduced unnaturally, and produced a grotesque effect instead of an attractive quaintness. Moreover, her slovenly elisions, indiscriminate mixture of old and new verbal inflections, eccentric rhymes, forced accents, wearisome repetition of favored words to a degree that almost implied poverty of thought, —

such matters justly were held to be an outrage upon the beauty and dignity of metrical art. An occasional discord has its use and charm, but harshness in her verse was the rule rather than the exception. When she had a felicitous refrain — a peculiar grace of her lyrics — she frequently would mar the effect and give a shock to her readers by the introduction of some whimsical or repulsive image. Her passion was spasmodic; her sensuousness lacked substance; as for simplicity, it was at one time questionable whether she was not to be classed among those who, with a turbulent desire for utterance, really have nothing definite to say. Her sonnet on "The Soul's Expression" showed that the only thing clear to her mind was that she could state nothing clearly: — *Clouded vision.*

> "With stammering lips and insufficient sound
> I strive and struggle to deliver right
> That music of my nature, day and night
> With dream and thought and feeling interwound."

Metaphysical reading aggravated her natural vagueness and what is termed transcendentalism, — perilous qualities in the domain of art. Long afterward she herself spoke of "the weakness of these earlier verses, which no subsequent revision has succeeded in strengthening." *Cp. "Poets of America": pp. 168, 169, 249, 253.*

In "A Drama of Exile," where she had a more definite object, these faults are less apparent, and her genius shines through the clouds; so that we catch glimpses of the brightness which eventually lighted her to a station in the Valhalla of renown. *"A Drama of Exile," 1844.*

During her years of illness she had added some knowledge of Hebrew to her acquirements, and could read the Old Testament in the original. The grander elements of her imagination received a new stimulus from the sacred text, with which, after all, her mind was more in sympathy than with the serene beauty of the Greek. In the " Drama of Exile " she aimed at the highest, and failed ; but such failures are impossible to smaller poets. It contains wonderfully fine passages ; is a chaotic mass, from which dazzling *Fervent im-* lustres break out so frequently that a critic aptly *agination.* spoke of the " flashes " of her " wild and magnificent genius," the " number and close propinquity of which render her book one flame." My review presupposes the reader's familiarity with her writings, so that citation of passages does not fall within its intention. Yet, let me ask what other female poet has risen to such language as this of Adam to Lucifer ?

> " The prodigy
> Of thy vast brows and melancholy eyes
> Which comprehend the heights of some great fall.
> I think that thou hast one day worn a crown
> Under the eyes of God."

And where in modern verse is there a more vigorous and imaginative episode than Lucifer's remembrance of the couched lion, " when the ended curse left silence in the world " ?

> " Right suddenly
> He sprang up rampant and stood straight and stiff,
> As if the new reality of death
> Were dashed against his eyes, — and roared so fierce
> (Such thick carnivorous passion in his throat
> Tearing a passage through the wrath and fear)
> And roared so wild, and smote from all the hills
> Such fast, keen echoes crumbling down the vales
> Precipitately, — that the forest beasts,
> One after one, did mutter a response
> Of savage and of sorrowful complaint

> Which trailed along the gorges. Then, at once,
> He fell back, and rolled crashing from the height
> Into the dusk of pines."

Miss Barrett in this drama displayed a true conception of the sublime ; though as yet she had neither grace, logic, nor sustained power. The most fragile and delicate of beings, she essayed, with more than man's audacity, to reach the infinite and soar to "the gates of light."

That she was a tender woman, also, and that her hand had been somewhat trained by varied lyrical efforts, was manifest from some of those minor pieces through which she now began to attract the popular regard. Among those not previously mentioned, the tributes to Mrs. Hemans and Miss Landon, "Catarina to Camoens," "Crowned and Wedded," "Cowper's Grave," "The Sea-Mew," "To Flush, my Dog," and "The Swan's Nest," were more simple and open to general esteem than their companion pieces. "An Island," "The Lost Bower," and "The House of Clouds" are pure efforts of fancy, for the most part charmingly executed. "Bertha in the Lane" is treasured by the poet's admirers for its virginal pathos, — the sacred revelation of a dying maiden's heart, — an exquisite poem, but greatly marred in the closing. It was difficult for the author, however fine her beginnings, to end a poem, once begun, or to end it well under final compulsion. "The Cry of the Human," with its impassioned refrain and almost agonized plea that the ancient curse may be lightened, evinced her recognition of the sorrows and mysteries of existence : — all these things she "kept in her heart," and uttered brave invectives against black or white slavery, and other social wrongs. "The Cry of the Children,"

Successful lyrical efforts.

Humanitarian poems.

6* I

uneven as it is, takes its place beside Hood's "Song of the Shirt," for sweet pity and frowning indignation. In behalf of the little factory-slaves, after reading Horne's report of his Commission, her soul took fire and she did what she could. If the British mill-owners were little likely to be impressed by her imaginative ode, with its Greek motto, it certainly affected the minds of public writers and speakers, who could fashion their more practical agitation after the pattern thus given them in the Mount.

Her most popular ballad.

But "Lady Geraldine's Courtship" was the ballad — and often a poet has one such — which gained her a sudden repute among lay-readers. It is said that she composed it in twelve hours, and not improbably; for, although full of melodious sentiment and dainty lines, the poem is marred by commonplaces of frequent occurrence. Many have classed it with "Locksley Hall," but, while certain stanzas are equal to Tennyson's best, it is far from displaying the completeness of that enduring lyric. I value it chiefly as an illustration of the greater freedom and elegance to which her poetic faculty had now attained, and as her first open avowal, and a brave one in England, of the democracy which generous and gifted spirits, the round world over, are wont to confess. As for her story, she only succeeded in showing how meanly a womanish fellow might act, when enamored of one above him in social station, and that the heart of a man possessed of healthy self-respect was something she had not yet found out. Her Bertram is a dreadful prig, who cries, mouths, and faints like a school-girl, allowing himself to eat the bread of the Philistines and betray his sense of inequality, and upon whom Lady Geraldine certainly throws herself away. He is a libel upon the whole race of poets. The romance, none the less, met with instant popularity on both sides of the Atlantic, and has passed into literature, somewhat pruned by later touches, as one of its author's more conspicuous efforts.

Miss Barrett now, at the relatively mature age of thirty-five, appeared to have completed her intellectual growth. It was a chance whether her future should be greater than her past. Thus far I regard her experience as merely formative. Much of her vagueness and gloom had departed with the physical prostration that so long had borne her down. For her improving health showed that study and authorship, though against the wishes of her attendants, were the best medicine for a body and mind diseased. *End of her formative career.*

As the scent of the rose came back "above the mould," she was to emerge upon a new life, different from that which we hitherto have considered as the day is from the night. She was not to be enrolled among the mournful sisterhood of women, who

> " sit still
> On winter nights by solitary fires
> And hear the nations praising them far off."

The dearest common joys were yet to be hers, and that full development which a woman's genius needs to make it rounded and complete. There is a pretty story of her first meeting with the poet Browning, based upon the lines referring to him in " Lady Geraldine's Courtship." This, however, is not credited by Theodore Tilton, her American editor, who wrote the Memorial prefixed to the collection of her " Last Poems." Four lyrics, thrown off at this time, — en- *Robert Browning* *" Memorial," by Theodore Tilton, 1862.*

titled " Life and Love," " A Denial," " Proof and Disproof," and " Inclusions," — go far to show Miss Barrett's humility, and inability to comprehend the happiness which had come to her. But, nevertheless, the poet wooed and won her ; and in 1846, her

Her marriage, London, 1846.

thirty-seventh year, she was taken from her couch to the altar, and at once borne away by her husband from her native land. Some facts in my possession with respect to this event have too slight a bearing upon the record of her literary achievements to warrant their insertion here. It is well known that the marriage was opposed by her father, but she builded better than he knew. Her cloister-life of maidenhood in England was at an end. Fifteen happy and illustrious years in Italy lay before her ; and in her

Married life.

case the proverb *Cœlum, non animum,* was unfulfilled. Never was there a more complete transmutation of the habits and sympathies of life than that which she experienced beneath the blue Italian skies. Still, before all and above all, her refined soul remained in allegiance to the eternal Muse.

III.

HE is but a shallow critic who neglects to take into his account of a woman's genius a factor representing the master-element of Love. The chief event

Influence of love upon a woman's genius.

in the life of Elizabeth Barrett was her marriage, and causes readily suggest themselves which might determine the most generous parent to oppose such a step on her part. The dedication of her edition of 1844 shows how close was the relation existing between her father and herself, and I am told by one who knew her for many years, that Mr. Barrett " was a man of intellect and culture, and she had been his pride, as well as the light of his eyes, after he became a widower." To such a parent, now well in the vale of years, a marriage which was to lift his fragile daughter from the couch to' which she had been bound as a picture to its frame must have seemed a rash experiment, and a cruel blow to himself, however eminent and devoted the suitor who had claimed her. But when the long-closed tide-ways of a woman's heart are opened, the torrent comes with double force at last, sweeping kith and kin away by Nature's inexorable law. If the old West India merchant had not afterwards acted with utter selfishness in respect to the marriage of another daughter, I should be disposed to estimate his wounded love for Elizabeth, as she herself did, by his steadfast refusal, despite her "frequent and heart-moving" appeals, to be reconciled to her throughout the remainder of his darkened life.

Her father's opposition to the nuptials.

Wedlock was so thoroughly a new existence to her, that her kindred well might fear for the result. A veritable Lady of Shalott, she now entered the open highways of a peopled world. She left a polar region of dreams, solitude, introspection, for the equatorial belt of outer and real life. The beneficent sequel shows how wise are the instincts of a refined nature. To Mrs. Browning, love, marriage, travel, were happiness, desire of life, renewed bodily and spiritual health; and when, in her fortieth year, the sacred and mysterious functions of maternity were given her to realize, there also came that ripe fruition of a genius that hitherto, blooming in the night, had yielded fragrant and impassioned, but only sterile flowers.

Complete womanhood.

The question of an artist's married life, it seems

Relations of art and marriage:
to me, has wholly different bearings when considered from the opposite standing-points of the two sexes. A discerning writer has recently mentioned an artist whose view was, that a man devoted to art might marry " either a plain, uneducated woman devoted to household matters, or else a woman quite capable of entering into his artistic life"; but no one between the two extremes. The former would be less perilous than to marry a daughter of the Philistines, "equally incapable of comprehending his pursuits, but much more likely to interfere with them." Yet in behalf

As they affect, 1, the husband;
of a man of artistic genius and sensibility, who is born to a career if he chooses to pursue it, I would not accept even the first-named alternative, unless he has sufficient wealth to insure him perfect independence or seclusion. An author's growth, and the happiness of both parties, are vastly imperilled by his union with the most affectionate of creatures, if she has an inartistic nature and a dull or commonplace mind. The Laureate makes the simple wife exclaim: "I cannot understand: I love!"—but there is no perfect love without mutual comprehension; at the best, a wearisome, unemotional forbearance takes its place. On the one part jealousy, active or disguised, of the other's wider range, too often exerts a restrictive influence, by which the art-impulse, and the experiences it should feed upon, are modified or repressed. It is a law of psychological mathematics that the constant force of dulness will in the end overcome any varying force resisting it; and when Pegasus can be driven in harness, one generally finds him yoked with a brood-mare, — ay, and broken-in when young and more or less defenceless.

Again, we so readily persuade ourselves to lapse

from the efforts of creative labor, when temptation puts on the specious guise of duty! The finest kind of art — that possessing originality — is unremunerative for years; and who has the courage to pursue it, while responsible for the conventional ease and happiness of those who possibly regret that he is not so practical as other men, and look with distrust upon his habits of life and labor? Ordinary people can more easily attain to that perfect mating which is the sum of bliss. But let an artist marry art, and be true to it alone, unless by some rare chance he can find a companion whose soul is kindred with his own, who can sympathize with his tastes, and aid him with tact and circumstance in his social and professional career. If she has genius of her own, and her own purposes in any department of art, then all obligations can be entirely mutual, and under favorable auspices the highest wedded felicity should be the result.

The relations of art and marriage, where the development of female genius is concerned, are of a distinctive character, and must be so considered. It is no doubt true that a woman, also, can only arrive at extreme happiness by wedlock founded upon entire congeniality of mind and purpose; and yet there are conditions under which it may become essential to her complete development as an artist that she should marry out of her own ideal, rather than not be married at all. So closely interwrought are her physical and spiritual existences, that otherwise the product of her genius may be little more than a beautiful fragment at the most. We must therefore esteem Mrs. Browning doubly fortunate, and protected by the gods themselves. For marriage not only had given her, by one of Nature's charming miracles, a precious lease

As they affect, 2, the wife.

The wedded poets.

of life, but had united her with a fellow-artist whose disposition and pursuits were in absolute harmony with her own, — the one man in the world whom she would have chosen, yet who sought her out, and deemed it his highest joy to possess her as a wife, and cherish her as companion, lover, and friend. In this life of incongruities it is encouraging to find such an instance of the serene fitness of things. The world is richer for their union, than which none more distinguished is of record in the annals of authorship.

Summit of Mrs. Browning's greatness.

The ten years following the date of Mrs. Browning's marriage were the noonday of her life, and three master-works, embraced in this period, represent her at her prime. *Casa Guidi Windows* appeared in 1851, the same volume including the matchless " Sonnets from the Portuguese." *Aurora Leigh* was published in 1856. None of her later or earlier compositions were equal to these in scope, method, and true poetical value.

Her powers fully developed.

At first the influence of her new life was of a complex nature. It opened a sealed fountain of love within her, which broke forth in celestial song: it gave her a land and a cause to which she thoroughly devoted her woman's soul; finally, a surprising advance was evident in the rhythm, language, and all other constituents of her metrical work. The Saxon English, which she hitherto had quarried for the basis of her verse, now became conspicuous throughout the whole structure. Her technical gain was partly due to the stronger themes which now bore up her wing, — and partly, I have no doubt, to the companionship of Robert Browning. Even if he did not directly revise her works, neither could fail to profit by the other's genius and experience; and the blem-

ishes of his wife's earlier style were such as Browning
at this time would not relish, for they were of a different kind from his own. Besides, we are sensitive
to faults in those we love, while committing them ourselves as if by chartered right.

I am disposed to consider the *Sonnets from the Por-* "*Sonnets*
tuguese as, if not the finest, a portion of the finest *from the*
Portu-
subjective poetry in our literature.   Their form re- *guese*,"
minds us of an English prototype, and it is no sacri- 1850.
lege to say that their music is showered from a higher
and purer atmosphere than that of the Swan of Avon.
We need not enter upon cold comparison of their
respective excellences ; but Shakespeare's personal
poems were the overflow of his impetuous youth : — his
broader vision, that took a world within its ken,, was
absolutely objective ; while Mrs. Browning's Love Sonnets are the outpourings of a woman's tenderest emotions, at an epoch when her art was most mature,
and her whole nature exalted by a passion that to
such a being comes but once and for all. Here, indeed, the singer rose to her height. Here she is absorbed in rapturous utterance, radiant and triumphant
with her own joy.   The mists have risen and her
sight is clear. Her mouthing and affectation are forgotten, her lips cease to stammer, the lyrical spirit
has full control.   The sonnet, artificial in weaker
hands, becomes swift with feeling, red with a " veined
humanity," the chosen vehicle of a royal woman's
vows. Graces, felicities, vigor, glory of speech, here
are so crowded as to tread each upon the other's
sceptred pall.   The first sonnet, equal to any in our
tongue, is an overture containing the motive of the
canticle ; — " not Death, but Love " had seized her
unaware. The growth of this happiness, her worship

of its bringer, her doubts of her own worthiness, are the theme of these poems. She is in a sweet and, to us, pathetic surprise at the delight which at last had fallen to her : —

> "The wonder was not yet quite gone
> From that still look of hers."

Never was man or minstrel so honored as her "most gracious singer of high poems." In the tremor of her love she undervalued herself, — with all her feebleness of ·body, it was enough for any man to live within the atmosphere of such a soul! In fine, the Portuguese Sonnets, whose title was a screen behind which the singer poured out her full heart, are the most exquisite poetry hitherto written by a woman, and of themselves justify us in pronouncing their author the greatest of her sex, — on the ground that the highest mission of a female poet is the expression of love, and that no other woman approaching her in genius has essayed the ultimate form of that expression. An analogy with "In Memoriam" may be derived from their arrangement and their presentation of a single analytic theme ; but Tennyson's poem — though exhibiting equal art, more subtile reasoning and comprehensive thought — is devoted to the analysis of philosophic Grief, while the Sonnets reveal to us that Love which is the most ecstatic of human emotions and worth all other gifts in life.

Devotion to Italy. Mrs. Browning's more than filial devotion to Italy has become a portion of the history of our time. Independently of her husband's enthusiasm, everything in the aspect and condition of the country of her adoption was fitted to arouse this sentiment. It became a passion with her ; she identified herself with the Italian cause, and for fourteen years her oratory in Casa Guidi was vocal with the aspiration of that fair land struggling to be free. Its beauty and sorrow enthralled her; its poetry spoke through her voice; its grateful soil finally received her ashes, and will treasure them for many an age to come.

Nothing can be finer than the burst of song at the opening of her Italian poem, —

"*Casa Guidi Windows,*" 1851.

> "I heard last night a little child go singing,
>   'Neath Casa Guidi windows, by the church,
>   *O bella liberta, O bella!*" —

unless it be the passages which begin and close the second portion of the same work, composed after an interval of three years, when the hope of the first exultant outbreak was for the time obscured. Between the two extremes the chant is eloquently sustained, and is our best example of lucid, sonorous English verse composed in a semi-Italian *rima*. While full of poetry, its increase of intellectual vigor shows how a singer may be lifted by the occasion and capacity for pleading a noble cause. Deep voice, strong heart, fine brain, — the three must go together in the making of a great poet. "Casa Guidi Windows" won a host of friends to Italy, and gained for its devoted author an historic name. During the interval mentioned she had given birth to the child whose presence was the awakening of a new prophetic gift: —

> "The sun strikes through the windows, up the floor;
>   Stand out in it, my own young Florentine,
> Not two years old, and let me see thee more!
>   It grows along thy amber curls to shine
> Brighter than elsewhere. Now look straight before,
>   And fix thy brave blue English eyes on mine,
> And from thy soul, which fronts the future so

> With unabashed and unabated gaze,
> Teach me to hope for what the Angels know
> When they smile clear as thou dost! "

While experience of motherhood now had perfected her woman's nature, Mrs. Browning was also at the zenith of her lyrical career. Her minor verses of the period are admirable. She revised her earlier poetry for the edition of 1856, and Mr. Tilton has pointed out some of her fastidious and usually successful emendations. It was the happiest portion of her life, as well as the most artistic. The sunshine of an enviable fame enwreathed her ; rare and gifted spirits, wandering through Italy, were attracted to her presence and paid homage to its laurelled charm. Hence, as a secondary effect of her marriage, her knowledge of the world increased ; she became a keen though impulsive observer of men and women, and of the thought and action of her own time. Few social movements escaped her notice, whether in Europe or our own unrestful land ; her instincts were in favor of agitation and reform, and her imagination was ever looking forward to the Golden Year. And it was now that, summoning all her strength — alas ! how unequal was her frail body to the tasks laid upon it by the aspiring soul ! — with heroic determination and most persistent industry, she undertook and completed her *capo d'opera*, — the poem which, in dedicating to John Kenyon, she declares to be the most mature of her works, " and the one into which my highest convictions upon Life and Art have entered."

If Mrs. Browning's vitality had failed her before the production of " Aurora Leigh," — a poem comprising twelve thousand lines of blank-verse, — her generation certainly would have lost one of its repre-

Strength, happiness, and fame.

" Aurora Leigh," 1856.

sentative and original creations : representative in a versatile, kaleidoscopic presentment of modern life and issues ; original, because the most idiosyncratic of its author's poems. An audacious, speculative freedom pervades it, which smacks of the New World rather than the Old. Tennyson, while examining the social and intellectual phases of his era, maintains a judicial impassiveness ; Mrs. Browning, with finer dramatic insight, — the result of intense human sympathy, enters into the spirit of each experiment, and for the moment puts herself in its advocate's position. "Aurora Leigh" is a mirror of contemporary life, while its learned and beautiful illustrations make it, almost, a handbook of literature and the arts. As a poem, merely, it is a failure, if it be fair to judge it by accepted standards. One may say of it, as of Byron's "Don Juan" (though loath to couple the two works in any comparison), that, although a most uneven production, full of ups and downs, of capricious or prosaic episodes, it nevertheless contains poetry as fine as its author has given us elsewhere, and enough spare inspiration to set up a dozen smaller poets. The flexible verse is noticeably her own, and often handled with as much spirit as freedom ; it is terser than her husband's, and, although his influence now began to grow upon her, is not in the least obscure to any cultured reader. The plan of the work is a metrical concession to the fashion of a time which has substituted the novel for the dramatic poem. Considered as a "novel in verse," it is a failure by lack of either constructive talent or experience on the author's part. Few great poets invent their myths ; few prose character-painters are successful poets ; the epic songsters have gone to tradition for their themes,

A characteristic production.

the romantic to romance, the dramatic to history and
incident. Mrs. Browning essayed to invent her whole
story, and the result was an incongruous framework,
covered with her thronging, suggestive ideas, her
flashing poetry and metaphor, and confronting you by
whichever gateway you enter with the instant presence
of her very self. But either as poem or novel, how
superior the whole, in beauty and intellectual power,
to contemporary structures upon a similar model,
which found favor with the admirers of parlor romance or the lamb's-wool sentiment of orderly British
life! As a social treatise it is also a failure, since
nothing definite is arrived at. Yet the poet's sense
of existing wrongs is clear and exalted, and if her
exposition of them is chaotic, so was the transition
period in which she found herself involved. Upon
the whole, I think that the chief value and interest of
" Aurora Leigh " appertain to its marvellous illustrations of the development, from childhood on, of an
æsthetical, imaginative nature. Nowhere in literature
is the process of culture by means of study and passional experience so graphically depicted. It is the
metrical and feminine complement to Thackeray's
" Pendennis " ; a poem that will be rightly appreciated by artists, thinkers, poets, and by them alone.

Landor to
J Forster,
1857.

Landor, for example, at once received it into favor,
and also laid an unerring finger upon its weakest
point : " I am reading a poem," he wrote, " full of
thought and fascinating with fancy. In many pages
there is the wild imagination of Shakespeare. . . . .
I had no idea that any one in this age was capable of such poetry. . . . . There are, indeed, even
here, some flies upon the surface, as there always
will be upon what is sweet and strong. I know not

yet what the story is. Few possess the power of construction."

The five remaining years of Mrs. Browning's life were years of self-forgetfulness and devotion to the heroic and true. Her beautiful character is exhibited in her correspondence, and in the tributes ,of those who were privileged to know her. What poetry she wrote is left to us, and I am compelled to look upon it as belonging to her period of decline. However *Mrs.* fine its motive, " we are here," as M. Taine has said, *Browning's period of* to judge of the product alone, and " to realize, not an *decline.* ode, but a law." Physical debility was the main cause of this lyrical falling off. Her exhausted frame was now, more than ever, what Hillard had pronounced it, " nearly a transparent veil for a celestial and' immortal spirit." Her feelings were again more imperative than her mastery of art ; her hand trembled, her voice quavered with that emotion which is not strength. She now, as I have said, unconsciously began to yield *Secondary* to the prolonged influence of her husband's later style, *influence of her married* and it affected her own injuriously, though it must *life.* be acknowledged that her poetry acquired, toward the last, a new and genuine, but painful, dramatic quality. Her " Napoleon III. in Italy," and the minor lyrics *" Poems be-* upon the Italian question, are submitted in evidence *fore Congress,"* 1860. of the several points just made. Some of her later poems were contributed to a New York newspaper, *" The Inde-* with whose declared opinions she was in sympathy, *pendent."* and which was the mouthpiece of her warmest American admirers ; and, in the effort to promptly meet her engagements, she tendered unrevised and faulty work. At intervals the production of some gracious, healthful hour would be a truly effective poem, and such lyrics as " De Profundis," " A Court Lady," " The

Forced Recruit," " Parting Lovers," and " Mother and
Poet," made the world realize how rich and tuneful
could be the voice still left to her. One evening it
was my fortune to listen to a recitation of the last-
named poem, from the lips of a beautiful girl who
looked the very embodiment of the lyric Muse, and I
was struck with the truthfulness and strength displayed
in the poet's dramatic conception of the mingled patriotism and anguish in a bereaved Italian mother's
heart. But the dominant roughness which too gen-
" Last
Poems,"
1860 – 1861.
erally pervades her *Last Poems* shows how completely
she now had accepted Browning's theory of entire
subordination, in poetry, of the art to the thought,
and his method of giving expression to the latter, no
matter how inchoate, at any cost to the finish and
effectiveness of the work in hand.

IV.

Final esti-
mate of Mrs.
Browning's
genius.
IN a former chapter I wrote of " an inspired singer,
if there ever was one, — all fire and air, — her song
and soul alike devoted to liberty, aspiration, and love."
The career of this gifted woman has now been traced.
In conclusion, let us attempt to estimate her genius
and discover the position to be assigned to her
among contemporary poets.

Her art.
And first, with regard to her qualities as an
artist. She was thought to resemble Tennyson in
some of her early pieces, but this was a mistake, if
anything beyond form is to be considered. In read-
Tennyson
and Mrs.
Browning.
ing Tennyson you feel that he drives stately and
thoroughbred horses, and has them always under
control ; that he could reach a higher speed at pleasure ; while Mrs. Browning's chargers, half-untamed,

prance or halt at their own will, and often bear her away over some rugged, dimly lighted tract. Her verse was the perfect exponent of her own nature, including a wide variety of topics in its range, but with the author's manner injected through every line of it. Health is not its prominent characteristic. Mrs. Browning's creative power was not equal to her capacity to feel; otherwise there was nothing she might not have accomplished. She evinced *over-possession,* and certainly had the contortions of the Sibyl, though *Over-posses-sion.* not lacking the inspiration. We feel that she must have expression, or perish, — a lack of restraint common to female poets. She was somewhat deficient in æsthetic conscientiousness, and we cannot say of her works, as of Tennyson's, that they include nothing which has failed to receive the author's utmost care. She had that distrust of the " effect " of her produc- *Incertitude.* tions which betrays a clouded vision; and in truth, much of her vaguer work well might be distrusted. Her imagination was radiant, but seldom clear; it was the moon obscured by mists, yet encircled with a glorious halo.

Her metres came by chance, and this often to her detriment; she rarely had the patience to discover those best adapted to her needs, but gave voice to the first strain which occurred to her. Hence she had a spontaneity which is absent from the Laureate's work. *Spontaneity.* This charming element has its drawbacks: she found herself hampered by difficulties which a little fore-thought would have avoided, and her song, though as fresh, was too often as purposeless, as that of a forest-bird. There is great music in her voice, but one wishes that it were better trained. She had a gift of *Her re-* melodious and effective refrains : " The Nightingales, *frains.*

7   J

Cp. " Poets of America": p. 245.

the Nightingales," "Margret, Margret," "You see we're tired, my Heart and I," "Toll slowly!" "The River floweth on," "Pan, Pan is dead!"—these and other examples captivate the memory, but occasionally the burden is the chief sustainer of the song. One of her repetends, "He giveth His beloved Sleep," is the motive of an almost celestial lyric, faultless in holy and melodious design. It is a poem to read by the weary couch of some loved one passing away, and doubtless in many a heart is already associated with memories that "lie too deep for tears."

Undue facility.

Her spontaneous and exhaustless command of words gave her a large and free style, but likewise a dangerous facility, and it was only in rare instances, like the one just cited, that she attained to the strength and sweetness of repose. Her intense earnestness spared her no leisure for humor, a feature curiously absent *Lack of humor.* from her writings: she almost lacked the sense of the ludicrous, as may be deduced from some of her two-word rhymes, and from various absurdities solemnly indulged in. But of wit and satire she has more than enough, and lashes all kinds of tyranny and hypocrisy with supernal scorn. It is perhaps due to her years of indoor life that the influence of landscape-scenery is not more visible in her poetry. Her girlhood, nevertheless, was partly spent in Herefordshire, among the Malvern Hills, and we find in "Aurora Leigh," and in some of her minor pieces, not only reminiscences of that region, but other landscape, both English and Italian, executed in a broad and *Slight idyllic tendency.* admirable manner. But when she follows the idyllic method, making the tone of the background enhance the feeling of a poem, she uses by preference the works of man rather than those of Nature: architecture, furniture, pictures, books above all, rather than water, sky, and forest. Men and women were the chief objects of her regard, — her genius was more dramatic than idyllic, and lyric first of all.

The instinct of worship and the religion of humanity were pervading constituents of Mrs. Browning's nature, and demand no less attention than the love which dictated her most fervent poems. A spiritual trinity, of zeal, love, and worship, presided over her work. If in her outcry against wrong she had nothing decisive to suggest, she at least sounded a clarion note for the incitement of her comrades and successors, and this was her mission as a reformer. Religious exaltation breathes through every page of her compositions. Her eulogist aptly called her the Blaîse Pascal of women, and said that her books were prayer-books. She had a profound faith in Christian revelation, interpreted in its most catholic sense. Her broad humanity and religion, her defence of her sex, her subtile and tender knowledge of the hearts of children, her abnegation, hope, and faith, seemed the apotheosis of womanhood and drew to her the affection of readers in distant lands. She was the most beloved of minstrels and women. Jean Paul said of Herder that he was less a poet than a poem, but in Mrs. Browning the two were blended : she wrote herself into her works, and I have closely reviewed her experience, because it is inseparable from her lyrical career. The English love to call her Shakespeare's Daughter, and in truth she bears to their greatest poet the relation of Miranda to Prospero. Her delicate genius was purely feminine and subjective, attributes that are made to go together. Most introspective poetry, in spite of Sidney's injunction, wearies us,

Her sympathetic and religious nature.

Cp. " Poets of America" : pp. 123-128.

The most beloved of poets.

Subjective quality of her genius.

Cp. " Poets of Amer- ica " : p. 146.

because it so often is the petty or morbid sentiment of natures little superior to our own. Men have more conceit, with less tact, than women, and, as a rule, when male poets write objectively they are on the safer side. But when an impassioned woman, yearning to let the world share her poetic rapture or grief, reveals the secrets of her burning heart, generations adore her, literature is enriched, and grosser beings have glimpses of a purity with which we invest our conceptions of disenthralled spirits in some ideal sphere.

Her repre- sentative position.

I therefore regard Mrs. Browning as the representative of her sex in the Victorian era, and a luminous example of the fact that " woman is not undeveloped man, but diverse " ; as the passion-flower of the century ; the conscious medium of some power beyond the veil. For, if she was wanting in reverence for the form and body of the poet's art, she more than all her tuneful brethren revered the poet's *inspiration.* To her poets were

Belief in inspiration. Cp. " Poets of Amer- ica " : p. 129.

> " the only truth-tellers now left to God ;
> The only speakers of essential truth,
> Opposed to relative, comparative,
> And temporal truths ; the only holders by
> His sun-skirts."

And this in a period when technical refinement has caused the mass of verse-makers to forget that art is vital chiefly as a means of expression. Like her Hebrew poets, she was obedient " to the heavenly vision," and I think that the form of her religion, which was in sympathy with the teachings of Emanuel Swedenborg, enables us clearly to understand her genius and works. I have no doubt that she surrendered herself to the play of her imagination, as if

Her exalta- tion and rapture.

some angelic voice were speaking through her, — and of what other modern poet can this be said? With equal powers of expression, such a faith exalts the bard to an apocalyptic prophet, — to the consecrated interpreter, of whom Plato said in "Ion," "A poet is a thing light, with wings, and unable to compose poetry until he becomes inspired and is out of his sober senses, and his imagination is no longer under his control; for he does not compose by art, but through a divine power."

At the close of the first summer month of 1861, a memorable year for Italy, the land of song was free, united, once more a queen among the nations; but the voice of its sweetest singer was hushed, the golden harp was broken; the sibylline minstrel lay dying in the City of Flowers. She was at the last, as ever, the enraptured seer of celestial visions. Some efflux of imperishable glory passed before her eyes, and she said that it was beautiful. It seemed, to those around her, as if she died beholding

> "in jasper-stone as clear as glass,
> The first foundations of that new, near Day
> Which should be builded out of Heaven to God."

Died in Florence, June 29, 1861.

CHAPTER V.

ALFRED TENNYSON.

I.

Alfred Tennyson, Poet-Laureate: born at Somerby, Lincolnshire, Aug. 5, 1809.

THAT a new king should arise "over Egypt, which knew not Joseph," was but the natural order of events. The wonder is that nothing less than the death of one Pharaoh, and the succession of another, could oust a favorite from his position. Statesman or author, that public man is fortunate who does not find himself subjected to the neglectful caprices of his own generation, after some time be past and the duration of his influence unusually prolonged. There is a law founded in our dread of monotony, in that weariness of soul which we call *ennui*, — the spiritual counterpart of a loathing which even the manna that fell from heaven at last bred in the Israelites: a law that affects, as surely as death, statesmen, moralists, heroes, — and equally the renowned artist or poet. The law is Nature's own, and man's perception of it is the true apology for each fashion as it flies. But Nature, with all her changes, is secure in certain noble, recurrent types; and so there are elevated modes of art, to which we sometimes not unwillingly bid farewell, knowing that after a time they will return, and be welcome again and forever.

Law of change in public taste. Cp. "Poets of America": pp. 39, 273.

A case in point.

At present we have only to observe the working of this law with respect to the acknowledged leader, by influence and laurelled rank, of the Victorian poetic hierarchy. He, too, has verified in his recent experience the statement that, as admired poets advance in years, the people and the critics begin to mistrust the quality of their genius, are disposed to revise the laudatory judgments formerly pronounced upon them, and, finally, to claim that they have been overrated, and are not men of high reach. Such is the result of that long familiarity whereby a singer's audience becomes somewhat weary of his notes, and it is exaggerated in direct ratio with the potency of the influence against which a revolt is made. In fact, the grander the success the more trying the reaction. It is what the ancients meant by the envy of the gods, unto which too fortunate men were greatly subjected. Alternate periods of favor and rejection not only follow one another in cycles, by generations, or by centuries even ; but the individual artist, during a long career, will find himself tested by minor perturbations of the same kind, varying with his successive achievements, and the varying conditions of atmosphere and time.

The influence of Alfred Tennyson has been almost unprecedentedly dominant, fascinating, extended, yet of late has somewhat vexed the public mind. Its reposeful charm has given it a more secure hold upon our affections than is usual in this era, whose changes are the more incessant because so much more is crowded into a few years than of old. Even of this serene beauty we are wearied ; a murmur arises ; rebellion has broken out ; the Laureate is irreverently criticised, suspected, no longer worshipped as a demigod. Either because he is not a demi-god, or that through long security he has lost the power to take the buffets and rewards of fortune "with equal

Recent strictures.

thanks," he does not move entirely contented within
the shadow that for the hour has crossed his tri-
umphal path.   A little poem, " The Flower," is the
expression of a genuine grievance : his plant, at first
novel and despised, grew into a superb flower of art,
was everywhere glorious and accepted, yet now is
again pronounced a weed because the seed is common, and men weary of a beauty too familiar.   The
petulance of these stanzas reveals a less edifying matter, to wit, the failure of their author in submission
to the inevitable, the lack of a philosophy which he
is not slow to recommend to his fellows.   If he verily
hears " the roll of the ages," as he has declared in
his answer to " A Spiteful Letter," why then so rest-
ive?   Why not recognize, even in his own case, the
benignity of a law which, as Cicero said of death,
must be a blessing because it is universal?   He himself has taught us, in the wisest language of our time,
that

> " God fulfils himself in many ways,
>   Lest one good custom should corrupt the world."

No change, no progress.   Better to decline, if need
be, upon some inferior grade, that all methods may
be tested.   Ultimately, disgust of the false will bring
a reaction to something as good as the best which
has been known before.

Last of all, the world's true and enduring verdict.
In calmer moments the Laureate must needs reflect
that a future age will look back, measure him as he
is, and compare his works with those of his contem-

poraries.   To forestall, as far as may be, this steadfast judgment of posterity, is the aim and service of
the critic.   Let us separate· ourselves from the adu-
lation and envy of the moment, and search for the

true relation of Tennyson to his era, — estimating his poetry, not by our appetite for it, but by its inherent quality, and its lasting value in the progress of British song.

There have been few comprehensive reviews of Tennyson's poetical career. The artistic excellence of his work has been, from the first, so distinguished that lay critics are often at a loss how to estimate this poet. We have had admirable homilies upon the spirit of his teachings, the scope and nature of his imagination, his idyllic quality, — his landscape, characters, language, Anglicanism, — but nothing adequately setting forth his technical superiority. I am aware that professional criticism is apt to be unduly technical ; to neglect the soul, in its concern for the body, of art. My present effort is to consider both ; nevertheless, with relation to Tennyson, above all other modern poets, how little can be embraced within the limits of an essay! The specialist-reviewer has the advantage of being thorough as far as he goes. All I can hope is to leave no important point untouched, though my reference to it may be restricted to a single phrase. *Dual nature of art.*

II.

It seems to me that the only just estimate of Tennyson's position is that which declares him to be, by eminence, the representative poet of the recent era. Not, like one or another of his compeers, representative of the melody, wisdom, passion, or other partial phase of the era, but of the time itself, with its diverse elements in harmonious conjunction. Years have strengthened my belief that a future age will *Tennyson represents his era.*

7 *

regard him, independently of his merits, as bearing this relation to his period. In his verse he is as truly " the glass of fashion and the mould of form " of the Victorian generation in the nineteenth century as Spenser was of the Elizabethan court, Milton of the Protectorate, Pope of the reign of Queen Anne. During his supremacy there have been few great leaders, at the head of different schools, such as belonged to the time of Byron, Wordsworth, and Keats. His poetry has gathered all the elements which find vital expression in the complex modern art.

Has the influence of Tennyson made the recent British school, or has his genius itself been modified and guided by the period ? It is the old question of the river and the valley. The two have taken shape together ; yet the beauty of Tennyson's verse was so potent from the first, and has so increased in potency, that we must pronounce him an independent genius, certainly more than the mere creature of his surroundings.

*E. A. Poe's
essay on
" The Poetic
Principle."*
Years ago, when he was yet comparatively unknown, an American poet, himself finely gifted with the lyrical ear, was so impressed by Tennyson's method, that, " in perfect sincerity," he pronounced him " the noblest poet that ever lived." If he had said " the noblest artist," and confined this judgment to lyrists of the English tongue, he possibly would have made no exaggeration. Yet there have been artists with a less conscious manner and a broader style. The Laureate is always aware of what he is doing ; he is his own *daimon*, — the inspirer and controller of his own utterances. He sings by note no less than by ear, and follows a score of his own inditing. But, acknowledging his culture, we have no right to assume

that his ear is not as fine as that of any poet who gives voice with more careless rapture. His average is higher than that of other English masters, though there may be scarcely one who in special flights has not excelled him. By Spencer's law of progress, founded on the distribution of values, his poetry is more eminent than most which has preceded it.

I have inferred that the very success of Tennyson's art has made it common in our eyes, and rendered us incapable of fairly judging it. When a poet has length of days, and sees his language a familiar portion of men's thoughts, he no longer can attract that romantic interest with which the world regards a genius freshly brought to hearing. Men forget that he, too, was once new, unhackneyed, appetizing. But recall the youth of Tennyson, and see how complete the revolution with which he has, at least, been coeval, and how distinct his music then seemed from everything which had gone before. *Hindrances to correct appreciation.*

He began as a metrical artist, pure and simple, and with a feeling perfectly unique, — at a long remove, even, from that of so absolute an artist as was John Keats. He had very little notion beyond the production of rhythm, melody, color, and other poetic effects. Instinct led him to construct his machinery before essaying to build. Many have discerned, in his youthful pieces, the influence of Wordsworth and Keats, but no less that of the Italian poets, and of the early English balladists. I shall hereafter revert to "Oriana," "Mariana," and "The Lady of Shalott," as work that in its kind is fully up to the best of those Pre-Raphaelites who, by some arrest of development, stop precisely where Tennyson made his *A born artist.* *The Pre-Raphaelites.*

second step forward, and censure him for having gone beyond them.

Meaningless as are the opening melodies of his collected verse, how delicious they once seemed, as a change from even the greatest productions which then held the public ear. Here was something of a new kind! The charm was legitimate. Tennyson's immediate predecessors were so fully occupied with the mass of a composition that they slighted details: what beauty they displayed was not of the parts, but of the whole. Now, in all arts, the natural advance is from detail to general effect. How seldom those who begin with a broad treatment, which apes maturity, acquire subsequently the minor graces that alone can finish the perfect work! By comparison of the late and early writings of great English poets, — Shakespeare and Milton, — one observes the process of healthful growth. Tennyson proved his kindred genius by this instinctive study of details in his immature verses. In marked contrast to his fellows, and to every predecessor but Keats, — " that strong, excepted soul," — he seemed to perceive from the outset, that *Poetry is an art, and chief of the fine arts: the easiest to dabble in, the hardest in which to reach true excellence;* that it has its technical secrets, its mysterious lowly paths that reach to aërial outlooks, and this no less than sculpture, painting, music, or architecture, but even more. He devoted himself, with the eager spirit of youth, to mastering this exquisite art, and wreaked his thoughts upon expression, for the expression's sake. And what else should one attempt, with small experiences, little concern for the real world, and less observation of it? He had dreams rather than thoughts; but was at the

His early study of details.

Poetry chief of the fine arts.

most sensitive period of life with regard to rhythm, color, and form. In youth feeling is indeed " deeper than all thought," and responds divinely to every sensuous confrontment with the presence of beauty.

It is difficult now to realize how chaotic was the notion of art among English verse-makers at the beginning of Tennyson's career. Not even the example of Keats had taught the needful lesson, and I look upon his successor's early efforts as of no small importance. These were dreamy experiments in metre and word-painting, and spontaneous after their kind. Readers sought not to analyze their meaning and grace. The significance of art has since become so well understood, and such results have-been attained, that " Claribel," " Lilian," " The Merman," " The Dying Swan," " The Owl," etc., seem slight enough to us now ; and even then the affectation pervading them, which was merely the error of a poetic soul groping for its true form of expression, repelled men of severe and established tastes ; but to the neophyte they had the charm of sighing winds and babbling waters, a wonder of luxury and weirdness, inexpressible, not to be effaced. How we lay on the grass, in June, and softly read them from the white page ! To this day what lyrics better hold their own than " Mariana " and the " Recollections of the Arabian Nights." In these pieces, however, as in the crude yet picturesque " Ode to Memory," the poet exhibited some distinctness of theme and motive, and, in a word, seemed to feel that he had something to express, if it were but the arabesque shadows of his fancy-laden dreams. Of a mass of lyrics, sonnets, and other metrical essays, published theretofore, — some contained in the *Poems by Two Brothers*, and

A transition period, 1820–1830.

Charm of Tennyson's early lyrics.

" Poems, chiefly Lyrical," 1830.

" Poems by Two Brothers," 1827.

others in the original volume of 1830, — I say nothing, for they show little of the purpose that characterizes the few early pieces which our poet himself retains in his collected works. One of them, " Hero and Leander," is too good in its way to be discarded ; the greater number are juvenile, often imitative, and the excellent judgment of Tennyson is shown by his rejection of all that have no true position in his lyrical rise and progress.

" Poems,"
1832 - 33.

The volume of 1832, which began with " The Lady of Shalott," and contained " Eleänore," " Margaret," " The Miller's Daughter," " The Palace of Art," " The May Queen," " Fatima," " The Lotos-Eaters," and " A Dream of Fair Women," was published in his

Sudden and delightful poetic growth.

twenty-second year. All in all, a more original and beautiful volume of minor poetry never was added to our literature. The Tennysonian manner here was clearly developed, largely pruned of mannerisms. The command of delicious metres ; the rhythmic susurrus of stanzas whose every word is as needful and studied as the flower or scroll of ornamental architecture, — yet so much an interlaced portion of the whole, that the special device is forgotten in the general excellence ; the effect of color, of that music which is a passion in itself, of the scenic pictures which are the counterparts of changeful emotions ; all are here, and the poet's work is the epitome of

An expression of the beautiful.

every mode in art. Even if these lyrics and idyls had expressed nothing, they were of priceless value as guides to the renaissance of beauty. Thenceforward slovenly work was impossible, subject to instant rebuke by contrast. The force of metrical elegance made its way and carried everything before it. From this day Tennyson confessedly took his place at the head of what some attempt to classify as the art-school : that is, of poets who largely produce their effect by harmonizing scenery and detail with the emotions or impassioned action of their verse.

The "art-school."

The tendency of his genius was revealed in this volume. The author plainly was a college-man, a student of many literatures, and, though. an English-man to the core, alive to suggestions from Italian and Grecian sources. His Gothic feeling was mani fest in "The Lady of Shalott" and "The Sisters"; his classicism in "Œnone"; his idyllic method, es-pecially, now defined itself, making the scenery of a poem enhance the central idea, — thought and land-scape being so blended that it was difficult to deter-mine which suggested the other.

Tendency of the poet's genius.

I shall elsewhere examine with some care the rela-tions between Tennyson and Theocritus, and the gen-eral likeness of the Victorian to the Alexandrian period, and at present need not enter upon this spe-cial ground. Enough to say that the Greek influence is visible in many portions of the volume of 1832, sometimes through almost literal translations of clas-sical passages. "Œnone," modelled upon the new-Doric verse, ranks with "Lycidas" as an Hellenic study. While this most chaste and beautiful poem fascinated every reader, the wisest criticism found more of genuine worth in the purely English quality of those limpid pieces in which the melody of the lyric is wedded to the sentiment and picture of the idyl, — "The Miller's Daughter," "The May Queen," and "Lady Clara Vere de Vere." More dewy, fresh, pathetic, native verse had not been written since the era of "As You Like It" and "A Winter's Tale." During ten years this book accomplished its auspi-

See Chapter VI.

Classicism.

Purely Eng-lish idyls.

cious work, until the author's fame and influence had
so extended that he was encouraged to print the vol-

"Poems,"
1842.

ume of 1842, wherein he first gave the name of idyls
to poems of the class that has brought him a distinctive reputation.

At the present day, were this volume to be lost,
we possibly should be deprived of a larger specific
variety of Tennyson's most admired poems than is
contained in any other of his successive ventures.   It

*A treasury
of represent-
ative poems.*

is an assortment of representative poems.   To an art
more restrained and natural we here find wedded a
living soul.   The poet has convictions : he is not a
pupil, but a master, and reaches intellectual greatness.
His verses still bewitch youths and artists by their
sentiments and beauty, but their thought takes hold of
thinkers and men of the world.   He has learned not
only that art, when followed for its own sake, is al-
luring, but that, when used as a means of expressing
what cannot otherwise be quite revealed, it becomes
seraphic.   We could spare, rather than this collection,
much which he has since given us : possibly " Maud,"
—without doubt, idyls like "The Golden Supper" and
" Aylmer's Field."   Look at the material structure of
the poetry.   Here, at last, we observe the ripening

Blank-verse.

of that blank-verse which had been suggested in the
" Œnone."   Consider Tennyson's handling of this
measure, — the domino of a poetaster, the state garment of a lofty poet.   It must be owned that he now
enriched it by a style entirely his own, and as well-
defined as those already established.   Foremost of

*Previous
styles.*

the latter was the Elizabethan, marked by freedom
and power, and never excelled for dramatic composition.   Next, the Miltonic or Anglo-Epic, with its
sonorous grandeur and stately Roman syntax, of which

"Paradise Lost" is the masterpiece, and "Hyperion" the finest specimen in modern times. That it really has no place in our usage is proved by the fact that Keats, with true insight, refused, after some experience, to complete "Hyperion," on the ground that it had too many "Miltonic inversions." Meanwhile blank-verse had been used for less imaginative or less heroical work; notably, for didactic and moralizing essays, by Cowper, Wordsworth, and other leaders of the contemplative school.

Cp. "Poets of America": pp. 79, 87, 374.

Tennyson's is of two kinds, one of which is suited to the heroic episodes in his idyllic poetry,—the first important example being the "Morte d'Arthur," which opened the volume of 1842, and is now made a portion of the "Idyls of the King." I hold the verse of that poem to be his own invention, derived from the study of Homer and his natural mastery of the Saxon element in our language. Milton's Latinism is so pronounced as to be un-English; on the other hand, there is such affinity between the simple strength of the Homeric Greek and that of the English in which Saxon words prevail, that the former can be rendered into the latter with great effect. Tennyson recognizes this in his prelude to "Morte d'Arthur," deprecating his heroics as "faint Homeric echoes, nothing-worth." But almost with the perusal of the first two lines,

Originality and perfection of Tennyson's blank-verse.

"Morte d'Arthur."

Homeric and Saxon qualities.

> "So all day long the noise of battle roll'd
> Among the mountains by the winter sea,"

we see that this style surpasses other blank-verse in strength and condensation. It soon became the model for a score of younger aspirants; in short, impressed itself upon the artistic mind as a new and vigorous form of our grandest English measure.

K

*The Victo-
rian idyllic
verse.*

The other style of Tennyson's blank-verse is found in his purely idyllic pieces, — "The Gardener's Daughter," "Dora," "Godiva," and, upon a lower plane, such eclogues as "Audley Court" and "Edwin Morris." "St. Simeon Stylites" and "Ulysses" have each a special manner. In the first-named group, the poet brought to completeness the Victorian idyllic verse. The three are models from which he could not advance: in surpassing beauty and naturalness unequalled, I say, by many of his later efforts. What

Crabbe.

Crabbe essayed in a homely fashion, now, at the touch of a finer artist, became the perfection of rural,

"Dora."

idyllic tenderness. "Dora" is like a Hebrew pastoral, the paragon of its kind, with not a quotable detail, a line too much or too little, but faultless as a whole. Who can read it without tears? "Godiva"

"Godiva."
*"The Gardener's
Daughter."*

and "The Gardener's Daughter" demand no less praise for descriptive felicity of another kind. But, for virile grandeur and astonishingly compact expression, there is no blank-verse poem, equally restricted

"Ulysses."

as to length, that approaches the "Ulysses": conception, imagery, and thought are royally imaginative, and the assured hand is Tennyson's throughout.

*Comprehensive range.
of "English
Idyls and
Other
Poems."*

I reserve for later discussion the poet's general characteristics, fairly displayed in this volume. The great feature is its comprehensive range; it includes a finished specimen of every kind of poetry within the author's power to essay. The variety is surprising, and the novelty was no less so at the date of

"The Talking Oak."

its appearance. Here is "The Talking Oak," that marvel of grace and fancy, the nonpareil of sustained lyrics in quatrain verse; as exquisite in filigree-work as "The Rape of the Lock," with an airy beauty and rippling flow, compared with which the motion of

Pope's couplets is that of partners in an eighteenth-century minuet. Here is the modern lover reciting "Locksley Hall," which, despite its sentimental egotism and consolation of the heart by the head, has fine metrical quality, is fixed in literature, and furnishes genuine illustrations of the poet's time. In "The Two Voices" and "The Vision of Sin" the excess of his speculative intellect makes itself felt: but the second of these seems to me a strained and fantastic production ; for which very reason, perchance, it drew the attention of semi-metaphysical persons who have no perception of the true mission of poetry, and, by a certain affectation, mistaken for subtilty, has excited more comment and analysis than it deserves. "The Day-Dream," like "The Talking Oak," gives the poet an opportunity for dying falls, mellifluous cadences, and delicately fanciful pictures. The story is made to his hand ; he rarely invents a story, though often, as in the last-named poem, chancing upon the conceit of a dainty and original theme. Here, too, are "Lady Clare," "The Lord of Burleigh," and "Edward Gray," each a simple, crystalline, and flawless ballad. Nor has Tennyson ever composed, in his minor key, more enduring and suggestive little songs than "Break, break, break!" and "Flow down, cold Rivulet, to the Sea!" both, also, in this volume. His humor, which seldom becomes him, is at its best in that half-pensive, half-rollicking, wholly poetic composition, dear to wits and dreamers, "Will Waterproof's Lyrical Monologue." In this collection, too, we find his early experiments in the now famous measure of "In Memoriam." Purest and highest of all the lyrical pieces are "St. Agnes" and "Sir Galahad," full of white light, and each a stain-

"Locksley Hall."

"The Two Voices."

"The Vision of Sin."

"The Day-Dream."

Ballads.

Songs.

The "Lyrical Monologue."

"St. Agnes" and "Sir Galahad."

less idealization of its theme. " Sir Galahad " must be recited by a clarion voice, ere one can fully appreciate the sounding melody, the knightly, heroic ring. The poet has never chanted a more ennobling strain.

A composite and influential volume.

Such is the excellence, and such the unusual range of a volume in which every department of poetry, except the dramatic, is exhibited in great perfection, if not at the most imaginative height. To the author's students it is a favorite among his books, as the one that fairly represents his composite genius. It powerfully affected the rising group of poets, giving their work a tendency which established its general character for the ensuing thirty years.

Climacterics in art.

There comes a time in the life of every aspiring artist, when, if he be a painter, he tires of painting cabinet-pictures, — however much they satisfy his admirers ; if a poet, he says to himself : " Enough of lyrics and idyls ; let me essay a masterpiece, a sustained production, that shall bear to my former work the relation which an opera or oratorio bears to a composer's sonatas and canzonets." It may be that some feeling of this kind impelled Tennyson to write

" The Princess : a Medley," 1847.

The Princess, the theme and story of which are both his own invention. At that time he had not learned the truth of Emerson's maxim that " Tradition supplies a better fable than any invention can " ; and that it is as well for a poet to borrow from history or romance a tale made ready to his hands, and which his genius must transfigure. The poem is, as

A romantic composition.

he entitled it, " A Medley," constructed of ancient and modern materials, — a show of mediæval pomp and movement, observed through an atmosphere of latter-day thought and emotion ; so varying, withal, in the scenes and language of its successive parts,

that one may well conceive it to be told by the group
of thoroughbred men and maidens who, one after
another, rehearse its cantos to beguile a festive summer's day. I do not sympathize with the criticisms
to which it has been subjected upon this score, and
which is but the old outcry of the French classicists
against Victor Hugo and the romance school. The
poet, in his prelude, anticipates every stricture, and The Prel-
ude.
to me the anachronisms and impossibilities of the
story seem not only lawful, but attractive. Like those
of Shakespeare's comedies, they invite the reader
off-hand to a purely ideal world ; he seats himself
upon an English lawn, as upon a Persian enchanted
carpet, — hears the mystic word pronounced, and,
presto ! finds himself in fairy-land. Moreover, Tennyson's special gift of reducing incongruous details
to a common structure and tone is fully illustrated
in a poem made

> "to suit with Time and place,
> A Gothic ruin and a Grecian house,
> A talk of college and of ladies' rights,
> A feudal knight in silken masquerade.
>
> .   .   .   .   .
>
> This *were* a medley ! we should have him back
> Who told the ' Winter's Tale ' to do it for us."

But not often has a lovelier story been recited. After
the idyllic introduction, the body of the poem is
composed in a semi-heroic verse. Other works of our
poet are greater, but none is so fascinating as this
romantic tale : English throughout, yet combining the
England of Cœur de Leon with that of Victoria in
one bewitching picture. Some of the author's most
delicately musical lines — " jewels five words long "

— are herein contained, and the ending of each canto is an effective piece of art.

Epic swift-
ness of
movement.
Cp. " Poets
of Amer-
ica" : p.
88.

The tournament scene, at the close of the fifth book, is the most vehement and rapid passage to be found in the whole range of Tennyson's poetry. By an approach to the Homeric swiftness, it presents a contrast to the laborious and faulty movement of much of his narrative verse. The songs, added in the second edition of this poem, reach the high-water mark of lyrical composition. Few will deny that, taken together, the five melodies : " As through the land," " Sweet and low," " The splendor falls on castle walls," " Home they brought her warrior dead," and " Ask me no more ! " — that these constitute the finest group of songs produced in our century ; and the third, known as the " Bugle Song," seems to many the most perfect English lyric since the time of Shakespeare. In " The Princess " we also find Tennyson's most successful studies upon the model of the Theocritan isometric verse. He was the first to enrich our poetry with this class of melodies, for the burlesque pastorals of the eighteenth century need not be considered. Not one of the blank-verse songs in his Arthurian epic equals in structure or feeling the " Tears, idle tears," and " O swallow, swallow, flying, flying south ! " Again, what witchery of landscape and action ; what fair women and brave men, who, if they be somewhat stagy and traditional, at least are more sharply defined than the actors in our poet's other romances ! Besides, " The Princess " has a distinct purpose, — the illustration of woman's struggles, aspirations, and proper sphere ; and the conclusion is one wherewith the instincts of cultured people are so thoroughly in accord, that some are used to an-

A notable group of lyrics.

Isometric songs.

swer, when asked to present their view of the " woman question," " You will find it at the close of
' The Princess.' " Those who disagree with Tennyson's presentation acknowledge that if it be not true
it is well told. His Ida is, in truth, a beautiful and
heroic figure : —

> " She bow'd as if to veil a noble tear.
>
> .   .   .   .   .
>
> Not peace she looked, the Head : but rising up
> Robed in the long night of her deep hair, so
> To the open window moved.   .   .   .
> .   .   .   She stretched her arms and call'd
> Across the tumult and the tumult fell."

Of the author's shortcomings in this and other poems
we have to speak hereafter. I leave " The Princess,"
deeming it the most varied and interesting of his
works with respect to freshness and invention. All
mankind love a story-teller such as Tennyson, by this
creation, proved himself to be.

In the youth of poets it is the material value of
their work that makes it precious, and for certain
gifts of language and color we esteem one more
highly than another. When a sweet singer dies pre-
maturely, we lament his loss ; but in a poet's later
years character and intellect begin to tell. His other
gifts being equal, he who has the more vigorous mind
will draw ahead of his fellows, and take the front
position. Tennyson, like Browning and Arnold, has
that which Keats was bereft of, and which Wordsworth,
Landor, and Procter possessed in full measure, — the
gift of years, and must be judged according to his
fortune. In mental ability he comes near to the
greatest of the five, and in synthetic grasp surpasses
them all. Arnold's thought is wholly included ın

Tennyson ; if you miss Browning's psychology, you find a more varied analysis, qualified by wise restraint. His intellectual growth has steadily progressed, and is reflected in the nature of his successive poems.

The prime of life.

At the age of forty a man, blessed with a sound mind in a sound body, should reach the maturity of his intellectual power. At such a period Tennyson

"In Memoriam," 1850.

produced *In Memoriam*, his most characteristic and significant work : not so ambitious as his epic of King Arthur, but more distinctively a poem of this century, and displaying the author's genius in a sub-

His most unique and distinctive production.

jective form. In it are concentrated his wisest reflections upon life, death, and immortality, the worlds within and without, while the whole song is so largely uttered, and so pervaded with the singer's manner, that any isolated line is recognized at once. This work stands by itself : none can essay another upon its model, without yielding every claim to personality and at the risk of an inferiority that would be appalling. The strength of Tennyson's intellect has full sweep in this elegiac poem, — the great threnody of

Elegiac masterpieces.

our language, by virtue of unique conception and power. "Lycidas," with its primrose beauty and varied lofty flights, is but the extension of a theme set by Moschus and Bion. Shelley, in "Adonais," despite his spiritual ecstasy and splendor of lament, followed the same masters, — yes, and took his landscape and imagery from distant climes. Swinburne's dirge for Baudelaire is a wonder of melody ; nor do we forget the "Thyrsis" of Arnold, and other modern ventures in a direction where the sweet and absolute

This poem the greatest of them all.

solemnity of the Saxon tongue is most apparent. Still, as an original and intellectual production, "In Memoriam" is beyond them all : and a more important, though possibly no more enduring, creation of rhythmic art.

The metrical form of this work deserves attention. The author's choice of the transposed-quatrain verse was a piece of good fortune. Its hymnal quality, finely exemplified in the opening prayer, is always impressive, and, although a monotone, no more monotonous than the sounds of nature, — the murmur of ocean, the soughing of the mountain pines. Were "In Memoriam" written in direct quatrains, I think the effect would grow to be unendurable. The work as a whole is built up of successive lyrics, each expressing a single phase of the poet's sorrow-brooding thought ; and here again is followed the method of nature, which evolves cell after cell, and, joining each to each, constructs the sentient organization. But Tennyson's art-instincts are always perfect ; he does the fitting thing, and rarely seeks through eccentric and curious movements to attract the popular regard. *Its metrical and stanzaic arrangement.*

As to scenery, imagery, and general treatment, "In Memoriam" is eminently a British poem. The grave, majestic, hymnal measure swells like the peal of an organ, yet acts as a brake on undue spasmodic outbursts of discordant grief. A steady, yet varying *marche funèbre;* a sense of passion held in check, of reserved elegiac power. For the strain is everywhere calm, even in rehearsing a bygone violence of emotion, along its passage from woe to desolation, and anon, by tranquil stages, to reverence, thought, aspiration, endurance, hope. On sea and shore the elements are calm ; even the wild winds and snows of winter are brought in hand, and made subservient, as the bells ring out the dying year, to the new birth of Nature and the sure purpose of eternal God. *A thoroughly national poem.* *Rhythmic grandeur and solemnity.*

8

Incorrect estimates.

Critical objections are urged against " In Memo-riam "; mostly, in my opinion, such as more fitly apply to poems upon a lower grade. It is said to present a confusion of religion and skepticism, an attempt to reconcile faith and knowledge, to blend the feeling of Dante with that of Lucretius ; but, if

Faith and doubt.

this be so, the author only follows the example of his generation, and the more faithfully gives voice to its spiritual questionings. Even here he is accused of "idealizing the thoughts of his contemporaries"; to which we rejoin, in the words of another, "that great writers do not anticipate the thought of their age ; they but anticipate its expression." His scien-

Poetic use of scientific material.

tific language and imagery are censured also, but do not his efforts in this direction, tentative as they are, constitute a merit? Failing, as others have failed, to reconcile poetry and metaphysics, he succeeds better in speculations inspired by the revelations of lens and laboratory. Why should not such facts be taken into account? The phenomenal stage of art is pass-ing away, and all things, even poetic diction and metaphor, must endure a change. It is absurd to think that a man like Tennyson will rest content with ignoring or misstating what has become every-day knowledge. The spiritual domain is still the poet's own ; but let his illustrations be derived from living truths, rather than from the worn and ancient fables of the pastoral age. A certain writer declares that Tennyson shows sound sense instead of imaginative power. Not only sense, methinks, but "the sanity of true genius"; and the Strephon-and-Chloë singers must change their tune, or be left without a hearing. A charge requiring more serious consideration is that the sorrow of "In Memoriam" is but food for thought, a passion of the head, not of the heart. The poet, however, has reached a philosophical zenith of his life, far above ignoble weakness, and performs the office which an enfranchised spirit might well require of him ; building a mausoleum of immortal verse, — conceiving his friend as no longer dead, but as having solved the mysteries they so often have discussed together. If there is didacticism in the poem, it is a teaching which leads *ad astra*, by a path strictly within the province of an elegiac minstrel's song. *Wisdom spiritualized by grief.*

For the rest, "In Memoriam" is a serene and truthful panorama of refined experiences ; filled with pictures of gentle, scholastic life, and of English scenery through all the changes of a rolling year ; expressing, moreover, the thoughts engendered by these changes. When too sombre, it is lightened by sweet reminiscences ; when too light, recalled to grief by stanzas that have the deep solemnity of a passing bell. Among its author's productions it is the one most valued by educated and professional readers. Recently, a number of authors having been asked to name three leading poems of this century which they would most prefer to have written, each gave "In Memoriam" either the first or second place upon his list. Obviously it is not a work to read at a sitting, nor to take up in every mood, but one in which we are sure to find something of worth in every stanza. It contains more notable sayings than any other of Tennyson's poems. The wisdom, yearnings, and aspirations of a noble mind are here ; curious reasoning, for once, is not out of place ; the poet's imagination, shut in upon itself, strives to irradiate with inward light the mystic problems of life. At the close, Nature's eternal miracle is made symbolic *General quality of this noble poem.* *Admired by men of letters.*

of the soul's palingenesis, and the tender and beautiful marriage-lay tranquillizes the reader with the thought of the dear common joys which are the heritage of every living kind.

III.

Poet-Laureate of England, Nov. 21, 1850.

IN the year 1850 Tennyson received the laurel, and almost immediately was called upon by the national sentiment to exercise the functions of his poetic office. The "Ode on the Death of the Duke of Wellington" was the first, and remains the most ambitious, of his patriotic lyrics. This tribute to the

The Wellington Ode.

"last great Englishman" may fairly be pronounced equal to the occasion ; a respectable performance for Tennyson, a strong one for another poet. None but a great artist could have written it, yet it scarcely is a great poem, and certainly, though Tennyson's most important ode, is not comparable with his predecessor's lofty discourse upon the "Intimations of Immortality." Several passages have become folk-words, such as "O good gray head which all men knew!" and

> "This is England's greatest son, —
> He that gain'd a hundred fights,
> Nor ever lost an English gun!"

but the ode, upon the whole, is labored, built up of high-sounding lines and refrains after the manner of Dryden, in which rhetoric often is substituted for imagination and richness of thought.

Forced quality of his occasional pieces.

The Laureate never has been at ease in handling events of the day. To his brooding and essentially poetic nature such matters seem of no more moment, beside the mysteries of eternal beauty and truth,

than was the noise of catapults and armed men to
Archimedes studying out problems during the city's
siege. If he succeeds at all with them, it is by
sheer will and workmanship. Even then his voice
is hollow, and his didacticism, as in " Maud," artificial and insincere. The laurel, and the fame which
now had come to him, seemed for a time to bring
him more in sympathy with his countrymen, and he
made an honest endeavor to rehearse their achievements in his song. The result, seen in the volume
Maud, and Other Poems, illustrates what I say. Here
are contained his prominent occasional pieces, " The
Charge of the Light Brigade," the Wellington ode,
and the metrical romance from which the volume
takes its name. After several revisions, the Balaklavan lyric has passed into literature, but ranks
below the nobler measures of Drayton and Campbell.
" Maud," however, with its strength and weakness,
has divided public opinion more than any other of
the author's works. I think that his judicious
students will not demur to my opinion that it is
quite below his other sustained productions ; rather,
that it is not sustained at all, but, while replete
with beauties, weak and uneven as a whole, — and
that this is due to the poet's having gone outside
his own nature, and to his surrender of the joy of
art, in an effort to produce something that should
at once catch the favor of the multitude. " Maud "
is scanty in theme, thin in treatment, poor in
thought ; but has musical episodes, with much fine
scenery and diction. It is a greater medley than
" The Princess," shifting from vague speculations to
passionate outbreaks, and glorying in one famous
and beautiful nocturne, — but all intermixed with

*The volume
of* 1855.

" *Maud.*"

cheap satire, and conspicuous for affectations unworthy of the poet. The pity of it was that this
production appeared when Tennyson suddenly had
become fashionable, in England and America, through
his accession to the laureate's honors, and for this
reason, as well as for its theme and eccentric qualities, had a wider reading than his previous works :
not only among the masses, to whom the other volumes had been sealed books, but among thoughtful
people, who now first made the poet's acquaintance
and received " Maud " as the foremost example of
his style. First impressions are lasting, and to this
day Tennyson is deemed, by many of the latter
class, an apostle of tinsel and affectation. In our
own country especially, his popular reputation began
with " Maud," — a work which, for lack of constructive beauty, is the opposite of his other narrative
poems.

*Lyric and
idyllic
verse.*

A pleasing feature of the volume of 1855 was an
idyl, " The Brook," which is charmingly finished and
contains a swift and rippling inter-lyric delightful to
every reader. A winsome, novel stanzaic form, possibly of the Laureate's own invention, is to be found
in " The Daisy," and in the Horatian lines to his
friend Maurice. Here, too, is much of that felicitous
word-painting for which he is deservedly renowned : —

> " O Milan, O the chanting quires,
>   The giant windows' blazon'd fires,
>   The height, the space, the gloom, the glory !
>   A mount of marble, a hundred spires !
>
>   .   .   .   .   .   .
>
> " How faintly-flush'd, how phantom-fair,
>   Was Monte Rosa, hanging there
>   A thousand shadowy-pencill'd valleys
>   And snowy dells in a golden air."

We come at last to Tennyson's master-work, so recently brought to a completion after the labor of twenty years, — during which period the separate *Idyls of the King* had appeared from time to time. Nave and transept, aisle after aisle, the Gothic minster has extended, until, with the addition of a cloister here and a chapel yonder, the structure stands complete. I hardly think that the poet at first expected to compose an epic. It has grown insensibly, under the hands of one man who has given it the best years of his life, — but somewhat as Wolf conceived the Homeric poems to have grown, chant by chant, until the time came for the whole to be welded together in heroic form. Yet in other great epics the action rarely ceases, the links are connected, and the movement continues from day to day until the end. Here, we have a series of idyls, — like the tapestry-work illustrations of a romance, scene after scene, with much change of actors and emotions, yet all leading to one solemn and tragic close. It is the epic of chivalry, — the Christian ideal of chivalry which we have deduced from a barbaric source, — our conception of what knighthood should be, rather than what it really was ; but so skilfully wrought of high imaginings, faery spells, fantastic legends, and mediæval splendors, that the whole work, suffused with the Tennysonian glamour of golden mist, seems like a chronicle illuminated by saintly hands, and often blazes with light like that which flashed from the holy wizard's book when the covers were unclasped. And, indeed, if this be not the greatest narrative-poem since "Paradise Lost," what other English production are you to name in its place ? Never so lofty as the grander portions of Milton's epic,

" Idyls of the King," 1859-72.

An epic of ideal chivalry.

it is more evenly sustained and has no long prosaic passages ; while " Paradise Lost " is justly declared to be a work of superhuman genius impoverished by dreary wastes of theology.

Malory's
" Le Morte
Darthur,"
1485.

Tennyson early struck a vein in the black-letter compilation of Sir Thomas Malory. A tale was already fashioned to his use, from which to derive his legends and exalt them with whatsoever spiritual meanings they might require. The picturesque qualities of the old Anglo-Breton romance fascinated his

Tennyson a
Pre-Raph-
aelite in
youth.

youth, and found lyrical expression in the weird, melodious, Pre-Raphaelite ballad of " The Lady of Shalott." The young poet here attained great excellence in a walk which Rossetti and his pupils have since chosen for their own, and his early studies are on a level with some of their masterpieces. Until recently, they have made success in this direction a special aim, while Tennyson would not be restricted even to such attractive work, but went steadily on, claiming the entire field of imaginative research as the poet's own.

His love of
allegory.

His strong allegorical bent, evinced in that early lyric, was heightened by analysis of the Arthurian legends. The English caught this tendency, long since, from the Italians ; the Elizabethan era was so charged with it, that the courtiers of the Virgin Queen hardly could speak without a mystical double-meaning, — for an illustration of which read the dialogue in certain portions of Kingsley's " Amyas Leigh." From Sidney and Spenser down to plain John Bunyan, and even to Sir Walter Scott, allegory is a natural English mode ; and, while adopted in several of Tennyson's pieces, it finds a special development in the " Idyls of the King."

The name thus bestowed upon the early instalments of this production seems less adapted to its complete form. Like the walls of Troy, it

> " Rose slowly to a music slowly breathed,
> A cloud that gathered shape."

The shape no longer is idyllic, and doubt no longer exists whether a successful epic can be written in a mature period of national literature. We have one here, but subdivided into ten distinct poems, each of which suits the canonical requirement, and may be read at a single sitting.

To my mind, there is a marked difference in style between the original and later portions of this work. The " Morte d'Arthur " of 1842 is Homeric to the farthest degree possible in the slow, Saxon movement of the verse ; grander, with its " hollow oes and aes," than any succeeding canto, always excepting " Guinevere." Nor do I think the later idyls equal to those four which first were issued in one volume, and which so cleared the Laureate's fame from the doubts suggested by " Maud, and Other Poems." " Vivien " is a bold and subtle analysis, a closer study of certain human types than Tennyson is wont to make. " Elaine " still remains, for pathetic sweetness and absolute beauty of narrative and rhythm, dearest to the heart of maiden, youth, or sage. " Enid," while upon the lower level of " Pelleas and Ettarre " and " Gareth and Lynette," is clear and strong, and shows a freedom from mannerism characteristic of the author's best period. It would seem that his creative vigor reached its height during the composition of these four idyls ; certainly, since the production of " Enoch Arden,"

Distinction between the early and later blank-verse.

" Vivien."

" Elaine."

" Enid."

" Pelleas and Et-tarre."

8* L

*" Guine-
vere " the
Laureate's
most dra-
matic and
imaginative
work.*

at an early subsequent date, he has not advanced in freshness and imagination. His greatest achievement still is that noblest of modern episodes, the canto entitled " Guinevere," surcharged with tragic pathos and high dramatic power. He never has so reached the *passio vera* of the early dramatists as in this imposing scene. There is nothing finer in modern verse than the interview between Arthur and his remorseful wife ; nothing loftier than the passage beginning —

> " Lo ! I forgive thee, as Eternal God
> Forgives : do thou for thine own soul the rest.
> But how to take last leave of all I loved ?
> O golden hair, with which I used to play
> Not knowing ! O imperial-moulded form,
> And beauty such as never woman wore,
> Until it came a kingdom's curse with thee —
> I cannot touch thy lips, they are not mine,
> But Lancelot's : nay, they never were the King's."

When this idyl first appeared, what elevation seized upon the soul of every poetic aspirant as he read it ! What despair of rivalling a passion so imaginative, an art so majestic and supreme !

I have referred to the Homeric manner of the fragment now made the conclusion of the epic, and

*" The Pass-
ing of Ar-
thur."*

entitled " The Passing of Arthur." The magnificent battle-piece, by which it is here preluded, is so different in manner from the original " Morte d'Arthur," that both are injured by their juxtaposition. The canto, moreover, plainly weakens at the close. The epic properly ends with the line,

> " And on the mere the wailing died away."

The poet's sense of proportion here works injuriously, urging him to bring out fully the moral of his allegory, albeit the effect really is harmed by this addition of the sequel, down to the line which finishes the work : —

" And the new sun rose bringing the new year."

In conclusion, observe the technical features of " Gareth and Lynette," a canto recently added to the poem. It displays Tennyson's latest, not his best manner, carried to an extreme ; the verse is clamped together, with every conjunction omitted that can be spared, yet interspersed with lines of a galloping, redundant nature, as if the Laureate were somewhat influenced by Swinburne and adapting himself to a fashion of the time. A special fault is the substitution of alliteration for the simple excellence of his standard verse. This may be a concession to the modern school, or a result of his mousing among Pre-Chaucerian ballads. It palls on the ear, as does the poet's excessive reiteration and play upon words. We are compensated for all this by a stalwart presentation of that fine old English which Emerson has pronounced " a stern and dreadful language." The public is indebted to Tennyson for a restoration of precious Saxon words, too long forgotten, which, we trust, will hereafter maintain their ground. He is a purifier of our tongue : a resistant to the novelties of slang and affectation intruded upon our literature by the mixture of races and the extension of English-speaking colonies to every clime and continent in the world.

It is not probable that another sustained poem will hereafter be written upon the Arthurian legends. Milton's dream inconsonant with his own time and

"Gareth and Lynette."

Recent mannerisms.

Tennyson's English.

higher aspirations, has, at last, its due fulfilment. The subject waited long, a sleeping beauty, until the "fated fairy-prince" came, woke it into life, and the spell is forever at an end. But who shall say whether future generations will rate this epic as highly as we do; whether it will stand out like "The Faery Queene" and "Paradise Lost," as one of the epochal compositions by which an age is symbolized? More than one poem, or series of poems, — Drayton's "The Barons' Wars," for instance, — has wrongly in its own time been thought a work of this class, though now men say of it that only the shadow of its name remains. At present we have no right to declare of the "Idyls of the King," as of "In Memoriam," that it is so original, so representative both of the author and of his period, as to defy the dust of time.

Resolute and fortunate advance in work and fame.

A famous life often falls short of its promise. Temperament and circumstance hedge it with obstacles; or, perhaps, the "Fury with the abhorred shears" slits its thin-spun tissue before the decisive hour. In the case of Tennyson this has been reversed. He has advanced by regular stages to the highest office of a poet. More fortunate than Landor, he was suited to the time, and the time to his genius; he has been happier than Keats or Shelley in length of years, and, in ease of circumstances, than Wordsworth, Coleridge, or Hood. Had he died after completing the epic, his work would still seem rounded and complete. Surely a poet's youthful dream never was more fully realized, and we must regard the Laureate's genius as developed through good fortune to the utmost degree permitted by inherent limitations.

During the growth of this epic he has, however, produced a few other poems which take high rank. Of these, *Enoch Arden*, in sustained beauty, bears a relation to his shorter pastorals similar to that existing between the epic and his minor heroic-verse. Coming within the average range of emotions, it has been very widely read. This poem is in its author's purest idyllic style; noticeable for evenness of tone, clearness of diction, successful description of coast and ocean, — finally, for the loveliness and fidelity of its *genre* scenes. In study of a class below him, hearts "centred in the sphere of common duties," the Laureate is unsurpassed. A far different creation is "Lucretius," a brooding character with which Tennyson is quite in sympathy. He has invested it with a certain restless grandeur, yet hardly, I should conceive, wrought out the work he thought possible when the theme was first suggested to his mind. He found its limits and contented himself with portraying a gloomy, isolated figure, as strongly and subtly as Browning would have drawn it, and with a terseness beyond the latter's art.

I have already spoken of "The Golden Supper" and "Aylmer's Field." Among other and better pieces, "Sea-Dreams," — a poem of measureless satire and much idyllic beauty, — "Tithonus," "The Voyage," — a fine lyric, and such masterly ballads as "The Victor," "The Captor," and "The Sailor-Boy," will not be forgotten. It is worth while to observe the few dialect poems which Tennyson has written, — thrown off, as if merely to show that he could be easily first in a field which he resigns to others. The "Northern Farmer" ballads, old and

Marginal notes:

"*Enoch Arden, and Other Poems,*" 1864.

"*Lucretius.*"

Miscellaneous pieces.

Dialect poems, etc.

new, are the best English dialect studies of our time. Among his minor diversions are light occasional pieces and some experiments in classical measures, — often finished sketches, germs of works to which he has given no further attention. He saw that " Boadicea " offered no such field as that afforded by the Arthurian legends, and wisely gave it over. Again, he unquestionably could have made a great blank-verse translation of Homer, but chose the better part in devoting his middle life solely to creative work. The world can ill afford to lose a poet's golden prime in the labors of a translator.

IV.

*Character-
istics of
Tennyson's
genius.*

In whatsoever light we examine the characteristics of the Laureate's genius, the complete and even balance of his poetry is from first to last conspicuous. It exhibits that just combination of lyrical elements which makes a symphony, wherein it is difficult to say what quality predominates. Reviewing minor poets, we think this one attractive for the wild flavor of his unstudied verse ; another, for the gush and music of his songs ; a third, for idyllic

*Synthetic
perfection.*

sweetness or tragic power ; but in Tennyson we have the strong repose of art, whereof — as of the perfection of nature — the world is slow to tire. It has become conventional, but remember that nothing endures to the point of conventionalism which is not based upon lasting rules ; that it once was new and refreshing, and is sure, in future days, to regain the early charm.

*Lack of
spirit and
quality.*

The one thing longed for, and most frequently missed, in work of this kind, is the very wilding flavor of which I speak. We are not always broad enough and elevated enough to be content with symphonic art. Guinevere wearies of Arthur. There are times when a tart apple, a crust of bread, a bit of wild honey, are worth more to us than all the delicacies of the larder. We wish more rugged outbreaks, more impetuous discords; we listen for the sudden irregular trill of the thicket songster. The fulness of Tennyson's art evades the charm of spontaneity. How rarely he takes you by surprise! His stream is sweet, assured, strong; but how seldom the abrupt bend, the plunge of the cataract, the thunder and the spray! Doubtless he has enthusiasms, but all are held in hand; college-life, study, restraint, comfort, reverence, have done their work upon him. He is well broken, as we say of a thoroughbred, — proud and true, and, though he makes few bursts of speed, keeps easily forward, and is sure to be first at the stand.

We come back to the avowal that in technical excellence, as an artist in verse, Alfred Tennyson is the greatest of modern poets. Other masters, old or new, have surpassed him in special instances; but he is the one who rarely nods, and who *always* finishes his verse to the extreme. Not that he is free from weaknesses: to the present day, when pushed for inspiration, he resorts to inventions as disagreeable as the affectation which repelled many healthy minds from his youthful lyrics. Faults of this sort, in "Maud" and later poems, have somewhat prejudiced another class of readers, — people who, with what a critic denominates their "eighteenth century" taste, still pay homage to the genius of Pope for merits which the Laureate has in even

A great and conscientious artist.

greater excess. A question recently has been
mooted, whether Milton, were he living in our time,
could write " Paradise Lost "? A no less interesting
conjecture would relate to the kind of poetry that
we should have from Pope, were he of Tennyson's

*Points of
resemblance
between
Tennyson
and Pope.*

generation. The physical traits of the two men
being so utterly at variance, no doubt many will
scout my suggestion that the verse of the former
might closely resemble that of the latter. Pope
excelled in qualities which, *mutatis mutandis,* are
noticeable in Tennyson : finish and minuteness of
detail, and the elevation of common things to fanciful beauty. Here, again, compare " The Rape of
the Lock " with " The Sleeping Beauty," and especially with " The Talking Oak." A faculty of " saying things," which, in Pope (his being a cruder age,
when persons needed that homely wisdom which
seems trite enough in our day), became didacticism,
in Tennyson is sweetly natural and poetic. Since
the period of the " Essay on Man," from what writer
can you cull so many wise and fine proverbial
phrases as from the poet who says : —

" ' T is better to have loved and lost,
Than never to have loved at all " ;

" Kind hearts are more than coronets,
And simple faith than Norman blood " ;

" There lives more faith in honest doubt,
Believe me, than in half the creeds " ;

who puts the theory of evolution in a couplet when
he sings of

" one far-off divine event,
To which the whole creation moves " ;

who so tersely avows that

> " Knowledge comes, but wisdom lingers ";

> " Things seen are mightier than things heard ";

and, again : —

> " Old age hath yet his honor and his toil ";

from whom else so many of these proverbs, which are not isolated, but, as in Pope's works, recur by tens and scores? Curious felicities of verse : —

> " Laborious orient ivory sphere in sphere ";

lines which record the most exquisite thrills of life : —

> " Our spirits rush'd together at the touching of the lips ";

and unforgotten similes : —

> " Dear as remembered kisses after death "; —

such beauties as these occur in multitudes, and literally make up the body of the Laureate's song. In feeling, imagination, largeness of heart and head, the diminutive satirist can enter into no comparison with our poet, but the situation is otherwise as respects finish and moralistic power. The essence of Pope's art was false, because it was the product of a false age ; Dryden had been his guide to the stilted heroics of the French school, which so long afterwards, Pope lending them such authority, stalked through English verse. In this day he would, like Tennyson, have found his masters among the early, natural poets, or obtained, in a direct manner, what classicism he needed, and not through Gallic filters. Yet it is not long since I heard an eminent man lauding Pope for the very characteristics which, as here

Points of difference, subjective and objective.

shown, are conspicuous in Tennyson; and decrying the latter, misled by that chance acquaintance with his poetry which is worse than no acquaintance at all. In *suggestiveness* Pope was singularly deficient: his constructive faculty so prevailed, that he left nothing to the reader's fancy, but explained to the end. He had no such moods as those evoked by "Tears, idle tears," and "Break, break, break!" and therefore his verses never suggest them. In irony Tennyson would equal Pope, had he not risen above it. The man who wrote "The New Timon and the Poets," and afterwards rebuked himself for so doing, could write another "Dunciad," or, without resort to any models, a still more polished and bitter satire of his own.

Supreme and complex modern art.

Tennyson's original and fastidious art is of itself a theme for an essay. The poet who studies it may well despair; he never can excel it, and is tempted to a reactionary carelessness, trusting to make his individuality felt thereby. Its strength is that of perfection; its weakness, the over-perfection which marks a still-life painter. Here is the absolute sway of metre, compelling every rhyme and measure needful to the thought; here are sinuous alliterations, unique and varying breaks and pauses, winged flights and falls, the glory of sound and color, everywhere present, or, if missing, absent of the poet's free will. Art so complex was not possible until centuries of literature had passed, and an artist could overlook the field, essay each style, and evolve a metrical result, which should be to that of earlier periods what the music of Meyerbeer and Rossini is to the narrower range of Piccini or Gluck. In Tennyson's artistic conscientiousness, he is the opposite of that compeer who approaches him most nearly in years and strength of intellect, Robert Browning. His gift of language is not so copious as Swinburne's, yet through its use the higher excellence is attained. But I shall elsewhere write of these matters. Let me conclude my remarks upon the Laureate's art with a reference to his unfailing taste and sense of the fitness of things. This is neatly exemplified in the openings, and especially in the endings, of his idyls. " Audley Court" very well illustrates what I mean. Observe, also, the beautiful dedication of his collected works to the Queen, and the solemn and faithful character-painting of the tribute to Prince Albert which forms the prelude to the Idyls of the King. The two dedications are equal to the best ever written, and each is a poem by itself. They fully sustained the wisdom of Victoria's choice of a successor to

> " This laurel greener from the brows
> Of him that uttered nothing base."

Leaving the architecture of Tennyson's poetry and coming to the sentiment which it seeks to express, we are struck at once by the fact that an idyllic, or picturesque mode of conveying that sentiment is the one natural to this poet, if not the only one permitted by his limitations. In this he surpasses all the poets since Theocritus ; and his work is greater than the Syracusan's, because his thought and period are greater. His eyes are his purveyors ; with " wisdom at one entrance quite shut out " he would be helpless. To use the lingo of the phrenologists, his locality is better than his individuality. He does not, like Browning, catch the secret of a master-passion, nor, like the old dramatists, the very life of action ;

Browning.

Swinburne.

Taste.

The Laureate an idyllist.

on the contrary, he gives us an ideal picture of an ideal person, but set against a background more tangible than other artists can draw, — making the accessories, and even the atmosphere, convey the meaning of his poem. As we study his verse, and the sound and color of it enter our souls, we think with him, we partake of his feeling, and are led to regions which he finds himself unable to open for us except in this suggestive way. The fidelity of his accessories is peculiar to the time : realistic, without the Flemish homeliness ; true as Pre-Raphaelitism, but mellowed with the atmosphere of a riper art. This idyllic method is not that of the most inspired poets and the most impassioned periods. But, merely

His descriptive faculty. as a descriptive writer, who is so delightful as Tennyson? He has the unerring first touch, which in a single line proves the artist; and it justly has been remarked that there is more true English landscape in many an isolated stanza of "In Memoriam" than in the whole of "The Seasons," — that vaunted descriptive poem of a former century. A paper has been written upon the Lincolnshire scenery depicted in his poems, and we might have others, just as well, upon his marine or highland views. He is a born observer of physical nature, and, whenever he applies an adjective to some object, or passingly alludes to some phenomenon which others have not noted, is almost infallibly correct. Possibly he does this too methodically, but his opponents cannot deny that his outdoor rambles are guided by their eloquent apostle's "Lamp of Truth."

Limitations. His limitations are nearly as conspicuous as his abundant gifts. They are indicated, first, by a style pronounced to the degree of mannerism, and, secondly, by failure, until within a very recent date, to *Cp. page* 191. produce dramatic work of the genuine kind.

With respect to his style, it may be said that *Style.* Tennyson — while objective in the variety of his themes, and in ability to separate his own experience from their development — is the most subjective of poets in the distinguishable flavor of his language and rhythm. Reading him you might not guess his life and story, — the reverse of which is true with Byron, whom I take as a familiar example of the subjective in literature ; nevertheless, it is impossible to observe a single line, or an entire specimen, of the Laureate's poems, without feeling that they are in the handwriting of the same master, or of some disciple who has caught his fascinating and contagious style.

I speak of his second limitation, with a full *Lack of the true dramatic gift.* knowledge that many claim a dramatic crown for the author of the " Northern Farmer," " Tithonus," " St. *Cp. " Poets of America" : pp. 204, 467.* Simeon Stylites," — for the poet of the Round Table and the Holy Grail. But isolated studies are not sufficient: a group of living men and women is necessary to broad dramatic action. Tennyson forces his characters to adapt themselves to preconceived, statuesque ideals of his own. His chief success is with those in humble life ; in " Enoch Arden," and elsewhere, he has very sweetly depicted the emotions of simple natures, rarely at a sublime height or depth of passion. He also draws — with an easy touch occasionally found in the prose of the author of " The Warden " — a group of sturdy, refined, comfortable fellows upon their daily rambles, British and modern in their wholesome talk. But the true dramatist instinctively portrays either exceptional characters, or ordinary beings in impassioned and extraordinary moods. This Tennyson rarely essays to do, except when presenting imaginary heroes of a visioned past. A great master of contemplative, descriptive, or lyrical verse, he falls short in that combination of action and passion which we call dramatic, and often gives us a series of marvellous tableaux in lieu of exalted speech and deeds.

Effect of a secluded life.

Cp. " Poets of America": pp. 155, 156.

This lack of individuality is somewhat due to the influence of the period; largely, also, to the habit of solitude which the poet has chosen to indulge. His life has been passed among his books or in the seclusion of rural haunts; when in town, in the company of a few chosen friends. This has heightened his tendency to reverie, and unfitted him to distinguish sharply between men and men. The great novelists of our day, who correspond to the dramatists of a past age, have plunged into the roar of cities and the thick of the crowd, touching people closely and on every side. It must be owned that we do not find in their works that close knowledge of inanimate nature for which Tennyson has foregone "the proper study of mankind." The one seems to curtail the other, Wordsworth's writings being another example in point. "Men my brothers, men the workers," sings the Laureate, and is pleased to watch and encourage them, but always from afar.

His ideal personages.

With few exceptions, then, his most poetical types of men and women are not substantial beings, but beautiful shadows, which, like the phantoms of a stereopticon, dissolve if you examine them too long and closely. His knights are the old bequest of chivalry, yet how stalwart and picturesque! His early ideals of women are cathedral-paintings, — scarcely flesh and blood, but certain attributes personified and made angelical. Where a story has been made for him he is more dramatic. Arthur, Lancelot, Merlin, Guinevere, are strong, wise, or beautiful, and so we find them in the chronicle from which the poet drew his legend. He has advanced them to the requirements of modern Christianity, yet hardly created them anew. It is not improbable that Tennyson may force himself to compose some notably dramatic work ; but only through skill and strength of purpose, in this age, and with his habit of life. In a dramatic period he might find himself as sadly out of place as Beddoes, Darley, Landor, have been in his own century. By sheer good fortune he has flourished in a time calling for tenderness, thought, excellent workmanship, and not for wild extremes of power. So chaste, varied, and tuneful are his notes, that they are scornfully compared to piano-music, in distinction from what he himself has entitled the "God-gifted organ voice of England." Take, however, the piano as an instrumental expression of recent musical taste, and see to what a height of execution, of capacity to give almost universal pleasure, the art of playing it has been carried. A great pianist is a great artist ; and it is no light fame which holds, with relation to poetry, the supremacy awarded to Liszt or Schumann by the refined musicians of our time.

The cast of Tennyson's intellect is such, that his social rank, his training at an old university, and his philosophic learning have bred in him a liberal conservatism. Increase of ease and of fame has strengthened his inclination to accept things as they are, and, while recognizing the law of progress, to make no undue effort to hasten the order of events. He

He may yet write a fine drama.

P. S. See p. 413, and cp. "Poets of America": p. 467.

Perfectly adapted to his time.

A liberal conservative:

In politics, sees that "the thoughts of men are widened with the process of the suns," but is not the man to lead a reform, or to disturb the pleasant conditions in which his lot is cast. No personal wrong has allied him to the oppressed and struggling classes, yet he is too intellectual not to perceive that such wrongs exist. It must be remembered that Shakespeare and Goethe were no more heroic. Just so with his re-

and in re- ligious attitude. Reverence for beauty would of itself
ligion. dispose him to love the ivied Church, with all its art, and faith, and ancestral legendary associations ; and therefore, while amply reflecting in his verse the doubt and disquiet of the age, his tranquil sense of order, together with the failure of iconoclasts to substitute any creed for that which they are breaking down, have brought him to the position of stanch Sir William Petty (*obiit* 1687), who wrote in his will these memorable words : " As for religion, I die in the profession of that Faith, and in the practice of such Worship, as I find established by the law of my country, not being able to believe what I myself please, nor to worship God better than by doing as I would be done unto, and observing the laws of my country, and expressing my love and honor unto Almighty God by such signs and tokens as are understood to be such by the people with whom I live, God knowing my heart even without any at all."

Artistic So far as the " religion of art " is concerned, Ten
reverence. nyson is the most conscientious of devotees. Throughout his work we find a pure and thoughtful purpose, abhorrent of the mere licentious passion for beauty,

> "such as lurks
> In some wild Poet, when he works
> Without a conscience or an aim."

In my remarks upon " In Memoriam " I have shown that in one direction he readily keeps pace with the advance of modern thought. A leading mission of his art appears to be that of hastening the transition of our poetic nomenclature and imagery from the old or phenomenal method to one in accordance with knowledge and truth. His laurel is brighter for the fact that he constantly avails himself of the results of scientific discovery, without making them prosaic. This tendency, beginning with " Locksley Hall " and " The Princess," has increased with him to the present time. If modern story-writers can make the wonders of chemistry and astronomy the basis of tales more fascinating to children than the Arabian Nights, why should not the poet explore this field for the creation of a new imagery and expression? There is a remarkable passage in Wordsworth's preface to the second edition of his poems ; a prophecy which, half a century ago, could only have been uttered by a man of lofty intellect and extraordinary premonition of changes even now at hand : —

His verse conformed to modern progress and discovery.

" The objects of the poet's thoughts are everywhere ; though the eyes and senses of men are, it is true, his favorite guides, yet he will follow wheresoever he can find an atmosphere of sensation in which to move his wings. Poetry is the first and last of all knowledge, — it is immortal as the heart of man. If the labors of the men of science should ever create any material revolution, direct or indirect, in our condition, and in the impressions which we habitually receive, the poet will sleep then no more than at present ; he will be ready to follow the steps of the man of science, not only in those general indirect effects, but he will be at his side, carrying sensation

Wordsworth upon the future relations of Science and Poetry. See also page 15.

into the midst of the objects of the science itself. The remotest discoveries of the chemist, the botanist, or mineralogist will be as proper objects of the poet's art as any upon which it can be employed, *if the time should ever come when these things shall be familiar to us, and the relations under which they are contemplated by the followers of the respective sciences shall be manifestly and palpably material to us as enjoying and suffering beings. If the time should ever come when what is now called science, thus familiarized to men, shall be ready to put on, as it were, a form of flesh and blood, the poet will lend his divine spirit to aid the transfiguration, and will welcome the Being thus produced, as a dear and genuine inmate of the household of man.*"

It is not unlikely that Tennyson was early impressed by these profound observations; at all events, he has seen the truths of science becoming familiar "to the general," and has governed his art accordingly. The poet and man of science have a common ground, since few discoveries are made without the exercise of the poet's special gift, — the imagination. This faculty is required to enable a child to comprehend any scientific paradox: for instance, that of the rotation of the Earth upon its axis. The imagination of an investigator advances from one step to another, and thus, in a certain sense, the mental processes of a Milton and a Newton are near akin. A plodding, didactic intellect is not strictly scientific; nor will great poetry ever spring from a merely phantasmal brain: "best bard because the wisest," sings the poet.

Taine's analysis: M. Taine's chapter upon Tennyson shows an intelligent perception of the Laureate's relations to his time,

and especially to England; but though containing a
fine interlude upon the perennial freshness of a poet
and the zest which makes nature a constant surprise
to him, — declaring that the poet, in the presence of
this world, is as the first man on the first day, — with
all this excellence the chapter fails to rightly appreciate Tennyson, and overestimates Alfred de Musset
in comparison. M. Taine's failure, I think, is due to *Its defects.*
the fact that no one, however successful in mastering
a foreign language, can fully enter into that nicety
of art which is the potent witchery of Tennyson's
verse. The minute distinction between one poem
and another, where the ideas are upon a level, and
the difference is one of essential flavor, a foreigner
loses without perceiving his loss. Precisely this delicacy of aroma separates Tennyson from other masters
of verse. An English school-girl will see in his work
a beauty that wholly escapes the most accomplished
Frenchman: the latter may have ten times her knowledge of the language, but she "hears a voice he
cannot hear" and *feels* an influence he never can
fairly understand. Again, M. Taine does not allow
credit for the importance of the works actually produced by Tennyson. Largeness and proportion go
for something in edifices; and although De Musset, *De Musset.*
the errant, impassioned, suffering Parisian, had the
sacred fire, and gave out burning flashes here and
there, his light was fitful, nor long sustained, and we
think rather of what one so gifted ought to have
accomplished than of what he actually did.

But Taine's catholicity, and the very fact that he *Wherein*
is a foreigner, have protected him, on the other hand, *the French critic has*
from the overweening influence of Tennyson's art, that *succeeded.*
holds us

> "Above the subject, as strong gales
> Hold swollen clouds from raining ";

have made him a wiser judge of the poet's intellectual and imaginative position. In this matter he is
like a deaf man watching a battle, undisturbed by
the bewildering power of sound. His remarks upon
the limitations of a " comfortable, luxurious, English "
muse are not without reason ; all in all, he has a
just idea of Tennyson's representative attitude in the
present state of British thought and art. He has
laid too little stress upon the difference between
Tennyson and Byron, by observing which we gather
a clearer estimate of the former's genius than in any
other way.

*Tennyson
and Byron:*

Tennyson is the antithesis of Byron, in both the
form and spirit of his song. The Georgian poet,
with all the glow of genius, constantly giving utterance to condensed and powerful expressions, never
attempted condensation in his general style ; there
was nothing he so little cared for ; his inspiration
must have full flow and break through every barrier ;
it was the roaring of a mighty wind, the current of

A contrast.

a great river, — prone to overflow, and often to spread
thinly and unevenly upon the shoals and lowlands.
Tennyson, though composing an extended work, seeks
the utmost terseness of expression ; howsoever composite his verse, it is tightly packed and cemented,
and decorated to repletion with fretwork and precious
stones ; nothing is neglected, nothing wasted, nothing
misapplied. You cannot take out a word or sentence
without marring the structure, nor can you find a
blemish ; while much might be profitably omitted
from Byron's longer poems, and their blemishes are
frequent as the beauties. Prolixity, diffuseness, were

characteristic of Byron's time. Again, Tennyson is greater in analysis and synthesis, the two strong servitors of art. In sense of proportion Byron was all abroad. He struck bravely into a poem, and, trusting to the fire of his inspiration, let it write itself, neither seeing the end nor troubling his mind concerning it. Certainly this was true with regard to his greatest productions, " Childe Harold " and " Don Juan " ; though others, such as " Manfred," were exceptions through dramatic necessity. In Tennyson's method, as in architecture, we are sure that the whole structure is foreseen at the outset. Every block is numbered and swings into an appointed place ; often the final portions are made first, that the burden of the plan may be off the designer's mind. Leaving the matter of art, there is no less difference between the two poets as we consider their perceptive and imaginative gifts, and here the largeness of Byron's vision tells in his favor. Tennyson, sometimes grand and exalted, is equally delicate, — an artist of the beautiful in á minute way. Of this Byron took little account ; his soul was exalted by the broad and mighty aspects of nature ; for mosaic-work he was unfitted : a mountain, the sea, a thunder-storm, a glorious woman, — such imposing objects aroused his noble rage. You never could have persuaded *him* that the microcosm is equal to the macrocosm. Again, his subjectivity, so intense, was wholly different from Tennyson's, in that he became one with Nature, — a part of that which was around him. Tennyson is subjective, so far as a pervading sameness of style, a landscape seen through one shade of glass, can make him, yet few have stood more calmly aloof from Nature, and viewed

1. Their difference in method;

2. In perception and imagination;

3. In subjectivity;

her more objectively. He contemplates things without identifying himself with them. In these respects, Tennyson and Byron not only are antithetical, but — each above his contemporaries — reflect the antithetical qualities of their respective eras. In con-

4. In the matter of influence.

clusion, it should be noticed that, although each has had a host of followers, Byron affected the spirit of the people at large, rather than the style of his brother poets; while Tennyson, through the force of his admirable art, has affected the poets themselves, who do not sympathize with his spirit, but show themselves awed and instructed by his mastery of technics. Byron's influence was national; that of Tennyson is professional to an unprecedented degree.

An ideal poetic career.

If the temperament of Byron or of Mrs. Browning may be pronounced an ideal poetic temperament, certainly the career of Tennyson is an ideal poetic career. He has been less in contact with the rude outer world than any poet save Wordsworth; again, while even the latter wrote much prose, Tennyson, "having wherewithal," and consecrating his life wholly to metrical art, has been a verse-maker and nothing else. He has passed through all gradations, from obscurity to laurelled fame; beginning with the lightest lyrics, he has lived to write the one successful epic of the last two hundred years; and though he well might rest content, if contentment were possible to poets and men, with the glory of a far-reaching and apparently lasting renown, he still pursues his art, and seems, unlike Campbell and many another poet, to have no fear of the shadow of his own success. His lot has been truly enviable. We have observed the disadvantages of amateurship in the case of Landor, and noted the limitations

imposed upon Thomas Hood by the poverty which
clung to him through life ; but Tennyson has made
the former condition a vantage-ground, and thereby
carried his work to a perfection almost unattainable
in the experience of a professional, hard-working *lit-
térateur.* Writing as much and as little as he chose,
he has escaped the drudgery which breeds contempt.
His song has been the sweeter for his retirement,
like that of a cicada piping from a distant grove.

*Cp. " Poets
of Amer-
ica " : pp.
222, 223.*

V.

REVIEWING our analysis of his genius and works,
we find in Alfred Tennyson the true poetic irritability,
a sensitiveness increased by his secluded life, and displayed from time to time in "the least little touch
of the spleen"; we perceive him to be the most
faultless of modern poets in technical execution, but
one whose verse is more remarkable for artistic perfection than for dramatic action and inspired fervor.
His adroitness surpasses his invention. Give him a
theme, and no poet can handle it so exquisitely,—yet
we feel that, with the Malory legends to draw upon,
he could go on writing "Idyls of the King" forever.
We find him objective in the spirit of his verse, but
subjective in the decided manner of his style; possessing a sense of proportion, based upon the highest analytic and synthetic powers,—a faculty that can
harmonize the incongruous thoughts, scenes, and general details of a composite period; in thought resembling Wordsworth, in art instructed by Keats, but
rejecting the passion of Byron, or having nothing in
his nature that aspires to it; finally, an artist so perfect in a widely extended range, that nothing of his

*Summary
of the fore-
going analy-
sis.*

work can be spared, and, in this respect, approaching
Horace and outvying Pope; not one of the great
wits nearly allied to madness, yet possibly to be accepted as a wiser poet, serene above the frenzy of
the storm; certainly to be regarded, in time to come,
as, all in all, the fullest representative of the refined,
speculative, complex Victorian age.

CHAPTER VI.

TENNYSON AND THEOCRITUS.

H AVING acknowledged Tennyson as master of the idyllic school, — and having seen that his method, during the last thirty years, whatever its strength or weakness, has been conspicuous in the prevailing form and spirit of English verse, — it does not seem amiss, in the case of this poet, to supplement my review of his genius and works by some remarks upon the likeness which he bears to the Dorian father of idyllic song, and upon the relations of both the ancient and modern poets to their respective eras.

Supplemental notice of Tennyson and the idyllic school.

I.

UNTIL within a very recent period, the text of the Greek idyls was not embraced in the course of study at our foremost American colleges. Nevertheless, the Greek Reader which, a score of years ago, was largely in use for the preparatory lessons of the high schools, contained, amidst an assorted lot of passages from various writers, that wonderful elegy, "The Epitaph of Bion," whose authorship is attributed to Moschus. The novelty, the beauty, the fresh and modern thought of this undying poem were visible even to the school-fagged intellect of youths to whom poetry was a vague

" The Epitaph of Bion." Moschus, III.

9 *

delight. Well might they be, for this elegy, — in which the pain and passion of lamentation for a brother-minstrel are sung in strains echoing those which Bion himself had chanted in artificial sorrow for the mystic Adonis, — this perpetual elegy was the mould, if not the inspiration, of four great English dirges : laments beyond which the force of poetic anguish can no further go, and each of which is but a later affirmation that the ancient pupil of Theocritus found the one key-note to which all high idyllic elegy should be attuned thenceforth.

Having made a first acquaintance with the work of Tennyson, — and who does not remember how new and delicious the lyrics of the rising English poet seemed to us, half surfeited, as we were, with the fulness of his predecessors ? — I could not fail to observe a resemblance between certain portions of his verse and the only Greek idyl which I then knew. For example, in the use of the elegiac refrain, in the special imagery, in the adaptation of landscape and color to the feeling of a poem, and, often, in the suggestion of the feeling by the mere scenic effect. It was not till after that thorough knowledge of the English master's art, which has been no less absorbing and perilous than instructive to the singers of our period, that I *Obligations* was led to study the entire relics of the Greek idyllic *to the Greek* *idyllic poets.* poets. Then, for the first time, I became aware of the immense obligations of Tennyson to Theocritus, not only for the method, sentiment, and purpose, but for the very form and language, which render beautiful much of his most widely celebrated verse.

Three points were distinctly brought in view : —

1. The likeness of the Victorian to the Alexandrian age.

2. The close study made by Tennyson of the Syracusan idyls, resulting in the adjustment of their structure to English theme and composition, and in the artistic imitation of their choicest passages.

3. Hence, his own discovery of his proper function as a poet, and the gradual evolution and shaping of his whole literary career.

II.

THE design of this supplemental chapter is to exhibit some of the evidences on which the foregoing points are taken. They may interest the student of comparative minstrelsy, as an addition to his list of "Historic Counterparts" in literature, and are worth the attention of that host of readers, so wonted _to the faultless art of Tennyson that each trick and turn of his verse, his every image and thought, are more familiar to them than were the sentimental ditties of Moore and the romantic cantos of Scott and Byron to the poetic taste of an earlier generation. And how few, indeed, of his pieces could we spare! so few, that when he does trifle with his art the critics laugh like school-boys delighted to catch the master tripping for once; not wholly sure but that the matter may be noble, because, forsooth, he composed it. Yet men, wont to fare sumptuously, will now and then leave their delicate viands untasted, and hanker with lusty appetite for ruder and more sinewy fare. We turn again to Byron for sweep and fervor, to Coleridge and Shelley for the music that is divine; and it is through Wordsworth that we commune with the very spirits of the woodland and the misty mountain winds.

Illustration of the foregoing points.

It will not harm the noble army of verse-readers to be guided for a moment to the original fountain of that stream from which they take their favorite draughts. The Sicilian idyls were very familiar to the dramatists and songsters of Shakespeare's time, and a knowledge of them was affected, at least, by the artificial jinglers of the seventeenth and eighteenth centuries. Nowadays, we have Homer and Horace by heart; but Theocritus, to most of us, is but the echo of a melodious name. As the creator of the fourth great order of poetry, the composite, or idyllic, he bears to it the relation of Homer to epic, Pindar to lyric, Æschylus to dramatic verse; and if he had not sung as he sang, in Syracuse and Alexandria, two thousand years ago, it is doubtful whether modern English fancy would have been under the spell of that minstrelsy by which it was of late so justly and delightfully enthralled.

The father of idyllic song.

I do not know that any extended references to our topic were brought together before the appearance of a monograph, by the present writer, in which the substance of this chapter first appeared in print; nevertheless, within the last decade, during a revival of the study and translation of the Greek poets, allusions to the relations of Tennyson and Theocritus have been made, and parallel passages occasionally noted, — as by Thackeray in his Anthology, and by Snow in his appendix to the Clarendon school edition of Theocritus, — such waifs confirming me in my recognition of the evidence on which the foregoing statements are adventured. But, even now, many of the Laureate's reviewers, while noticing the "iteration" of his refrains, the arrangement of his idyllic songs, etc., seem to be unconscious of the influences under which these at the outset were produced.

Let us briefly consider the likeness of the Victorian to the Alexandrian age. The latter covered the time wherein the city, by which Alexander marked the splendor of his western conquests, was the capital of a new Greece, and had grouped within it all that was left of Hellenic philosophy, beauty, and power. Latin thought and imagination were still in their dawning, and Alexandria was the centre, the new Athens, of the civilized world. But the period, if not that of a decadence, was reflective, critical, scholarly, rather than creative ; a comfortable era, in which to live and enjoy the gathered harvests of what had gone before. All the previous history of Greece led up to the high Alexandrian refinement. Her literature had completed a round of four hundred years, of which the first three centuries, in the slower progress of national adolescence, comprised an epic and lyric period, reaching from Homer and Hesiod to Anacreon and Pindar. The remainder was the golden Attic age, the time of the Old, Middle, and New Comedy, of the dramatists from Æschylus to Aristophanes. Greek poetry then passed its noontide ; the Alexandrian school arose, flourishing for two centuries before the birth of Christ.

Comparison of the Victorian and Alexandrian eras.

Literary accomplishments now were widely diffused. There was a mob of gentlemen who wrote with ease. Tact and scholarship so abounded, that it was difficult to draw the line between talent and genius. We see a period of scholia and revised and annotated editions of the elder writers; wherein was done for Homer, Plato, the Hebrew Scriptures, what is now doing for Dante, Shakespeare, and Goethe. Philology came into being, and criticism began to clog the fancy. Schoell says that " the poets were

Cp. Matter: Hist. de l'École d'Alexandrie.

Schoell:
Hist. de la
Litt.
Grecque
Profane.

deeply read, but wanting in imagination, and often also in judgment." It was impossible for most to rise above the influence of the time. Science, however, made great strides. In material growth it was indeed a "wondrous age," an era of inventions, travel, and discovery: the period of Euclid and Archimedes; of Ptolemy with his astronomers; of Hiero, with his galleys long as clipper-ships; of academies, museums, theatres, lecture-halls, gymnasia; of a hundred philosophies; of geographers, botanists, casuists, scholiasts, reformers, and what not, — all springing into existence and finding support in the luxurious, speculative, bustling, news-devouring hurly-burly of that strangely modern Alexandrian time.

Distinction
between the
Greek and
English
tongues.

It is unnecessary to dwell upon the analogy which my readers already have drawn for themselves. It is not an even one. There is no parallel between the Greek and English languages. The former is copious, but simple, and a departure from the Attic purity was in itself a decline to vagueness and affectation. Our own tongue grows richer and stronger every year. Again, though England has also passed through great dramatic and lyric periods, our modern cycles are not of antique duration, but are likely to repeat themselves again and again. Our golden year is shorter, and the seasons in their turns come often round. Nevertheless, at the close of the poetical renaissance which marked the first quarter of the nineteenth century, English literature drifted into an indecisive, characterless period, bearing a resemblance to that of Alexandria when Ptolemy Philadelphus commenced his reign.

Ptolemy II.

That liberal and ambitious monarch confirmed the structure of an empire, and made the capital city

attractive and renowned. The wisest and most famous scholars resorted to his court, but not even
imperial patronage could restore the lost spirit of
Greek creative art. There was a single exception.
A poet of original and abounding genius, nurtured *Theocritus.*
in the beautiful island of Sicily, where the sky and
sea are bluer, the piny mountains, with Ætna at
their head, more kingly, the breezes fresher, the
rivulets more musical, and the upland pastures greener
than upon any other shores which the Mediterranean
borders, — such a poet felt himself inspired to utter
a fresh and native melody, even in that over-learned
and bustling time. Disdaining any feeble variations
of worn-out themes, he saw that Greek poetry had
achieved little in the delineation of common, every-
day life, and so flung himself right upon nature,
which he knew and reverenced well ; and erelong the
pastoral and town idyls of Theocritus, with their
amœbean dialogue and elegant occasional songs, won
the ear of both the fashionable and critical worlds.
Although his subjects were entirely novel, he availed
himself, in form, of all his predecessors' arts ; composing in the new Doric, the most liquid, colloquial,
and flexible of the dialects : and thus he fashioned *Birth of the*
his *eidullia*, — little pictures of real life upon the hill- *idyl.*
side and in the town, among the high and low, —
portraying characters with a few distinct touches in
lyric, epic, or dramatic form, and often by a combination of the whole. It is not my province here
to show who were his immediate teachers, or from
what rude island ditties and mimes he conceived and
shaped his art ; only, to state that Theocritus found
one field of verse then unworked, and so availed
himself of it as to make it his own, capturing the

hearts of those who still loved freshness and beauty, and forthwith attaining such excellence that the relics left us by him and two of his pupils are even now the wonder and imitation of mankind. A few sentences from Charles Kingsley's reference to the father of idyllic poetry tell the truth as simply and clearly as it can be told : —

Kingsley's "Alexandria and her Schools."

"One natural strain is heard amid all this artificial jingle, — that of Theocritus. It is not altogether Alexandrian. Its sweetest notes were learnt amid the chestnut-groves and orchards, the volcanic glens and sunny pastures of Sicily; but the intercourse between the courts of Hiero and the Ptolemies seems to have been continual. Poets and philosophers moved freely from one to the other, and found a like atmosphere in both. . . . . One can well conceive the delight which his idyls must have given to the dusty Alexandrians, pent up forever between sea and sand-hills, drinking the tank-water and never hearing the sound of a running stream; whirling, too, forever, in all the bustle and intrigue of a great commercial and literary city. To them and to us also. I believe Theocritus is one of the poets who will never die. He sees men and things, in his own light way, truly; and he describes them simply, honestly, with little careless touches of pathos and humor, while he floods his whole scene with that gorgeous Sicilian air, like one of Titian's pictures; . . . . and all this told in a language and a metre which shapes itself almost unconsciously, wave after wave, into the most luscious song."

It was in this wise that Theocritus founded and endowed the Greek idyllic school. Let us see how Tennyson, living in a somewhat analogous period, may be compared with him. How far has the representative idyllist of the nineteenth century profited by the example of his prototype? To what extent is the one indebted to the other for the structure, the manner, it may be even the matter, of many of his poems ?

We are uninformed of the year in which the boy Tennyson was entered at Trinity College, Cambridge, but find him there in 1829, taking the chancellor's gold medal for English verse ; this by the poem " Timbuctoo," a creditable performance for a lad of nineteen, and favored with the approval of the " Athenæum." It was thought to show traces of Milton, Shelley, and Wordsworth.   In the years 1826 – 1829 a Cambridge reprint was made of the Kiessling edition of Theocritus, Bion, and Moschus, including a Doric Lexicon, the whole in two octavo volumes ; an excellent text and commentary, and altogether the most noticeable English edition of the Sicilian poets since that superb Oxford Theocritus, edited by the laureate, Warton, which appeared in 1770.   The publication of a Cambridge text must have directed unusual attention to the study of these classics, and if Tennyson did not place them upon his list for the public examinations, there can be little doubt that he at this time familiarized himself with their difficult and exquisite verse. His present admiration of them is well known.

Tennyson at Cambridge.

I have shown that in his early poems we find an open loyalty to Wordsworth's canon of reliance upon nature, and occasionally Wordsworth's mannerism and language, with something of the music of Shelley and the sensuous beauty of Keats.   A study of old English ballad-poetry is also apparent.   The influence of the great Italian poets is quite marked ; whether by reflection from the Chaucerian and Elizabethan periods, or by more direct absorption, it is difficult to pronounce.   The truth was, that the poet began his career at an intercalary, transition period.   To quote

Formation of his style.

from a eulogistic book-note by E. A. Poe: "Matters were now verging to their worst; and, at length, in Tennyson, poetic inconsistency attained its extreme. But it was precisely this extreme which wrought in him a natural and inevitable revulsion; leading him first to contemn, and secondly to investigate, his early manner, and finally to winnow from its magnificent elements the truest and purest of all poetical styles."

The result an idyllic method.

In all that concerns *form* the young poet soon found himself in sympathy with the Greek idyllic compositions. He saw the opportunity for work after these models, and willingly yielded himself to their beautiful influence. It has never left him, but is present in his latest and most sustained productions. But there is a difference between his maturer work — which is the adjustment of the idyllic method to native, modern conceptions, with a delightful presentation of English landscape and atmosphere, and the manners and dialects of English life — and the experimental, early poems, which were written upon antique themes. Of these "Œnone" and "The Lotos-Eaters" appeared in the collection of 1832, and in the same volume are other poems appealing more directly to modern sympathies, which show traces of the master with whom Tennyson had put his genius to school.

III.

Two kinds of resemblance.

THERE are two modes in which the workmanship of one poet may resemble that of another. The first, while not subjecting an author to the charge of direct appropriation, in the vulgar sense of plagiarism, is

detected by critical analogy, and, of the two, is more
easily recognized by the skilled reader. It is the
mode which involves either a sympathetic treatment
of rhythmical breaks, pauses, accents, alliterations;
a correspondence of the architecture of two poems,
with parallel interludes and effects; correspondence
of theme, allowing for difference of place and period;
or, a correspondence of scenic and 'metrical purpose;
in fine, general analogy of atmosphere and tone.
The second, more obvious and commonplace, mode
is that displaying immediate coincidence of structure,
language, and thought; a mode which, in the hands
of inferior men, leaves the users at the mercy of their
dullest reviewers.

A citation of passages, exemplifying these two kinds
of resemblance between the Sicilian idyls and the
poetry of Tennyson, will confirm and illustrate the
statements upon which this chapter is based. The
instance first set forth is that of a general, and not
the special, .likeness; but no subsequent attempt is
made to classify the obligations of our modern poet
to the ancient, as it is believed that the reader will
easily distinguish for himself the significant analogies
in each collection.

"Hylas," the celebrated thirteenth idyl of Theocritus, is one of the most perfect which have come
down to our time. It is not a bucolic poem, but
classified as narrative or semi-epic in character, yet
exhibits many touches of the bucolic sweetness; is a
poem of seventy-five verses, written in the honey-
flowing pastoral hexameter, so distinct, in cæsura
and dactylic structure, from the verse of Homer, and
commencing thus : —

"Hylas"
and "Go-
diva."

> "Not only for ourselves the God begat
> Erôs — whoever, Nicias, was his sire —
> As once we thought; nor unto us the first
> Have lovely things seemed lovely; not to us
> Mortals, who cannot see beyond a day;
> But he, that heart of brass, Amphitryôn's son,
> Who braved the ruthless lion, — he, too, loved
> A youth, the graceful Hylas." [1]

A lovely poem.

As a counterpart to this, and directly modelled upon it in form, take the " Godiva " of Tennyson, — that lovely and faultless poem, whose rhythm is full of the melodious quality which gives specific distinction to the Laureate's blank-verse; a "flower," of which so many followers now have the "seed" that it has taken its place as the standard idyllic measure of our language.

"Godiva" is a narrative or semi-epic idyl, which, like the "Hylas," contains — after a didactic prelude, divided from the story proper — just seventy-five verses, and commences thus : —

> "Not only we, the latest seed of time,
> New men, that in the flying of a wheel

---

[1] This translation, and many which follow, I have rendered in blank-verse, not because I deem that measure at all adequate in effect to the original. But even a tolerable version in "English hexameter" would require more labor than is needful for our immediate purpose; and again, blank-verse is the form in which the English poet chiefly has availed himself of his Dorian models. I have translated most of the passages as rapidly as possible; only taking care, first, that my versions should be literal; secondly, that by no artifice they should seem to resemble the work of Tennyson any more closely than in fact they do.

Scholars will recall the fact that the text of the *Bucolicorum Græcorum Reliquiæ* is greatly in dispute. In some instances the editions which I have followed may differ from their wonted readings.

Cry down the past, not only we, that prate
Of rights and wrongs, have loved the people well,
And loathed to see them overtaxed; but she
Did more, and underwent, and overcame,
The woman of a thousand summers back,
Godiva, wife to that grim Earl, who ruled
In Coventry — "

But it is in the " Œnone " that we discover Tenny-son's earliest adaptation of that *refrain* which was a striking beauty of the pastoral elegiac verse.

> "O mother Ida, hearken ere I die,"

ıs the analogue of (Theocr., II.)

> " See thou, whence came my love, O lady Moon";

of the refrain to the lament of Daphnis (Theocr., I.),

> " Begin, dear Muse, begin the woodland song";

and of the recurrent wail in the "Epitaph of Bion" (Mosch., III.),

> "Begin, Sicilian Muses, begin the song of your sorrow!"

Throughout the poem the Syracusan manner and feel-ing are strictly and nobly maintained; and, while we are considering "Œnone," a few points of more exact resemblance may be noted: —

> *The Thalysia* (Theocr., VII. 21–23).
> " Whither at noonday dost thou drag thy feet?
> For now the lizard sleeps upon the wall,
> The crested lark is wandering no more — "

> *The Enchantress* (Theocr., II. 38–41).
> "Lo, now the sea is silent, and the winds
> Are hushed. Not silent is the wretchedness
> Within my breast; but I am all aflame
> With love for him who made me thus forlorn, —
> A thing of evil, neither maid nor wife."

"Œnone."

The elegiac refrain.

The Young Herdsman (Theocr., XX. 19, 20; 30, 31).

"O shepherds, tell me truth! Am I not fair?
Hath some god made me, then, from what I was,
Off-hand, another being? . . . .
Along the mountains all the women call
Me beautiful, all love me."

Œnone.

"For now the noonday quiet holds the hill :
The grasshopper is silent in the grass :
The lizard, with his shadow on the stone,
Rests like a shadow, and the cicala sleeps.
The purple flowers droop : the golden bee
Is lily-cradled : I alone awake.
My eyes are full of tears, my heart of love,[1]
My heart is breaking, and my eyes are dim,
And I am all aweary of my life.

.   .   .   .   .

"Yet, mother Ida, hearken ere I die.
Fairest — why fairest wife? Am I not fair?
My love hath told me so a thousand times.
Methinks I must be fair, for yesterday," etc.

"The Lotos-
Eaters."

"The Lotos-Eaters," another imaginative presentment of an antique theme, — full of Tennyson's excellences, no less than of early mannerisms since foregone, — while Gothic in some respects, is charged
from beginning to end with the effects and very language of the Greek pastoral poets. As in "Œnone,"
there is no consecutive imitation of any one idyl; but
the work is curiously filled out with passages borrowed here and there, as the growth of the poem
recalled them at random to the author's mind. The
idyls of Theocritus often have been subjected to this

---

[1] "Mine eyes are full of tears, my heart of grief."
Second Part of King Henry VI, Act II. Sc. 3.

process; first, by Virgil, in several of whose eclogues the component parts were culled from his master, as one selects from a flower-plot a white rose, a red, and then a sprig of green, to suit the exigencies of color, while the wreath grows under the hand. Pope, among moderns, has followed the method of Virgil, as may be observed in either of his four "Pastorals." The process used by Pope is tame, artificial, and avowed; in "The Lotos-Eaters" it is subtile, masterly, yet of a completeness which only parallel quotations can display.

A culling process.

The Argonauts (Theocr., XIII.) come in the afternoon unto a land of cliffs and thickets and streams; of meadows set with sedge, whence they cut for their couches sharp flowering-rush and the low galingale. "In the afternoon" the Lotos-Eaters "come unto a land" where

> "Through mountain clefts the dale
> Was seen far inland, and the yellow down
> Bordered with palm, and many a winding vale
> And meadow, set with slender galingale."

Except the landscape, all this, in either poem, is after Homer, from the ninth book of the Odyssey. The "Choric Song" follows, of them to whom

> "Evermore
> Most weary seemed the sea, weary the oar,
> Weary the wandering fields of barren foam";

and in this, the feature of the poem, are certain coincidences to which I refer: —

Europa (Mosch., II. 3, 4).

> "When Sleep, that sweeter on the eyelids lies
> Than honey, and doth fetter down the eyes
> With gentle bond."

The Wayfarers (Theocr., V. 50, 51).

"Here, if you come, your feet shall tread on wool,
  The fleece of lambs, softer than downy Sleep."

·Ibid. (45–49).

"Here are the oaks, and here is galingale,
  Here bees are sweetly humming near their hives;
  Here are twin fountains of cool water; here
  The birds are prattling on the trees, — the shade
  Is deeper than beyond; and here the pine
  From overhead casts down to us its cones."

Ibid. (31, 34).

        "More sweetly will you sing
  Propt underneath the olive, in these groves.
  Here are cool waters plashing down, and here
  The grasses spring; and here, too, is a bed
  Of leafage, and the locusts babble here."

·The Choice (Mosch., V. 4–13).

'When the gray deep has sounded, and the sea
  Climbs up in foam and far the loud waves roar,
  I seek for land and trees, and flee the brine,
  And earth to me is welcome: the dark wood
  Delights me, where, although the great wind blow,
  The pine-tree sings. An evil life indeed
  The fisherman's, whose vessel is his home,
  The sea his toil, the fish his wandering prey.
  But sweet to me to sleep beneath the plane
  Thick-leaved; and near me I would love to hear
  The babble of the spring, that murmuring
  Perturbs him not, but is the woodman's joy."

The Lotos-Eaters.

"Music, that gentlier on the spirit lies
  Than tired eyelids upon tired eyes;
  Music that brings sweet sleep down from the blissful skies.

" Here are cool mosses deep,
  And through the moss the ivies creep,

Passages rearranged (for examination) in the order of the foregoing translations.

And in the stream the long-leaved flowers weep,
And from the craggy ledge the poppy hangs in sleep.

.   .   .   .   .

Lo! sweetened with the summer light
The full-juiced apple, waxen over-mellow,
Drops in a silent autumn night.

.   .   .   .   .

But, propt on beds of amaranth and moly,
How sweet (while warm airs lull us, blowing lowly)

.   .   .   .   .

To watch the emerald-colored water falling
Through many a woven acanthus-wreath divine!
Only to hear and see the far-off sparkling brine,
Only to hear were sweet, stretched out beneath the pine.

.   .   .   .   .

Hateful is the dark blue sky,
Vaulted o'er the dark blue sea.

.   .   .   .   .

            Is there any peace
In ever climbing up the climbing wave?

.   .   .   .   .

All day the wind breathes low with mellower tone.

.   .   .   .   .

How sweet it were, hearing the downward stream,
With half-shut eyes ever to seem
Falling asleep in a half-dream."

Dismissing these two poems, the earlier of Tenny- *His modern* *idyls.*
son's experiments upon classical myths, let us look at
another class of idyls, wherein the Theocritan method
is adapted to modern themes; where the form is Dorian, but the feeling, color, and thought are thoroughly
and naturally English. Of "Godiva" I have already
spoken, and the Laureate's rural compositions in
blank-verse are directly in point, reflecting every feature of the so-called "pastoral idyls" of Theocritus.
"The Gardener's Daughter," "Audley Court," "Walk-

10

ing to the Mail," " Edwin Morris, or the Lake," and
"The Golden Year" are modelled upon such patterns
as "The Thalysia," "The Singers of Pastorals," "The
Rival Singers," and "The Triumph of Daphnis." In
all of them, cultured and country-loving friends are
sauntering, resting, singing, sometimes lunching in
the open air among the hills, the waters, and the
woods; in all of them there is dialogue, healthful
philosophy, a wealth of atmosphere and color; and
in nearly all we see for the first time successfully
handled in English and made really melodious the

*The isomet-
ric song.*

true *isometric song* as found in Theocritus. The effects
of this are not produced by any change to a strictly
lyrical measure, but it is composed in the metre of
the whole poem; the Greek, of course, in hexameter, the English, in unrhymed iambic-pentameter
verse. Still, it is a song, with stanzaic divisions into
distiches, triplets, quatrains, etc., as the case may be.

*Amœbean
contests.*

As in Theocritus, so in Tennyson, two songs by rival
comrades sometimes are balanced against each other:
a love-ditty against a proverbial or worldly-wise lyric,
— the latter, in the modern idyl, frequently rising to
the height of modern faith and progress. These
" blank-verse songs," as they are termed, are a special beauty of the Laureate's verse. Where each
stanza has a refrain or burden, as in " Tears, idle
tears," " Our enemies have fallen, have fallen," etc.,
they partake both of the bucolic and elegiac manner;
but elsewhere Tennyson's personages discourse against
each other as in the eclogues proper. For example,
the two songs in " Audley Court,"

" Ah! who would fight and march and countermarch?"

"Sleep, Ellen Aubrey, sleep and dream of me!"

are the *Doppelgänger*, so to speak, of the ditties sung respectively by Milo and Battus, in " The Harvesters " (Theocr., X.). Thirteen of these songs, many of them in " riddling triplets of old time," are scattered through " Audley Court," " The Golden Year," " The Princess," and the completed " Idyls of the King." And where Tennyson's rustic and civic graduates content themselves with jest and debate, it is after a semi-amœbean fashion, which no student of the Syracusan idyls can fail to recognize.

Even in " The Gardener's Daughter " there are passages which respond to the verse of Theocritus. That simply perfect idyl, " Dora," and such pieces as " The Brook " and " Sea-Dreams," are more original, yet the legitimate outgrowth of the antique school. The blank-verse idyls of Tennyson, though connecting him with Theocritus, do not establish a ratio between the relations of the ancient and the modern poet to their respective periods. The Laureate is a more genuine, because more independent and English, idyllist and lyrist in " The May Queen," " The Miller's Daughter," " The Talking Oak," " The Grandmother," and " Northern Farmer, Old Style." *Theocritus created his own school*, with no models except those obtainable from the popular mimes and catches of his own region ; just as Burns, availing himself of the simple Scottish ballads, lifted the poetry of Scotland to an eminent and winsome individuality.

IV.

THE co-relations of Theocritus and Tennyson lie in the fact that our poet discovered years ago that a period had arrived for poetry of the idyllic or com-

" The May Queen," etc.

Burns.

Theocritus and Tennyson.

posite order; and that much of the manner, form, and language of the latter is directly taken from the former. Mr. Tennyson's maturer poems, "The Princess" and "The Idyls of the King," are written Dorian-wise. "The Holy Grail" and its associate legendary pieces occupy the same position in his life-work which those *semi-epic* poems, "The Dioscuri," "The Infant Heracles," and "Heracles the Lion-Slayer" hold in the relics of Theocritus. The "Morte d'Arthur" is written as he would have translated Homer, judging from his version of a passage in the Iliad, and was composed years before the other "Idyls of the King," and in a noticeably different style. For all this, — especially in the speech of the departing Arthur, — it is semi-idyllic, to say the least; a grand poem, a chant without a discord, strong throughout with ringing, monosyllabic Saxon verse.

The Swallow Song.

The Swallow Song, in "The Princess," is modelled upon the isometric songs in the third and eleventh idyls of Theocritus, bearing a special likeness to the lover's serenade in Idyl III., as divided by Ahrens and others into stanzas of three verses each. There is also some correspondence of imagery : —

The Serenade (Theocr., III. 12 – 14).

"Would that I were
The humming-bee, to pass within thy cave,
Thridding the ivy and the feather-fern
By which thou 'rt hidden."

Cyclops (Theocr., XI. 54 – 57).

"O that I had been born a thing with fins
To sink anear thee, and to kiss thy hands, —
If thou deniedst thy mouth, — and now to bring
White lilies to thee, and the red-leaved bloom
Of tender poppies!"

The Princess (Book IV.).

"O Swallow, Swallow, if I could follow, and light
Upon her lattice, I would pipe and trill,
And chirp and twitter twenty million loves."

"O were I thou that she might take me in,
And lay me in her bosom, and her heart
Would rock the snowy cradle till I died."

Throughout the work of Tennyson we meet with *Miscellaneous passages selected for comparison.* isolated passages which also seem to be reflections or reminiscences of verses in the relics of the Syracusan triad. Where the thought or image of such a passage is of a familiar type, common to many classical writers, there is often a flavor about it to indicate that its immediate inspiration was caught from Theocritus, Bion, or Moschus. One of the following comparisons, however, can only be made between the two poets from whom it is derived. Many have been struck by the novelty, no less than the fitness, of an image which I will quote from "Enid." Nothing in earlier English poetry suggests it, and I was surprised to find a conceit, which, with a shade of difference, is so akin, in the semi-epic fragment of "The Dioscuri." The modern verse and image are the more excellent : —

The Dioscuri (Theocr., XXII. 46 – 50).

"His massive breast and back were rounded high
With flesh of iron, like that of which is wrought
A forged colossus. On his stalwart arms,
Sheer over the huge shoulder, standing out
Were muscles, — like the rolled and spheric stones,
Which, in its mighty eddies whirling on,
The winter-flowing stream hath worn right smooth
This side and that."

Enid.

" And bared the knotted column of his throat,
The massive square of his heroic breast,
And arms on which the standing muscle sloped
As slopes a wild brook o'er a little stone,
Running too vehemently to break upon it."

Pastorals (Theocr., IX. 31, 32).

" Dear is cicala to cicala, dear
The ant to ant, and hawk to hawk, but I
Hold only dear to me the Muse and Song."

The Princess (Book III.).

" 'The crane,' I said, 'may chatter of the crane,
The dove may murmur of the dove, but I
An eagle clang an eagle to the sphere.'"

The Syracusan Gossips (Theocr., XV. 102 – 105).

" How fair to thee the gentle-footed Hours
Have brought Adonis back from Acheron !
Sweet Hours, and slowest of the Blessed Ones :
But still they come desired, and ever bring
Gifts to all mortals." [1]

Love and Duty.

" The slow, sweet Hours that bring us all things good,
The slow, sad Hours that bring us all things ill,
And all things good from evil."

The Bridal of Helen (Theocr., XVIII. 47, 48).

" In Dorian letters on the bark
We 'll carve for men to see,
*Pay honor to me, all who mark,
For I am Helen's tree.*"

---

[1] " I thought how once Theocritus had sung
Of the sweet years, the dear and wished-for years,
Who each one in a gracious hand appears
To bear a gift for mortals, old or young."
MRS. BROWNING, *Sonnets from the Portuguese.*

The Talking Oak.

"But tell me, did he read the name
   I carved with many vows,
When last with throbbing heart I came
   To rest beneath thy boughs?

   .   .   .   .   .

"And I will work in prose and rhyme,
   And praise thee more in both,
Than bard has honored beech or lime," etc.

The Little Heracles (Theocr. XXIV., 7 – 9).

(Alcmene's Lullaby.)

"Sleep ye, my babes, a sweet and healthful sleep!
Sleep safe, ye brothers twain that are my life:
Sleep, happy now, and happy wake at morn."

"Cradle Song," in *The Princess.*

"Sleep and rest, sleep and rest,
   Father will come to thee soon!
Rest, rest, on mother's breast,
   Father will come to thee soon!

   .   .   .   .   .

Sleep, my little one, sleep, my pretty one, sleep."

Epitaph of Bion (Mosch., III. 68, 69).

"Thee Cypris holds more dear than that last kiss
She gave Adonis, as he lay a-dying."

Tears, Idle Tears.

"Dear as remembered kisses after death."

Bion (III. 16).

"Where neither cold of frost, nor sun, doth harm us."

Morte d'Arthur.

"Where falls not hail, or rain, or any snow."

*Cp., also,
Tibul. III.
4. 31 and
Catul.
LXII.
20–23.*

The Triumph of Daphnis (Theocr., VIII. 90, 91).

" But as the other pined, and in his heart
Smouldered with grief, even so a girl betrothed
Still feels regret."

("A maid first parting from her home might wear as sad a face."
— *Calverley's Transl.*)

In Memoriam (XXXIX.).

" When crowned with blessing she doth rise
To take her latest leave of home,
And hopes and light regrets that come
Make April of her tender eyes."

The Distaff (Theocr., XXVIII. 24, 25).

" For, seeing thee, one to his friend shall say :
Lo, what a grace enriches this poor gift !
All gifts from friends are ever gifts of worth."

Elaine.

" Diamonds for me ! they had been thrice their worth,
Being your gift, had you not lost your own.
To loyal hearts the value of all gifts
Must vary as the giver's." [1]

Cyclops (Theocr., XI. 25–29).

(Love at first sight.)

" For I have loved you, maiden, since you first,
A-gathering hyacinths from yonder mount,
Came with my mother, and I was your guide.
So, having seen you once, I could not cease
To love you from that time, nor can I now."

The Gardener's Daughter.

" But she, a rose
In roses, mingled with her fragrant toil,

---

[1] But see, also, *Hamlet* (III. 1) : —
" And with them, words of so sweet breath composed
As made the things more rich : their perfume lost,
Take these again ; for to the noble mind
Rich gifts wax poor, when givers prove unkind."

Nor heard us come, nor from her tendance turned
Into the world without. . . . .
So home I went, but could not sleep for joy,
Reading her perfect features in the gloom.

.　　.　　.　　.　　.

Love at first sight, first-born and heir of all,
Made this night thus."

There are passages of another class, in Mr. Ten- *Minor re-
nyson's verse, which bear a common likeness to the *semblances.*
work of various classical poets, his university studies
retaining their influence over him through life. In
some of these, by brief touches, he reproduces the
whole picture of a Greèk idyl : —

Europa (Mosch., II. 125 - 130).
" But she, upon the ox-like back of Zeus
Sitting, with one hand held the bull's great horn,
And with the other her garment's purple fold
Drew upward, that the infinite hoary spray
Of the salt ocean might not drench it through ;
The while Europa's mantle by the winds
Was filled and swollen like a vessel's sail,
Buoying the maiden onward."

The Palace of Art.
" Or sweet Europa's mantle blew unclasped
From off her shoulder backward borne :
From one hand drooped a crocus ; one hand grasped
The wild bull's golden horn."

Elsewhere, in the " Europa," the heroine is said to
" shine most eminent, as the Foam-Born among her
Graces three." Tennyson's classical feeling is so
strong, that, in the closing scene of " The Princess,"
at the height of his dramatic passion, he stops to
draw a picture of Aphrodite coming "from barren
deeps to conquer all with love," and follows the god-
　　10 *　　　　　　　　o

dess even to her Graces, who "decked her out for worship without end." Both the ancient and modern idyllists are mindful of the second Homeric Hymn to Aphrodite ; and the excursus of the latter poet is so beautiful that we forgive him for delaying the action of his poem. In his other classical allusions such phrases as "the cold-crowned snake," "the charm of married brows," "softer than sleep," "like a dog he hunts in dreams," "thou comest, much wept for ! " and "sneeze out a full God-bless-you right and left," repeat not only the language of Theocritus and his pupils, but of Homer, Anacreon, and the Latin Lucretius and Catullus.

The lover's song, "It is the Miller's Daughter," is an exquisite imitation of the sixteenth ode of Anacreon. Often, however, the Laureate enriches his romantic and epic poems with effects borrowed from Gothic, mediæval sources. A reference, for example, to the "Théâtre Français au Moyen Age," printed by Monmerqué in 1839, will discover the miracle-play from which he obtained something more than a hint for the isometric burden, — " Too late, too late! ye cannot enter now."

Similar effects of rhythm.

Alliterations and rhymes within lines, graces of poetry in which Tennyson has excelled English predecessors, are a continuous excellence of his Syracusan teachers. There is a wandering melody, wholly different from the sounding Homeric rhythm, and impossible for a translator to reproduce, which the author of " The Princess " has approached in such lines as these : —

" O Swallow, Swallow, if I could follow, and light."

" Fly to her, and pipe and woo her, and make her mine."

"Laborious, orient ivory, sphere in sphere."

"The lime a summer home of murmurous wings."

"Ran riot, garlanding the gnarled boughs
With bunch and berry and flower through and through."

"The flower of all the west and all the world."

"And in the meadow tremulous aspen-trees
And poplars made a noise of falling showers."

"Sweeter thy voice, but every sound is sweet,
Myriads of rivulets hurrying through the lawn,
The moan of doves in immemorial elms,
And murmuring of innumerable bees."

These effects, which the Laureate employs with such variation and continuance that the resultant style is known as Tennysonian, were Dorian first of all. *Dorian music.* Whole idyls of Theocritus, composed in the flexible bucolic hexameter, are a succession of melodies which are simply consonant with the genius of the new Doric tongue. The four English verses last cited above are curiously imitated from the musical passage in the first idyl (Theocr., I. 7, 8).

"Sweeter thy song, O shepherd, than the sound
Of yon loud stream, falling adown, adown,"

combined with the alliterative line, which mimics the murmuring of bees (Theocr., V. 46),

ὧδε καλὸν βομβεῦντι ποτὶ σμάνεσσι μέλισσαι.

It may be said, generally, that our poet imitates the Sicilians, and them alone, of all his classical models, in the persistent ease with which sound, color, form, and meaning are allied in his compositions. False notes are never struck, and no discordant hues are admitted.

V.

THIS chapter has extended beyond its proposed limits, but, ere dismissing the theme, I will cite two more examples in which Mr. Tennyson has very closely followed his prototype. The first is that "small sweet idyl" in the seventh division of "The Princess"; possibly, so far as objective beauty and finish are concerned, the nonpareil of the whole poem. It is an imitation of the apostrophe of Polyphemus to Galatea, and never were the antique and modern feelings more finely contrasted: the one, clear, simple, childlike, perfect (in the Greek) as regards melody and tone; the other, nobler, more intellectual, the antique body with the modern soul. The substitution of the mountains for the sea, as the haunt of the beloved nymph, is the Laureate's only departure from the *material* employed by Theocritus: —

Cyclops (Theocr., XI. 42–49, 60–66).

"Come thou to me, and thou shalt have no worse;
Leave the green sea to stretch itself to shore!
More sweetly shalt thou pass the night with me
In yonder cave; for laurels cluster there,
And slender-pointed cypresses; and there
Is the dark ivy, the sweet-fruited vine;
There the cool water, that from shining snows
Thick-wooded Ætna sends, a draught for gods.
Who these would barter for the sea and waves?

   .   .   .   .   .

There are oak fagots and unceasing fire
Beneath the ashes. . . . .
Now will I learn to swim, that I may see
What pleasure thus to dwell in water depths
Thou findest! Nay, but, Galatea, come!
Come thence, and having come, forget henceforth,
As I (who tarry here), to seek thy home!

And mayst thou love with me to feed the flocks
And milk them, and to press the cheese with me,
Curdling their milk with rennet."

The Princess (Book VII.).

"Come down, O maid, from yonder mountain height:
What pleasure lives in height (the shepherd sang),
In height and cold, the splendor of the hills?
But cease to move so near the heavens, and cease
To glide a sunbeam by the blasted pine,
To sit a star upon the sparkling spire;
And come, for Love is of the valley, come,
For Love is of the valley, come thou down
And find him; by the happy threshold he,
Or hand in hand with Plenty in the maize,
Or red with spurted purple of the. vats,
Or fox-like in the vine: . . . .

     .   .   .
. . . . . Let the torrent dance thee down
To find him in the valley; let the wild
Lean-headed eagles yelp alone, *and leave*
The monstrous ledges there to slope . . . .
. . . . *but come;* for all the vales
Await thee; azure pillars of the hearth
Arise to thee; the children call, and I,
Thy shepherd, pipe, and sweet is every sound."

The closing example is from "The Thalysia," or Harvest-Home, which has furnished Mr. Tennyson with the design for portions of "The Gardener's Daughter" and "Audley Court." There is no exact reproduction, but in outline and spirit the passages herewith compared will be seen to resemble each other more nearly than others already given, where the expressions of the Greek text are repeated in the English adaptation: —

"The Thalysia," and its counterparts.

The Thalysia (Theocr., VII. 1, 2, 130–147).
"It was the day when I and Eucritus
  Strolled from the city to the river-side:
  With us a third, Amyntas."

(After this opening follows a eulogy of the poet's friends, Phrasidamus and Antigénes.)

" He, leftward turning, sauntered on the road
To Pyxa ; as for Eucritus and me
With handsome young Amyntas, — having gained
The house of Phrasidamus, and lain down
On beds of fragrant rushes and on leaves
Fresh from the vines, — we took our fill of joy.
Poplars and elms were rustling in the wind
Above us, and a sacred rivulet
From the Nymphs' cave was murmuring anigh.
The red cicalas ceaselessly amid
The shady boughs were chirping; from afar
The tree-frog in the briers chanted shrill ;
The crest-larks and the thistle-finches sang,
The turtle-dove was plaining; tawny bees
Were hovering round the fountain. *All things near*
Smelt of the ripened summer, all things smelt
Of fruit-time. Pears were rolling at our feet,
And apples for the taking ; to the ground
The plum-tree staggered, burdened with its fruit ;
And we, meanwhile, brushed from a wine-jar's mouth
The pitch, four years unbroken."

The Gardener's Daughter.

"This morning is the morning of the day
When I and Eustace from the city went
To see the Gardener's Daughter :

(After this opening follows a eulogy of Eustace and Juliet.)

" .   .   .   . All the land in flowery squares,
Beneath a broad and equal-blowing wind,
Smelt of the coming summer. .   .   .   .
.   .   .   . From the woods
Came voices of the well-contented doves.
The lark could scarce get out his notes for joy,
But shook his song together as he neared

"*His happy home, the ground. To left and right*
The cuckoo told his name to all the hills;
The mellow ouzel fluted in the glen;
The red-cap whistled; and the nightingale
Sang loud, as though he were the bird of day."

Audley Court.

"There, on a slope of orchard, Francis laid
A damask napkin wrought with horse and hound,
Brought out a dusky loaf that smelt of home,
And, half cut down, a pasty costly made,
Where quail and pigeon, lark and leveret, lay
Like fossils of the rock, with golden yolks
Imbedded and injellied; last, with these,
A flask of cider from his father's vats
Prime, which I knew."

Each portion of the foregoing English Idyls, so far as quoted, is a reminiscence of some portion of the "Thalysia" (*mutatis mutandis*, with regard to theme, season, and country), and the general analogy is equally spirited and remarkable. As for the two lunches, the one is pure Sicilian, of the fruits of the orchard and the vine; the other, pure Briton, smacking of the cook and the larder. Your true Englishman, while sensible of the beauty of the song of the lark, who can "scarce get out his notes for joy," appreciates him none the less when lying "imbedded and injellied" beneath the crust of "a pasty costly made." It should be remembered, however, that the bird does not appear under these differing conditions in the same idyl.

A close analogy.

VI.

A sufficient number of analogous passages have now been cited to illustrate the homage which the Laureate has paid to the example of Theocritus, and the perfection of that art by which he has wedded his master's method to the spirit and resources of the English tongue. I have written with genuine reverence for Tennyson's work, and with a gratitude, felt by all who take pleasure in noble verse, for the delight imparted through many years by the successive

Tennyson none the less an original poet.

productions of his genius. In study of the Sicilian models he has been true to his poetic instinct, and fortunate in discernment of the wants of his day and generation. Emerson, in an essay on " Imitation and Originality," has said : " We expect a great man to be a good reader; or in proportion to the spontaneous power should be the assimilating power"; and again, " There are great ways of borrowing. Genius borrows nobly. When Shakespeare is charged with debts to his authors, Landor replies : 'Yet he was more original than his originals. He breathed upon dead bodies and brought them to life.' "

It must be acknowledged that somewhat of this applies to Tennyson's variations upon Theocritus. To him, also, may be adjudged the credit of being the first to catch the manner of the classical idyls and reproduce it in modern use and being. Before his time Milton and Shelley were the only poets who measurably succeeded in this attempt, and neither of them repeated it after a single trial. Other reproduc-

Pseudo-pastoral verse.

tions of the Greek idyllic form have been by a kind of filtration through the Latin medium; and often, by a third remove, after a redistillation of the French product. The odious result is visible in the absurd pastorals of " standard British poets," from Dryden himself and Pope, to Browne, Ambrose Philips, Shenstone, and Gay. Their bucolics have made us sicken at the very mention of such names as Daphnis and

Corydon, soiled as these are with all ignoble use.   Tennyson revived the true idyllic purpose, adopting the form mainly as a structure in which to exhibit, with *The true idyl.* equal naturalness and beauty, the scenery, thought, manners, of his own country and time.   Assuming the title of idyllic poet, he made the term "idyl" honored and understood ; but carried his method to such perfection, that its cycle seems already near an end, and a new generation is calling for work of a different order, for more vital passion and dramatic power.

CHAPTER VII.

THE GENERAL CHOIR.

An era fairly represented by its miscellaneous poets.

THE choral leaders are few in number, and it is from a blended multitude of voices that we derive the general tone and volume, at any epoch, of a nation's poetic song. The miscellaneous poets, singly or in characteristic groups, give us the pervading quality of a stated era. Great singers, lifted by imagination, make style secondary to thought; or, rather, the thought of each assumes a correlative form of expression. Younger or minor contemporaries catch and reflect the fashion of these forms, even if they fail to create a soul beneath. It is said that very great poets never, through this process, have founded schools, their art having been of inimitable loftiness or simplicity; but who of the accepted few, during recent years, has thus held the unattainable before the vision of the facile English throng?

I.

The early situation and outlook.

Accession of Victoria: June 20, 1837.

AT the beginning of the present reign Tennyson was slowly obtaining recognition, and his influence had not yet established the poetic fashion of the time. Wordsworth shone by himself, in a serene and luminous orbit, at a height reached only after a prolonged career. The death of Byron closed a splendid but tempestuous era, and was followed by years of reaction, — almost of sluggish calm. At least, the group of poets was without a leader, and was composed of men who, with few great names among them, utilized their gifts, — each after his own method or after one of that master, among men of the previous generation, whom he most affected. A kind of interregnum occurred. Numbers of minor poets and scholars survived their former compeers, and wrote creditable verse, but produced little that was essentially new. Motherwell had died, at the early age of thirty-eight, having done service in the revival of Scottish ballad-minstrelsy: and with the loss of the author of that exquisite lyric, " Jeanie Morrison," of " The Cavalier's Song," and " The Sword-Chant of Thorstein Raudi," there passed away a vigorous and sympathetic poet. Southey, Moore, Rogers, Frere, Wilson, James Montgomery, Campbell, James and Horace Smith, Croly, Joanna Baillie, Bernard Barton, Elliott, Cunningham, Tennant, Bowles, Maginn, Peacock, poor John Clare, the translators Cary and Lockhart,[1] — all these were still alive, but had outlived their generation, and, as far as verse was concerned,

William Wordsworth, Poet Laureate: born April 7, 1770; died April 23, 1850.

William Motherwell: 1797 – 1835.

The retired list.

---

[1] Robert Southey, *Poet Laureate*, 1774 – 1843 ; Thomas Moore, 1779 – 1852 ; Samuel Rogers, 1763 – 1855 ; Rt. Hon. John Hookham Frere, 1769 – 1846 ; John Wilson, 1785 – 1854 ; Rev. James Montgomery, 1771 – 1854 ; Thomas Campbell, 1777 – 1844 ; James Smith, 1775 – 1839 ; Horace Smith, 1779 – 1849 ; Rev. George Croly, 1780 – 1860 ; Joanna Baillie, 1762 – 1851 ; Bernard Barton, 1784 – 1849 ; Ebenezer Elliott, 1781 – 1849 ; Allan Cunningham, 1784 – 1842 ; William Tennant, 1785 – 1848 ; Rev. William Lisle Bowles, 1762 – 1850; William Maginn. 1793 – 1842 ; Thomas Love Peacock, 1785 – 1866 ; John Clare, 1793 – 1864 ; Rev. Henry Francis Cary, 1772 – 1844 ; John Gibson Lockhart, 1794 – 1854.

Leigh Hunt. See page 103.

Rev. Henry Hart Milman: 1791 – 1868.

Sir Thomas Noon Talfourd: 1795 – 1854.

James Sheridan Knowles: 1784 – 1862.

Mary Russell Mitford: 1786 – 1855.

"Strayed singers."

George Darley: 1785 – 1849.

were more or less superannuated. What Landor, Hood, and Procter were doing has passed already under review. Leigh Hunt continued his pleasant verse and prose, and did much to popularize the canons of art exemplified in the poetry of his former song-mates, Coleridge, Shelley, and Keats. Milman, afterward Dean of St. Paul's, a pious and conventional poet who dated his literary career from the success of an early drama, " Fazio," still was writing plays that did credit to a churchman and Oxford professor. Talfourd's " Ion " and " The Athenian Captive " also had made a stage-success : the poets had not yet discovered that a stage which the talent of Macready exactly fitted, and a histrionic feeling of which the plays of Sheridan Knowles had come to be the faithful expression, were not stimulating to the production of the highest grade of dramatic poetry. Various dramas and poems, by that cheery, versatile authoress, Miss Mitford, had succeeded her tragedies of " Julian " and " Rienzi." It must be owned that these three were good names in a day of which the fashion has gone by. At this distance we see plainly that they were minor poets, or that the times were unfriendly to work whose attraction should be lasting. Doubtless, were they alive and active now, they would contend for favor with many whom the present delights to honor.

Meanwhile a few men of genius, somewhat out of place in their generation, had been essaying dramatic work for the love of it, but had little ambition or continuity, finding themselves so hopelessly astray. Darley, after his first effort, " Sylvia," — a crude but poetical study in the sweet pastoral manner of Jonson and Fletcher, — was silent, except for some occasional song, full of melody and strange purpose-lessness. Beddoes, a stronger spirit, author of "The Bride's Tragedy" and "Death's Jest-Book," wandered off to Germany, and no collection of his wild and powerful verse was made until after his decease. Taylor, whose noble intellect and fine constructive powers were early affected by the teachings of Words-worth, entered a grand protest against the sentimen-talism into which the Byronic passion now had de-generated. He would, I believe, have done even better work, if this very influence of Wordsworth had not deadened his genuine dramatic power. He saw the current evils, but could not substitute a potential excellence or found an original school. As it is, "Philip van Artevelde" and "Edwin the Fair" have gained a place for him in English literature more enduring than the honors awarded to many popular authors of his time.

The sentimental feeling of these years was nurtured on the verse of female writers, Mrs. Hemans and Miss Landon, whose deaths seemed to have given their work, always in demand, a still wider reading. It had been fashionable for a throng of humbler imitators, including some of gentle blood, to con-tribute to the "annuals" and "souvenirs" of Alaric Watts, but their summer-time was nearly over and the chirping rapidly grew faint. The Hon. Mrs. Norton, styled "the Byron of poetesses," was at the height of her popularity. A pure religious sentiment in-spired the sacred hymns of Keble. Young Hallam had died, leaving material for a volume of literary remains ; if he did not live to prove himself great, his memory was to be the cause of greatness in others, and is now as abiding as any fame which

Thomas Lovell Beddoes: 1803–49.

Sir Henry Taylor: 1800–86.

The senti-mentalists.

The "An-nuals."

Alaric Alexander Watts: 1799–1864.

Caroline Elizabeth Sarah Norton: 1808–77.

Rev. John Keble: 1792–1866.

Arthur Henry Hallam: 1811–33.

*Rev. Rich-
ard Harris
Barham:
1788 – 1845.*

*Winthrop
Mackworth
Praed:
1802 – 39.*

maturity could have brought him.   Besides the comic
verse of Hood, noticed in a previous chapter, other
jingling trifles, like Barham's *Ingoldsby Legends*, a cross
between Hood's whimsicality and that of Peter Pindar,
were much in vogue, and serve to illustrate the broad
and very obvious quality of the humor of the day.
Lastly, Praed, a sprightly and delicate genius, soon to
die and long to be affectionately lamented, was restor-
ing the lost art of writing society-verse, and, in a style
even now modern and attractive, was lightly throwing off stanzas neater than anything produced since
the wit of Canning and the fancy of Tommy Moore.

All this was light enough, and now seems to us to
have betokened a shabby, profitless condition.   From
it, however, certain elements were gradually to crys-
tallize and to assume definite purpose and form.   The
influence of Wordsworth began to deepen and widen ;
and erelong, under the lead of Tennyson, composite
groups and schools were to arise, having clearer ideas
of poetry as an art, and adorning with the graces of
a new culture studies after models derived from the
choicest poetry of every literature and time.

II.

*A critical
analogy.*

THE cyclic aspect of a nation's literary history has
been so frequently observed that any reference to it
involves a truism.   The analogy between the courses
through which the art of different countries advances
and declines is no less thoroughly understood.   The
country whose round of being, in every department
of effort, is most sharply defined to us, was Ancient
Greece.   The rise, splendor, and final decline of her
imaginative literature constitute the fullest paradigm

of a nation's literary existence and of the supporting
laws. In the preceding chapter I have enlarged upon *See pages*
205, 206.
the active, critical, and learned Alexandrian period,
which succeeded to the three creative stages of Hellenic song. I have said that during this epoch the
Hellenic spirit grew elaborately feeble ; what was
once so easily creative became impotent, and at last
entirely died away. Study could not supply the force
of nature. A formidable circle of acquirements must
be formed before one could aspire to the title of an
author. Verbal criticism was introduced ; researches
were made into the Greek tongue ; antique and quaint
words were sought for by the poets, and, to quote
again from Schoell, " they sought to hide their defects
beneath singularity of idea, and novelty and extravagance of expression ; while the bad taste of some
displayed itself in their choice of subjects still more
than in their manner of treating them."

In modern times, when more events are crowded *Contrast be-*
tween an-
cient and
modern lit-
erary cycles.
into a decade than formerly occurred in a century,
and when civilization ripens, mellows, and declines,
only to repeat the process in successively briefer
periods, men do not count a decline in national literature a symptom that the national glory is approaching
its end.   Still, more than one recurring cycle of English literature has its analogue in the entire course
of that of Ancient Greece.   And, when we come to
the issue of supremacy in poetic creation, the question arises whether Great Britain has not recently
been going through a period similar to the Alexandrian in other respects than the production of a fine
idyllic poet. It is difficult to estimate our own time,
so insensibly does the judgment ally itself to the
graces and culture in vogue. Take up any well-

Skill and refinement of the minor poets.

edited selection from English minor poetry of the last thirty years, and our first thought is, — how full this is of poetry, or at least of poetic material! What refined sentiment! what artistic skill! what elaborate metrical successes! From beginning to end, how very readable, high-toned, close, and subtile in thought! Here and there, also, poems are to be found of the veritable cast, — simple, sensuous, passionate; but not so often as to give shape and color to the whole. With the same standard in view, one could not cull such a garland from the minor poetry of any portion of the last century; nor, indeed, from that of any interval later than the generation after Shakespeare, and earlier than the great revival, which numbered Burns, Wordsworth, Byron, and Keats among the leaders of an awakened chorus of natural English minstrelsy.

The Georgian revival: 1790-1824.

That revival, in its minor and major aspects, was truly glorious and inspiring. The poets who sustained it were led, through the disgust following a hundred years of false and flippant art, and by something of an intellectual process, to seek again that full and limpid fountain of nature to which the Elizabethan singers resorted intuitively for their draughts. But the unconscious vigor of that early period was still more brave and immortal than its philosophical counterpart in our own century. Ah, those days of Elizabeth! of which Mrs. Browning said, in her exult-

Essay on " The Book of the Poets," E. B. B.

ant, womanly way, — that "full were they of poets as the summer days are of birds. . . . . Never since the first nightingale brake voice in Eden arose such a jubilee-concert; never before nor since has such a crowd of true poets uttered true poetic speech in one day. . . . . Why, a common man, walking through the earth in those days, grew a poet by position."

Now, have freshness, synthetical art, and sustained imaginative power been the prominent endowments of the recent schools of British minor poets? For an answer we must give attention to their blended or distinctive voices, remembering that certain of the earliest groups have recruited their numbers, and prolonged their vitality, throughout the middle and even the latest divisions of the period under review.

A question before the reader.

III.

THE tone of the first of these divisions upon the whole was suggested by Wordsworth, while the poetic form had not yet lost the Georgian simplicity and profuseness. Filtered through the intervening period of which we have spoken, its eloquence had grown tame, its simplicity somewhat barren and prosaic. Still, both tone and form, continuing even to our day, are as readily distinguished, by the absence of elaborate adornment and of curious nicety of thought, from those of either the Tennysonian or the very latest school, as the water of the Mississippi from that of the Missouri for miles below their confluence. The poets of the group before us are not inaptly thought to constitute the Meditative School, characterized by seriousness, reflection, earnestness, and, withal, by religious faith, or by impressive conscientious bewilderment among the weighty problems of modern thought.

Influence of Wordsworth.

The Meditative School.

The name of Hartley Coleridge here may be recalled. His poetry, slight in force and volume, yet relieved by half-tokens of his father's sudden melody and passion, is cast in the mould and phrase of his father's life-long friend. This mingled quality came by descent and early association. The younger Coleridge

Rev. Hartley Coleridge : 1796–1849.

*Rev. John
Mitford:
1811-58.*

*Richard
Chenevix
Trench:
1807-86.*

*Henry
Alford:
1810-71.*

*Aubrey
Thomas de
Vere:
1814-*

(whose beautiful child-picture by Wilkie adds a touching interest to his memoirs) inherited to the full the
physical and psychological infirmities of the elder, with
but a limited portion of that "rapt one's" divine gift.
The atmosphere of his boyhood was full of learning
and idealism.   He had great accomplishments, and
had the poetic temperament, with all its weaknesses
and dangers, yet without a coequal faculty of reflection and expression.   Hence the inevitable and pathetic tragedy of a groping, clouded life, sustained
only by piteous resignation and faith.   Several moralistic poets date from this early period, — Mitford,
Trench, Alford, and others of a like religious mood.
Archbishop Trench's work is careful and scholarly,
marked by earnestness, and occasionally rises above
a didactic level.   Dean Alford's consists largely of
Wordsworthian sonnets, to which add a poem modelled upon "The Excursion"; yet he has written a
few sweet lyrics that may preserve his name.   The
devotional traits of these writers gave some of them
a wider reading, in England and America, than their
scanty measure of inspiration really deserved.   Gradually they have fallen out of fashion, and again illustrate the truth that no ethical virtue will compensate
us in art for dulness, didacticism, want of imaginative
fire.   Aubrey de Vere, a later disciple of the Cumber-
land school, is of a different type, and has shown versatility, taste, and a more natural gift of song.   This
gentle poet and scholar, though hampered by too rigid
adoption of Wordsworth's theory, often has an attractive manner of his own.   Criticized from the artistic
point of view, a few studies after the antique seem
very terse when compared with his other work.   A
late drama, "Alexander the Great," has strength of

language and construction. The earnestness and purity of his patriotic and religious verses give them exaltation, and, on the whole, the Irish have a right to be proud of this most spiritual of their poets, — one who, unlike Hartley Coleridge, has improved upon an inherited endowment. Returning on our course, we see in the verse of Burbidge another reflection of Wordsworth, but also something that reminds us of the older English poets. As a whole, it is of middle quality, but so correct and finished that it is no wonder the author never fulfilled the dangerous promise of his boyhood. He was a schoolfellow of Clough, and I am not aware that he ever published any volume subsequent to that by which this note is suggested, and which bears the date of 1838. The relics of Sterling, the subject of Carlyle's familiar memoir, like those of Hallam, do not of themselves exhibit the full ground of the biographer's devotion. The two names, nevertheless, have given occasion respectively for the most characteristic poem and the finest prose memorial of recent times. A few of Sterling's minor lyrics, such as "Mirabeau," are eloquent, and, while defaced by conceits and prosaic expressions, show flashes of imagination which brighten the even twilight of a meditative poet. Between the deaths of Sterling and Clough a long interval elapsed, yet there is a resemblance between them in temperament and mental cast. It may be said of Clough, as Carlyle said of Sterling, that he was "a remarkable soul, ... who, more than others, sensible to its influences, took intensely into him such tint and shape of feature as the world had to offer there and then ; fashioning himself eagerly by whatsoever of noble presented itself." It may be said of

Thomas Burbidge: born about 1816.

John Sterling: 1806-44.

Arthur Hugh Clough: 1819-61.

Cp. "Poets of Amer- ica" : pp. 339, 340.

him, likewise, that in his writings and actions "there is for all true hearts, and especially for young noble seekers, and strivers towards what is highest, a mirror in which some shadow of themselves and of their immeasurably complex arena will profitably present itself. Here also is one encompassed and struggling even as they now are." Clough must have been a rare and lovable spirit, else he could never have so wrapped himself within the affections of true men. Though he did much as a poet, it is doubtful whether his genius reached anything like a fair development. Intimate as he was with the Tennysons, his style, while often reflective, remained essentially his own. His fine original nature was never quite subservient to passing influences. His free temperament and radical way of thought, with a manly disdain of all factitious advancement, made him a force even among the choice companions attached to his side; and he was valued as much for his character and for what he was able to do, as for the things he actually accomplished. There was nothing second-rate in his mould,

Clough's hexameter poem.

and his *Bothie of Tober-na-Vuolich*, which bears the reader along less easily than the billowy hexameters of Kingsley, is charmingly faithful to its Highland theme, and has a Doric simplicity and strength. His shorter pieces are uneven in merit, but all suggestive and worth a thinker's attention. If he could have remained in the liberal American atmosphere, and have been spared his untimely taking-off, he might have come to greatness; but he is now no more, and with him departed a radical thinker and a living protest against the truckling expedients of the mode.

The poetry of Lord Houghton is of a modern contemplative type, very pure, and often sweetly lyrical.

Emotion and intellect blend harmoniously in his delicate, suggestive verse, and a few of his songs — among which "I wandered by the brookside" at once recurs to the memory — have a deserved and lasting place in English anthology. This beloved writer has kept within his limitations. He has the sincere affection of men of letters, who all honor his free thought, his catholic taste, and his generous devotion to authors and the literary life. To the friend and biographer of Keats, the thoughtful patron of David Gray, and the progressive enthusiast in poetry and art, I venture to pay this cordial tribute, knowing that I but feebly repeat the sentiments of a multitude of authors on either side of the Atlantic.

Richard Monckton Milnes: 1809–85.

Dr. Newman has lightened the arduous labors and controversies of his distinguished career by the composition of many thoughtful hymns, imbued with the most devotional spirit of his faith. As representing the side of obedience to tradition these *Verses of Many Years* have their significance. At the opposite pole of theological feeling, Palgrave, just as earnest and sincere, seems to illustrate the Laureate's saying, —

Rev. John Henry Newman: 1801 –

Francis Turner Palgrave: 1824 –

> " There lives more faith in honest doubt,
> Believe me, than in half the creeds."

Nevertheless, in " The Reign of Law," one of his best and most characteristic pieces, he argues himself into a reverential optimism, that seems, just now, to be the resting-place of the speculative religious mind. He may be said to represent the latest attitude of the meditative poets, and in this closely resembles Arnold, of whom I have already spoken as the most conspicuous and able modern leader of their school.

Indeed, there is scarcely a criticism which I have made upon the one that will not apply to the other. Palgrave, with less objective taste and rhythmical skill than are displayed in Arnold's larger poems, is in his lyrics equally searching and philosophical, and occasionally shows evidence of a musical and more natural ear. The Biblical legends and narrative poems of Dr. Plumptre are simple, and somewhat like those of the American Willis, but didactic and of a kind going out of vogue. His hymns are much better, but it is as a classical translator that we find him at his best. Among the later religious poets Myers deserves notice for the feeling, careful finish, and poetic sentiment of his longer pieces. A few of his quatrain-lyrics are exceedingly delicate ; his sonnets, more than respectable. From the resemblance of the artist Hamerton's descriptive poetry to that of Wordsworth, I refer, in this place, to his volume, *The Isles of Loch Awe, and Other Poems,* issued in 1859. This dainty book, with its author's illustrations, is interesting as the production of one who has since achieved merited popularity both as an artist and prose author, — in either of which capacities he probably is more at home than if he had followed the art which gave vent to the enthusiasm of his younger days. He may, however, be called the tourist's poet ; his book is an excellent companion to one travelling northward ; the poems, though lacking terseness and force, and written on a too obvious theory, are picturesque, and, as the author claimed for them in an appendix, "coherent, and easily understood."

Regarding Palgrave and Arnold, then, as advanced members of the contemplative group, I renew the question concerning the freshness and creative in-

Rev. Edward Hayes Plumptre : 1821 –

Frederic William Henry Myers : 1843 –

Philip Gilbert Hamerton : 1834 –

Spirit of the contemplative poets. See also pp. 96 – 98.

stinct of this recent school. The unconscious but uppermost emotion of both is one of doubt and indecision : a feeling, I have said, that they were born too late. They are awed and despondent before the mysteries of life and nature. As to art, their conviction is that somehow the glory and the dream have left our bustling generation for a long, long absence, and may not come again. Palgrave's " Reign of Law," after all, is but making the best of a dark matter. It reasons too closely to be highly poetical. The doubts and refined melancholy of his other poetry reflect the sentiment of the still more subtile Arnold, from whose writings many a passage such as this may be taken, to show a dissatisfaction with his mission and the time : —

Attitude of Palgrave and Arnold.

> " Who can see the green Earth any more
> As she was by the sources of Time ?
> Who imagine her fields as they lay
> In the sunshine, unworn by the plough ?
> Who thinks as they thought,
> The tribes who then lived on her breast,
> Her vigorous, primitive sons ?
>
> What Bard,
> At the height of his vision, can dream
> Of God, of the world, of the soul,
> With a plainness as near,
> As flashing as Moses felt,
> When he lay in the night by his flock
> On the starlit Arabian waste ?
> Can rise and obey
> The beck of the Spirit like him ?
>
> And we say that repose has fled
> Forever the course of the River of Time," etc.

Great or small, the meditative poets lack that elas-

ticity which is imparted by a true lyrical period, —
whose very life is gladness, with song and art for an
undoubting, blithesome expression. The better class,
thus sadly impressed, and believing it in vain to
*Weakness
and decline
of the school.* grasp at the skirts of the vanishing Muse, are impelled to substitute choice *simulacra,* which culture
and artifice can produce, for the simplicity, sensuousness, and passion, declared by Milton to be the elements of genuine poetry. They are what training
has made them. Some of the lesser names were
cherished by their readers, in a mild and sterile time,
for their domestic or religious feeling, — very few
really for their imagination or art. At last even
sentiment has failed to sustain them, and one by one
they have been relegated to the ever-increasing collection of unread and rarely cited "specimen" verse.

IV.

*A few inde-
pendent
singers.* So active a literary period could not fail to develop, among its minor poets, singers of a more fresh
and genuine order. Here and there one may be discovered whose voice, however cultivated, has been
less dependent upon culture, and more upon emotion
and unstudied art. One of the finest of these, un-
*Richard
Hengist
Horne:
born
1802–03,
died
March* 13,
1884. questionably, is Horne, author of "Cosmo de' Medici,"
"Gregory the Seventh," "The Death of Marlowe,"
and "Orion." I am not sure that in natural gift he
is inferior to his most famous contemporaries. That
he here receives brief attention is due to the dispro-
portion between the sum of his productions and the
length of his career, — for he still is an occasional
and eccentric contributor to letters. There is something Elizabethan in Horne's writings, and no less in

a restless love of adventure, which has borne him
wandering and fighting around the world, and breaks
out in the robust and virile, though uneven, character
of his poems and plays.   He has not only, it would
seem, dreamed of life, but lived it.   Taken together,
his poetry exhibits carelessness, want of tact and wise
method, but often the highest beauty and power.   A
fine erratic genius, in temperament not unlike Beddoes and Landor, he has not properly utilized his
birthright.   His verse is not improved by a certain
transcendentalism which pervaded the talk and writings of a set in which he used to move.   Thus
Orion was written with an allegorical purpose, which
luckily did not prevent it from being one of the noblest poems of our time ; a complete, vigorous, highly
imaginative effort in blank-verse, rich with the antique imagery, yet modern in thought, — and full of
passages that are not far removed from the majestic
beauty of " Hyperion."   The author's *Ballad Romances*,
issued more lately, is not up to the level of his
younger work.   While it seems as if Horne's life has
been unfruitful, and that he failed — through what
cause I know not — to conceive a definite purpose
in art, and pursue it to the end, it must be remembered that a poet is subject to laws over which we
have no control, and in his external relations is a
law unto himself.   I think we fairly may point to
this one as another man of genius adversely affected
by a period not suited to him, and not as one who
in a dramatic era would be incapable of making any
larger figure.   He was the successor of Darley and
Beddoes, and the prototype of Browning, but capable
at his best of more finish and terseness than the last-
named poet.   In most of his productions that have

*A fine er-
ratic genius.*

*His
" Orion,"
etc.*

*Horne un-
suited to his
period.*

11 *

reached me, amidst much that is strange and grotesque, I find little that is sentimental or weak.

*Thomas
Babington
Macaulay:
1800 – 59.*

Lord Macaulay's *Lays of Ancient Rome* was a literary surprise, but its poetry is the rhythmical outflow
of a vigorous and affluent writer, given to splendor
of diction and imagery in his flowing prose.   He
spoke once in verse, and unexpectedly.   His themes
were legendary, and suited to the author's heroic cast,
nor was Latinism ever more poetical than under his
thoroughly sympathetic handling.   I am aware that
the Lays are criticised as being stilted and false to the
antique, but to me they have a charm, and to almost
every healthy young mind are an immediate delight.
Where in modern ballad-verse will you find more
ringing stanzas, or more impetuous movement and
action ?   Occasionally we have a noble epithet or
image.   Within his range — little as one who met
him might have surmised it — Macaulay was a poet,
and of the kind which Scott would have been first to
honor.   " Horatius " and " Virginius," among the Roman lays, and that resonant battle-cry of " Ivry," have
become, it would seem, a lasting portion of English

*William
Edmond-
stoune Ay-
toun: 1813 –
65.*

verse.   In the work of Professor Aytoun, similar in
kind, but more varied, and upon Scottish themes, we
also discern what wholesome and noteworthy verse
may be composed by a man who, if not a poet of
high rank, is of too honest a breed to resort to un-
wonted styles, and to measures inconsonant with the
English tongue.   The ballads of both himself and
Macaulay rank among the worthiest of their class.
Aytoun's " Execution of Montrose " is a fine production.   In " Bothwell," his romantic poem in the metre
and manner of Scott, he took a subject above his
powers, which are at their best in the lyric before

named. Canon Kingsley, as a poet, had a wider range. His "Andromeda" is an admirable composition, — a poem laden with the Greek sensuousness, yet pure as crystal, and the best-sustained example of English hexameters produced up to the date of its composition. It is a matter of indifference whether the measure bearing that name is akin to the antique model, for it became, in the hands of Kingsley, Hawtrey, Longfellow, and Howells, an effective form of English verse. The author of "Andromeda" repeated the error of ignoring such quantities as do obtain in our prosody, and relying upon accent alone; but his fine ear and command of words kept him musical, interfluent, swift. In "St. Maura," and the drama called "The Saint's Tragedy," the influence of Browning is perceptible. Kingsley's true poetic faculty is best expressed in various sounding lyrics for which he was popularly and justly esteemed. These are new, brimful of music, and national to the core. "The Sands o' Dee," "The Three Fishers," and "The Last Buccaneer" are very beautiful; not studies, but a true expression of the strong and tender English heart.

Here we observe a suggestive fact. With few exceptions the freshest and most independent poets of the middle division — those who seem to have been born and not made — have been, by profession and reputation, first, writers of prose; secondly, poets. Their verses appear to me, like their humor, "strength's rich superfluity." Look at Macaulay, Aytoun, and Arnold, — the first a historian and critic, the others, essayists and college professors. Kingsley and Thackeray might have been dramatic poets in a different time and country, but accepted the romance and

Rev. Charles Kingsley: 1819–75.

English hexameter verse. Cp. " Poets of America": pp. 90, 91, and pp. 195–199.

Kingsley's ballads.

Fresh and genuine poetry by notable writers of prose.

Cp. " Poets of America": pp. 462–464.

George
Walter
Thorn-
bury:
1828-76.

novel as affording the most dramatic methods of
the day. Thornbury is widely known by his prose
volumes, but has composed some of the most fiery
and rhythmical songs in the English tongue. His
Ballads of the New World are inferior to his *Songs
of the Cavaliers and Roundheads*, and to his other lyrics
of war and revolution in Great Britain and France,
which are full of unstudied lyrical power. Some of
these remind us of Browning's "Cavalier Tunes";
but Browning may well be proud of the pupil who
wrote "The Sally from Coventry" and "The Three

A true lyri-
cal poet.

Scars." He is hasty and careless, and sometimes
coarse and extravagant; his pieces seem to be struck
off at a heat, — but what can be better than "The
Jester's Sermon," "The Old Grenadier's Story," and
"La Tricoteuse"? How unique the *Jacobite Ballads!*
Read "The White Rose over the Water." "The
Three Troopers," a ballad of the Protectorate, has a
clash and clang not often resonant in these piping
times: —

> "Into the Devil tavern
>   Three booted troopers strode,
> From spur to feather spotted and splashed
>   With the mud of a winter road.
> In each of their cups they dropped a crust,
>   And stared at the guests with a frown;
> Then drew their swords and roared, for a toast,
>   'God send this Crum-well-down!'"

I have a feeling that this author has not been
fairly appreciated as a ballad-maker. Equally perfect

William
Makepeace
Thackeray:
1811-63.

of their sort are "The Mahogany-Tree," "The Ballad
of Bouillabaise," "The Age of Wisdom," and "The
End of the Play," — all by the kindly hand of Thackeray, which shall sweep the strings of melody no

more ; yet their author was a satirist and novel-writer, never a professed poet. Nor can one read the collection made, late in life, by Doyle, another Oxford professor, of his occasional verse, without thinking that "The Return of the Guards," "The Old Cavalier," "The Private of the Buffs," and other soldierly ballads are the modest effusions of a natural lyrist, who probably has felt no great encouragement to perfect a lyrical gift that has been crowded out of fashion by the manner of the latter-day school.

The success of these unpretentious singers again illustrates the statement that *spontaneity* is an essential principle of the art. The poet should carol like the bird : —

> " He knows not why nor whence he sings,
>   Nor whither goes his warbled song ;
>   As Joy itself delights in joy,
>   His soul finds strength in its employ,
>   And grows by utterance strong."

The songs of minstrels in the early heroic ages displayed the elasticity of national youth. When verses were recited, not written, a pseudo-poet must have found few listeners. In a more cultivated stage, poetry should have all this unconscious freshness, refined and harmonized with the thought and finish of the day.

V.

MANY of the novelists have written verse, but usually, with the foregoing exceptions, by a professional effort rather than a born gift. The Brontë sisters began as rhymesters, but quickly found their true field. Mrs. Craik has composed tender stanzas

---

Sir Francis Hastings Doyle: 1810–

Spontaneity an essential principle of lyric art. Cp. " Poets of America ": pp. 316, 317.

Inferior novelist-poets.

The Brontë sisters.

Dinah Maria Mu-lock Craik: 1826–

Marian Evans Lewes (Mrs. Cross): 1819–80.

resembling those of Miss Procter, and mostly of a grave and pleasing kind. George Eliot's metrical work has special interest, coming from a woman acknowledged to be, in her realistic yet imaginative prose, at the head of living female writers. She has brought all her energies to bear, first upon the construction of a drama, which was only a *succès d' estime,* and recently upon a new volume containing "The Legend of Jubal" and other poems. The result shows plainly that Mrs. Lewes, though possessed of great intellect and sensibility, is not, in respect to metrical expression, a poet. Nor has she a full conception of the simple strength and melody of English verse, her polysyllabic language, noticeable in the moralizing passages of *Middlemarch,* being very ineffective in her poems. That wealth of thought which atones for all her deficiencies in prose does not seem to be at her command in poetry. *The Spanish Gypsy* reads like a second-rate production of the Byronic school. "The Legend of Jubal" and "How Lisa loved the King" suffer by comparison with the narrative poems, in rhymed pentameter, of Morris, Longfellow, or Stoddard. A little poem in blank-verse, entitled "O may I join the choir invisible!" and setting forth her conception of the "religion of humanity," is worth all the rest of her poetry, for it is the outburst of an exalted soul, foregoing personal immortality and compensated by a vision of the growth and happiness of the human race.

Edward, Lord Lyt-ton: 1805–73.

Bulwer was another novelist-poet, and one of the most persistent. During middle age he renewed the efforts made in his youth to obtain for his metrical writings a recognition always accorded to his ingenious and varied prose-romance; but whatever he did in verse was the result of deliberate intellect and culture. The fire was not in him, and his measures do not give out heat and light. His shorter lyrics never have the true ring; his translations are somewhat rough and pedantic; his satires were often in poor taste, and brought him no great profit; his serio comic legendary poem of *King Arthur* is a monument to industry, but never was labor more hopelessly thrown away. In dramas like "Richelieu" and "Cromwell" he was more successful; they contain passages which are wise, eloquent, and effective, though rarely giving out the subtile aroma which comes from the essential poetic principle. Yet Bulwer had an honest love for the beautiful and sublime, and his futile effort to express it was almost pathetic.

Many of his odes and translations were contributed, I think, to *Blackwood's* magazine. This suggests mention of the ephemeral groups of lyrists that gathered about the serials of his time. Among the Blackwood writers, Moir, Aird, — a Scotsman of some imagination and fervor, — Simmons, and a few greater or lesser lights, are still remembered. *Bentley's* was the mouthpiece of a rollicking set of pedantic and witty rhymesters, from whose diversions a book of comic ballads has been compiled. *Fraser's, The Dublin University,* and other magazines, attracted each its own staff of verse-makers, besides receiving the frequent assistance of poets of wide repute. I may say that throughout the period much creditable verse has been produced by studious men who have given poetry the second place as a vocation. Among recent productions of this class the historical drama of *Hannibal,* by Professor Nichol, of Glasgow, may be taken as a type and a fair example.

The magazines and their contributors.

David Macbeth Moir: 1798–1851.

Thomas Aird: 1802–76.

B. Simmons: died 1850.

John Nichol: 1833–

*Diffusion of
inferior
verse.*

With respect to poetry, as to prose, the coarser and less discriminating appetite is the more widely diffused. Create a popular taste for reading, and an inferior article comes to satisfy it, by the law of supply and demand. Hence the enormous circulation of didactic artificial measures, adjusted to the moral and intellectual levels of commonplace, like those of Hervey, Tupper, and Robert Montgomery: while other poets of the early and middle divisions, who had sparks of genius in them, but who could not adapt themselves to either the select or popular markets of their time, found the struggle too hard for them, and have passed out of general sight and mind. At the very beginning of the period Wade gave promise of something fine. A copy of his *Mundi et Cordis* lies before me, dated 1835. It is marked with the extravagance and turgidity which soon after broke out among the rhapsodists, yet shows plainly the sensitiveness and passion of the poet. The contents are in sympathy with, and like, the early work of Shelley, and various poems are of a democratic, liberal stripe, inspired by the struggle then commencing over Europe. As long ago as 1837 Domett was contributing lyrics to *Blackwood* which justly won the favor of the burly editor. From a young poet who could throw off a glee like " Hence, rude Winter, crabbed old fellow ! " or " All who 've known each other long," his friends had a right to expect a brilliant future. But he was an insatiable wanderer, and could "not rest from travel " His productions dated from every portion of the globe ; finally he disappeared altogether, and ceased to be heard from, but his memory was kept green by Browning's nervous characterization of him, — " What 's become of Waring ? " After three dec-

*Thomas
Kibble
Hervey :
1799 – 1859.*

*Martin
Farquhar
Tupper :
1810 –*

*Rev. Robert
Montgom-
ery : 1807 –
55.*

*A few men
of early
promise.*

*Thomas
Wade :
1805 – 75.*

*Alfred
Domett :
1811 –*

*His Black-
wood lyrics.*

ades the question is answered, and our vagrant bard returns from Australia with a long South Sea idyl, *Ranolf and Amohia,* — a poem justly praised by Browning for varied beauty and power, but charged with the diffuseness, transcendentalism, defects of art and action, that were current among Domett's radical brethren so many years ago. The world has gone by him. The lyrics of his youth, and chiefly a beautiful "Christmas Hymn," are, after all, the best fruits, as they were the first, of his long and restless life. But doubtless the life itself has been a full compensation. There also was Scott, who wrote *The Year of the World,* a poem commended by our Concord Brahmin for its faithful utilization of the Hindoo mythology. The author, a distinguished painter and critic, is now one of the highest authorities upon matters pertaining to the arts of design.[1] There were women too: among them, Mrs. Adams, author of remembered hymns, and of that forgotten drama of *Vivia Perpetua,* — a creature whose beauty and enthusiasm drew around her the flower of the liberal party; the friend of Hunt and Carlyle and W. J. Fox, and of Browning in his eager youth. Of many such as these, in whom the lyrical aspiration was checked by too profuse admixture with a passion for affairs, for active life, for arts of design, or for some ardent cause to which they became devoted, or who failed, through extreme sensibility, to be calm among the turbid elements about them, — of such it may be asked, where are they and their

Thirty-five years later.

William Bell Scott: 1811–

Sarah Flower Adams: 1805–48.

---

[1] Mr. Scott has now published his miscellaneous ballads, studies from nature, etc., — many of them written years ago, — in a volume to which his own etchings, and those of Alma Tadema, give additional beauty.

Poetry a jealous mistress. Cp. "Poets of America": pp. 75, 409.

productions, except in the tender memory and honor of their early comrades and friends? Poetry is a jealous mistress: she demands life, worship, tact, the devotion of our highest faculties; and he who refuses all of this and more never can be, first, and above his other attributes, an eminent or in any sense a true and consecrated poet.

VI.

The song-writers.

WE come to a brood of minstrels scattered numerously as birds over the meadows of England, the rye-fields of Scotland, and the green Irish hills. They are of a kind which in any active poetic era it is a pleasure to regard. They make no claims to eminence. Their work, however, though it may be faulty and uneven, has the charm of freshness, and comes from the heart. The common people must have songs; and the children of a generation that had found pleasure in the lyrics of Moore and Haynes Bayley have not been without their simple warblers. One of the most lovable and natural has but lately passed

Samuel Lover: 1797 - 1868.

away; Lover, a versatile artist, blitheful humorist and poet. In writing of Barry Cornwall I have referred to the essential nature of the song, as distinguished from that of the lyric, and in Lover's melodies the former is to be found. The office of such men is to give pleasure in the household, and even if they are not long to be held of account (though no one can safely predict how this shall be), they gain a prompt reward in the affection of their living countrymen.

William Allingham: 1828 -

We find spontaneity, also, in the rhymes of Allingham, whose "Mary Donnelly" and "The Fairies" have that intuitive grace called quality, — a grace which no amount of artifice can ever hope to produce, and for whose absence mere talent can never compensate us. The ballads of Miss Downing, Waller, and MacCarthy, all have displayed traces of the same charm ; the last-named lyrist, a man of much culture and literary ability, has produced still more attractive work of another kind. Bennett, within his bounds, is a true poet, who not only has composed many lovely songs, but has been successful in more thoughtful efforts. A few of his poems upon infancy and childhood are sweetly and simply turned. Dr. Mackay, in the course of a long and prolific career, has furnished many good songs. Some of his studied productions have merit, but his proper gift is confined to lyrical work. Among the remaining Scottish and English song-makers, Eliza Cook, the Howitts, Gilfillan, and Swain probably have had the widest recognition ; all have been simple, and often homely, warblers, having their use in fostering the tender piety of household life. Miller, a mild and amiable poet, resembling the Howitts in his love for nature, wrote correct and quiet verse thirty years ago, and was more noticeable for his rural and descriptive measures than for a few conventional songs.

It will be observed that, as in earlier years, the most characteristic and impressive songs are of Irish and Scottish production ; and, indeed, lyrical genius is a special gift of the warm-hearted, impulsive Celtic race. Nations die singing, and Ireland has been a land of song, — of melodies suggested by the political distress of a beautiful and unfortunate country, by the poverty that has enforced emigration and brought pathos to every family, and by the traditional loves, hates, fears, that are a second nature to the humble

Mary Downing: 1830 -

John Francis Waller: 1810 -

Denis Florence MacCarthy: 1817 - 82.

William Cox Bennett: 1820 -

Charles Mackay: 1814 -

Eliza Cook: 1817 -

William Howitt: 1795 - 1879.

Mary Howitt: 1798 -

Robert Gilfillan: 1798 - 1850.

Charles Swain: 1803 - 74.

Thomas Miller: 1809 - 74.

Irish and Scottish songs.

Patriotic ballads.

The Dublin newspaper press.

Gerald Griffin: 1803-40.

John Banim: 1798-1842.

Helen Selina, Lady Dufferin: 1807-67.

Thomas D'Arcy McGee: 1825-68.

John Kells Ingram: 1820-

Thomas Davis: 1814-45.

Sir Charles Gavan Duffy: 1816-

John Keegan: 1809-49.

Linton (see Chap. VIII.).

Mrs. Varian ("Finola").

Lady Wilde (" Speranza ").

James Clarence Mangan: 1803-49.

Other democratic rhymesters.

peasant. All Irish art is faulty and irregular, but often its faults are endearing, and in its discords there is sweet sound. That was a significant chorus which broke out during the prosperous times of *The Nation*, thirty years ago, and there was more than one tuneful voice among the patriotic contributors to the Dublin newspaper press. Griffin and Banim, novelists and poets, flourished at a somewhat earlier date, and did much to revive the Irish poetical spirit. Read Banim's " Soggarth Aroon "; in fact, examine the mass of poetry, old and recent, collected in Hayes' " Ballads," with all its poverty and riches, and, amid a great amount of rubbish, we find many genuine folk-songs, brimming with emotion and natural poetic fire. Certain ballads of Lady Dufferin, and such a lyric as McGee's "Irish Wife," are not speedily forgotten. Among the most prominent of the songmakers were the group to which I have referred, — Ingram, Davis, Duffy, Keegan, McGee, Linton (the English liberal), Mrs. Varian, Lady Wilde, and others, not forgetting Mangan, in some respects the most original of all. These political rhymers truthfully represented the popular feeling of their own day. Their songs and ballads will be the study of some future Macaulay, and are of the kind that both makes and illustrates national history. Their object was not art; some of their rhymes are poor indeed; but they fairly belong to that class of which Fletcher of Saltoun wrote: " If a man were permitted to make all the ballads, he need not care who should make the laws of a nation."

Here, too, we may say a word of a contemporary tribe of English democratic poets, many of them springing from the people, who kept up such an alarum during the Chartist agitation. After Thom, the "Inverury poet," who mostly confined himself to dialect and *genre* verses, and young Nicoll, who, at the beginning of our period strayed from Scotland down to Leeds, and poured out stirring liberal lyrics during the few months left to him, — after these we come to the bards of Chartism itself. This movement lasted from 1836 to 1850, and had a distinct school of its own. There was Cooper, known as "the Chartist poet." Linton, afterward to become so eminent as an artist and engraver, was equally prolific and more poetical, — a born reformer, who relieved his eager spirit by incessant poetizing over the pseudonym of "Spartacus," and of whom I shall have occasion to speak again. Ebenezer Jones was another Chartist rhymester, but also composed erotic verse ; a man of considerable talent, who died young. These men and their associates were greatly in earnest as agitators, and often to the injury óf their position as artists and poets.

William Thom: 1799 – 1850.

Robert Nicoll: 1814 – 37.

Chartism.

Thomas Cooper: 1805 –

"Spartacus."

Ebenezer Jones: 1820 – 60.

CHAPTER VIII.

THE SUBJECT CONTINUED.

Recent errors and affectations.

FEW of the minor poets belonging to the middle division of our period have been of the healthy and independent cast of Kingsley, Thackeray, Thornbury, or Aytoun. Some have servilely followed the vocal leaders, or even imitated one another,—the law of imitation involving a lack of judgment, and causing them to copy the heresies, rather than the virtues of their favorites ; and we are compelled to observe the devices by which they have striven, often unconsciously, to resist adverse influences or to hide the poverty of their own invention.

I.

The Rhapsodists ; or the "Spasmodic" school.

THE Chartist or radical poets, of whom we have just spoken, were the forerunners of a more artistic group whose outpourings the wits speedily characterized by the epithet "spasmodic." Their work constantly affords examples of the knack of substitution. Mention of Aytoun reminds us that he did good service, through his racy burlesque, *Firmilian*, in turning the laugh upon the pseudo-earnestness of this rhapsodical school. Its adherents, lacking perception and synthesis, and mistaking the materials of poetry for

"Firmilian."

poetry itself, aimed at the production of quotable passages, and crammed their verse with mixed and conceited imagery, gushing diction, interjections, and that mockery of passion which is but surface-deep.

Bailey was one of the most notable of this group, and from his earliest production may be termed the founder of the order. *Festus* certainly made an impression upon a host of readers, and is not without inchoate elements of power. The poet exhausted himself by this one effort, his later productions wanting even the semblance of force which marked it and established the new emotional school. The poets that took the contagion were mostly very young. Alexander Smith years afterward seized Bailey's mantle, and flaunted it bravely for a while, gaining by *A Life-Drama* as sudden and extensive a reputation as that of his master. This poet wrote of

> " A Poem round and perfect as a star,"

but the work from which the line is taken is not of that sort. With much impressiveness of imagery and extravagant diction that caught the easily, but not long, tricked public ear, it was vicious in style, loose in thought, and devoid of real vigor or beauty. In after years, through honest study, Smith acquired better taste and worked after a more becoming purpose. His prose essays were charming, and his *City Poems,* marked by sins of omission only, may be rated as negatively good. " Glasgow " and " The Night before the Wedding " really are excellent. The poet became a genuine man of letters, but died young, and when he was doing his best work. Massey, another emotional versifier, came on (like Ernest Jones, — who went out more speedily) in the wake of the Chartist

Philip James Bailey: 1816 –

Alexander Smith: 1830 – 67.

Gerald Massey: 1828 –

movement, to which its old supporters vainly sought to give new life with the hopes aroused by the continental revolutions of 1848. He made his sensation by cheap rhetoric, and the substitution of sentiment for feeling, in an otherwise laudable championship of the working-classes from which he sprang. Sympathy for his cause gained his social verses a wide hearing; but his voice sounds to better advantage in his songs of wedded love and other fireside lyrics, which often are earnest and sweet. He also has written an unusually good ballad, " Sir Richard Grenville's Last Fight."

George Macdonald: 1824 -

The latest of the transcendental poets is Macdonald, who none the less has great abilities as a preacher and novelist, and in various literary efforts has shown himself possessed of deep emotion and a fertile, delicate fancy. Some of his realistic, semi-religious tales of Scottish life are admirable. " Light," an ode, is imaginative and eloquent, but not well sustained, and his poetry too often, when not commonplace, is vague, effeminate, or otherwise poor. Is it defective vision, or the irresistible tendency of race, that inclines even the most imaginative North-Country writers to what is termed mysticism? A " Celtic glamour " is veiling the muse of Buchanan, — of whom I shall write more fully hereafter, — so that she is in danger of confusing herself with the forgotten phantoms of the spasmodic school. The touching story and writings of poor

David Gray: 1838 – 61.

Gray — who lived just long enough to sing his own dirges, and died with all his music in him — reveal a sensitive temperament unsustained by co-ordinate power. Possibly we should more justly say that his powers were undeveloped, for I do not wholly agree with those who deny that he had genius, and who think his work devoid of true promise. The limitless conceit involved in his estimate of himself was only what is secretly cherished by many a bantling poet, who is not driven to confess it by the horror of impending death. His main performance, " The Luggie," shows a poverty due to the want of proper literary models in his stinted cottage-home. It is an eighteenth-century poem, suggested by too close reading of Thomson and the like. Education, as compared with aspiration, comes slowly to low-born poets. The sonnets entitled " In the Shadows," written during the gradual progress of Gray's disease, are far more poetical, because a more genuine expression of feeling. They are indeed a painful study. Here is a subjective monody, uttered from the depths, but rounded off with that artistic instinct which haunts a poet to the last. The self pity, struggle, self discipline, and final resignation are inexpressibly sorrowful and tragic. Gray had the making of a poet in him, and suffered all the agonies of an exquisite nature contemplating the swift and surely coming doom.

II.

AFTER the death of Wordsworth the influence of Tennyson and that of Browning had more effect upon the abundant offerings of the minor poets. In the work of many we discover the elaboration and finesse of an art-method superadded by the present Laureate to the contemplative philosophy of his predecessor; while not a few, impressed by Browning's dramatic studies, assume an abrupt and picturesque manner, and hunt for grotesque and mediæval themes. Often the former class substitute a commonplace realism

Influence of Tennyson and Browning.

False simplicity.

12

for the simplicity of Tennyson's English idyls, just as the latest aspirants, trying to cope with the Pre-Raphaelite leaders, whose work is elevated by genius, carry the treatment beyond conscientiousness into sectarianism, and divide the surface of Nature from her perspective, laying hold upon her body, yet evaded by her soul.

Balzac on the true mission of Art.

Balzac makes a teacher say to his pupil: "The mission of Art is not to copy Nature, but to express her. You are not a vile copyist, but a poet!

Cp. " Poets of America ": pp. 367-369.

Take a cast from the hand of your mistress ; place it before you ; you will find it a horrible corpse without any resemblance, and you will be forced to resort to the chisel of an artist, who, without exactly copying it, will give you its movement and its life. We have to seize the spirit, the soul, the expression, of beings and things."

Aphorisms of William Blake.

Many of Blake's aphorisms express the same idea. "Practice and opportunity," he said, "very soon teach the language of art. Its spirit and poetry, centred in the imagination alone, never can be taught ; and these make the artist. . . . . Men think they can copy Nature as correctly as I copy the imagination. This they will find impossible. . . . . Nature and Fancy are two things, and never can be joined ; neither ought any one to attempt it, for it is idolatry, and destroys the soul."

Coventry Kearsey Dighton Patmore: 1823 -

Coventry Patmore, not fully comprehending these truths, has made verses in which, despite a few lovely and attractive passages, the simplicity is affected and the realism too bald. A carpet-knight in poetry, as the younger Trollope latterly is in prose, he merely photographs life, and often in its poor and commonplace forms. He thus falls short of that aristocracy of art which by instinct selects an elevated theme. It is better to beautify life, though by an

illusive reflection in a Claude Lorraine mirror, than
to repeat its every wrinkle in a sixpenny looking-
glass, after the fashion of such lines as these : —

> " Restless, and sick of long exile
>   From those sweet friends, I rode to see
> The church repairs ; and, after a while,
>   Waylaying the Dean, was asked to tea.
> They introduced the Cousin Fred
>   I 'd heard of, Honor's favorite : grave,
> Dark, handsome, bluff, but gently bred,
>   And with an air of the salt wave.
> He stared, and gave his hand, and I
>   Stared too," etc.

This is not the simplicity of Wordsworth in his better
moods, nor of the true idyllists, nor of him who was
the simplest of all poets, yet the kingliest in manner
and theme.

Sydney Dobell, a man of an eccentric yet very *Sydney Dobell: 1824-74.*
poetic disposition, had the faults of both the spas-
modic and realistic modes, and these were aggravated
by a desire to maintain a separate position of his
own.   His notes were pitched on a strident key,
piping shrill and harsh through all the clamor of his
fellow-bards.   " Balder " is the very type of a spasmodic drama.   " The Roman " is a healthier, though
earlier, production, at least devoid of egotism and
gush.   His lyrics constantly strive for effect.   In
" How 's My Boy? " and " Tommy 's Dead," he struck
pathetic, natural chords, but more often his measures
and inversions were disagreeably strange, while his
sentiment was tame and his action slighted.   " Owen *Robert, Lord Lytton: 1831-*
Meredith," — what shall be said of the author of
" The Wanderer," " Clytemnestra," and " The Apple
of Life "?   Certainly not that " Chronicles and Char-

acters," "Orval," and others of his maturer poems are an advance upon these early lyrics which so pleased young readers half a generation ago. They are not open to criticism that will apply to "The Wanderer," etc., but incur the severer charge of dulness which must preclude them from the welcome given to his first books. "Lucile," with all its lightness, remains his best poem, as well as the most popular: a really interesting, though sentimental, parlor-novel, written in fluent verse, — a kind of production exactly suited to his gift and limitations. It is quite original, for Lytton adds to an inherited talent for melodramatic tale-writing a poetical ear, good knowledge of effect, and a taste for social excitements. His society-poems, with their sensuousness and affected cynicism, present a later aspect of the quality that commended *Ernest Maltravers* and *Pelham* to the young people of a former day. Some of his early lyrics are tender, warm, and beautiful ; but more are filled with hot-house passion, — with the radiance, not of stars, but of chandeliers and gas-lights. The Bulwers always have been a puzzle. Their cultured talent and cleverness in many departments have rivalled the genius of other men. We admire their glittering and elaborate structures, though aware of something hollow or stuccoed in the walls, columns, and ceilings, and even suspicious of the floor on which we stand. Father and son, — their love of letters, determination, indomitable industry, have commanded praise. The son, writing in poetry as naturally as his father wrote in prose, has the same adroitness, the same unbounded ambition, the same conscientiousness in labor and lack of it in method. In his metaphysical moods we see a reflection of the

"Lucile."

The two Bulwers.

clearer Tennysonian thought; and, indeed, while interesting and amusing us, he always was something of an imitator. His lyrics were like Browning's dramatic stanzas; his blank-verse appropriated the breaks and cadences of Tennyson, and ventured on subjects which the Laureate was long known to have in hand. The better passages of "Clytemnestra" were taken almost literally from Æschylus. Those versed in Oriental poetry have alleged that his wanderings upon its borders are mere forays in "fresh woods and pastures new." His voluminous later works, in which every style of poetry is essayed, certainly have not fulfilled the promise of his youth, and those friends are disappointed who once looked to him for signs of a new poetical dawn.

III.

THE merits and weakness of the idyllic method, as compared with that of a time when a high lyric or epic feeling has prevailed, can best be studied in the productions of the Laureate's followers, rather than in his own verse; for the latter, whatever the method, would derive from his intellectual genius a glory and a charm. The idyl is a picturesque, rather than an imaginative, form of art, and calls for no great amount of invention or passion. It invariably has the method of a busy, anxious age, seeking rest rather than excitement. Through restrained emotion, music, and picturesque simplicity it pleases, but seems to betoken absence of creative power. The minor idyllists hunt for themes, — they do not write because their themes compel them; they construct poems as still-life artists paint their pictures, becoming thorough workmen, but

Minor idyllic poets.

The idyl.

at last we yearn for some swift heroic composition whose very faults are qualities, and whose inspiration fills the maker's soul.

Frederick Tennyson.

Frederick Tennyson, for example, treats outdoor nature with painstaking and curious discernment, repeating every shadow; but the result is a pleasantly illustrated catalogue of scenic details. It is nature refined by a tasteful landscape-gardener. Few late poets, however, have shown more elegance in verse-structure and rhythm. An artistic motive runs through his poems, all of which are carefully finished and not marred by the acrobatism of the rhapsodic school.

Charles (Tennyson) Turner: 1808-79.

Edwin Arnold: 1832-

Roden Noel. But see Supplement.

Thomas Woolner, R. A.: 1826-

Turner, another of the Tennyson brothers, was the least modern of them in his cast. His sonnets do not conform to either the Italian or English requirements, but have some poetical value. Edwin Arnold's verse is that of a scholarly gentleman. The books of Roden Noel may pass without comment. *My Beautiful Lady*, by Woolner, is a true product of the art-school, with just that tinge of gentle affectation which the name implies. It has a distinct motive, — to commemorate the growth, maintenance, and final strengthening by death, of a pure and sacred love, and is a votive tribute to its theme: a delicate volume of such verse as could have been produced in no other time. Lin-

William James Linton: 1812- See page 261.

ton's *Claribel and Other Poems*, 1865, distinctly belongs to the same school, and is noteworthy as an early specimen of a method frequently imitated by the latest poets. At the date of its appearance this pretty volume was almost unique, — the twofold work of the author, as artist and poet, and dedicated to William Bell Scott, a man of sympathetic views and associations. We have seen that Linton's early writings were devoted to liberal and radical propagandism. The

volume before me is a collection of more finished
poetry, imbued with an artistic purpose, and with
beauty of execution and design.   Few men have so
much individuality as its author, or are more versatile
in acquirements and adventure.   He is a famous engraver, and his work as a draughtsman and painter
is full of meaning.   These gifts are used to heighten
the effect of his songs ; fanciful and poetical designs
are scattered along the pages of this book ; nor can
it be said that such aids are meretricious, in these
latter days, when poetry is addressed not only to the
ear but also to the eye.   Some of the verse requires
no pictures to sustain it.   A " Threnody " in memory
of Albert Darasz is an addition to the few good and
imaginative English elegiac poems ; and it may be
said of whatever Linton does, that, if sometimes eccentric, it shows a decisive purpose and a love of art
for its own sake.   Westwood's "The Quest of the Sanc- *Thomas Westwood : 1814–*
greall " marks him for one of Tennyson's pupils.   His
minor lyrics are more pleasing.   All these poets turn
at will from one method to another, and may be
classed as of the composite school.   Meredith's verse *George Meredith : 1828–*
is a further illustration ; he is dramatic and realistic,
but occasionally ventures upon a classical or romantic
study.   He often fails of his purpose, though usually
having one.   The *Poems of the English Roadside* seem
to me his most original work, and of them "Juggling
Jerry " is the best.   Ashe is one of those minor *Thomas Ashe : 1836–*
poets who catch and reflect the prevailing mode : he
belongs to the chorus, and is not an independent
singer.   His *Poems*, 1859, are mildly classical and
idyllic ; but in 1867 he gave us *The Sorrows of Hyp-
sipyle*, — after *Atalanta in Calydon* had revived an interest in dramatic poetry modelled upon the antique.

IV.

OF those patrician rhymes which, for want of an English equivalent, are termed *vers de société*, the gentle Praed, who died at the commencement of the period, was an elegant composer. In verse under this head may also be included, for the occasion, epigrammatic couplets, witty and satirical songs, and all that metrical badinage which is to other poetry what the *feuilleton* is to prose. During the first half of our retrospect it was practised chiefly by scholarly and fluent wits. In the form of satire and parody it was cleverly employed, we have seen, by Aytoun, in his "spasmodic tragedy" of "Firmilian"; merrily, too, by Aytoun and Martin in the *Bon Gualtier* ballads; by Thackeray in "Love-Songs made Easy," "Lyra Hibernica," the ballads of "Pleaceman X.," etc.; by Hood in an interminable string of mirth and nonsense; and with mock-heroic scholarship by the undaunted Irish wit, poet, and Latinist, "Father Prout," and the whole jovial cohort that succeeded to the foregoing worthies in the pages of the monthly magazines. But with the restrained manners of the present time, and the finish to which everything is subjected, we have a revival of the more select order of society-verse. This is marked by an indefinable aroma which elevates it to the region of poetic art, and owing to which, as to the imperishable essence of a subtle perfume, the lightest ballads of Suckling and Waller are current to this day. In fine, true *vers de société* is marked by humor, by spontaneity, joined with extreme elegance of finish, by the quality we call breeding, — above all, by *lightness of touch*. Its composer holds a place in the Parnassian hemicycle as legitimate as that of Robin Goodfellow

Vers de société,

including satire, parody, etc. Cp. "Poets of America": pp. 284, 285, 448.

Rev. Francis Mahoney: 1805–66.

Qualities of good society-verse.

in Oberon's court. The dainty lyrics of Locker not unfrequently display these characteristics : he is not strikingly original, but at times reminds us of Praed or of Thackeray, and again, in such verses as "To my Grandmother," of an American, — Dr. Holmes. But his verse is light, sweet, graceful, gayly wise, and sometimes pathetic. Calverley and Dobson are the best of the new *farceurs*. *Fly-Leaves*, by the former, contains several burlesques and serio-comic translations that are excellent in their way, with most agreeable qualities of fancy and thought. Dobson's *Vignettes in Rhyme* has one or two lyrics, besides lighter pieces equal to the best of Calverley's, which show their author to be not only a gentleman and a scholar, but a most graceful poet, — titles that used to be associated in the thought of courtly and debonair wits. Such a poet, to hold the hearts he has won, not only must maintain his quality, but strive to vary his style ; because, while there is no work, brightly and originally done, which secures a welcome so instant as that accorded to his charming verse, there is none to which the public ear becomes so quickly wonted, and none from which the world so lightly turns upon the arrival of a new favorite with a different note.

Society-verse, then, has been another symptom of cultured and refined periods, — of the times of Horace, Catullus, Theocritus, Waller, Pope, Voltaire, Tennyson, and Thackeray. The intense mental activity of our own era is still more clearly evinced by the great number of recent English versions of the poetic masterpieces of other tongues. Oxford and Cambridge have filled Great Britain with scholars, some of whom, acquiring rhythmical aptness, have produced

Frederick Locker-Lampson: 1821-

Charles Stuart Calverley: 1831-84.

Austin Dobson: 1840-

Other tokens of a refined and scholarly period.

Recent translators, and the new theory of translation.

12 *   R

good work of this kind. Modern translations differ noticeably, in their scholastic accuracy, from those of earlier date, — among which Chapman's are the noblest, Pope's the freest, and those by Hunt, Shelley, and Frere scarcely inferior to the best. The theory of translation has undergone a change ; the old idea having been that as long as the spirit of a foreign author was reproduced an exact rendering need not be attempted. But to how few it is given to catch that spirit, and hence what wretched versions have appeared from time to time! Only natural poets worked successfully upon the earlier plan. The modern school possibly go too near the extreme of conscientiousness, yet a few have found the art of seizing upon both the spirit and the text. The amount produced is amazing, and has given the public access, in our own language, to the choicest treasures of almost every foreign literature, be it old or new.

Sir John Bowring: 1792–1872.

In the earlier division, Bowring was the most prolific, and he has also published several volumes of a very recent date. His excursions into the fields of continental literature have had most importance ; but his versions, however valuable in the absence of better, rarely display any poetic fire. The elder Lytton

The elder Lytton.

was a fair type of the elegant Latinists and minor translators belonging to the earlier school. His best performance was a recent version of Horace, in metres resembling, but not copied from, the original, — a translation more faithful than Martin's paraphrases, but not approaching the latter in elegance. Martin's

Sir Theodore Martin: 1816– See p. 272.

Horace, Homer, and their translators.

Horace has the flavor and polish of Tennyson, and plainly is modelled upon the Laureate's verse. Of all classical authors Horace is the Briton's favorite. The statement of Bulwer's preface is under the truth when it says: "Paraphrases and translations are still more numerous than editions and commentaries. There is scarcely a man of letters who has not at one time or other versified or imitated some of the odes; and scarcely a year passes without a new translation of them all." Upon Homer, also, the poetic scholars have expended immense energy, and various theories as to the proper form of measure have given birth to several noble versions, — distinguished from a multitude of no worth. Those of Wright, Worsley, Professor Newman, Professor Blackie, and Lord Derby may be pronounced the best; though admirable bits have been done by Arnold, Dr. Hawtrey, and the Laureate. I do not, however, hesitate to say — and believe that few will deny — that the ideal translation of Homer, marked by swiftness, simplicity, and grandeur, has yet to be made; nor do I doubt that it ultimately will be, having already stated that our Saxon-Norman language is finely adapted to reproduce the strength and sweetness of the early Ionic Greek. Professor Conington's Virgil, in the measure of "Marmion," was no advance, all things considered, upon Dryden's, nor equal to that of the American, Cranch. Some of the best modern translations have been made by women, who, following Mrs. Browning, mostly affect the Greek. Miss Swanwick and Mrs. Webster, among others, nearly maintain the standard of their inspired exemplar. M. P. Fitz-Gerald's versions of Euripides, and of the pastoral and lyric Greek poets, may be taken as specimens of the general excellence now attained, and I will not omit mention of Calverley's complete rendition of Theocritus, — undoubtedly as good as can be made by one who fears to undertake the original metres. Among me-

Ichabod Charles Wright: 1795 – 1871.

Philip Stanhope Worsley: died 1866.

Francis William Newman: 1805 –

John Stuart Blackie: 1809 –

Edward, Lord Derby: 1799 – 1869.

Rev. Edward Craven Hawtrey: 1789 – 1862. See page 251.

John Conington: 1825 –69.

Anna Swanwick.

Augusta Webster.

Maurice Purcell Fitz-Gerald.

Calverley. See page 273.

diæval and modern writers Dante and Goethe have received the most attention; but Longfellow and Taylor, in their translations of the Divine Comedy and of Faust, — and Bryant in his stately version of the Iliad and the Odyssey, — bear off the palm for America in reproduction of the Greek, Italian, and German poems.

*Rossetti and Morris.
See Chap. X.*

Of Rossetti's exquisite presentation of the Early Italian Poets, and Morris's Icelandic researches, I shall speak elsewhere, and can only make

*MacCarthy.
See page 259.*

a passing reference to MacCarthy's extended and beautiful selections from Calderon, rendered into English asonante verse. Martin has made translations from the Danish, and, together with Aytoun, of the ballads of Goethe. Of modern Oriental explorations, altogether the best is a version of the grave and imaginative *Rubáiyát* of Omar Khayyám, by E. Fitz-

Edward FitzGerald: 1808-83.

Gerald, who has made other successful translations from the Persian, as well as from the Spanish and the Attic Greek.

The foregoing are but a few of the host of translators; but their labors fairly represent the richness and excellence of this kind of work in our time, and are cited as further illustrations of the critical spirit of an age in which it would almost seem as if the home-field were exhausted, such researches are

*See Chap.
VI., page
205.*

made into the literature of foreign tongues. I again use the language of those who describe the Alexandrian period of Greek song: men "of tact and scholarship greatly abound," and by elegant studies endeavor to supply the force of nature. Early and strictly non-creative periods of English literature have been similarly characterized, — notably the century which included Pitt, Rowe, Cooke, West, and Fawkes among its scholars and poets.

In glancing at the lyrical poetry of the era, its hymnology should not be overlooked. Religious verse is one of the most genuine forms of song, inspired by the loftiest emotion, and rehearsed wherever the instinct of worship takes outward form. Written for music, it is lyrical in the original sense, and representative, even more than the domestic folk-songs, of our common life and aspiration. We are not surprised to find the work of recent British hymn-writers displaying the chief qualities of contemporary secular poetry, to wit, finish, tender beauty of sentiment and expression, metrical variety, and often culture of a high grade. What their measures lack is the lyrical fire, vigor, and passionate devotion of the earlier time. Within their province they reflect the method of Tennyson, and — with all their polish and subtilty of thought — write devotional verse that is somewhat tame beside the fervid strains of Watts, at his best, and the beautiful lyrics of the younger Wesley. In place of strength, exaltation, religious ecstasy, we have elaborate sweetness, refinement, emotional repose. Many hymn-writers of the transition period have held over to a recent time, such as James Montgomery, Keble, Lyte, Edmeston, Bowring, Milman, and Moir, and the stanzas of the first-named two have become an essential portion of English hymnody. The best results accomplished by recent devotional poets — and this also is an outgrowth of the new culture — have been the profuse and admirable translations of the ancient and mediæval Latin hymns by the English divines, Chandler, Neale, and Caswall, — the last-named being the deftest workman of the three, although the others may be credited with equal poetic glow. Among the most successful origi-

Recent hymnology:

Its characteristics.

The early and later composers of sacred verse.

Watts and C. Wesley.

Montgomery, Keble, and others.

The translators:

Rev. John Chandler (Church of England): 1806–76.

Rev. John Mason Neale (Ritualist): 1818–66.

Rev. Edward Caswall (Church of Rome): 1814–78.

Original composers:

Rev. Hora-
tius Bonar :
1808- (Scot-
tishChurch.)
Rev. Fred-
erick W. Fa-
ber : 1814-63
(Church of
Rome.)
Mrs. Adams.
(Unitarian.)
See page 257.
Charlotte
Elliott :
1789-1871.
Rev. Christo-
pher Words-
worth :
1807-85.
Rev. Arthur
Penrhyn
Stanley :
1815-81.
Rev. Sabine
Baring-
Gould :
1834-
Rev. Ed-
ward Henry
Bickersteth :
1825-
Hymns
from the
German,
and their
translators.
Catherine
Winkworth:
1829-78.
Frances
Elizabeth
Cox.
Jane Both-
wick : 1813-
Mrs. Eric
Bothwick
Findlater.
Richard
Massie :
1800-

nal composers Dr. Bonar should be mentioned, many of whose hymns are so widely and favorably known ; Faber, also, is one of the best and most prolific of this class of poets, notable for the sweetness and beauty of his sacred lyrics. Others, such as Dr. Newman, Dean Trench, Dean Alford, Palgrave, and Mrs. Adams, have been named elsewhere. I will barely refer, among a host of lesser note, to Miss Elliott, that pure and inspired sibyl, to Dr. Wordsworth, Dean Stanley, and Baring-Gould. Bickersteth, whose longest poem, like the writings of Tupper, has had a circulation strictly owing to its theme and in inverse proportion to its poetic merits, has composed a few hymns that have passed into favor. Excellent service also has been rendered by those who work the German field, and it is noticeable that, while the strongest versions from the Latin have been made by the divines before named, the most successful Germanic translators have been women. Among them, Miss Winkworth, who in 1855 and 1858 published the two series of the *Lyra Germanica ;* Miss Cox, editor of *Sacred Hymns from the German,* 1841 ; and the Bothwick sisters, whose *Hymns from the Land of Luther* appeared in several series, from 1854 to 1862. Massie, translator of *Luther's Spiritual Songs,* 1854, has been the chief competitor of these skilful and enthusiastic devotees. With respect to English hymnody, I may add that probably there never was another period when the sacred lyrics of all ages were so carefully edited, brought together, and arranged for the use and enjoyment of the religious world.

The success of the dialect-poets is a special mark

of an idyllic period. The novel and pleasing effect of the more musical dialects often has been used to give an interest to mediocre verse ; and close attention is required to discriminate between the true and the false pretensions of lyrics composed in the Scotch, that liquid Doric, or even in the rougher phrases of Lancashire, Dorsetshire, and other counties of England. Several Scottish bards, of more or less merit, — Thom, Ballantine, Maclagan, Janet Hamilton, — figure in the period. Professor Shairp's highland and border lyrics, faithful enough and painstaking, scarcely could be ranked with natural song. In England, Lancashire maintains her old reputation for the number and sweetness of her provincial songs and ballads. Waugh is by far the best of her recent dialect-poets. To say nothing of many other little garlands of poesy which have their origin in his knowledge of humble life in that district, the *Lancashire Songs* have gained a wide reception by pleasing, truthful studies of their dialect and themes. Barnes, an idyllic and learned philologist, has done even better work in his bucolic poems of Dorsetshire, and his *Poems of Rural Life* (in common English) are very attractive. The minor dialect-verses of England, such as the street-ballads and the sea-songs of many a would-be Dibdin, are unimportant and beyond our present view.

Dialect-verse.

Cp. " Poets of America ": p. 455.

Thom. See page 261.

James Ballantine: 1808–77.

Alexander Maclagan: 1811–79.

Janet Hamilton: 1795–1873.

John Campbell Shairp: 1819–85.

Edwin Waugh: 1818–

Rev. William Barnes: 1801–86.

V.

LEAVING the specialists, it is observable that the voices of the female poets, if not the best-trained, certainly are as natural and independent as any. Their utterance is less finished, but also shows less of Tennyson's influence, and seems to express a truly feminine

Female poets.

Jean Inge-low: 1830-

emotion and to come from the heart. As the voice of Mrs. Browning grew silent, the songs of Miss Inge-low began, and had instant and merited popularity. They sprung up suddenly and tunefully as skylarks from the daisy-spangled, hawthorn-bordered meadows of old England, with a blitheness long unknown, and in their idyllic underflights moved with the tenderest currents of human life. Miss Ingelow may be termed an idyllic lyrist, her lyrical pieces having always much idyllic beauty, and being more original than her recent ambitious efforts in blank-verse. Her faults are those common to her sex, — too rapid composition, and a diffuseness that already has lessened her reputation. But "The High Tide on the Coast of Lincolnshire" (with its quaint and true sixteenth-century dialect), "Winstanley," "Songs of Seven," and "The Long White Seam," are lyrical treasures, and their author especially may be said to evince that sincerity which is poetry's most enduring warrant. The gentle stanzas

Adelaide Anne Proc-ter: 1825–64. *See page* 107.

of Miss Procter also are spontaneous, as far as they go, but have had less significance as part of the litera-ture of the time. Yet it is like telling one's beads, or reading a prayer-book, to turn over her pages, — so beautiful, so pure and unselfish a spirit of faith, hope, and charity pervades and hallows them. These women, with their melodious voices, spotless hearts, and holy aspirations, are priestesses of the oracle. Their ministry is sacred ; in their presence the most irreverent become subdued. I do not find in the

Isa Craig Knox: 1831-

Christina Georgina Rossetti: 1830 -

lyrics of Mrs. Knox, the Scottish poetess, anything better than the ode in honor of Burns, which took the centenary prize. Miss Rossetti demands closer atten-tion. She is a woman of genius, whose songs, hymns, ballads, and various lyrical pieces are studied and original. I do not greatly admire her longer poems, which are more fantastic than imaginative; but elsewhere she is a poet of a profound and serious cast, whose lips part with the breathing of a fervid spirit within. She has no lack of matter to express; it is that expression wherein others are so fluent and adroit which fails to serve her purpose quickly; but when, at last, she beats her music out, it has mysterious and soul-felt meaning. Another woman-poet is Mrs. Webster, already mentioned as a translator. For many poetic qualities this lady's work is nearly equal, in several departments of verse, to that of the best of her sister artists; and I am not sure but her general level is above them all. She has a dramatic faculty unusual with women, a versatile range, and much penetration of thought; is objective in her dramatic scenes and longer idyls, which are thinner than Browning's, but less rugged and obscure; shows great culture, and is remarkably free from the tricks and dangerous mannerism of recent verse.

Augusta Webster: born about 1840-

VI.

THE minor poetry of the last few years is of a strangely composite order, vacillating between the art of Tennyson and the grotesqueness of Browning, while the latest of all illustrates, in rhythmical quality, the powerful effect Swinburne's manner already has had upon the poetic ear. We can see that the long-unpopular Browning at length has become a potent force as the pioneer of a half-dramatic, half-psychological method, whose adherents seek a change from the idyllic repose of the Laureate and his followers. With this intent, and with a strong leaning toward the art-

The latest schools.

Psychological and Neo-Romantic poets.

studies and convictions of the Rossetti group, a Neo-Romantic School has arisen, and many of the promising younger aspirants are upon its roll.

Sebastian Evans: 1830–

Among recent volumes decidedly in the manner of Browning may be mentioned *Brother Fabian's Manuscript; and Other Poems,* by Evans. On the other side, Simcox's *Poems and Romances* are elaborate and curious romantic studies, resembling works of this sort by Morris and Rossetti. P. B. Marston inherits a poetic gift from his father (Dr. Westland Marston, author of " The Patrician's Daughter " and many other plays). The son is of the new school. I do not remember any experimental volume that has shown more artistic perfection than his *Song-Tide and Other Poems.* His sonnets and lyrics approach those of Rossetti in terseness and beauty, and, while he possesses more restraint than others of his group, there is extreme feeling, pathetic yearning, and that self-pity which is consolation, in his sonnets of a love that has been, and is gone, — of " the joy that was, is not, and cannot be." It is said that Marston is blind, but not from birth ; and certainly his imagination finely supplies the want of outward vision in these picturesque and deeply emotional poems.

George Augustus Simcox: 1841–

Westland Marston: 1819–

Philip Bourke Marston: 1850–87.

Sometimes, in a garden that has changed owners and has been replanted with exotics of brilliant and various hues, the visitor is struck with surprise to see a sweet and sturdy native flower sprung up of itself, amid the new-fangled exuberance, from seed dropped in a season long gone by. It is with a kindred feeling that we examine Dr. Hake's volume, *Madeline, and Other Poems and Parables,* so strangely and pleasantly different from the contemporary mode. It is filled with quaint, grave, thoughtful measures, that

Thomas Gordon Hake, M. D.: 1809–

remind us, by their devotion, of Herbert or Vaughan, — by their radical insight, of the plain-spoken homilies of a time when England's clergymen believed what they preached, — and, by their emblematic and symbolic imagery, of Francis Quarles. " Old Souls," " The Lily of the Valley," and other parables, are well worth close reading, and possibly are the selectest portion of this very original writer's verse. Warren's *Philoctetes*, an antique drama, is a good example of the excellence attained in this kind of work by the new men. It is close, compact, Grecian, less rich with poetry and music than " Atalanta," but even more statuesque and severe. This poet is of the most cultured type. His *Rehearsals* is a collection of verses that generally show the influence of Swinburne, but include a few psychological studies in a widely different vein. He is less florid and ornate than his favorite master ; all of his work is highly finished, and much of it very effective. Among his other successes must be reckoned an admirable use of the stately Persian quatrain. Payne is a more open and pronounced disciple of the Neo-Romantic school. His first book, *The Masque of Shadows*, is a collection of mystical " romaunts," containing much old-fashioned diction, in form reminding us of Morris's octo-syllabic measures, but pervaded by an allegorical spirit. In his *Intaglios* we have a series of sonnets inscribed, like those of Rossetti, to their common master, Dante. Finally, the volume entitled *Songs of Life and Death* shows the influence of Swinburne, so that his works, if brought together, would present a curious mixture and reflection of styles. Nevertheless, this young poet has fire, imagination, and other inborn qualities, and should be entirely competent

John Leicester Warren: 1835-

John Payne: 1842-

Arthur W. E. O'Shaugh- nessy: 1844-81.

to achieve distinction in a manner plainly original. His friend O'Shaughnessy, another man who appears to have the natural faculty, is moving on a parallel line. *Music and Moonlight*, his latest volume, is no advance upon the *Lays of France*, — a highly poetical, though somewhat extravagant adaptation of the *Lais de Marie*, composed in the new manner, but showing, in style and measure, that the author has a person- ality of his own. The "Lays" resemble the work of Morris rather than that of Swinburne ; but "Music and Moonlight," and the author's first venture, *An Epic of Women*, are full of the diction and sugges- tions of the last-named poet. When this romancer becomes lyrical, he is vague and far less pleasing than in his narrative-verse. He, too, needs to shake off external influences, and acquire a definite purpose, before we can attempt to cast his horoscope. Both Payne and O'Shaughnessy have thus far shown themselves, by culture and affinity, to be pupils of the French Romantic school, so elaborate in style and subtile in allusions, but not really broad or healthy in manner and design. Its romanticism, as a new element added to English poetry, is worth something, and I hope that its beauty will survive its defects. It is an exotic, but English literature (like English architecture, sculpture, and music) is so thickly grafted with exotic scions as to yield little fruit that comes wholly from the parent stock.

The new method car- ried to an extreme.

Theophile Marzials: 1850-

In order to test the new method, let us study it when carried to an extreme. This is done by Mar- zials, whose poems are the result of Provençal studies. In *The Gallery of Pigeons, and other Poems*, he turns his back upon a more serene deity, and vows alle- giance to the Muse of Fantasy, or (as he prefers to write it) "Phantasy." At first sight his volume seems a burlesque, and certainly would pass for as clever a satire as "Firmilian." How else can we interpret such a passage as this, which is neither more nor less affected than the greater portion of our author's work? —

> "They chase them each, below, above, —
>   Half maddened by their minstrelsy, —
>   Thro' garths of crimson gladioles;
>   And, shimmering soft like damoisels,
>   The angels swarm in glimmering shoals,
>   And pin them to their aurioles,
>   And mimick back their ritournels."

Poetry of the fantastic and grotesque.

The long poem of which this is a specimen is aptly named "A Conceit." Then we have a pastoral of "Passionate Dowsabella," and her rival Blowselind. Again, "A Tragedy," beginning,

> "Death!
> Plop.
> The barges down in the river flop,"

and ending,

> "Drop
> Dead.
> Plop, flop.
> Plop."

Were this written by a satirist, it would be deemed the wildest caricature. Read closely, and you see that this fantastic nonsense is the work of an artist; that it has a logical design, and is composed in serious earnest. Throughout the book there is melody, color, and much fancy of a delicate kind. Here is a minstrel, with his head turned by a false method, and in very great danger, I should say. But lyrical absurdities are so much the fashion just now in Eng-

Want of wholesome criticism.

land, that reviewers seem complacently to accept them. It is enough to make us forgive the Georgian critics their brutality, and cry out for an hour of Jeffrey or Gifford ! To see how these fine fellows plume themselves ! They intensify the mannerism of their leader, but do not sustain it by his imagination, fervor, and tireless poetic growth.

" Scholar's work in poetry."

Every effort is expended upon decoration rather than construction, and upon construction rather than invention, by the minor adherents of the romance school. In critical notices, which the British publishers are wont to print on the fly-leaves of their books of verse, praise is frequently bestowed upon the contents as " excellent scholar's work in poetry." Poetry is treated as an art, not as an inspiration.

See pages 205, 206.

Moreover, just as in the Alexandrian period, researches are made into the early tongue; " antique and quaint words " are employed ; study endeavors to supply the force of nature, and too often hampers the genius of true poets. Renaissance, and not creation, is the aim and process of the day.

VII.

The foregoing list of poets selected to represent the mass.

IN the foregoing review of the course of British minor poetry during the present reign I have not tried to be exhaustive, nor to include all the lesser poets of the era. The latter would be a difficult task, for the time, if not creative, has been abundantly prolific. Of modern minstrels, as of a certain class of heroes, it may be said, that " every year and month sends forth a new one"; the press groans with their issues. My effort has been to select from the large number, whose volumes are within my reach, such names as represent the various phases considered. Although I have been led insensibly to mention more than were embraced in my original design, doubtless some have been omitted of more repute or merit than others that have taken their place. But enough has been said to enable us to frame an answer to the questions implied at the outset: The *Questions originally suggested.* spirit of later British poetry; is it fresh and proud with life, buoyant in hope, and tuneful with the melody of unwearied song? Again; has the usage of the time eschewed gilded devices and meretricious effect? Is it essentially simple, creative, noble, and enduring?

Certainly, with respect to what has been written by *Tone of the minor philosophic poets.* poets of the meditative school, the former question cannot be answered in the affirmative. With much simplicity and composure of manner, they havè been tame, perplexed, and more or less despondent. The second test, applied to those guided by Tennyson, Browning, and Swinburne, — and who have more or less succeeded in catching the manner of these greater poets, — is one which their productions fail to undergo successfully. It may be said that the characteristics of the early Victorian schools — distinguished from those of famous poetic epochs — have been reflective, sombre, metaphysical, rather than fruitful, spontaneous, and joyously inspired ; while those of the later section are more related to culture and elegant artifice, than to the interpretation of nature or the artistic presentation of essential truth. The minor *The idyllists, romancers, and others.* idyllists, romancers, and dramatic lyrists have possessed much excellence of expression, but do not subordinate this to what is to be expressed. They laboriously, therefore, hunt for themes, and in various ways endeavor to compromise the want of virile imagi-

Ruskin upon Art as a means of expression.

nation. Ruskin, who always has made an outcry against this frigid, perverted taste, established a correct rule in the first volume of *Modern Painters*, applying it to either of the fine arts : " Art," he said, " with all its technicalities, difficulties, and particular ends, is nothing but a noble and expressive language, invaluable as the vehicle of thought, but by itself nothing. . . . . Rhythm, melody, precision, and force are, in the words of the orator and poet, necessary to their greatness, but not the tests of their greatness. It is not by the mode of representing and saying, but by what is represented and said, that the respective greatness either of the painter or writer is to be finally determined. . . . . It is not, however, always easy, either in painting or literature, to determine where the influence of language stops and where that of thought begins. . . . . But the highest thoughts are those which are least dependent on language, and the dignity of any composition and the praise to which it is entitled are in exact proportion to its independency

His own word-painting.

of language or expression." Ruskin's own rhetorical gifts are so eminent, formerly leading him into word-painting for their display, that he pronounces decisively on this point, as one who does penance for a besetting fault. He might have added that the highest thought naturally finds a noble vehicle of expression, though the latter does not always include the former. To a certain extent he implies this, in his statement of a difference (which frequently confronts the reader of these late English poets) between what is ornamental in language and what is expressive : this distinction " is peculiarly necessary in painting : for in the language of words it is nearly impossible for that which is not expressive to be beautiful, except by mere rhythm or melody, any sacrifice to which is immediately stigmatized as error." Upon this point Arnold well calls attention to Goethe's statement that "what distinguishes the artist from the amateur is *architectoniké* in the highest sense ; that power of execution which creates, forms, and constitutes : not the profoundness of single thoughts, not the richness of imagery, not the abundance of illustration."

Goethe's statement.

The rule of architecture may safely be applied to poetry, — that construction must be decorated, not decoration constructed. The reverse of this is practised by many of these writers, who are abundantly supplied with poetical material, with images, quaint words, conceits, and dainty rhymes and alliteration, and who laboriously seek for themes to constitute the groundwork over which these allurements can be displayed. Having not even a definite purpose, to say nothing of real inspiration, their work, however curious in technique, fails to permanently impress even the refined reader, and never reaches the heart of the people, — to which all emotional art is in the end addressed. Far more genuine, as poetry, is the rude spontaneous lyric of a natural bard, expressing the love, or patriotism, or ardor, to which the common pulse of man beats time. The latter outlasts the former ; the former, however acceptable for a while, inevitably passes out of fashion, — being but a fashion, — and is sure to repel the taste of those who, in another age, may admire some equally false production that has come in vogue.

Construction and decoration. See also page 286. Cp. " Poets of America": p. 459.

Judged by the severe rule which requires soul, matter, and expression, all combined, does the character of recent minor poetry of itself give us cause to expect a speedy renewal of the imaginative periods

The present outlook.

*British and
American
minor poets
contrasted.
Cp. " Poets
of Amer-
ica " : p.
456.*

of British song? To apply another test which is like holding a mirror up to a drawing, suppose that the younger American singers were wholly devoted to work of the scholastic dilettant sort, would not their poetry be subjected to still more neglect and contumely than it has received from English critics? On the whole, our poets do not occupy themselves with mediæval and classical studies, with elaborate alliterations, curious measures, and affected refrains. Yet they have a perfect right to do this, — or, at least, every right that an English poet possesses, under the canon that the domain of the artist is boundless, and that the historic themes and treasures of all ages and places are at his disposal. America has no traditional period, except her memories of the motherland. She has as much right to British history, antedating Queen Anne's time, as the modern British poet. Before that epoch, her history, laws, relations, all were English, and her books were printed across the sea. The story of Mary Stuart, for instance, is as proper a theme for an American as for the author

*Freshness
and individ-
uality of the
latter.*

of *Bothwell.* Yet even our most eminent poets do not greatly avail themselves of this usufruct, and the minor songsters, who are many and sweet, sing to express some emotion aroused by natural landscape, patriotism, friendship, religion, or love. There is much originality among those whose note is harsh, and much sweetness among those who repeat the note of others. And the notes of what foreign bard do they repeat with a servility that merits the epithet

*See Chap.
XI.*

of " mocking-birds," applied to them by a poet whom I greatly admire, and often hinted at by others? There is far less imitation of Tennyson, Browning, and Swinburne in the minor poetry of America than in that of Great Britain; the former always has sweetness, and often strength, — and not seldom a freshness and simplicity that are the garb of fresh and simple thoughts. America has been passing through the two phases which precede the higher forms of art: the landscape period, and the sentimental or emotional; and she is now establishing her figure-schools of painting and song. A dramatic element is rapidly coming to light. The truth is that our minor poetry, with a few exceptions, is not well known abroad; a matter of the less importance, since this is the country, with its millions of living readers, to which the true American bard must look for the affectionate preservation of his name and fame. After a close examination of the minor poets of Britain, during the last fifteen years, I have formed, most unexpectedly, the belief that an anthology could be culled from the miscellaneous poetry of the United States equally lasting and attractive with any selected from that of Great Britain. I do not think that British poetry is *The recent aspect, and its true meaning.* to decline with the loss of Tennyson, Arnold, Browning, and the rest. There is no cause for dejection, none for discouragement, as to the imaginative literature of the motherland. The sterility in question is not symbolical of the over-ripening of the historical and aged British nation; but is rather the afternoon lethargy and fatigue of a glorious day, — the product of a critical, scholarly period succeeding a period of unusual splendor, and soon to be followed, as I shall hereafter show, by a new cycle of lyrical and dramatic achievement; England, the mother of nations, renews *Reflex influence of America upon the motherland.* her youth from her children, and hereafter will not be unwilling to receive from us fresh, sturdy, and vigorous returns for the gifts we have for two centuries obtained from her hands. The catholic thinker derives from the new-born hope and liberty of our own country the prediction of a jubilant and measureless art-revival, in which England and America shall labor hand to hand. If we have been children, guided by our elders, and taught to repeat lispingly their antiquated and timorous words, we boast that we have attained majority through fire and blood, and even now are learning to speak for ourselves. I believe that the day is not far distant when the fine and sensitive lyrical feeling of America will swell into floods of creative song. The most musical of England's younger poets — those on whom her hopes depend — are with us, and inscribe their works to the champions of freedom and equality in either world. Thus our progress may exert a reflex influence upon the mother-country; and to the land from which we inherit the wisdom of Shakespeare, the rapture of Milton, and Wordsworth's insight of natural things, our own shall return themes and forces that may animate a new-risen choir of her minstrels, while neither shall be forbidden to follow melodiously where the other may be inspired to lead.

CHAPTER IX.

ROBERT BROWNING.

IN a study of Browning, the most original and unequal of living poets, three features obviously
present themselves. His dramatic gift, so rare in
these times, calls for recognition and analysis; his
method — the eccentric quality of his expression —
constantly intrudes upon the reader; lastly, the moral
of his verse warrants a closer examination than we
give to the sentiments of a more conventional poet.
My own perception of the spirit which his poetry,
despite his assumption of a purely dramatic purpose,
has breathed from the outset, is one which I shall
endeavor to convey in simple and direct terms.

Various other examples have served to illustrate
the phases of a poet's life, but Browning arouses
discussion with respect to the elements of poetry as
an art. Hitherto I have given some account of an
author's career and writings before proffering a critical estimate of the latter. But this man's genius is
so peculiar, and he has been so isolated in style and
purpose, that I know not how to speak of his works
without first seeking a key to their interpretation, and
hence must reverse in some measure the order hitherto
pursued.

*Robert
Browning:
born in
Camberwell,
near Lon-
don, 1812.*

I.

It is customary to call Browning a dramatist, and without doubt he represents the dramatic element, such as it is, of the recent English school.   He counts among his admirers many intellectual persons, some of whom pronounce him the greatest dramatic poet since Shakespeare, and one has said that "it is to him we must pay homage for whatever is good, and great, and profound, in the second period of the Poetic Drama of England."

This may be true ; nevertheless, it also should be declared, with certain modifications, that Robert Browning, in the original sense of the term, is not a dramatic poet at all.

Procter, in the preface to a collection of his own songs, remarks with precision and truth : "It is, in fact, this power of forgetting himself, and of imagining and fashioning characters different from his own, which constitutes the dramatic quality.   A man who can set aside his own idiosyncrasy is half a dramatist."   Although Browning's earlier poems were in the form of plays, and have a dramatic purpose, they are at the opposite remove, in spirit and method, from the models of the true histrionic era, — the work of Fletcher, Webster, and Shakespeare.   They have the sacred rage and fire, but the flame is that of Browning, and not of the separate creations which he strives to inform.

The early drama was the mouthpiece of a passionate and adventurous era.   The stage bore to the period the relations of the modern novel and newspaper to our own, not only holding the mirror up to nature, but showing the "very age and body of the time." It was a vital growth, sprung from the people, and having a reflex action upon their imagination and conduct. Even in Queen Anne's day the theatre was the meeting-place of wits, and, if the plays were meaner, it was because they copied the manners of an artificial world. But, in either case, the playwrights were in no more hazard of representing their own natures, in one rôle after another, than are the leader-writers in their versatile articles upon topics of our day. They invented a score of characters, or took them from real life, grouped them with consummate effect, placed them in dramatic situations, lightened tragedy with mirth, mellowed comedy with pathos, and produced a healthful and objective dramatic literature. They looked outward, not inward : their imagination was the richer for it, and of a more varied kind.

The stage still has its office, but one more subsidiary than of old. Our own age is no less stirring than was the true dramatic period, and is far more subtle in thought. But the poets fail to represent it objectively, and the drama does not act as a safety-valve for the escape of extreme passion and desire. That office the novelists have undertaken, while the press brings its dramas to every fireside. Yet the form of the play still seems to a poet the most comprehensive mould in which to cast a masterpiece. It is a combination of scenic and plastic art; it includes monologue, dialogue, and song, — action and meditation, — man and woman, the lover, the soldier, and the thinker, — all vivified by the imagination, and each essential to the completeness of the whole. Even to poets like Byron, who have no perception of natures differing from their own, it has a fascination

The modern stage.

Cp. " Poets of America " : pp. 467–469.

as a vehicle of expression, and the result is seen in "Sardanapalus" and "Cain." Hence the closet-drama ; and although praiseworthy efforts, as in " Virginius " and "Ion," have been made to revive the early method, these modern stage-plays often are unpoetical and tame. Most of what is excellent in our dramatic verse is to be found in plays that could not be successfully enacted.

Browning's subjectivity. While Browning's earlier poems are in the dramatic form, his own personality is manifest in the speech and movement of almost every character of each piece. His spirit is infused, as if by metempsychosis, within them all, and forces each to assume a strange Pentecostal tone, which we discover to be that of the poet himself. Bass, treble, or recitative, — whether in pleading, invective, or banter, — the voice still is there. But while his characters have a common manner and diction, we become so wonted to the latter that it seems like a new dialect which we have mastered for the sake of its literature. This feeling is acquired after some acquaintance with his poems, and not upon a first or casual reading of them.

The brief, separate pieces, which he terms " dramatic lyrics," are just as properly dramas as are many of his five-act plays. Several of the latter were intended for stage-production. In these we feel that the author's special genius is hampered, so that the student of Browning deems them less rich and rare than his strictly characteristic essays. Even in the most conventional, this poet cannot refrain from the long monologues, stilted action, and metaphysical discursion, which mark the closet-drama and unfit a composition for the stage. His chief success is in the portrayal of single characters and specific moods.

I would not be understood to praise his originality *His special mission.* at the expense of his greatness. His mission has been that of exploring those secret regions which generate the forces whose outward phenomena it is for the playwrights to illustrate. He has opened a new field for the display of emotional power, — founding, so to speak, a sub-dramatic school of poetry, whose office is to follow the workings of the mind, to discover the impalpable elements of which human motives and passions are composed. The greatest forces are the most elusive, the unseen mightier than the seen ; modern genius chooses to seek for the under-currents of the soul rather than to depict acts and situations. Browning, as the poet of psychology, escapes to that stronghold whither, as I have said, science and materialism are not yet prepared to follow him. How shall the chemist read the soul ? No former poet has so relied upon this province for the excursions of his muse. True, he explores by night, stumbles, halts, has vague ideas of the topography, and often goes back upon his course. But, though others complete the unfinished work of Columbus, it is to him that we award the glory of discovery, — not to the engineers and colonists that succeed him, however firmly they plant themselves and correctly map out the now undisputed land.

II.

BROWNING'S manner is so eccentric as to challenge *Analysis of Browning's method.* attention and greatly affect our estimate of him as a poet. Eccentricity is not a proof of genius, and even an artist should remember that originality consists not only in doing things differently, but also in " doing

13 *

things better." The genius of Shakespeare and Mo-
lière enlarged and beautified their style ; it did not
distort it.   Again, the grammarian's statement is true,
that Poetry is a means of Expression.   A poet may
differ from other men in having profounder emotions
and clearer perceptions, but this is not for him to
assume, nor a claim which they are swift to grant.
The lines,

> "O many are the poets that are sown
> By Nature ! men endowed with highest gifts,
> The vision and the faculty divine ;
> Yet wanting the accomplishment of verse,"

imply that the recognized poet is one who gives voice,
in expressive language, to the common thought and
feeling which lie deeper than ordinary speech.   He
is the interpreter : moreover, he is the maker, — an
artist of the beautiful, the inventor of harmonious
numbers which shall be a lure and a repose.

A poet, however emotional or rich in thought, must
not fail to express his conception and make his work
attractive.   Over-possession is worth less than a more
commonplace faculty ; he that has the former is a
sorrow to himself and a vexation to his hearers,
while one whose speech is equal to his needs, and
who knows his limitations, adds something to the
treasury of song, and is able to shine in his place,
" and be content."   Certain effects are suggested by
nature ; the poet discovers new combinations within
the ground which these afford.   Ruskin has shown
that in the course of years, though long at fault, the
masses come to appreciate any admirable work.   By
inversion, if, after a long time has passed, the world
still is repelled by a singer, and finds neither rest
nor music in him, the fault is not with the world ;

there is something deficient in his genius, — he is so much the less a poet.

The distinction between poetry and prose must be sharply observed. Poetry is an art, — a specific fact, which, owing to the vagueness fostered by minor wits, we do not sufficiently insist upon. We hear it said that an eloquent prose passage is poetry, that a sunset is a poem, and so on. This is well enough for rhetorical effect, yet wholly untrue, and no poet should permit himself to talk in that way. Poetry is poetry, because it differs from prose; it is artificial, and gives us pleasure because we know it to be so. It is beautiful thought expressed in rhythmical form, not half expressed or uttered in the form of prose. It is a metrical structure; a spirit not disembodied, but in the flesh, — so as to affect the senses of living men. Such is the poetry of Earth; what that of a more spiritual region may be I know not. Milton and Keats never were in doubt as to the meaning of their art. It is true that fine prose is a higher form of expression than wretched verse; but when a distinguished young English poet thus writes to me, —

Poetry.
Misuse of
the term.

Cp. " Poets
of Amer-
ica" : pp.
327, 373.

" My own impression is that Verse is an inferior, or infant, form of speech, which will ultimately perish altogether. . . . . The Seer, the Vates, the teacher of a new truth, is single, while what you call artists are legion,"

Letter from
a rising
English
poet.

— when I read these words, I remember that the few great seers have furnished models for the simplest and greatest forms of art; I feel that this poet is growing heretical with respect, not to the law of custom, but to a law which is above us all; I fear to discover a want of beauty, a vague transcendentalism, rather than a clear inspiration, in his verse, —

Dangers of
transcen-
dentalism.

Cp. " Poets
of Amer-
ica" : pp.
168, 169,
249, 253.

to see him become prosaic and substitute rhetoric for passion, realism for naturalness, affectation for lofty thought, and, "having been praised for bluntness," to "affect a saucy roughness." In short, he is on the edge of danger. Yet his remark denotes a just impatience of forms so hackneyed that, once beautiful, they now are stale and corrupt. It may be necessary, with the Pre-Raphaelites, to escape their thraldom and begin anew. But the poet is a creator, not an iconoclast, and never will tamely endeavor to say in prose what can only be expressed in song. And I have faith that my friend's wings will unfold, in spite of himself, and lift him bravely as ever on their accustomed flights.

Impression produced by Browning's work.

Has the lapse of years made Browning any more attractive to the masses, or even to the judicious few? He is said to have "succeeded by a series of failures," and so he has, as far as notoriety means success, and despite the perpetuation of his faults. But what is the fact which strikes the admiring and sympathetic student of his poetry and career? Distrusting my own judgment, I asked a clear and impartial thinker, — "How does Browning's work impress you?" His reply, after a moment's consideration, was: "Now that I try to formulate the sensation which it always has given me, his work seems that of a grand intellect painfully striving for adequate use and expression, and never quite attaining either." This was, and is, precisely my own feeling. The question arises, What is at fault? Browning's genius, his chosen mode of expression, his period, or one and all of these? After the flush of youth is over, a poet must have a wise method, if he would move ahead. He must improve upon instinct by experience and common-sense. There is something amiss in one who has to grope for his theme and cannot adjust himself to his period ; especially in one who cannot agreeably handle such themes as he arrives at. More than this, however, is the difficulty in Browning's case. Expression is the flower of thought ; a fine imagina- tion is wont to be rhythmical and creative, and many passages, scattered throughout Browning's works, show that his is no exception. It is a certain caprice or perverseness of method, that, by long practice, has injured his gift of expression ; while an abnormal power of ratiocination, and a prosaic regard for de- tails, have handicapped him from the beginning. Be- sides, in mental arrogance and scorn of authority, he has insulted Beauty herself, and furnished too much excuse for small offenders. What may be condoned in one of his breed is intolerable when mimicked by every jackanapes and self-appointed reformer.

Defective and capri- cious ex- pression.

A group of evils, then, has interfered with the greatness of his poetry. His style is that of a man caught in a morass of ideas through which he has to travel, — wearily floundering, grasping here and there, and often sinking deeper until there seems no prospect of getting through. His latest works have been more involved and excursive, less beautiful and elevating, than most of those which preceded them. Possibly his theory is that which was his wife's instinct, — a man being more apt than a woman with some reason for what he does, — that poetry is valuable *only* for the statement which it makes, and must always be subordinate thereto. Nevertheless, Emerson, in this country, seems to have followed a kindred method ; and who of our poets is greater, or so wise?

His recent productions.

III.

BROWNING'S early lyrics, and occasional passages of recent date, show that he has melodious intervals, and can be very artistic with no loss of original power. Often the ring of his verse is sonorous, and overcomes the jagged consonantal diction with stirring lyrical effect. The " Cavalier Tunes " are examples. Such choruses as

> "Marching along, fifty-score strong,
> Great-hearted gentlemen, singing this song ! "

> " King Charles, and who 'll do him right now ?
> King Charles, and who 's ripe for fight now ?
> Give a rouse : here 's, in Hell's despite now,
> King Charles ! "

— these, with, " Boot, saddle, to horse, and away ! " show that Browning can put in verse the spirit of a historic period, and has, or had, in him the making of a lyric poet. How fresh and wholesome this work ! Finer still that superb stirrup-piece, best of its class in the language, " How they brought the good news from Ghent to Aix." " Ratisbon " and " The Lost Leader," no less, are poems that fasten themselves upon literature, and will not be forgotten. The old fire flashes out, thirty years after, in " Hervé Riel," another vigorous production, — unevenly sustained, but superior to Longfellow's legendary ballads and sagas. From among lighter pieces I will select for present mention two, very unlike each other ; one, as delightful a child's poem as ever was written, in fancy and airy extravagance, and having a wildness and pathos all its own, — the daintiest bit of folk-lore in English verse, — to what should I refer but " The Pied Piper of Hamelin?" The author made a strong bid for the love of children, when he placed " By Robert Browning " at its head, in the collection of his poems. The other,

> "Beautiful Evelyn Hope is dead!
> Sit and watch by her side an hour,"

appeals, like Wordsworth's " She dwelt among the untrodden ways," and Landor's " Rose Aylmer," to the hearts of learned and unlettered, one and all.

Browning's style is the more aggressive, because, in *Evils of his general style.* compelling beauty itself to suffer a change and conform to all exigencies, it presents such a contrast to the refined art of our day. I have shown that much of this is due to natural awkwardness,— but that the author is able, on fortunate occasions, to better his work, has just been amply illustrated. More often he either has let his verse have its way, or has shaped a theory of art by his own restrictions, and with that contempt for the structure of his song which Plato and St. Paul entertained for their fleshly bodies. If the mischief ceased here, it would not be so bad, but his genius has won pupils who copy his vices without his strength. He and his wife injured each *The two Brownings.* the other's style as much as they sustained their common aspiration and love of poesy. To be sure, there was a strange similarity, by nature, between their modes of speech ; and what I have said of the woman's obscurity, affectations, elisions, will apply to the man's — with his *i'thes* and *o'thes*, his dashes, breaks, halting measures, and oracular exclamations that convey no dramatic meaning to the reader. Her verse is the more spasmodic ; his, the more metaphysical, and, while effective in the best of his dramatic lyrics, is constantly running into impertinences worse than those of his poorest imitators, and which would not be tolerated for a moment in a lesser poet. Parodies on his style, thrown off as burlesques, are more intelligible than much of his " Dramatis Personæ."

Disregard of the fitness of things. Unlike Tennyson, he does not comprehend the *limits* of a theme ; nor is he careful as to the relative importance either of themes or details; his mind is so alert that its minutest turn of thought must be uttered; he dwells with equal precision upon the meanest and grandest objects, and laboriously jots down every point that occurs to him, — parenthesis within parenthesis, — until we have a tangle as intricate as the line drawn by an anemometer upon the recording-sheet. The poem is all zigzag, criss-cross, at odds and ends, — and, though we come out right at last, strength and patience are exhausted in mastering it. Apply the rule that nothing should be told in verse which can be told in prose, and half his measures would be condemned ; since their chief metrical purpose is, through the stress of rhythm, to fix our attention, by a certain unpleasant fascination, upon a process of reasoning from which it otherwise would break away.

Irreverence. For so much of Browning's crudeness as comes from inability to express himself, or to find a proper theme, he may readily be forgiven ; but whatever is due to real or assumed irreverence for the divine art, among whose votaries he stands enrolled, is a grievous wrong, unworthy of the humble and delightful spirit of a true craftsman. He forgets that art is the bride of the imagination, from whose embraces true creative work

Crude realism. must spring. Lastly, concerning realism, while poets are, as Mrs. Browning said, "your only truth-tellers,' it is not well that repulsive or petty facts should always be recorded ; only the high, essential truths demand a poet's illumination. The obscurity wherein Browning disguises his realism is but the semblance of imagination,—a mist through which rugged details jut out, while the central truth is feebly to be seen.

IV.

AFTER a period of study at the London University young Browning, in 1832, went to Italy, and acquired a remarkable knowledge of the Italian life and language. He mingled with all classes of the people, mastered details, and rummaged among the monasteries of Lombardy and Venice, studying mediæval history, and filling his mind with the relics of a bygone time. All this had much to do with the bent of his subsequent work, and possibly was of more benefit to his learning than to his ideality. *Browning's dramas, and "Sordello."*

At the age of twenty-three he published his first drama, *Paracelsus;* a most unique production,—strictly speaking, a metaphysical dialogue, as noticeable for analytic power as the romances of Keats for pure beauty. It did not find many readers, but no man of letters could peruse it without seeing that a genuine poet had come to light. From that time the author moved in the literary society of London, and was recognized as one who had done something and might do something more. The play is " Faust," with the action and passion, and much of the poetry and music,—upon which the fascination of the German work depends,— omitted ; the hero resembles " Faust " in the double aspiration to know and to enjoy, to search out mystical knowledge, yet drink at all the fountains of pleasure, — lest, after a long struggle, *"Paracelsus." 1835-36.*

T

failing of knowledge, he should have lived in vain. It must be understood that Mr. Browning's Paracelsus was his own creation : a man of heroic longings, observed at various intervals, from his twentieth year, in which he leaves his native hamlet, until he dies at the age of forty-eight, — obscure, and with his ideal seemingly unattained ; not the juggler, empiric, and charlatan of history, whose record the poet frankly gives us in a foot-note.

This poem has every characteristic of Browning's genius. The verse is as strong and as weak as the best and worst he has composed during thirty years, and is pitched in a key now familiar to us all. "Paracelsus," the fruit of his youth, serves as well for a study of this poet as any later effort, and, though inferior to "Pippa Passes" and "In a Balcony," is much better than his newest romance in blank verse. I cannot agree with critics who say that he did his poorest work first and has been moving along an ascending scale ; on the contrary, his faults and beauties have been somewhat evenly distributed throughout his career. We are vexed in "Paracelsus" by a vice that haunts him still, — that tedious garrulity which, however relieved by beautiful passages, palls on the reader and weakens the general effect. As an offset, he displays in this poem, with respect to every kind of poetic faculty except the sense of proportion, gifts equal to those of any compeer. By turns he is surpassingly fine. We have strong dramatic diction : —

*Character-
istic merits
and defects.*

> "Festus, strange secrets are let out by Death,
> Who blabs so oft the follies of this world :
> And I am Death's familiar, as you know.

I helped a man to die, some few weeks since;

   .   .   . . .   No mean trick
He left untried ; and truly wellnigh wormed
All traces of God's finger out of him.
Then died, grown old; and just an hour before —
Having lain long with blank and soulless eyes —
He sate up suddenly, and with natural voice
Said, that in spite of thick air and closed doors
God told him it was June ; and he knew well,
Without such telling, harebells grew in June ;
And all that kings could ever give or take
Would not be precious as those blooms to him."

The conception is old as Shakespeare, but the manner is large and effective. Few authors vary the breaks and pauses of their blank verse so naturally as Browning, and none can so well dare to extend the proper limits of a poem. Here, as in later plays, he shows a more realistic perception of scenery and nature than is common with dramatic poets. We have a bit of painting at the outset, in the passage beginning, *Browning's blank verse.*

"Nay, Autumn wins you best by this its mute
Appeal to sympathy for its decay!"

and others, equally fine and true, are scattered throughout the dialogue.

"Paracelsus" is meant to illustrate the growth and progress of a lofty spirit, groping in the darkness of his time. He first aspires to knowledge, and fails ; then to pleasure and knowledge, and equally fails — to human eyes. The secret ever seems close at hand : —

"Ah, the curse, Aprile, Aprile!
We get so near — so very, very near!
'T is an old tale : Jove strikes the Titans down
Not when they set about their mountain-piling,
But when another rock would crown their work!"

Now, it is a part of Browning's life-long habit, that
he here refuses to judge by ordinary standards, and
makes the hero's attainment lie even in his failure
and death. There are few more daring assertions of
the soul's absolute freedom than the words of Festus,
impressed by the nobility of his dying friend : —

> "I am for noble Aureole, God!
> I am upon his side, come weal or woe!
> His portion shall be mine! He has done well!
> I would have sinned, had I been strong enough,
> As he has sinned! Reward him, or I waive
> Reward! If thou canst find no place for him
> He shall be king elsewhere, and I will be
> His slave forever! There are two of us!"

The drama is well worth preserving, and even now
a curious and highly suggestive study. Its lyrical
interludes seem out of place. As an author's first
drama, it promised more for his future than if it had
been a finished production, and in any other case
but that of the capricious, tongue-tied Browning, the
promise might have been abundantly fulfilled.

*"Straf-
ford,"* 1837.

In "Strafford," his second drama, the interest also
centres upon the struggles and motives of one heroic
personage, this time entangled in a fatal mesh of
great events. Apparently the poet, after some experience of authorship, wished to commend his work
to popular sympathy, and tried to write a play that
should be fitted for the stage ; hence a tragedy, dedicated to Macready, of which the chief character, — the
hapless Earl of Strafford, — was assumed by that
tragedian. The piece is said to have been well received, but ran for five nights only, one of the chief
actors suddenly withdrawing from the cast. The
characters are eccentrically drawn, and are more

serious and mystical than even the gloom of their period would demand. It is hard to perceive the motives of Lady Carlisle and the Queen; there is no underplot of love in the play, to develop the womanly element, nor has it the humor of the great play-wrights, — so essential to dramatic contrast, and for which the Puritans and the London populace might afford rich material. Imagine Macready stalking portentously through the piece, the audience trying to follow the story, and listening with patience to the solemn speeches of Pym and Strafford, which answer for a death-scene at the close. The language is more natural than is usual with Browning, but here, where he is least eccentric, he becomes tame — until we see that he is out of his element, and prefer his striking psychology to a forced attempt at writing of the academic kind.

Something of this must have struck the poet himself, for, as if chagrined at his effort, he swung back to the other extreme, and beyond his early starting-place: farther, happily, than any point he since has ventured to reach. In no one of his recent works has he been quite so "hard," loquacious, and impracticable as in the renowned nondescript entitled *Sordello*. Twenty-three years after its appearance he owned that its "faults of expression were many," and added, "but with care for a man or book such would be surmounted." The acknowledgment was partial. "Sordello" is a fault throughout, in conception and execution: nothing is "expressed," not even the "incidents in the development of a soul," though such incidents may have had some nebulous origin in the poet's mind. It is asking too much of our care for a book or a man that we should surmount this chaotic

"*Sordello*,"
1840.

mass of word-building. Carlyle's " Sartor Resartus "
is a hard study, but, once entered upon, how poetical ! what lofty episodes ! what wisdom, beauty,
and scorn ! Few such treasures await him that would
read the eleven thousand verses into which the fatal
facility of the rhymed-heroic measure has led the
muse of Browning. The structure, by its very ugli-
ness and bulk, like some half-buried colossus in the
desert, may survive a lapse of time. I cannot persuade myself to solicit credit for deeper insight by
differing from the common judgment with regard to
this unattractive prodigy.

It had its uses, seemingly, in acting as a purge to
cleanse the visual humors of the poet's eyes and to
leave his general system in an auspicious condition.
His next six years were devoted to the composition
of a picturesque group of dramas, — the exact order
of which escapes me, but which finally were collected
in *Bells and Pomegranates*, a popular edition, issued
in serial numbers, of this maturer work. " Luria,"
" King Victor and King Charles," and " The Return
of the Druses," are stately pieces, historical or legendary, cast in full stage-form. In Luria we again see
Browning's favorite characterization, from a different
point of view. This is a large-moulded, suffering hero,
akin, if disturbed in conscience, to Wallenstein, —
if devoted and magnanimous, to Othello. Luria, the
Moor, is like Othello in many ways: a brave and skilful general, who serves Florence (instead of Venice),
and declares,

> "I can and have perhaps obliged the state,
> Nor paid a mere son's duty."

He is so true and simple, that Domizia says of
him,

" Bells and Pomegranates," 1840-46.

" Luria."

> "How plainly is true greatness charactered
> By such unconsciousness as Luria's here,
> And sharing least the secret of itself!"

Browning makes devotion to an ideal or trust, how- ever unworthy of it, the chief trait of this class of personages. Strafford dies in behalf of ungrateful Charles ; Luria is sacrificed by the Florence he has saved, and destroys himself at the moment when love and honor are hastening, too late, to crown him. Djabal, false to himself, is true to the cause of the Druses, and at last dies in expiation of his fault. Valence, in " Colombe's Birthday," shows devotion of a double kind, but is rewarded for his fidelity and honor. Luitolfo, in " A Soul's Tragedy," is of a kindred type. But I am anticipating. The language of " Luria " often is in the grand manner. In depicting the Moorish general and his friend Husain, — brooding, generous children of the sun, — the soldierly Tiburzio, painted with a few master-strokes, — and in the element of Italian craft and intrigue, the author is at home and well served by his knowledge of mediæval times. That is an eloquent speech of Domizia, near the end of the fourth act. Despite the poverty of action, and the prolonged harangues, this drama is worthy of its dedication to Landor and the wish that it might be " read by his light": almost worthy (Landor always weighed out gold for silver!) of the old bard's munificent return of praise : —

> "Shakespeare is not our poet but the world's,
> Therefore on him no speech ! and brief for thee,
> Browning ! Since Chaucer was alive and hale,
> No man hath walked along our roads with step
> So active, so inquiring eye, or tongue
> So varied in discourse. But warmer climes

Give brighter plumage, stronger wing : the breeze
Of Alpine heights thou playest with, borne on
Beyond Sorrento and Amalfi, where
The Siren waits thee, singing song for song."

*"The Re-
turn of the
Druses."*
"The Return of the Druses," with its scenic and
choric effects, is like some of Byron's plays : the
scene, an isle of the Sporades ; the legend, half-
Venetian, half-Oriental, one that only Browning could
make available. The girl Anael is an impassioned
character, divided between adoration for Hakeem, the
god of her race, — whom she believes incarnate in
Djabal, — and her love for Djabal as a man. The
tragedy, amid a good deal of trite and pedantic language, is marked by heroic situations and sudden
dramatic catastrophes. Several brilliant points are
made : one, where the Prefect lifts the arras, on the
other side of which death awaits him, and says, —

"This is the first time for long years I enter
Thus, without feeling just as if I lifted
The lid up of my tomb ! . . . .

.   .   .   .   .

Let me repeat — for the first time, no draught
Coming as from a sepulchre salutes me ! "

A moment, and the dagger is through his heart.
Another such is the wonder and contempt of Anael
at finding Djabal no deity, but an impostor ; while
perhaps the most telling point in the whole series of
Browning's plays is her cry of *Hakeem !* made when
she comes to denounce Djabal, but, moved by love,
proclaims him as the god, and falls dead with the
effort. The poet, however, is justly censured for too
frequently taking off his personages by the intensity
of their own passions, without recourse to the dagger

and bowl. He rarely does it after the "high Roman
fashion."

This tragedy observes the classic unities of time
and place. A hall in the Prefect's palace is made to
cover its entire action, which occupies only one day.
In its earnest pitch and lack of sprightly underplot, *The Classi-*
cal and
it also is Greek or Italian. Not long ago, listening *Gothic meth-*
ods in dra-
to Salvini in "Samson" and other plays, I was struck *matic art.*
by their likeness, in simplicity of action and costume,
to the antique dramas. The actors were sufficient to
themselves, and the audience was intent upon their
lofty speech and passion ; there was no lack of
interest, but a refreshing spiritual elevation. The
Gothic method better suits the English stage, nevertheless we need not refuse to profit by the experience of other lands. Our poetry, like the language,
should draw its riches from all tongues and races,
and well can endure a larger infusion of the ancient
grandeur and simplicity. In the play before us
Browning has but renewed the debt, long since in-
curred, of English literature to the Italian, — greater
than that to all other sources combined. Not without reason, in "De Gustibus," he sang, —

> "Open my heart and you will see,
> Graved inside of it, 'Italy.'
> Such lovers old are I and she ;
> So it always was, so it still shall be ! "

"King Victor" is one of those conventional plays *"King Vic-*
tor and
in which he appears to ordinary advantage. His *King*
Charles."
three dramatic masterpieces are "Pippa Passes," "A
Blot in the 'Scutcheon," and "Colombe's Birthday."

The last-named play, inscribed to Barry Cornwall, *"Colombe's*
Birthday."
really is a fresh and lovely little drama. The fair

14

young heroine has possessed her duchy for a single year, and now, upon her birthday, as she unsuspectingly awaits the greetings of her courtiers, is called upon to surrender her inheritance to Prince Berthold, decreed to be the lawful heir. At the same time Valence, a poor advocate of Cleves, seeks audience in behalf of his suffering townsmen, and ends by defending the Duchess's title to her rank. She loves him, and is so impressed by his nobility and courage as to decline the hand of the Prince, and surrender her duchy, to become the wife of Valence, with whom she joyfully retires to the ruined castle where her youth was spent. This play might be performed to the great interest of an audience composed exclusively of intellectual persons, who could follow the elaborate dialogue and would be charmed with its poetry and subtile thought. Once accept the manner of Browning, and you must be pleased with the delineation of the characters. " Colombe " herself is exquisite, and like one of Shakespeare's women. Valence seems too harsh and dry to win her, and her choice, despite his loyalty and intellect, is hardly defensible. Still, " Colombe's Birthday " is the most natural and winsome of the author's stage-plays.

" A Blot in the 'Scutch- eon."   " A Blot in the 'Scutcheon " was brought out at Drury Lane, in 1843. It is full of poetry and pathos, but there is little in it to relieve the human spirit, — which cannot bear too much of earnestness and woe added to the mystery and burden of our daily lives. Yet the piece has such tragic strength as to stamp the author as a great poet, though in a narrow range. One almost forgets the singular improbabilities of the story, the *blasé* talk of the child-lovers (an English Juliet of fourteen is against nature), the stiff language

of the retainers, and various other blemishes. There is a serenade in which, unchecked by his fear of detection, Mertoun is made to sing under Mildred's window, —

"There 's a woman like the dew-drop, she 's so purer than the purest!"

This song, composed seven years before the poet's meeting with Miss Barrett, is precisely in the style of "Lady Geraldine's Courtship," and other ballads of the gifted woman who became his wife.

The most simple and varied of his plays — that which shows every side of his genius, has most lightness and strength, and all in all may be termed a representative poem — is the beautiful drama with the quaint title of "Pippa Passes." It is a cluster of four scenes, with prologue, epilogue, and interludes; half prose, half poetry, varying with the refinement of the dialogue. Pippa is a delicately pure, good, blithesome peasant-maid. "'T is but a little black-eyed, pretty, singing Felippa, gay silk-winding girl,"— though with token, ere the end, that she is the child of a nobleman, put out of the way by a villain, Maffeo, at instigation of the next heir. Pippa knows nothing of this, but is piously content with her life of toil. It is New Year's Day at Asolo. She springs from bed, in her garret chamber, at sunrise, — resolved to enjoy to the full her sole holiday: she will not "squander a wavelet" of it, not a "mite of her twelve hours' treasure." Others can be happy throughout the year: haughty Ottima and Sebald, the lovers on the hill; Jules and Phene, the artist and his bride; Luigi and his mother; Monsignor, the Bishop; but Pippa has only this one day to enjoy. She envies these great

"Pippa Passes."

ones a little, but reflects that God's love is best, after all. And yet, how little can she do! How can she possibly affect the world? Thus she muses, and goes out, singing, to her holiday and the sunshine. Now, it so happens that she passes, this day, each of the groups or persons we have named, at an important crisis in their lives, and they hear her various carols as she trills them forth in the innocent gladness of her heart. Sebald and Ottima have murdered the latter's aged husband, and are unremorseful in their guilty love. Jules is the victim of a fraud practised by his rival artists, who have put in his way a young girl, a paid model, whom he believes to be a pure and cultured maiden. He has married her, and just discovered the imposture. Luigi is hesitating whether to join a patriotic conspiracy. Monsignor is tempted by Maffeo to overlook his late brother's murder, for the sake of the estates, and utterly to ruin Pippa.

Intense passion and beauty.

The scene between Ottima and Sebald is the most intense and striking passage of all Browning's poetry, and, possibly, of any dramatic verse composed during his lifetime up to the date of this play. A passionate esoteric theme is treated with such vigor and skill as to free it from any debasing taint, in the dialogue from which I quote : —

> " *Ottima.* . . . . The past, would you give up the past
> Such as it is, pleasure and crime together?
> Give up that noon I owned my love for you —
> The garden's silence — even the single bee,
> Persisting in his toil, suddenly stopt,
> And where he hid you only could surmise
> By some campanula's chalice set a-swing
> As he clung there — ' Yes, I love you !'
>   *Sebald.*   And I drew
> Back ; put far back your face with both my hands

Lest you should grow too full of me — your face
So seemed athirst for my whole soul and body!

See "*Pippa Passes,*" *Scene I.*

. . . . .

Ottima. Then our crowning night —
Sebald. The July night?
Ottima. The day of it too, Sebald!
When the heaven's pillars seemed o'erbowed with heat,
Its black-blue canopy seemed let descend
Close on us both, to weigh down each to each,
And smother up all life except our life.
So lay we till the storm came.
Sebald. How it came!
Ottima. Buried in woods we lay, you recollect;
Swift ran the searching tempest overhead;
And ever and anon some bright white shaft
Burnt thro' the pine-tree roof, — here burnt and there,
As if God's messenger thro' the close wood screen
Plunged and replunged his weapon at a venture,
Feeling for guilty thee and me : then broke
The thunder like a whole sea overhead —
Sebald. Yes!

. . . .

How did we ever rise?
Was it that we slept? Why did it end?
Ottima. I felt you,
Fresh tapering to a point the ruffled ends
Of my loose locks 'twixt both your humid lips —
(My hair is fallen now — knot it again!)
Sebald. I kiss you now, dear Ottima, now, and now!
This way? Will you forgive me — be once more
My great queen?
Ottima. Bind it thrice about my brow;
Crown me your queen, your spirit's arbitress,
Magnificent in sin. Say that!
Sebald. I crown you
My great white queen, my spirit's arbitress,
Magnificent — "

But here Pippa passes, singing

"God's in his heaven, —
All 's right with the world!"

Sebald is stricken with fear and remorse; his para-
mour becomes hideous in his eyes; he bids her dress
her shoulders, wipe off that paint, and leave him, for
he hates her! She, the woman, is at least true to
her lover, and prays God to be merciful, not to her,
but to him.

The scene changes to the post-nuptial meeting of
Jules and Phene, and then in succession to the other
passages and characters we have mentioned. All
these persons are vitally affected, — have their lives
changed, merely by Pippa's weird and suggestive
songs, coming, as if by accident, upon their hearing
at the critical moment. With certain reservations this
is a strong and delicate conception, admirably worked
out. The usual fault is present : the characters,

*Too intel-
lectual.*

whether students, peasants, or soldiers, all talk like
sages ; Pippa reasons like a Paracelsus in panta-
lets, — her intellectual songs are strangely put in the
mouth of an ignorant silk-winding girl ; Phene is
more natural, though mature, even for Italy, at fourteen. Browning's children are old as himself ; — he
rarely sees them objectively. Even in the songs he is
awkward, void of lyric grace ; if they have the wilding flavor, they have more than need be of specks
and gnarledness. In the epilogue Pippa seeks her
garret, and, as she disrobes, after artlessly running
over the events of her holiday, soliloquizes thus : —

> " Now, one thing I should like really to know :
> How near I ever might approach all these
> I only fancied being, this long day —
> — Approach, I mean, so as to touch them — so
> As to . . in some way . . move them — if you please,
> Do good or evil to them some slight way."

Finally, she sleeps, — unconscious of her day's mission, — and of the fact that her own life is to be something more than it has been, — but not until she has murmured these words of a hymn : —

> "All service is the same with God, —
> With God, whose puppets, best and worst,
> Are we : there is no last nor first."

"Pippa Passes" is a work of pure art, and has a wealth of original fancy and romance, apart from its wisdom, to which every poet will do justice. Its faults are those of style and undue intellectuality. To quote the author's words, in another drama, *A rare and exquisite production.*

> "Ah? well! he o'er-refines, — the scholar's fault!"

As it is, we accept his work, looking upon it as upon some treasured yet *bizarre* painting of the mixed school, whose beauties are the more striking for its defects. The former are inherent, the latter external and subordinate.

Everything from this poet is, or used to be, of value and interest, and "A Soul's Tragedy" is of both: first, for a masterly distinction between the action of sentiment and that founded on principle, and, secondly, for wit, satire, and knowledge of affairs. Ogniben, the Legate, is the most thorough man of the world Browning has drawn. That is a matchless stroke, at the close, where he says: "I have seen four-and-twenty leaders of revolts." It is a consolation to recall this when a pretender arises ; his race is measured, — his fall will surely come. *"A Soul's Tragedy."*

With "Luria," in 1845–6, Browning, whose plays had been briefly performed, and whose closet-dramas had found too small a reading, made his "last attempt, for the present, at dramatic poetry." It

remains to examine his miscellaneous after-work, including the long poems which have appeared within
the last five years, — thus far the most prolific, if not
the most creative, period of his untiring life.

V.

*Dramatic
nature of
Browning's
lyrics.*

SOMETHING of a dramatic character pertains to
nearly all of Browning's lyrics. Like his wife, he has
preferred to study human hearts rather than the
forms of nature. A note to the first collection of
his briefer poems places them under the head of
Dramatic Pieces. This was at a time when English
poets were enslaved to the idyllic method, and forgot
that their readers had passions most suggestive to art
when exalted above the tranquillity of picturesque repose. Herein Browning justly may claim originality.
Even the Laureate combined the art of Keats with
the contemplative habit of Wordsworth, and adapted
them to his own times ; while Browning was the
prophet of that reaction which holds that the proper
study of mankind is man. His effort, weak or able,
was at figure-painting, in distinction from that of

*Founder of
the new life-
school.*

landscape or still-life. It has not flourished during
the recent period, but we are indebted to him for
what we have of it. In an adverse time it was
natural for it to assume peculiar, almost morbid
phases ; but of this ·struggling, turbid figure-school, —
variously represented by the younger Lytton, Rossetti,
Swinburne, and others, he was the long-neglected
progenitor. His genius may have been unequal to
his aims. It is not easy for him to combine a score
of figures upon the ample canvas : his work is at its
best in separate ideals, or, rather, in portraits, — his

dramatic talent being more realistic than imaginative. Still, portraiture, in a certain sense, is the highest form of painting, and Browning's personal studies must not be undervalued. As usual, even here he is unequal, and, while some of them are matchless, in others, like all men of genius who aim at the highest, he conspicuously fails. A man of talent may never fail, yet never rise above a fixed height. Yet if Browning were a man of great genius his failures would not so outnumber his successes that half his lyrics could be missed without injury to his reputation.

The shorter pieces, "Dramatic Romances and Lyrics," in the first general collection of his works, are of a better average grade than those in his latest book of miscellanies. One of the best is "My Last Duchess," a masterly sketch, comprising within sixty lines enough matter to furnish Browning, nowadays, with an excuse for a quarto. Nothing can be subtler than the art whereby the Duke is made to reveal a cruel tragedy of which he was the relentless villain, to betray the blackness of his heart, and to suggest a companion-tragedy in his betrothal close at hand. Thus was introduced a new method, applied with such coolness as to suggest the idea of vivisection or morbid anatomy. *"My Last Duchess."*

But let us group other lyrics in this collection with the matter of two later volumes, *Men and Women*, and *Dramatis Personæ*. These books, made up of isolated poems, contain the bulk of his work during the eighteen years which followed his marriage in 1846. While their contents include no long poem or drama, they seem, upon the whole, to be the fullest expression of his genius, and that for which he is *"Men and Women,"* 1855. *"Dramatis Personæ,"* 1864.

14*   U

likeliest to be remembered. Every poet has limitations, and in such briefer studies Browning keeps within the narrowest bounds allotted to him. Very

Inferiority of the last-named volume.

few of his best pieces are in "Dramatis Personæ," the greater part of which book is made up of his most ragged, uncouth, and even puerile verse ; and it is curious that it appeared at a time when his wife was scribbling the rhetorical verse of those years which I have designated as her period of decline. But observe the general excellence of the fifty poems in "Men and Women,"— collected nine years earlier, when the author was forty-three years old, and at his prime. In the chapter upon Tennyson it was stated that almost every poet has a representative book, showing him at full height and variety. "Men and

"Men and Women" a representative work.

Women," like the Laureate's volume of 1842, is the most finished and comprehensive of the author's works, and the one his readers least could spare. Here we find numbers of those thrilling, skilfully dramatic studies, which so many have imitated without catching the secret of their power.

The general effect of Browning's miscellaneous poems is like that of a picture-gallery, where cabinet-paintings, by old and modern masters, are placed at random upon the walls. Some are rich in color ; others, strong in light and shade. A few are elaborately finished,— more are careless drawings, fresh, but hurriedly sketched in. Often the subjects are repulsive, but occasionally we have the solitary, impressive figure of a lover or a saint.

"Andrea del Sarto."

The poet is as familiar with mediæval thought and story as most authors with their own time, and adapts them to his lyrical uses. "Andrea del Sarto" belongs to the same group with "My Last Duchess."

It is the language of "the faultless painter," addressed to his beautiful and thoughtless wife, for whom he has lowered his ideal — and from whose chains he cannot break, though he knows she is unworthy, and even false to him. He moans before one of Rafael's drawings, excusing the faults, in envy of the genius : —

> "Still, what an arm! and I could alter it.
> But all the play, the insight and the stretch —
> Out of me! out of me! And wherefore out?
> Had you enjoined them on me, given me soul,
> We might have risen to Rafael, I and you.
>
> .   .   .   .   .
>
> But had you — O, with the same perfect brow,
> And perfect eyes, and more than perfect mouth,
> And the low voice my soul hears, as a bird
> The fowler's pipe, and follows to the snare, —
> Had you, with these the same, but brought a mind!
> Some women do so. Had the mouth there urged
> 'God and the glory! never care for gain!'
>
> .   .   .   .   .
>
> I might have done it for you."

Were it indeed "all for love," then were the "world well lost"; but even while he dallies with his wife she listens for her gallant's signal. This poem is one of Browning's finest studies : of late he has given us nothing equal to it. The picture of the rollicking "Fra Lippo Lippi" is broad, free-handed, yet scarcely so well done. "Pictor Ignotus" is upon another art-theme, and in quiet beauty differs from the poet's usual manner. Other old-time studies, good and poor, which served to set the fashion for a number of minor poets, are such pieces as "Count Gismond," "Cristina," "The Laboratory," and "The Confessional."

"Fra Lippo Lippi," etc.

"Christmas Eve" and "Easter Day," 1850.

How perilous an easy rhymed-metre is to this author was discernible in "Sordello." After the same manner he is tempted to garrulity in the semi-religious poems, "Christmas Eve" and "Easter Day." It is difficult otherwise to account for their dreary flow, since they are no more original in theology than poetical in language and design.

It would be strange if Browning were not indebted, for some of his most powerful themes, to the superstition from which mediæval art, politics, and daily life took their prevailing tone. In his analysis of

Excellent mediæval church studies.

its quality he seems to me extremely profound. Monasticism in Spain even now is not so different from that of the fifteenth century, and the repulsive imagery of a piece like the "Soliloquy of the Spanish Cloister," written in the harshest verse, well consorts with a period when the orders, that took their origin in exalted purity, had become degraded through lust, gluttony, jealousy, and every cardinal sin. Browning draws his monks, as Doré in the illustrations to "Les Contes Drôlatiques," with porcine or wolfish faces, monstrous, seamed with vice, defiled in body and soul. "The Bishop orders his Tomb" has been criticised as not being a faithful study of the Romish ecclesiastic, A. D. 15—; but, unless I misapprehend the spirit of that period, this is one of the poet's strongest portraitures. Religion then was often a compound of fear, bigotry, and greed ; its officers, trained in the Church, seemed to themselves invested with something greater than themselves ; their ideas of good and evil, after years of ritualistic service, — made gross with pelf, jealousy, sensualism, and even blood-guiltiness, — became strangely intermixed. The poet overlays this groundwork with that love of art and luxury — of jasper, peach-blossom marble, and lazuli — inbred in every Italian, — and even with the scholar's desire to have his epitaph carved aright : —

> "Choice Latin, picked phrase, Tully's every word,
> No gaudy ware like Gandolf's second line, —
> Tully, my masters? Ulpian serves his need!
> And then how I shall lie through centuries,
> And hear the blessed mutter of the mass,
> And see God made and eaten all day long,
> And feel the steady candle-flame, and taste
> Good, strong, thick, stupefying incense-smoke! "

All this commanded to his bastards! And for the rest, were ever suspicion, hatred, delight at outwitting a rival in love and preferment, and every other loathsome passion strong in death, more ruthlessly and truthfully depicted?

Of strictly mediæval church studies, "The Heretic's Tragedy" and "Holy-Cross Day," with their grotesque diction, annotations, and prefixes, are the most skilful reproductions essayed in our time. Browning alone could have conceived or written them. In "A Grammarian's Funeral," "Abt Vogler," and "Master Hugues," early scholarship and music are commemorated. The language of the simplest of these is so intricate that we have to be educated in a new tongue to comprehend them. Their value lies in the human nature revealed under such fantastic, and, to us, unnatural aspects developed in other times.

"Artemis Prologuizes," the poet's antique sketch, is as unclassical as one might expect from its affected title. "Saul," a finer poem, may have furnished hints to Swinburne with respect to anapestic verse and the Hebraic feeling. Three poems, which strive to reproduce the early likeness and spirit of Christianity,

" The Heretic's Tragedy," etc.

Studies upon themes taken from the first century.

merit close attention. One describes the raising of Lazarus, narrated in an " Epistle of Karshish, the Arab Physician." The pious, learned mage sees in the miracle

> "but a case of mania — subinduced
> By epilepsy, at the turning-point
> Of trance prolonged unduly some three days."

"Cleon." "Cleon" is an exposition of the highest ground reached by the Pagan philosophy, set forth in a letter written, by a wise poet, to Protos, the King. At the end he makes light of the preachings of Paul, who is welcome to the few proselytes he can make among the ignorant slaves : —

> "And (as I gathered from a bystander)
> Their doctrines could be held by no sane man."

The reader is forced to stop and consider what despised doctrines even now may be afloat, which in time may constitute the whole world's creed. The *"A Death in the Des-ert."* most elaborate of these pieces is "A Death in the Desert," the last words of St. John, the Evangelist, recorded by Pamphylax, an Antiochene martyr. The prologue and epilogue are sufficiently pedantic, but, like the long-drawn narrative, so characteristic, that this curious production may be taken as a representative poem. A similar bit of realism is the sketch of a great poet, seen in every-day life by a fellow-townsman, entitled, "How it Strikes a Contemporary." And now, having selected a few of these miscellaneous pieces to represent the mass, how shall we define their true value, and their influence upon recent art?

Browning is justified in offering such works as a substitute for poetic treatment of English themes, since he is upon ground naturally his own. Yet as *poems* they fail to move us, and to elevate gloriously the soul, but are the outgrowth of minute realism and speculation. To quote from one who is reviewing a kindred sort of literature, they sin " against the spirit of antiquity, in carrying back the modern analytic feeling to a scene where it does. not belong." It is owing precisely to this sin that several of Browning's longer works are literary and rhythmical prodigies, monuments of learning and labor rather than ennobling efforts of the imagination. His hand is burdened by too great accumulation of details, — and then there is the ever-present spirit of Robert Browning peering from the eyes of each likeness, however faithful, that he portrays. *Defect of the fore-cited poems.*

He is the most intellectual of poets, Tennyson not excepted. Take, for example, " Caliban," with its text, " Thou thoughtest I was altogether such an one as thyself." The motive is a study of anthropomorphism, by reflection of its counterpart in a lower animal, half man, half beast, possessed of the faculty of speech. The "natural theology" is food for thought; the poetry, descriptive and otherwise, realism carried to such perfection as to seem imagination. Here we have Browning's curious reasoning at its best. But what can be more vulgar and strictly unpoetical than " Mr. Sludge, the Medium," a composition of the same period? Our familiarity with such types as those to which the author's method is here applied enables us to test it with anything but satisfaction. Applied to a finer subject, in " Bishop Blougram's Apology," we heartily admire its virile analysis of the motives actuating the great prelate, who after due reflection has rejected *Browning's subtilty of intellect.* *" Caliban."* *" Mr. Sludge."* *" Bishop Blougram."*

> "A life of doubt diversified by faith
> For one of faith diversified by doubt."

Cardinal Wiseman is worldly and insincere; the poet, Gigadibs, is earnest and on the right side; yet, somehow, we do not quite despise the churchman nor admire the poet. This piece is at once the foremost defence and arraignment cf Philistinism, drawn up by a thinker broad enough to comprehend both sides. As an intellectual work, it is meat and wine; as a poem, as a thing of beauty, — but that is quite another point in issue.

Occasional lyrics:

Browning's offhand, occasional lyrics, such as "Waring," "Time's Revenges," "Up in a Villa," "The Italian in England," "By the Fireside," "The Worst of It," etc., are suggestive, and some of them widely familiar. His style has been caught by others. The picturesqueness and easy rhythm of "The Flight of the Duchess," and the touches in briefer lyrics, are repeated by minnesingers like Owen Meredith and Dobell. There is a grace and turn that still evades them, for sometimes their master can be as sweet and tuneful as Lodge, or any other of the skylarks. Witness "In a Gondola," that delicious Venetian cantata,

Their excellence and faults.

full of music and sweet sorrow, or "One Way of Love," for example, — but such melodies are none too frequent. When he paints nature, as in "Home Thoughts, from Abroad," how fresh and fine the landscape!

> "And after April, when May follows,
> And the white-throat builds, and all the swallows, —
> Hark! where my blossomed pear-tree in the hedge
> Leans to the field and scatters on the clover
> Blossoms, and dew-drops — at the bent spray's edge —
> That's the wise thrush; he sings each song twice over
> Lest you should think he never could recapture
> The first fine careless rapture!"

Having in mind Shakespeare and Shelley, I nevertheless think the last three lines the finest ever written
touching the song of a bird.   Contrast therewith the
poet's later method, — the prose-run-mad of stanzas
such as this : —

> " Hobbs hints blue, — straight he turtle eats.
>   Nobbs prints blue, — claret crowns his cup.
>   Nokes outdares Stokes in azure feats, —
>   Both gorge.   Who fished the murex up ?
>   What porridge had John Keats ? "

And this by no means the most impertinent of kindred
verses in his books, — poetry that neither gods nor
men can endure or understand, and yet interstrewn
with delicate trifles, such as " Memorabilia," which for
suggestiveness long will be preserved.   Who so deft to
catch the one immortal moment, the fleeting exquisite word ?   Who so wont to reach for it, and wholly
fail ?

VI.

We come, at last, to a class of Browning's poems
that I have grouped for their expression of that dominating sentiment, to which reference was made at the
beginning of this review.   Their moral is that of the
apothegm that " Attractions are proportional to destinies " ; of rationalistic freedom, as opposed to Calvin-
ism ; of a belief that the greatest sin does not consist
in giving rein to our desires, but in stinting or too
prudently repressing them.   Life must have its full
and free development.   And, as love is the master-
passion, he is most earnest in illustrating this belief
from its good or evil progress, and to this end has
composed his most impressive verse.

*Moral of his
emotional
verse.*

A main lesson of Browning's emotional poetry is that the unpardonable sin is "to dare something against nature." To set bounds to love is to commit that sin. Through his instinct for conditions which engender the most dramatic forms of speech and action, he is, at least, as an artist, tolerant of what is called an intrigue ; and that many complacent English and American readers do not recognize this, speaks volumes either for their stupidity, or for their hypocrisy and inward sympathy in a creed which they profess to abhor. Affecting to comprehend and admire Browning, they still refuse to forgive Swinburne, — whose crude earlier poems brought the lust of the flesh to the edge of a grossness too palpable to be seductive, and from which his riper manhood has departed altogether. The elder poet, from first to last, has appeared to defend the elective affinities against impediments of law, theology, or social rank. It is not my province to discuss the ethics of this matter, but simply to speak of it as a fact.

Its subjective undertone. It will not do to fall back upon Browning's protest, in the note to his "Dramatic Lyrics," that these are "so many utterances of so many imaginary persons," and not his own. For when he returns persistently to a certain theme, illustrates it in divers ways, and heaps the coals of genius upon it till it breaks out into flame, he ceases to be objective and reveals his secret thought. No matter how conservative his habit, he is to be judged, like any artist, by his work ; and in all his poems we see a taste for the joys and sorrows of a free, irresponsible life, — like that of the Italian lovers, of students in their vagrant youth, or of Consuelo and her husband upon the windy heath. Above all, he tells us : —

> "Thou shalt know, those arms once curled
> About thee, what we knew before,
> How love is the only good in the world."

"In a Balcony" is the longest and finest of his emotional poems: a dramatic episode, in three dialogues,
the personages of which talk at too great length, —
although, no doubt, many and varied thoughts flash
through the mind at supreme moments, and it is
Browning's custom to put them all upon the record.
How clearly the story is wrought! What exquisite
language, and passion triumphant over life and death!
Mark the transformation of the lonely queen, in the
one radiant hour of her life that tells her she is beloved, and makes her an angel of goodness and light.
She barters power and pride for love, clutching at
this one thing as at Heaven, and feels

> "How soon a smile of God can change the world."

Then comes the transformation, upon discovery of
the cruel deceit, — her vengeance and despair. The
love of Constance, who for it will surrender life, and
even Norbert's hand, is more unselfish ; never more
subtly, perhaps, than in this poem, has been illustrated Byron's epigram : —

> "In her first passion, woman loves her lover :
> In all the others, all she loves is love."

Here, too, is the profound lesson of the whole, that
a word of the man Norbert's simple, blundering truth
would have prevented all this coil.   But the poet is
at his height in treating of the master passion : —

> "Remember, I (and what am I to you?)
> Would give up all for one, leave throne, lose life,
> Do all but just unlove him! he loves me."

"*In a Bal-
cony.*"

With fine abandonment he makes the real worth so much more than the ideal : —

> "We live, and they experiment on life,
> These poets, painters, all who stand aloof
> To overlook the farther. Let us be
> The thing they look at!"

But in a large variety of minor lyrics it is hinted that our instincts have something divine about them ; that, regardless of other obligations, we may not disobey the inward monition. A man not only may forsake father and mother and cleave to his wife ; but forsake his wife and cleave to the predestined one. No sin like repression ; no sting like regret ; no requital for the opportunity slighted and gone by. In "The Statue and the Bust," — a typical piece, — had the man and woman seen clearly "the end" of life, though "a crime," they had not so failed of it : —

" The Statue and the Bust."

> "If you choose to play — is my principle !
> Let a man contend to the uttermost
> For his life's set prize, be it what it will !
>
> "The counter our lovers staked was lost
> As surely as if it were lawful coin :
> And the sin I impute to each frustrate ghost
>
> "Was, the unlit lamp and the ungirt loin.
> Though the end in sight was a crime, I say."

"A Light Woman" turns upon the right of every soul, however despicable, to its own happiness, and to freedom from the meddling of others. The words of many lyrics, attesting the boundless liberty and sovereignty of love, are plainly written, and to say the lesson is not there is to ape those commentators who discover an allegorical meaning in each Scriptural text that interferes with their special creeds.

Both Browning and his wife possessed by nature a radical gift for sifting things to the core, an heroic disregard of every conventional gloss or institution. They were thoroughly mated in this respect, though one may have outstripped the other in exercise of the faculty. Their union, apparently, was so absolute that neither felt any need of fuller emotional life. The sentiment of Browning's passional verse, therefore, is not the outgrowth of perceptions sharpened by restraint. The poetry addressed to his wife is, if anything, of a still higher order. He watches her

Wedded poets.

> " Reading by firelight, that great brow
>   And the spirit-small hand propping it
> Mutely — my heart knows how —

> " When, if I think but deep enough,
>   You are wont to answer, prompt as rhyme ";

and again and again addresses her in such lines as these : —

> "God be thanked, the meanest of his creatures
> Boasts two soul-sides, one to face the world with,
> One to show a woman when he loves her.
>
>   .   .   .   .   .
>
> This to you — yourself my moon of poets !
> Ah, but that's the world's side — there's the wonder —
> Thus they see you, praise you, think they know you."

In fine, not only his passional lyrics, but all the poems relating to the wedded love in which his own deepest instincts were thoroughly gratified, are the most strong and simple portion of his verse, — showing that luminous expression is still the product of high emotion, as some conceive the diamond to have been crystallized by the electric shock.

True passion ennobles art.

VII.

MANY of the lyrics in the volume of 1864 are so thin and faulty, and so fail to carry out the author's intent, — the one great failure in art, — as sadly to illustrate the progressive ills which attend upon a wrong method.

The gift still remained, however, for no work displays more of ill-diffused power and swift application

than Browning's longest poem, *The Ring and the Book.* It has been succeeded rapidly, within five years, by other works, — the whole almost equalling, in bulk, the entire volume of his former writings. Their special quality is affluence: limitless wealth of language and illustration. They abound in the material of poetry. A poet should condense from such star-dust the orbs which give light and outlast time. As in "Sordello," Browning again fails to do this; he gives us his first draught, — the huge, outlined block, yet to be reduced to fit proportions, — the painter's sketch, blotchy and too obscure, and of late without the early freshness.

Nevertheless, "The Ring and the Book" is a wonderful production, the extreme of realistic art, and considered, not without reason, by the poet's admirers, to be his greatest work. To review it would

require a special chapter, and I have said enough with respect to the author's style in my citation of his less extended poems; but as the product of sheer intellect this surpasses them all. It is the story of a tragedy which took place at Rome one hundred and seventy years ago. The poet seems to have found his thesis in an old book, — part print, part manuscript, — bought for eight pence at a Florence stall:—

> "A book in shape, but, really, pure crude fact
> Secreted from man's life when hearts beat hard,
> And brains, high-blooded, ticked two centuries since."

The versified narrative of the child Pampilia's sale to *Outline of the poem.* Count Guido, of his cruelty and violence, of her rescue by a young priest, — the pursuit, the lawful separation, the murder by Guido of the girl and her putative parents, the trial and condemnation of the murderer, and the affirmation of his sentence by the Pope, — all this is made to fill out a poem of twenty-one thousand lines ; but these include ten different versions of the same tale, besides the poet's prelude, — in which latter he gives a general outline of it, so that the reader plainly may understand it, and the historian then be privileged to wander as he choose. The chapters which contain the statements of the priest-lover and Pampilia are full of tragic beauty and emotion ; the Pope's soliloquy, though too prolonged, is a wonderful piece of literary metempsychosis ; but the speeches of the opposing lawyers carry realism to an intolerable, prosaic extreme. Each of these books, possibly, should be read by itself, and not too steadily nor too often. Observe that the author, in *The style of certain passages.* elevated passages, sometimes forgets his usual manner and breaks into the cadences of Tennyson's style ; for instance, the apostrophe to his dead wife, beginning

> "O lyric Love, half angel and half bird,
> And all a wonder and a wild desire ! "

But elsewhere he still leads the reaction from the art-school. His presentations are endless : in his architecture the tracery, scroll-work, and multifoil bewilder us and divert attention from the main design. Yet in presence of the changeful flow of his verse, and the facility wherewith he records the speculations of his various characters, we are struck with wonder. "The Ring and the Book" is thus far imaginative, and a rhythmical marvel, but is it a stronghold of poetic art? As a whole, we cannot admit that it is; and yet the thought, the vocabulary, the imagery, the wisdom, lavished upon this story, would equip a score of ordinary writers, and place them beyond danger of neglect.

"Balaustion's Adventure," 1871.

Balaustion's Adventure, the poet's next volume, displays a tranquil beauty uncommon in his verse, and it seems as if he sought, after his most prolonged effort, to refresh his mind with the sweetness and repose of Greek art. He treads decently and reverently in the buskins of Euripides, and forgets to be garrulous in his chaste semi-translation of the Alcestis. The girl Balaustion's prelude and conclusion are very neatly turned, reminding us of Landor; nor does the book, as a whole, lack the antique flavor and the blue, laughing freshness of the Trinacrian sea.

"Fifine at the Fair," 1872.

What shall be said of *Fifine at the Fair,* or of that volume, the last but one of Browning's essays, which not long ago succeeded it? Certainly, that they exhibit his steadfast tendency to produce work that is less and less poetical. There is no harder reading than the first of these poems; no more badly chosen, rudely handled measure than the verse selected for it; no pretentious work, from so great a pen, has less of the spirit of grace and comeliness. It is a pity that the author has not somewhat accustomed himself to write in prose, for he insists upon recording all of his thoughts, and many of them are essentially prosaic. Strength and subtilty are not enough in art: beauty, either of the fair, the terrible, or the grotesque, is its justification, and a poem that repels at the outset has small excuse for being. "Prince Hohenstiel-Schwangau, Savior of Society," is another of Browning's experiments in vivisection, the subject readily made out to be the late Emperor of the French. It is longer than "Bishop Blougram's Apology," but compare it therewith, and we are forced to perceive a decline in terseness, virility, and true imaginative power.

Red Cotton Night-Cap Country; or, Turf and Towers, —what exasperating titles Browning puts forth! this time under the protection of Miss Thackeray. That the habit is inbred, however, is proved by some absurd invention whenever it becomes necessary to coin a proper name. After "Bluphocks" and "Gigadibs," we have no right to complain of the title of his Breton romance. The poem itself contains a melodramatic story, and hence is less uninteresting than "Fifine." But to have such a volume, after Browning's finer works, come out with each revolving year, is enough to extort from his truest admirers the cry of "Words! Words! Words!" Much of the detail is paltry, and altogether local or temporal, so that it will become inexplicable fifty years hence. There is a constant "dropping into" prose; moreover, whole pages of wandering nonsense are called forth by some word, like "night-cap" or "fiddle," taken for a text, as if to show the poet's mastery of verse-building and how contemptible he can make it. Once he would have put the narrative of this poem into a brief dramatic sketch that would have had beauty and interest. "My Last Duchess" is a more genuine addition to literature than the two hundred pages of this tedious and affected romance. A pro-

"Prince Hohenstiel-Schwangau."

"Red Cotton Night-Cap Country," 1873.

Decline in poetic value.

15 v

longed career has not been of advantage to the reputation of Browning: his tree was well-rooted and reached a sturdy growth, but the yield is too profuse, of a fruit that still grows sourer from year to year.

Nevertheless, this poet, like all men of genius, has happy seasons in which, by some remarkable per-formance, he seems ·to renew his prime. *Aristopha-nes' Apology* continues the charm of "Balaustion's Adventure," to which poem it is a sequel. What I have said of the classical purity and sweetness of the earlier production, will apply to portions of " the last adventure of Balaustion," — which also includes " a transcript from Euripides." Besides, it displays the richness of scholarship, command of learned de-tails, skill in sophistry and analysis, power to recall, awaken, and dramatically inform the historic past, in all which qualifications this master still remains un-equalled by any modern writer, even by the most gifted and affluent pupil of his own impressive school.

"Aristopha-nes' Apol-ogy," 1875.

VIII.

A FAIR estimate of Browning may, I think, be de-duced from the foregoing review of his career. It is hard to speak of one whose verse is a metrical paradox. I have called him the most original and the most unequal of living poets ; he continually descends to a prosaic level, but at times is elevated to the Laureate's highest flights. Without realizing the proper functions of art, he nevertheless sympa-thizes with the joyous liberty of its devotees; his life may be conventional, but he never forgets the Latin Quarter, and often celebrates that freedom in love and song which is the soul of Béranger's

Final esti-mate of this poet.

Most origi-nal and unequal.

"Dans un grenier qu'on est bien à vingt ans."

Then, too, what working man of letters does not thank him when he says, —

> "But you are of the trade, my Puccio!
> You have the fellow-craftsman's sympathy.
> There's none knows like a fellow of the craft
> The all unestimated sum of pains
> That go to a success the world can see."

He is an eclectic, and will not be restricted in his themes ; on the other hand, he gives us too gross a mixture of poetry, fact, and metaphysics, appearing to have no sense of composite harmony, but to revel in arabesque strangeness and confusion. He has a barbaric sense of color and lack of form. Striving against the trammels of verse, he really is far less a master of expression than others who make less resistance. We read in "Pippa Passes": "If there should arise a new painter, will it not be in some such way by a poet, now, or a musician (spirits who have conceived and perfected an Ideal through some other channel), transferring it to this, and escaping our conventional roads by pure ignorance of them?" This is the Pre-Raphaelite idea, and, so far, good ; but Browning's fault is that, if he has "conceived," he certainly has made no effort to "perfect" an Ideal.

And here I wish to say, — and this is something which, soon or late, every thoughtful poet must discover, — that the structural exigencies of art, if one adapts his genius to them, have a beneficent reaction upon the artist's original design. By some friendly law they help the work to higher excellence, suggesting unthought-of touches, and refracting, so to speak, the single beam of light in rays of varied and delightful beauty.

The brakes which art applies to the poet's movement not only regulate, but strengthen its progress.
Their absence is painfully evinced by the mass of
Browning's unread verse. Works like "Sordello" and
"Fifine," however intellectual, seem, like the removal
of the Malvern Hills, a melancholy waste of human
power. When some romance like the last-named
comes from his pen, — an addition in volume, not in
quality, to what he has done before, — I feel a sadness like that engendered among hundreds of gloomy
folios in some black-letter alcove: books, forever closed,
over which the mighty monks of old wore out their
lives, debating minute points of casuistic theology,
though now the very memory of their discussions has
passed away. Would that Browning might take to
heart his own words, addressed, in "Transcendentalism," to a brother-poet: —

> "Song's our art:
> Whereas you please to speak these naked thoughts
> Instead of draping them in sights and sounds.
> — True thoughts, good thoughts, thoughts fit to treasure up!
> But why such long prolusion and display,
> Such turning and adjustment of the harp?
>
> .   .   .   .
>
> But here's your fault; grown men want thought, you think;
> Thought's what they mean by verse, and seek in verse:
> Boys seek for images and melody,
> Men must have reason, — so you aim at men.
> Quite otherwise!"

Incidentally we have noted the distinction between
the drama of Browning and that of the absolute
kind, observing that his characters reflect his own
mental traits, and that their action and emotion are
of small moment compared with the speculations to
which he makes them all give voice. Still, he has

dramatic insight, and a minute power of reading other men's hearts. His moral sentiment has a potent and subtile quality : — through his early poems he really founded a school, and had imitators, and, although of his later method there are few, the younger poets whom he has most affected very naturally began work by carrying his philosophy to a startling yet perfectly logical extreme.

Much of his poetry is either very great or very poor. It has been compared to Wagner's music, and entitled the "poetry of the future"; but if this be just, then we must revise our conception of what poetry really is. The doubter incurs the contemptuous enmity of two classes of the dramatist's admirers: first, of the metaphysical, who disregard considerations of passion, melody, and form ; secondly, of those who are sensitive to their master's failings, but, in view of his greatness, make it a point of honor to defend them. That greatness lies in his originality ; his error, arising from perverseness or congenital defect, is the violation of natural and beautiful laws. This renders his longer poems of less worth than his lyrical studies, while, through avoidance of it, productions, differing as widely as "The Eve of St. Agnes" and "In Memoriam," will outlive "The Ring and the Book." In writing of Arnold I cited his own quotation of Goethe's distinction between the dilettanti, who affect genius and despise art, and those who respect their calling though not gifted with high creative power. Browning escapes the limitations of the latter class, but incurs the reproach visited upon the former ; and by his contempt of beauty, or inability to surely express it, fails of that union of art and spiritual power which always characterizes a poet "entirely great."

The "poetry of the future."

What constitutes true greatness in art.

CHAPTER X.

LATTER-DAY SINGERS.

ROBERT BUCHANAN. — DANTE GABRIEL ROSSETTI. — WILLIAM MORRIS.

I.

A new departure. THROUGHOUT the recent poetry of Great Britain a new departure is indicated, and there are signs that the true Victorian era has nearly reached a close. To speak more fully, we approach the end of that time in which — although a composite school has derived its models from all preceding forms — the idyllic method, as represented by Tennyson, upon the whole has prevailed, and has been more successful than in earlier times, and than contemporary efforts in the higher scale of song.

All periods are transitional ; yet it may be said that the calling of the British poets, during the last fifteen years, has been a " struggle," not so much for recognition, as for the vital influence which consti- *The latter-day poets.* tutes a genuine " existence." The latter-day singers, who bear a special relation to the immediate future, are like those priests of the Sun, who, on hills over-looking the temples of strange gods, and above the tumult of a hostile nation, tend the sacred fire, in presence of their band of devotees, and wait for the coming of a fairer day. Not that the blood of Englishmen is more frigid, and their wants more sordid, than of old. The time is sufficiently imaginative. Love of excitement, the most persistent of human motives, is strong as ever. But the sources are various which now supply to the imagination that stimulus for which the new generation otherwise might resort to poetry. It is an age of journalism ; all the acts of all the world are narrated by the daily press. It is, we have seen, a time of criticism and scholarship, similar to the Alexandrian period of Greek thought. It is the very noontide of imaginative work in prose ; and so largely have great novelists supplanted the poets in general regard, that annalists designate the Victorian period as the " age of prose romance." Finally, and notably within the last decade, readers have been confronted with those wonders of science which have a double effect, — destroying the old poetic diction and imagery, and elevating the soul with beauty and sublimity beyond anything proffered by verse of the idyllic kind. The poets — especially Tennyson, in his recognition of modern science and the new theology — have tried to meet the exigency, but their efforts have been timid and hardly successful. Their art, though noble and refined, rarely has swayed the multitude, or even led the literary progress of the time, — that which verse was wont to do in the great poetic epochs. Year by year these adverse conditions have been more severely felt. To the latest poets, I say, the situation is so oppressive that there is reason to believe it must be near an end, and hence we see them striving to break through and out of the restrictions that surround them.

Where is the point of exit? This is the problem

Their embarrassments.

Cp. " Poets of America" : p. 437.

Remedial efforts.

which, singly or in groups, they are trying, perhaps unconsciously, to solve. Some return to a purely natural method, applying it to scenes whose freshness and simplicity may win attention ; others withdraw to the region of absolute art, and by new and studied forms of constructive beauty gratify their own taste, and at least secure a delight in labor which, of itself, is full compensation. Some have applied poetic investigation to the spiritual themes which float like shadows among the pillars and arches of recent materialism ; finally, all are agreed in attempting to infuse with more dramatic passion the over-cultured method of the day.

Need of a dramatic revival. Cp. " Poets of America " : pp. 466-469.

In this last endeavor I am sure their instinct is right. Modern art has carried restraint and breeding below the level of repose. Poetry, to recover its station, must shake off its luxurious sleep : the Philistines are upon it. It must stimulate feeling, arouse to life, love, and action, before there can be a true revival of its ancient power.

It would be invidious to lay any stress upon the fact that the body of recent English verse is supplied by those smaller lyrists, who, the poet tells us, never weary of singing the old eternal song. Socialists avow that Nature is unerring in the distribution of her groups. Among a thousand men are so many natural farmers, so many mechanics, a number of scholars, two or three musicians, — a single philanthropist, it may be. But we search groups of a hundred thousand for a tolerable poet, and of a million for a good one. The inspired are in the proportion of diamonds to amethysts, of gold to iron. If, in the generation younger than Tennyson and the Brownings, we discover three or four singers fit to aspire and lead the way, especially at this stage of competition with science and prose romance, there surely is no need that we should wholly despair.

I have spoken elsewhere of the minor poets, and of those specialists who excel in dialect-writing and society-verse, and have derived from their miscellaneous productions an idea of the tone and fashion of the period. As we seek for those who are distinguished, not only by power and individuality, but by the importance of their accomplished work, three or four, at most, require specific attention. Another year, and the position may be changed; for poets are like comets in the suddenness of their appearance, and too often also in brief glory, hyperbolic orbit, and abrupt departure to be seen no more.

Of the four whose names most readily occur to the mind, — Buchanan, Rossetti, Morris, and Swinburne, — the first holds an isolated position; the remaining three, though their gifts are entirely distinctive, have an appearance of association through sympathy in taste or studies, — so that, while to classify them as a school might be unphilosophical, to think of one is to recall the others. Such a group is not without precedent. It is not for this cause that I include the three under one review; if it were so, Buchanan, from his antagonistic position, well might be placed elsewhere. The fact is, that all are latter-day poets, and need not object to meet on the footing of guests in the house of a common friend. With the exception of Rossetti, these later poets are alike in at least one respect: they are distinguished from the Farringford school by a less condensed, more affluent order of work, — are prodigal of their verse, pouring it out in youth, and flooding the ear with rhythm. There is

Representative names.

15*

no nursing of couplets, and so fruitful a yield may be taken as the evidence of a rich and fertile soil.

II.

*Robert Bu-
chanan:
born in Scot-
land, Aug.
18, 1841.*

JUDGED either by his verse or by his critical writings, Robert Buchanan seems to have a highly developed poetic temperament, with great earnestness, strength of conviction, and sensitiveness to points of right and wrong. Upon the whole, he represents, possibly more than any other rising man, the Scottish element in literature,—an element that stubbornly retains its characteristics, just as Scotch blood manages to hold its own through many changes of emigration, intermarriage, or long descent. The most prosaic Scotsman has something of the imagination and warmth of feeling that belong to a poet; the Scottish minstrel has the latter quality, at least, to an extent beyond ordinary comprehension. He wears his heart upon his sleeve; his naïveté and self-consciousness subject him to charges of egotism; he has strong friends but makes as many enemies by tilting against other people's convictions, and by zealous advocacy of his own.

*His temper-
ament.*

It is difficult for such a man to confine himself to pure art, and Buchanan is no exception to the rule. He is a Scotsman all over, and not only in push and aggressiveness, but, let me add, in versatility, in genuine love and knowledge of nature, and in his religious aspiration. The latter does not manifest itself through allegiance to any traditional belief, but through a spirit of individual inquiry, resulting in speculations which he advances with all the fervor of Knox or Chalmers, and thus furnishes another illustration of the saying that every Scot has a creed of his own.

Great Britain can well afford to tolerate the metaphysics of Scotland for the sake of her poetry. Buchanan's transcendentalism is mentioned here, because
he has made his verse its exponent, and thus, in his
chosen quest after the knowledge of good and evil, has
placed himself apart from the other poets of his time.

The library edition of his writings, recently issued, *His writings.*
does not exhibit accurately the progress of his growth.
The poems are not arranged in the order of their
composition, but upon a system adapted to the author's taste. In their perusal this is not the only
feature to remind us of Wordsworth, whose arbitrary
classification of his works is familiar to all. Both the
early and the later writings of Buchanan show that
much of his tutelage came from a youthful study of
the bard of Rydal Mount, and he thus took a bent
in a direction quite separate from that of the modern
art-school. What he gained in freedom he lost in
reserve, acquiring Wordsworth's gravest fault, — the *Influence of Wordsworth and the Lake school.*
habit of versifying every thought that comes to mind.
A useful mission of the art-school has been to correct
this tendency. Like Wordsworth, also, Buchanan is
a natural sonneteer and idyllist, and he resembles the
whole Lake school in the Orphic utterance of his
opinions upon half the questions that fill the air.
Hence some notable mistakes and beliefs, subject
to revision ; hence, also, ill-conceived and spasmodic
work, like the " Napoleon Fallen " and " The Drama
of Kings," of which I believe that only a select
portion has been retained in a new edition of this
author's works.

Thus Robert Buchanan is one of the least restrained *An isolated position.*
and most unequal of the younger poets ; yet he is to
be placed by himself on the ground of his decided

purpose and originality. What he lacks is the faculty
of restraint. Stimulated, it may be, by his quick success, he has printed a great quantity of verse since
the day, fourteen years ago, when David Gray and
himself first started for London. That portion which
is most carefully finished is, also, the freshest and
most original; showing either that in his case the
labor limæ is not thrown away, or else that, if the
ruggedness of certain pieces is its result, he should
have left them as they came from his brain. Of
course his early efforts were experiments in verse

"Under-tones," 1860.
rather than new and sweet pipings of his own. *Under-tones* consisted chiefly of classical studies, — a kind of
work, I should say, apart from his natural turn, and
in which he was not very successful. We do not
find the true classical spirit in " Pan," nor in " The
Last Song of Apollo," good as both these pieces are
in a certain way. " Polypheme's Passion," imitated
from Euripides and Theocritus, is nearer the mark.
The strength, precision, and beauty of the antique
are what evade him. After Keats, Landor, Tennyson,
and Arnold, his classicism is no real addition to work
of this kind in English poetry.

"Idyls and Legends of Inverburn," 1865.
Five years later his Scottish idyls and legends
showed the touch and feeling of the real poet.
They introduced us to scenes and language before
almost unstudied, and were affecting, truthful, and
picturesque. His songs of Lowland superstition are
light with fancy, and sometimes musical as the chim-
ing of glass bells. The Inverburn tales, in rhymed-
heroic and blank verse, were rightly named idyls.
They are exquisite pictures of humble life, more full
of dialogue and incident than Wordsworth's, broader
in treatment than Tennyson's ; in short, composed in

their author's own style, and transcripts of the manners and landscape which he best knew. Few poems have more fairly deserved their welcome than "Willie Baird," "Poet Andrew," "John" ("The English Huswife's Gossip"), and "The Widow Mysie." Buchanan justly may be pronounced the most faithful poet of Nature among the new men. He is her familiar, and in this respect it would seem as if the mantle of Wordsworth had fallen to him from some fine sunset or misty height. He *knows* the country with that knowledge which is gained only in youth. Like an American poet, and like no British poet save himself, he knows the hills and valleys, the woods and rippling trout-streams. An artist is apt to underrate his special gift. Buchanan is said to place more value upon his town-poems; yet they do not affect us as these rural studies do, and the persons he best describes are those found in bucolic life. His four "Pastoral Pictures" rank with the pastorals of Bryant and Wordsworth in being so imaginative as to have the charm of more dramatic poems. "A Summer Pool" and "Up the River" are full of excellence. The following lines, taken almost at random, show what poetic beauty can be reached in purely descriptive verse: —

Fidelity to Nature.

Pastoral verse.

> "The air is hotter here. The bee booms by
>   With honey-laden thigh,
> Doubling the heat with sounds akin to heat;
>   And like a floating flower the butterfly
> Swims upward, downward, till its feet
> Cling to the hedge-rows white and sweet.
>
>   .   .   .   .   .
>
> The sunlight fades on mossy rocks,
> And on the mountain-sides the flocks
>   Are spilt, like streams; — the highway dips
> Down, narrowing to the path where lambs

Lay to the udders of their dams
　　Their soft and pulpy lips.
The hills grow closer; to the right
The path sweeps round a shadowy bay,
Upon whose slated fringes white
　　And crested wavelets play.
All else is still.　But list, O list!
Hidden by bowlders and by mist,
A shepherd whistles in his fist;
From height to height the far sheep bleat
In answering iteration sweet.
Sound, seeking Silence, bends above her,
Within some haunted mountain grot;
Kisses her, like a trembling lover,—
So that she stirs in sleep, but wakens not!"

As a writer of Scottish idyls, Buchanan was strictly within his limitations, and secure from rivalry.　There is no dispute concerning a specialist, but a host will rebuke the claims of one who aims at universal success, and would fain, like the hard-handed man of Athens, play all parts at once.　The young poet, however, having so well availed himself of these home-scenes, certainly had warrant for attempting other labors than those of a mere *genre* painter in verse. He took from the city various subjects for his maturer work, treating these and his North-coast pictures in a more realistic fashion, discarding adornment, and letting his art teach its lesson by fidelity to actual life.　A series of the lighter city-poems, suggested by early experiences in town, and entitled "London Lyrics" in the edition of 1874, is not in any way remarkable.　The lines "To the Luggie" are a more poetical tribute to his comrade, Gray, than is the lyric "To David in Heaven."　For poems of a later date he made studies from the poor of London and it required some courage to set before his comfortable readers

"London Poems," 1866.

the wretchedness of the lowest classes, — to introduce their woful phantoms at the poetic feast. "Nell" and "Liz" have the unquestionable power of truth; they are faithfully, even painfully, realistic. The metre is purposely irregular, that nothing may cramp the language or blur the scene. "Nell" — the plaint of a creature whose husband has just been hanged for murder, and who, over the corpse of her still-born babe, tells the story of her misery and devotion — is stronger than its companion-piece; but each is the striking expression of a woman's anguish put in rugged and impressive verse. "Meg Blane," among the North-coast pieces, is Buchanan's longest example of a similar method applied to a rural theme. I do him no wrong by not quoting from any one of these productions, whose force lies in their general effect, and which are composed in a manner directly opposite to that of the elaborate modern school.

As a presentment of something new and strong, these are remarkable poems. Nevertheless, and granting that propagandism is a legitimate mission of art, does not that poetry teach the most effectually which is the most attractive to a poet's audience? Have the great evangelists kept their hearers in an exalted state of anguish without frequent intermissions of relief? Hogarth, in his realistic pictures of low life, followed nature, and made their wretchedness endurable by seizing upon every humorous or grotesque point that could be made. "Nell," "Liz," and "Meg Blane" harrow us from first to last; there is no remission, — the poet is inexorable; the pain is continuous; we are willing to accept these lessons, but would be spared from others of the same cast.

Better as a poem, more tempting in its graphic

Their merits and defects.

A beautiful idyl.

pictures of coast-life and brave sailorly forms, more pathetic as a narrative, and told in verse at once sturdier and more sweet, is that dramatic and beautiful idyl, "The Scairth o' Bartle," in which we find a union of naturalism and realism at their best. The lesson is just as impressive as that of "Meg Blane," and the verse—how tender and strong! I think that other poets, of the rhetorical sort, might have written the one, while Buchanan alone could have so rendered the Scottish-sailor dialect of the other, and have given to its changeful scenery and detail those fine effects which warrant us in placing "The Scairth o' Bartle" at the high-water mark of the author's North-coast poems.

Among other realistic studies, "Edward Crowhurst" and "Jane Lawson" will repay attention. That this *Humor.* poet has humor of the Tam-o'-Shanter kind is shown in the racy sketch of Widow Mysie, and by the English and Scottish Eclogues. He also has done good work after Browning's lighter manner, of which "De Berny" (a life-like study of a French refugee in London) and "Kitty Kemble" may be taken as examples. The latter, by its flowing satire, reminds us of Swift, but is mellowed with the kindness and charity which redeem from cynicism the wit of a true poet. The ease and grace of these two poems are very noticeable.

It is in another direction that Buchanan has made his decided revolt against the modes and canons of *" The Book of Orm,"* 1870. the period. *The Book of Orm* invites us to a spiritual region, where fact and materialism cannot hamper his imaginings. To many it will seem that, in taking metaphysics with him, he but exchanges one set of hindrances for another. It is a natural outcome

of his Scottish genius that he should find himself
discussing the nature of evil, and applying mysticism
to the old theological problems. The "Book" itself
is hard to describe, being a study of the meaning of
good and evil, as observed through a kind of Celtic
haze ; and even the author, to explain his own purpose, resorts to the language of a friendly critic, who
pronounces it "a striking attempt to combine a quasi-
Ossianic treatment of nature with a philosophy of *Transcen-*
rebellion rising into something like a Pantheistic *dental and*
lacking sim-
vision of the necessity of evil." The poet himself *plicity ;*
adds that to him its whole scope is "to vindicate the
ways of God to Man [*sic*]." He thus brings the
great instance of Milton to sustain his propagandism,
but while poetry, written with such intent, may be
sensuous, and often is passionate, it never can be
entirely simple. The world has well agreed that
what is fine in "Paradise Lost" is the poetry ; what
is tiresome, the theology ; yet the latter certainly furnished the motive of England's greatest epic. In
adopting a theme which, after all, is didactics under
a spiritual glamour, Buchanan has chosen a distinctive ground. The question is, What sort of art is the
result ? Inevitably a strange mixture of poetry and
prose, — the relative proportions varying with the flow
of the poet's imagination. "The Book of Orm" is
largely made up of vague aspiration, rhetoric, padded
and unsatisfactory verse. It contains, withal, very *but fine here*
fine poetry, of which one or two specimens are as *and there.*
good as anything the author has composed. A portion of the work has a trace of the weird quality to
be found in nearly all of Blake's pictures, and in most
of his verse. The "Soul and Flesh," the "Flower of
the World," and the "Drinkers of Hemlock" are thus

characterized.   Two episodes are prominent among
the rest.   "The Dream of the World without Death"
is a strong and effective poem : a vision of the time
when

> "There were no kisses on familiar faces,
>   No weaving of white grave-clothes, no lost pondering
>   Over the still wax cheeks and folded fingers.

> "There was no putting tokens under pillows,
>   There was no dreadful beauty slowly fading,
>   Fading like moonlight softly into darkness.

> "There were no churchyard paths to walk on, thinking
>   How near the well-beloved ones are lying.
>   There were no sweet green graves to sit and muse on,

> "Till grief should grow a summer meditation,
>   The shadow of the passing of an angel,
>   And sleeping should seem easy, and not cruel.

> "Nothing but wondrous parting and a blankness."

Of a still higher order is " The Vision of the Man
Accurst," which is marked by fine imagination, though
conceits and artificial phrases somewhat lessen its
effect.   It seems to me the poet's strongest production thus far, and holds among his mystical pieces
the position of " The Scairth o' Bartle " among the
Scottish tales.

"Napoleon Fallen." and the "Drama of Kings," 1871.   In applying the Orphic method to contemporary
politics he makes a failure akin to that of Shelley
in " The Revolt of Islam."   Having perceived the
weakness of his poems upon the Franco-German war,
he gives them to us under new titles, and largely
pruned or otherwise remodelled.   Much of the political verse is written in a mouthing manner, inferior
to his narrative style.   The aspiration of Shelley's

writings doubtless went far to sustain the melody that renders them so exquisite. Whatever Buchanan's mission may be, it detracts from, rather than enhances, his genius as a poet. In reformatory lyrics and sonnets he does not rise so very far above the level of Massey and other spasmodic rhymesters. An American, living in a country where every mechanic is the peer of Buchanan as a reformer, and where poetry is considerably scarcer than "progress," is likely to care not so much for a singer's theories as for the quality of his song.

Buchanan's versatility, and desire to obtain a hearing in every province of his art, have impelled him to some curious ventures, among which are two romantic volumes upon American themes, published anonymously, but now acknowledged as his own. *St. Abe* and *White Rose and Red* have been commended for fidelity of local color and diction, but readers to the manner born will assure the author that he has succeeded only in being faithful to a British ideal of American frontier life. To compensate us, we have some thin poetry in his Maine romance, while in the Salt Lake extravaganza I can find none at all. His critical prose-writings are marked by eloquence and vigor, but those of a polemical order have, I should opine, entailed upon him more vexation than profit. He is said to figure creditably as a playwright, "The Witch-Finder" and "The Madcap Prince" having met with success upon the London stage.

As a result of his impulse to handle every theme that occurs to him, and to essay all varieties of style, much of his poetry, even after the winnowing to which it has been subjected, is not free from sterile and prosaic chaff. A lesser fault is the custom of

"St. Abe," 1871.

"White Rose and Red," 1873.

Prose writings.

Stage-plays

Faults of judgment and style.

handicapping his pieces with affected preludes, and his volumes with metrical statements of their purpose, — barbarisms taken from a period when people did not clearly see that Art must stand without crutches. Occasionally a theme which he selects, such as the description from Heine's " Reisebilder" of the vanishing of the old gods, is more of a poem than any verses that can be set to it. Nor do we care for such an excess of self-annunciation as is found in the prelude to " Bexhill." Faults of style are less common, yet he does not wholly escape the affectations of a school with which he is in open conflict. Still, he can be artistic to a degree not exceeded in *An impressive ballad.* the most careful poetry of his time. " The Ballad of Judas Iscariot," which he has done well to place at the opening of his collection, is equal in finish to anything written since " The Rime of the Ancient Mariner," and approaches that poem in weird impressiveness and power. Among his sonnets, those of the Coruisken series, sustained by lofty feeling and noble diction, are without doubt the best.

The past and future. In conclusion, it would appear that his work of the last five years is not an advance upon his Scottish idyls, and that a natural and charming poet has been retarded by conceiving an undue sense of his inspiration as a seer, a mystic, a prophet of the future. Moreover, like Southey, Buchanan has somewhat too carefully nursed his reputation. The sibyls confided their leaves to the winds, and knew that nothing which the gods thought worth preserving could be effaced by the wanton storm. His merits lie in his originality, earnestness, and admirable understanding of nature, in freedom of style and strength of general effect. His best poetry grows upon the reader.

He still is young, scarcely having begun the mature creative period, and, if he will study the graces of restraint, and cling to some department of art in which he is easily foremost, should not fail of a new and still more successful career.

III.

ROSSETTI is one of those men whose significant position is not so much due to the amount of work which they produce as to its quality, and to the principles it has suggested. Such leaders often are found, and influence contemporary thought by the personal magnetism that attracts young and eager spirits to gather around them. Sometimes a man of this kind, in respect to creative labor, is greater than his productions. But if Rossetti's special attitude has been of more account than his poetry, it is not because he lacks the power to equalize the two. He has chosen to give his energies to a kindred art of expression, for which his genius is no less decided. Yet his influence as a poet, judging from his writings, and from even a meagre knowledge of his life and associates, seems to be radical and more or less enduring.

A stream broadens as it flows. Already, in the careers of Morris and Swinburne, we see the forms of extension through which the indestructibility of nature is secured for a specific mode of art. The instinct is not so far wrong which connects these poets with Rossetti, and calls the circle by his name. Three men could not be more independent of one another in their essential gifts; yet there is some common chain between them to which the clew most

Dante Gabriel Rossetti: born in London, May 12, 1828.

His distinctive force and attitude.

Comrades in art.

likely was obtained first by Rossetti, — he being the eldest, and the first to seize it in his search after beauty's underlying laws. It is true that Morris, a comrade near his own age, dedicated a book of poetry to him long before the artist had compiled a volume of his own poems ; nevertheless, we gather the idea that the conversation and presence of Rossetti had a formative influence upon the author of "The Earthly Paradise," as well as upon that younger singer whose dramatic genius already has half determined what is to be the poetic tendency of the era now beginning. We turn to the young for confirmation of our views with regard to the immediate outlook ; for it is the privilege of youth to discern the freshest and most potential style. A prophetic sensitiveness, wiser than the dulled experience of age, unites it to the party of the future.

Recent poetry and the arts of design.

Since the master treatise of Lessing there has been no question of the impassable barriers betwixt the provinces of the artist and the poet. Poetry, however, furnishes themes to the painter ; and of late, painting, through study of elemental processes, has enriched the field of poetry, — to which Rossetti's contribution is the latest, if not the greatest, and has the charm of something rare that is brought to us from another land. He was an early member of the Pre-Raphaelite brotherhood in painting, Millais and Holman Hunt being his most famous associates. He also has had some connection with Morris in the decorative artwork to which the latter has been so enviably devoted. The element which Rossetti's verse and bearing have brought into English poetry holds to that art the relation of Pre-Raphaelite painting and decoration to painting and decoration of the academic

Pre-Raphaelitism: its use and abuse.

kind. As a figure-painter, his drawings, such as I have seen, are far above the strictly realistic work produced by acolytes of his order. The term realism constantly is used to cloak the mediocrity of artists whose designs are stiff, barren, and grotesque, — the form without the soul. They deal with the minor facts of art, unable to compass the major; their labor is scarcely useful as a stepping-stone to higher things; if it were not so unimaginative, it would have more value as a protest against conventionalism and a guide to something new. But Rossetti, a man of genius, has lighted his canvas and his pages with a quality that is more ennobling. He has discerned the spirit of beauty, wandering within the confines of a region whose landscape is visible, not to groundlings, but to the poet's finer sight. Even his strictly Pre-Raphaelite verse, odd and weird as it may at first appear, is full of exaltation and lyrical power.

Genius of Rossetti.

Such of his ballads as recall the Troubadour period are no more realistic than the ballads of the idyllic poets. They are studies of what the Pre-Chaucerian minstrels saw, and partly result from use of their materials. However rich and rare, they hold, in the youth of the new movement, no more advanced position than that of Tennyson's "Oriana" and "The Lady of Shalott" compared with his epic and philosophic masterpieces. This point is worth consideration. The Laureate's work of this kind was an effort, in default of natural themes, to borrow something from that old Romantic art which so long has passed away as again to have the effect of newness.

See page 176.

Much of Rossetti's verse is of this sort, yet possessing a quality which shows that his genius, if fully exercised, might lead him to far greater achievements as an English poet. Consecrated, from his Italian parentage, to learning, art, and song, — reared in a household over which the mediæval spirit has brooded, — he is thoroughly at home among romantic themes and processes, while a feeling like that of Dante exalts the maturer portion of his emblematic verse.

Transla-
tions from
"The Early
Italian
Poets."

In fact, he made his first appearance as a writer with a volume of translations, — *The Early Italian Poets*, published in 1861. In the new edition (1874), entitled "Dante and his Circle, with the Italian Poets preceding him," more stress is laid upon the arrangement of the book. Dante, through the "Vita Nuova" and many lyrics associated with his friends, is made the luminous central figure of a group of poets who shine partly by their own and partly by reflected light. Sonnets, lyrics, and canzonets are given also from more than forty additional writers, chiefly of an earlier date, and the whole volume is edited with patient learning and religious care. The time and poetry are elucidated with a fidelity and beauty not to be found in any English or Continental essays in the same field. An exquisite spirit possesses the workman and the work. An Anglo-Italian, he has a double nature, like that of the enchanter who understood the speech of birds. Whatever original work he might have produced with the same labor, it hardly could be a greater addition to our literature than this admirable transcript of Italy's most suggestive period and song.

"Poems,"
1870.

Rossetti's own poems are collected in a single volume. Twoscore ballads, songs, and studies, with thrice that number of sonnets, make up its contents; but there are not a few to maintain that here we have "infinite riches in a little room." A reviewer

is grateful to one who waits for songs that sing themselves, and does not force us to examine long cantos
for a satisfactory estimate of his power. Some of
these poems were composed years ago, but the author
does not specify them, " as nothing has been included
which he believes to be immature." Conscientiousness is a feature of this artist's work. A poet is not
to be measured by the quantity of his outpourings ; if
otherwise, what of Keats or Collins, and what of
Southey and Young ?

In this collection, then, I find no verse so realistic *Style and*
as to be unimaginative ; but I do find a quaint use *language.*
of old phraseology, and a revival of the early rhythmical accents. The result is a not unpleasant mannerism, of a kind that is visible in the poetry of
Morris and Swinburne, and also crops out frequently
in recent miscellaneous verse. Besides enriching, like
Tennyson, our modern English by the revival of obsolete yet effective Saxon and Norman words, Rossetti
adds to its flexibility by novel inversions and accentual endings. With regard to the diction, it should
be noted that such forms as " herseemed," though
here in keeping, would be unendurable in the verse
of an imitator. Throughout his poetry we discern a
finesse, a regard for detail, and a knowledge of color
and sound, that distinguish this master of the Neo-
Romantic school. His end is gained by simplicity
and sure precision of touch. He knows exactly what *Precision*
effect he desires, and produces it by a firm stroke of *of touch.*
color, a beam of light, a single musical tone. Herein
he surpasses his comrades, and exhibits great tact
in preferring only the best of a dozen graces which
either of them would introduce. In terseness he certainly is before them all.

16

We must accept a true poet for what he is, and be thankful. Rossetti is not the man to attract a dullard. His quaintness must seem to many as "outlandish" as the speech and garments of Christian and Faithful among the worldlings of Vanity Fair; and he is so indifferent to its outlandishness that some may deem him wanting in sense and humor. But he is too earnest, too absorbed in his own vision of things spiritual and lovely, to look at matters from the common point of view. To one willing to share his feeling, and apt to recognize the inspiration of Dürer, or William Blake, or John La Farge, the effect is not to be gainsaid. The strangeness passes away with a study of his poems. Yielding to their melody and illumination, we are bathed in the rich colors of an abbey-window and listen to the music of choristers chanting from some skyey, hidden loft.

The melody is indisputably fine, — whether from the lips of the transfigured maiden, of whom he tells us that, when

> "She spoke through the still weather,
> Her voice was like the voice the stars
> Had when they sang together";

or the witch-music of Lilith, the wife of Adam : —

> "Not a drop of her blood was human,
> But she was made like a soft, sweet woman."

It is difficult, however, to separate a single tone from the current harmony. Light and color are worthy of the music : —

> "Her eyes were deeper than the depth
> Of waters stilled at even ;
> She had three lilies in her hand,
> And the stars in her hair were seven."

> "Her hair, that lay along her back,
> Was yellow, like ripe corn."

> —"The clear-ranged unnumbered heads
> Bowed with their aureoles."

> —"She ceased.
> The light thrilled toward her, filled
> With angels in strong level flight."

Of Rossetti's lyrics in the Gothic or Romantic form, "The Blessed Damozel," from which I quote, is most widely known, and deserves its reputation. Nothing, save great originality and beauty, could win us over to its peculiar manner. It is full of imagination:—

> "Herseemed she scarce had been a day
> One of God's choristers;
> The wonder was not yet quite gone
> From that still look of hers";

> "And the souls mounting up to God
> Went by her like thin flames."

> "I'll take his hand and go with him
> To the deep wells of light,—
> We will step down as to a stream,
> And bathe there in God's sight."

The spell of this poem, I think, lies in the feeling that even in heaven the maiden, as on earth, is so real, so living, that

> "her bosom must have made
> The bar she leaned on warm";

and that her terrestrial love and yearning are more to her than all the joys of Paradise. The poet, moreover, in this brief, wild lyric, seems to have conceived, like Dante, an apotheosis of some buried

"*The Blessed Damozel.*"

Ballads.

mistress, — regarded, it may be, with worship, but no less with immortal passion and desire.

In three mediæval ballads of another class there is lyrical and dramatic power. I refer to "Troy Town," "Eden Bower," and "Sister Helen." These, with "Stratton Water" and "The Staff and Scrip," probably are as characteristic and successful as any late revival of the ballad forms.

Miscellaneous poems.

"A Last Confession" is a tragical Italian story, in blank-verse, not unlike what Browning — leaving out Rossetti's Italian song — might write upon a similar theme. "Dante at Verona" is a grave and earnest poem, sustained with dignity throughout, yet I prefer Dr. Parsons's lines "On a Bust of Dante," — that majestic lyric, the noblest of tributes to the great Florentine in our own or any other tongue. At the opposite extreme, and in a vein that differs from Rossetti's other works, we have a curious and vivid piece of realism entitled "Jenny." The poet moralizes, with equal taste and feeling, and much picturesqueness, over a beautiful but ignorant girl of the town, who no more than a child is aware of the train of thought she has inspired. A striking passage upon lust is specially effective and poetical.

Translations from the French.

I have said that as an Italian translator Rossetti is unsurpassed, and he is nearly as fine in renderings from the old French, of which both Swinburne and himself have made enthusiastic studies. Witness a stanza from "The Ballad of Dead Ladies," François Villon, 1450. The translator's inherent quaintness is suited to his task : —

> "Tell me now in what hidden way is
> Lady Flora the lovely Roman?

> Where 's Hipparchia, and where is Thais,
>   Neither of them the fairer woman?
> Where is Echo, beheld of no man,
> Only heard on river and mere, —
>   She whose beauty was more than human? . . . .
> But where are the snows of yester-year?"

His lyrical faculty is exquisite; not often swift, but *Melody.*
chaste, and purely English. "The Song of the
Bower," a most tuneful love-chant, reminding us of
George Darley, is a good specimen of his melody,
while "The Stream's Secret" has more music in it
than any *slow* lyric that I now remember. Dramatic
power is indicated by true lyrical genius, and we are
not surprised to find Rossetti's poems surcharged *Rossetti's sonnets.*
with it. As a sonneteer, also, he has no living equal.
Take the group written for pictures and read the
sonnet of "Mary Magdalene." It is a complete dramatic poem. The series belonging to "The House
of Life," in finish, spontaneity, and richness of feeling, is such as this man alone can produce. Mrs.
Browning's sonnets were the deathless revelation of
her own beautiful soul; if these are more objective,
they are equally perfect in another way. Finally, the
imagination to which I have alluded is rarely absent *Imagina-tion.*
from Rossetti's verse. His touches now are delicate,
and again have a broad sweep : —

> "As though mine image in the glass
>   Should tarry when myself am gone."

> "How then should sound upon Life's darkening slope,
> The ground-whirl of the perished leaves of Hope,
> The wind of Death's imperishable wing?"

In measuring his career as a poet, we at once per- *Aspects of his poetry and career.*
ceive that he has moved in a somewhat narrow range
with respect to both the thought and method of his

compositions ; but that he approaches Tennyson in simplicity, purity, and richness of tone.   His dramatic and lyrical powers are very marked, though not fully developed ; if he had been restricted to verse as a means of expression, he no doubt would have added greatly to our English song.   Sonnets like the " Bridal Birth " and " Nuptial Sleep," and poems so profoundly thoughtful as " The Sea-Limits " and " The Woodspurge," place him among his foremost contemporaries.   He has had a magnetic influence upon those who come within his aureole.   Should he complete " The House of Life " upon its original projection, he will leave a monument of beauty more lasting than the tradition of his presence.   His verse is compact of tenderness, emotional ecstasy, and poetic fire.   The spirit of the master whose name he *D. G. R.* bears clothes him as with a white garment.   And we *died at* should expect his associates to be humble lovers of *Birching-* the beautiful, first of all, and through its ministry to *ton-on-Sea,* rise to the lustrous upper heaven of spiritual art.
April 9,
1882.

I V.

William It is but natural, then, that we should find in *Morris :* William Morris a poet who may be described, to use *born near* the phrase of Hawthorne, as an Artist of the Beautiful. *London,* He delights in the manifestation of objective beauty. *1834.* Byron felt himself one with Nature.   Morris is absorbed in the loveliness of his romantic work, and *An artist of* as an artist seems to find enchantment and content. *the beautiful.*
In this serenity of mood he possesses that which has been denied to greater poets.   True, he sings of himself,

> "Dreamer of dreams, born out of my due time,
> Why should I strive to set the crooked straight?"

but what time could be to him more fortunate?
Amid the problems of our day, and the uncertainty
as to what kind of art is to result from its confused
elements, there is at least repose in the enjoyment of
absolute beauty. There is safety in an art without a
purpose other than to refresh and charm. People
who labor in "six counties overhung with smoke"
are willing enough to forget them. Morris's proffer
of the means to this end could not have been more
timely. Keats had juster cause for dissatisfaction:
he could not know how eagerly men would turn to
his work when the grandiloquent period, in which he
found himself so valueless, should have worn itself
away. Besides, he never fairly attained his ideal.
To him the pursuit of Beauty, rather than the possession, was a passion and an appetite. He followed
after, and depicted her, but was not at rest in her
presence. Had Keats lived, — had he lived to gain
the feeling of Morris, to pass from aspiration to attainment, and had his delicious poems been succeeded
by others, comparing with "Isabella" and "The Eve
of St. Agnes," as "The Earthly Paradise" compares
with "The Defence of Guenevere," then indeed the
world would have listened to a singer

> "Such as it had
> In the ages glad,
> Long ago!"

Morris and Keats.

Morris appears to have been devoted from youth
to the service of the beautiful. He has followed
more than one branch of art, and enjoys, besides his
fame as a poet, a practical reputation as an original

Taste, the parent of versatility in art.

and graceful designer in decorative work of many kinds. The present era, like the Venetian, and others in which taste has sprung from the luxury of wealth, seems to breed a class of handicraftsmen who are adepts in various departments of creative art. Rossetti, Morris, Linton, Scott, Woolner, Hamerton, among others, follow the arts of song or of design at will. Doubtless the poet Morris, while making his unique drawings for stained glass, wall-paper, or decorative tile-work, finds a pleasure as keen as that of the artist Morris in the construction of his metrical romances. There is balm and recreation to any writer in some tasteful pursuit which may serve as a foil to that which is the main labor and highest purpose of his life.

As for his poetry, it is of a sort which must be delightful to construct: wholly removed from self, breeding neither anguish nor disquiet, but full of soft music and a familiar olden charm. So easeful to read, it cannot be unrestful to compose, and to the maker must be its own reward. He keeps within his self-allotted region; if it be that of a lotos-eater's dream, he is willing to be deluded, and no longing for the real makes him "half sick of shadows." In this respect he is a wise, sweet, and very fortunate bard.

"The Defence of Guenevere," 1858.

Some years ago, judging of Morris by *The Defence of Guenevere, and Other Poems,* the only volume which he then had printed, I wrote of him: "Never a slovenly writer, he gives us pieces that repay close reading, but also compel it, for they smack of the closet and studio rather than of the world of men and women, or that of the woods and fields. He, too, sings the deeds of Arthur and Lancelot." Let me now say that there is no purer or fresher landscape, more clearly

visible both to the author and the reader, than is to
be found everywhere in the course of Morris's later
volumes. Not only are his descriptions of every aspect of Nature perfect, but he enters fully into the
effect produced by her changes upon our lives and
feelings. He sings of June,

> " And that desire that rippling water gives
>   To youthful hearts to wander anywhere " ;

of the drowsy August languor,

> " When men were happy, they could scarce tell why,
>   Although they felt the rich year slipping by."

A thousand similar examples may be selected from
his poems. But his first work was quite in sympathy
with that of Rossetti : an effort to disconnect poetry
from modern thought and purpose, through a return
not so much to nature as to models taken from the
age of ballad-romance. It was saturated with the
Pre-Chaucerian spirit. In mediæval tone, color, and
somewhat rigid drawing, it corresponded to the missal-
work style of the Pre-Raphaelites in art. The manner
was too studied to permit of swift movement or broad
scope ; the language somewhat ancient and obscure.
There is much that is fine, however, in the plumed
and heroic ballad, " Riding Together," and " The
Haystack in the Flood " is a powerful conception,
wrought out with historic truth of detail and grim
dramatic effect.

*Pre-Chau-
cerian bal-
lads.*

These thirty poems, fitly inscribed to Rossetti, made
up a work whose value somewhat depended upon its
promise for the future. The true Pre-Raphaelite is
willing to bury his own name in order to serve his
art ; to spend a life, if need be, in laying the ground-

16 *   x

wall upon which his successors can build a new temple that shall replace the time-worn structure he has
helped to tear away. But, to a man of genius, the
higher service often is given later in his own career.

Morris's second volume showed that he had left
the shadows of ballad minstrelsy, and entered the
pleasant sunlight of Chaucer. After seven years of
silence *The Life and Death of Jason* was a surprise,
and was welcomed as the sustained performance of
a true poet. It is a narrative poem, of epic proportions, all story and action, composed in the rhymed
pentameter, strongly and sweetly carried from the
first book to the last of seventeen. In this production, as in all the works of Morris, — in some respects
the most notable raconteur since the time of his
avowed master, Geoffrey Chaucer, — the statement is
newly illustrated, that imaginative poets do not invent
their own legends, but are wise in taking them from
those historic treasuries of fact and fiction, the out-
lines of which await only a master-hand to invest them
with living beauty. The invention of "Jason," for
instance, does not consist in the story of the Golden
Fleece, but in new effects of combination, and in the
melody and vigor of the means by which these old
adventurous Greeks again are made to voyage, sing,
love, fight, and die before us. Its author has a close
knowledge of antiquities. Here and there his method
is borrowed from Homer, — as in the gathering of the
chiefs, which occupies the third book. Octosyllabic
songs are interspersed, such as that of Orpheus,

> "O bitter sea, tumultuous sea,
> Full many an ill is wrought by thee!"

after which,

*"The Life
and Death
of Jason,"
1865.*

*Cp. "Poets
of Amer-
ica": p.
471.*

"Then shouted all the heroes, and they drove
 The good ship forth, so that the birds above,
 With long white wings, scarce flew so fast as they."

These three lines convey an idea of the general diction ; nor can any be selected from the ten thousand which compose the work that do not show how well our Saxon English is adapted for the transmission of the Homeric spirit. The poem is fresh and stirring, and the style befits the theme, though not free from harshness and careless rhymes ; moreover, it must be confessed that the reader often grows weary of the prolonged tale. This is an Odyssean epic, but written with continuity of effort; not growing of itself with the growth of a nation, nor builded at long intervals like the "Idyls of the King." The poet lacks variety. His voice is in a single key, and, although it be a natural one that does not tire the ear, we are content as we close the volume, and heave a sigh of satisfied appetite rather than of regret that the entertainment has reached an end.

In his learned taste for whatever is curious and rare Morris has made researches among the Sagas of Norse literature, especially those of Iceland. The admirable translations which he made, in company with E. Magnusson, from the Icelandic Grettis and Volsunga Sagas, show how thoroughly every class of work is fashioned by his hands, and illustrate the wealth of the resources from which he obtained the conception of his latest poem.[1] *The Story of Grettir the Strong*, and *The Story of the Volsungs and Niblungs*,

Translations from the Icelandic, 1869.

---

[1] He now is said to be engaged upon a lineal and literal translation of Virgil, — a work which he can hardly fail to execute speedily and well.

appeared in 1869; but in 1868, five years after the completion of "Jason," the public had been delighted with the early instalments of a charming production, which, whatever he may accomplish hereafter, fairly exhibits his powers in their most sustained and varied form.

"*The Earthly Paradise,*" 1868–70.

The plan of *The Earthly Paradise* was conceived in a day that should be marked with a white stone, since for this poet to undertake it was to complete it. The effort was so sure to adjust itself to his genius (which is epic rather than dramatic), that the only question was one of time, and that is now a question of the past. In this important work Morris reaches the height of his success as a relator. His poems always have been stories. Even the shortest ballads in his first book are upon themes from the old chronicles. "The Earthly Paradise" has the universe of fiction for a field, and reclothes the choicest and most famous legends of Asia and Europe with the delicate fabric of its verse. Greek and Oriental lore, the tales of the Gesta Romanorum, the romance of the Nibelungen-Lied, and even the myths of the Eddas, contribute to this thesaurus of narrative song. All these tales are familiar: many of a type from which John Fiske or Müller would prove their long descent, tracing them far as the "most eastern East"; but never before did they appear in more attractive shape, or fall so musically from a poet's honeyed mouth. Their fascination is beyond question. We listen to the narrator, as Arabs before the desert fire hang upon the lips of one who recites some legend of the good Haroun. Here is a successor to Boccaccio and to Chaucer. The verse, indeed, is exclusively Chaucerian, of which three styles are used, the heroic, sestina,

Historic myths and legends.

Cp. "*Poets of America*": *pp.* 108, 109.

and octosyllabic. Chance quotations show with what felicity and perfect ease the modern poet renews the cadences of his master. Take one from " Atalanta's Race ": —

"Through thick Arcadian woods a hunter went,
Following the beasts up, on a fresh spring day;
But since his horn-tipped bow, but seldom bent,
Now at the noontide naught had happed to slay,
Within a vale he called his hounds away,
Hearkening the echoes of his lone voice cling
About the cliffs, and through the beech-trees ring."

Another from " The Man Born to be King ": —

" So long he rode he drew anigh
A mill upon the river's brim,
That seemed a goodly place to him,
For o'er the oily, smooth millhead
There hung the apples growing red,
And many an ancient apple-tree
Within the orchard could he see,
While the smooth millwalls, white and black,
Shook to the great wheel's measured clack,
And grumble of the gear within ;
While o'er the roof that dulled that din
The doves sat crooning half the day,
And round the half-cut stack of hay
The sparrows fluttered twittering."

And this, from "The Story of Cupid and Psyche" :—

" From place to place Love followed her that day
And ever fairer to his eyes she grew,
So that at last when from her bower she flew,
And underneath his feet the moonlit sea
Went shepherding his waves disorderly,
He swore that of all gods and men, no one
Should hold her in his arms but he alone."

The couplet which I have italicized has an imaginative quality not frequent in Morris's verse, for the excellence of this poet lies rather in his clear vision and exquisite directness of speech. Examples, otherwise neither better nor worse than the foregoing, may be taken from any one of the sixteen hundred pages of his great work. I can give but the briefest statement of its method and range.

Clear expression.

In each of these metrical forms the verse is smooth and transparent, — the choice result of the author's Chaucerian studies, with what addition of beauty and suggestiveness his genius can bestow. His language is so pure that there absolutely is no resisting medium to obscure the interest of a tale. We feel that he enjoys his story as we do, yet the technical excellence, seen at once by a writer, scarcely is thought of by the lay reader, •to whom poetry is in the main addressed. Morris easily grasps the feeling of each successive literature from which his stories are derived. He is at will a pagan, a Christian, or a worshipper of Odin and Thor; and especially has caught the spirit of those generations which, scarcely emerged from classicism in the South, and bordered by heathendom on the North, peopled their unhallowed places with beings drawn from either source. Christ reigned, yet the old gods had not wholly faded out, but acted, whether fair or devilish, as subjects and allies of Satan. All this is magically conveyed in such poems as "The Ring given to Venus" and "The Lady of the Land." The former may be consulted (and any other will do almost as well) for evidence of the advantage possessed by Morris through his knowledge of mediæval costumes, armor, dances, festivals, and all the curious paraphernalia of days gone by. So well equipped a virtuoso, and so facile a rhythmist, was warranted in undertaking to write "The Earthly Paradise," broad as it is in scope, and extended to the enormous length of forty thousand lines. The result shows that he set himself a perfectly feasible task.

In this work he avoids the prolonged strain of "Jason," by making, with few exceptions, each story of a length that can be read at a sitting. His harmonic turn is shown in the arrangement of them all under the signs of the zodiac. We have one classical and one mediæval legend for each month of the year. I take it that the framework of the whole, the romance of voyagers in search of an earthly Paradise, is familiar to the reader. While Morris claims Chaucer, as Dante claimed Virgil, for his master, this only relates to the purpose and form of his poetry, for the freshness and sweetness are his own. He has gone to Chaucer, but also to nature, — to the earth whence sprang that well of English undefiled. His descriptive preludes, that serenely paint each phase of the revolving year, and the scenic touches throughout his stories, are truthful and picturesque. He uses but few and often-repeated adjectives; like the early rhapsodists, once having chosen an epithet for a certain thing, he clings to it, never introducing, for novelty's sake, another that is poorer than the best.

Morris fairly escapes from our turmoil and materialism by this flight to the refuge of amusement and simple art. A correlative moral runs through all of his poetry; one which, it must be owned, savors of pagan fatalism. The thought conveyed is that nothing should concern men but to enjoy what hollow good the gods award us, and this in the present, be-

A tinge of fatalism.

fore the days come when we shall say we have no
pleasure in them, — before death come, which closes
all. He not only chooses to be a dreamer of dreams,
and will not "strive to set the crooked straight," but
tells us, —

> "Yes, ye are made immortal on the day
>   Ye cease the dusty grains of time to weigh";

and in every poem has some passage like this: —

> "Fear little, then, I counsel you,
>   What any son of man can do;
>   Because a log of wood will last
>   While many a life of man goes past,
>   And all is over in slight space."

His hoary voyagers have toiled and wandered, as they
find, in vain: —

> "Lo,
> A long life gone, and nothing more they know,
> Why they should live to have desire and foil,
> And toil, that, overcome, brings yet more toil,
> Than that day of their vanished youth, when first
> They saw Death clear, and deemed all life accurst
> By that cold, overshadowing threat, — the End."

*"Carpe
diem."*

They have nothing left but to beguile the remnant of
their hours with story and repose, until the grave shall
be reached, in which there is neither device, nor knowledge, nor wisdom. The poet's constant injunction is
to seize the day, to strive not for greater or new
things, since all will soon be over, and who knoweth
what is beyond? In his epilogue to the entire work
he faithfully epitomizes its spirit: —

> "Death have we hated, knowing not what it meant;
>   Life have we loved, through green leaf and through sere,
>   Though still the less we knew of its intent:
>   The Earth and Heaven through countless year on year,

> Slow changing, were to us but curtains fair,
> Hung round about a little room, where play
> Weeping and laughter of man's empty day."

This tinge of fatalism has a saddening effect upon
Morris's verse, and thus far lessens its charm.   A
shadow falls across the feast.   One of his critics has
well said that " A poet, in this age of the world, who
would be immortal, must write as if he himself believed in immortality."   His personages, moreover, are
phantasmal, and really seem as if they issued from the
ivory gate.   Again, while his latest work is a marvel
of prolonged strength and industry, its length gives
it somewhat of an encyclopedic character.   The last
volume was not received so eagerly as the first.   I *Metrical
facility.*
would not quote against the author that saying of
Callimachus, " a great book is a great evil "; nevertheless we feel that he has a too facile power, — a
story once given him, — of putting it into rippling
verse as rapidly as another man can write it in prose.
Still, " The Earthly Paradise " is a library of itself,
and in yielding to its spell we experience anew the
delights which the " Arabian Nights " afforded to our
childhood.   What more tempting than to loll in such
an " orchard-close " as the poet is wont to paint for
us, and — with clover blooming everywhere, and the
robins singing about their nests — to think it a portion of that fairy-land " East of the Sun and West of
the Moon "; or to read the fay-legends of " The Watching of the Falcon " and " Ogier the Dane," or that
history of " The Lovers of Gudrun," which possibly
is the finest, as it is the most extended, of all our
author's romantic poems?   What more potent spell
to banish care and pain?   And let there be some
one near to sing: —

> " In the white-flowered hawthorn brake,
> Love, be merry for my sake ;
> Twine the blossoms in my hair,
> Kiss me where I am most fair, —
> Kiss me, love ! for who knoweth
> What thing cometh after death ? "

Sweet, but unimpassioned, measures.

We have seen that the poetry of William Morris is thoroughly sweet and wholesome, fair with the beauty of green fields and summer skies, and pervaded by a restful charm. Yet it is but the choicest fashion of romantic narrative-verse. The poet's imagination is clear, but never lofty ; he never will rouse the soul to elevated thoughts and deeds. His low, continuous music reminds us of those Moorish melodies whose delicacy and pathos come from the gentle hearts of an expiring race, and seem the murmurous echo of strains that had an epic glory in the far-away past. Readers who look for passion, faith, and high imaginings, will find his measures cloying in the end.

Relative positions of the Neo-Romantic poets.

Rossetti's work has been confined to Pre-Chaucerian minstrelsy, and to the spiritualism of the early Italian school. Morris advances to a revival of the narrative art of Chaucer. The next effort, to complete the cyclic movement, should renew the fire and lyric outburst of the dramatic poets. Let us estimate the promise of what already has been essayed in that direction ; — but to do this we must listen to the voice of the youngest and most impassioned of the group that stand with feet planted upon the outer circuit of the Victorian choir, and with faces looking eagerly toward the future.

CHAPTER XI.

LATTER–DAY SINGERS.

ALGERNON CHARLES SWINBURNE.

SOME years have passed since this poet took the critical outposts by storm, and with a single effort gained a laurel-crown, of which no public envy, nor any lesser action of his own, thenceforth could dispossess him. The time has been so crowded with his successive productions — his career, with all its strength and imprudence, has been so thoroughly that of a poet — as to heighten the interest which only a spirit of most unusual quality can excite and long maintain.

We have just observed the somewhat limited range of William Morris's vocabulary. It is composed mainly of plain Saxon words, chosen with great taste and musically put together. No barrenness, however, is perceptible, since to enrich that writer's language from learned or modern sources would disturb the tone of his pure English feeling. The nature of Swinburne's diction is precisely opposite. His faculty of expression is so brilliant as to obscure the other elements which are to be found in his verse, and constantly to lead him beyond the wisdom of art. Nevertheless, reflecting upon his genius and the chances of his future, it is difficult for any one to write with cold restraint who has an eye to see, an

Algernon Charles Swinburne: born in London, April 5, 1837.

His diction

ear to hear, and the practice which forces an artist to wonder at the lustre, the melody, the unstinted fire and movement, of his imperious song.

I.

His surprising command of rhythm.

I wish, then, to speak at some length upon the one faculty in which Swinburne excels any living English poet ; in which I doubt if his equal has existed among recent poets of any tongue, unless Shelley be excepted, or, possibly, some lyrist of the modern French school. This is his miraculous gift of rhythm, his command over the unsuspected resources of a language. That Shelley had a like power is, I think, shown in passages like the choruses of " Prometheus Unbound," but he flourished half a century ago, and did not have (as Swinburne has) Shelley for a predecessor ! A new generation, refining upon the lessons given by himself and Keats, has carried the art of rhythm to extreme variety and finish. Were Shelley to have a second career, his work, if no finer in single passages, would have, all in all, a range of musical variations such as we discover in Swinburne's. So close is the resemblance in quality of these two voices, however great the difference in development, as almost to justify a belief in metempsychosis. A master is needed to awake the spirit slumbering in any musical instrument. Before the advent of Swinburne we did not realize the full scope of English verse. In his hands it is like the violin of Paganini. The range of his fantasias, roulades, arias, new effects of measure and sound, is incomparable with anything hitherto known. The first emotion of one who studies even his immature work is that of wonder at the freedom and richness of his diction, the susurrus of his rhythm, his unconscious alliterations, the endless change of his syllabic harmonies, — resulting in the alternate softness and strength, height and fall, riotous or chastened music, of his affluent verse. How does he produce it? Who taught him all the hidden springs of melody? He was born a tamer of words: a subduer of this most stubborn, yet most copious of the literary tongues. In his poetry we discover qualities we did not know were in the language, — a softness that seemed Italian, a rugged strength we thought was German, a blithe and debonair lightness we despaired of capturing from the French. He has added a score of new stops and pedals to the instrument. He has introduced, partly from other tongues, stanzaic forms, measures and effects untried before ; and has brought out the swiftness and force of metres like the anapestic, carrying each to perfection at a single trial. Words in his hands are like the ivory balls of a juggler, and all words seem to be in his hands. His fellow-craftsmen, who alone can understand what has been done in their art, will not term this statement extravagance. Speaking only of his command over language and metre, I have a right to reaffirm, and to show by many illustrations, that he is the most sovereign of rhythmists. He compels the inflexible elements to his use. Chaucer is more limpid, Shakespeare more kingly, Milton loftier at times, Byron has an unaffected power, — but neither Shelley nor the greatest of his predecessors is so dithyrambic, and no one has been in all moods so absolute an autocrat of verse. With equal gifts, I say, none *could* have been, for Swinburne comes after and profits by the art of all. Poets often win distinction by

Unprecedented melody and freedom.

The most dithyrambic of poets.

producing work that differs from what has gone be-fore. It seems as if Swinburne, in this ripe period, resolved to excel others by a mastery of known melodies, adding a new magic to each, and going beyond the range of the farthest. His amazing tricks of rhythm are those of a gymnast outleaping his fellows. We had Keats, Shelley, and Coleridge, after Collins and Gray, and Tennyson after Keats, but now Swinburne adds such elaboration, that an art which we thought perfected seems almost tame. In the first place, he was born a prodigy, — as much so as Morphy in chess; added to this he is the product of these latter days, a phenomenon impossible before. It is safe to declare that at last a time has come when the force of expression can no further go.

I do not say that it has not gone too far. The fruit may be, and here is, too luscious; the flower is often of an odor too intoxicating to endure. Yet what execution! Poetry, the rarest poetic feeling, may be found in simpler verse. Yet again, what execution! The voice may not be equal to the grandest music, nor trained and restrained as it should be. But the voice is there, and its possessor has the finest natural organ to which this generation has listened.

Expression carried to fatiguing excess.

Right here it is plain that Swinburne, especially in his early poems, has weakened his effects by cloying us with excessive richness of epithet and sound: in later works, by too elaborate expression and redun-dancy of treatment. Still, while Browning's amplifi-cation is wont to be harsh and obscure, Swinburne, even if obscure, or when the thought is one that he has repeated again and again, always gives us unap-proachable melody and grace. It is true that his glo-ries of speech often hang upon the slightest thread of purpose. He so constantly wants to stop and sing that he gets along slowly with a plot. As we listen to his fascinating music, the meaning, like the libretto of an opera, often passes out of mind. The melody is unbroken: in this, as in other matters, Swinburne's fault is that of excess. He does not frequently admit the sweet discords, of which he is a master, nor relieve his work by simple, contrasting interludes. Until recently his voice had a narrow range; its effect resulted from changes upon a few notes. The richness of these permutations was a marvel, yet a series of them blended into mannerism. Shelley could be academic at times, and even humorous; but Swinburne's monotone, original and varied within its bounds, was thought to be the expression of a limited range of feeling, and restricted his early efforts as a dramatic lyrist.

The question first asked, with regard to either a poet or singer, is, Has he voice? and then, Has he execution? We have lastly to measure the passion, imagination, invention, to which voice and method are but ministers. From the quality of the latter, the style being the man, we often may estimate the higher faculties that control them. The principle here involved runs through all the arts of beauty and use A fine vocal gift is priceless, both for itself and for the spiritual force behind it. With this preliminary stress upon Swinburne's most conspicuous gift, let us briefly examine his record, bethinking ourselves how difficult it is to judge a poet who is obscured by his own excess of light, and whose earlier verses so cloyed the mind with richness as to deprive it of the judicial taste.

Voice and execution always essential.

II.

THERE is a resemblance, both of temperament and intellect, between Swinburne and what is known of Landor in his youth. The latter remained for a comparatively brief time at college, but the younger poet, like the elder, was a natural scholar and linguist. He profited largely by his four years at Oxford, and the five at Eton which preceded them, for his intuitive command of languages is so unusual, that a year of his study must be worth a lustrum of other men's, and he has developed this gift by frequent and exquisite usage. No other Englishman has been so able to vary his effects by modes drawn, not only from classical and Oriental literatures, but from the haunting beauty of mediæval song. I should suppose him to be as familiar with French verse, from Ronsard to Hugo, as most of us are with the poetry of our own language, — and he writes either in Greek or Latin, old and new, or in troubadour French, as if his thoughts came to him in the diction for the time assumed. No really admirable work, I think, can be produced in a foreign tongue, until this kind of lingui-naturalization has been attained.

His first volume, *The Queen Mother and Rosamond,* gave him no reputation. Possibly it was unnoticed amid the mass of new verse offered the public. We now see that it was of much significance. It showed the new author to be completely unaffected by the current idyllic mode. Not a trace of Tennyson; just a trace, on the other hand, of Browning; above all, a true dramatic manner of the poet's own, — like noth-

ing modern, but recalling the cadences, fire, and action of England's great dramatic period. There were

many faults of construction, but also very strong and
beautiful characterizations, in this youth's first essays :
a manifest living in his personages for the time ; such
fine language as this, in " Rosamond " : —

> " I see not flesh is holier than flesh,
>   Or blood than blood more choicely qualified
>   That scorn should live between them."

And this : —

> " I that have roses in my name, and make
>   All flowers glad to set their color by ;
>   I that have held a land between twin lips
>   And turned large England to a little kiss ;
>   God thinks not of me as contemptible."

" The Queen Mother " (time : the massacre of St.
Bartholomew) is a longer and more complex tragedy
than that from which the foregoing lines are taken.
Catherine de' Medici is strongly and clearly delineated,
— a cruel, relentless, yet imposing figure. The style
is caught from Shakespeare, as if the youth's pride
of intellect would let him go no lower for a model.
Study, for example, the language of Teligny, Act III.,
Scene 2 ; and that of Catherine, Act V., Scene 3,
where she avows that if God's ministers could see
what she was about to do, then

> " Surely the wind would be as a hard fire,
>   And the sea's yellow and distempered foam
>   Displease the happy heaven ; . . . .
>
>   .   .   .   .
>
>   . . . . towers and popular streets
>   Should in the middle green smother and drown,
>   And Havoc die with fulness."

In another scene the king says of Denise : —

17   Y

> " Yea, dead ?
> She is all white to the dead hair, who was
> So full of gracious rose the air took color,
> Turned to a kiss against her face."

The scene in which Catherine poisons her clown, and the whole of the closing portion of Act V., are full of strength and spirit. Scattered through the two plays are some of the curious Latin, old French, and old English lyrics which the author already was so deft at turning. The volume was inscribed to Rossetti. It reveals to a penetrative eye many traits of the genius that has since blazed out so finely, and shows the nature of Swinburne's studies and associates. The man had come who was to do what Browning had failed to do in a less propitious time, and make a successful diversion from the idyllic lead of Tennyson. The body of recent minor verse fully displays the swift and radical character of the change.

" Atalanta in Calydon," 1864.

Three years later Swinburne printed his classical tragedy, *Atalanta in Calydon.*[1] Whatever may be said of the genuineness of any reproduction of the antique, this is the best of its kind. One who undertakes such work has the knowledge that his theme is removed from popular sympathy, and must be content with a restricted audience. Swinburne took up the classical dramatic form, and really made the dry bones live, — as even Landor and Arnold had not; as no man had, before or after Shelley; that is to say, as no man has, for the " Prometheus Unbound," grand as it is, is classical only in some of its personages and in the

---

[1] During this time he also had written "Chastelard," but held it in reserve for future publication. "Atalanta" was begun on the day following the completion of the last-named poem.

mythical germ of its conception, — a sublime poem, full of absorbing beauty, but antique neither in spirit nor in form. "Atalanta" is upon the severest Greek model, that of Æschylus or Sophocles, and reads like an inspired translation. We cannot repeat the antique as it existed, though a poem may be better or worse. But consider the nearness of this success, and the very great poetry involved.

Poetry and all, this thing has for once been done as well as possible, and no future poet can safely attempt to rival it. "Atalanta" is Greek in unity and simplicity, not only in the technical unities, — utterly disregarded in "Prometheus Unbound," — but in maintenance of a single pervading thought, the impossibility of resisting the inexorable high gods. The hopeless fatalism of this tragedy was not the sentiment of the joyous and reverential Greeks, but reminds us of the Hebrews, whose God was of a stern and dreadful type. This feeling, expressed in much of Swinburne's early verse, is the outcome of a haughty and untamed intellect chafing against a law which it cannot resist. Here is an imperious mind, requiring years of discipline and achievement to bring it into that harmony with its conditions through which we arrive at strength, happiness, repose.

The best English reproduction of the antique.

The opening invocation of the Chief Huntsman, with its majestic verse and imagery, alone secures the reader's attention, and the succeeding chorus, at the height of Swinburne's lyric reach, resolves attention to enchantment : —

> "When the hounds of spring are on winter's traces,
>   The mother of months in meadow or plain
>   Fills the shadows and windy places
>   With lisp of leaves and ripple of rain ;

> And the brown bright nightingale amorous
> Is half-assuaged for Itylus,
> For the Thracian ships and the foreign faces,
> The tongueless vigil, and all the pain."

Read this divine chorus, and three others equally perfect of their kind, deepening in grandeur and impressiveness: "Before the beginning of years," "We have seen thee, O Love, thou art fair," "Who hath given man speech?"—and we have read the noblest verse of a purely lyric order that has appeared since the songs and choruses of the "Prometheus." How much more dithyrambic than the unrhymed measures of Arnold! Rhyme is free as the air, that chartered libertine, to this poet, and our language in his mouth becomes not only as strong, but as musical, as the Greek. The choric spirit is here, however inharmonious the thought that God is the "supreme evil," covering us with his "hate," or the conclusion of the whole matter:—

> "Who shall contend with his lords,
>   Or cross them or do them wrong?
> Who shall bind them as with cords?
>   Who shall tame them as with song?
> Who shall smite them as with swords?
>   For the hands of their kingdom are strong."

Finally, the conception of the drama is large, the imagination clear, elevated, of an even tone throughout. The herald's account of the hunt is finely poetic. The choric responses of the last dialogue form a resonant climax to the whole. As a work of art it still remains the poet's flawless effort, showing the most objective purpose and clarified by the necessity of restraint. It is good to know that a work of pure art could at once make its way. It appealed to a

select audience, but the verdict of the few was so
loud and instant as to gain for " Atalanta " a popular
reading,—especially in rude America, with her strange,
pathetic, misunderstood yearning for a rightful share
of the culture and beauty of the older world.

"Chastelard" appeared in the ensuing year; but
as I wish to mention this poem in some discussion of
the larger work to which it holds the relation of the
first division of a trilogy, and of Swinburne's character as a dramatist, let us pass to the miscellaneous
productions of the ten years intervening between "Atalanta" and "Bothwell."

III.

SWINBURNE'S work revived the interest felt in poetry. "*Poems and Ballads,*" 1866.
His power was so evident that the public looked to
see what else had come from his pen. This led to
the collection, under the title of *Poems and Ballads*,
of various lyrical pieces, some of which had been
contributed to the serials, while others now were
printed for the first time. Without fair consideration,
this volume was taken as a new and studied work of
the mature poet, and there was much astonishment
over its contents. Here began a notable literary discussion. If unmeasured praise had been awarded to
Swinburne for the chastity and beauty of " Atalanta,"
he now was made to feel how the critical breath could
shift to the opposite extreme and balance its early *Excitement created by this book.*
favor with reprehension of the severest kind. Here
was a series of wild and Gothic pieces, full of sensuous and turbid passion, lavishing a prodigious wealth
of music and imagery upon the most perilous themes,
and treating them in an openly defiant manner.

Sense was everywhere exalted above spirituality; and to them who did not consider the formative nature of the book and the dramatic purpose of the least restrained ballads, it seemed as if the young author was lusting after strange gods, and had plunged into adoration of Venus and Priapus; or that he had drunk of Circe's goblet, and was crowning himself with garlands ere his transformation into one of the beasts that follow in her train. Rebukes were freely uttered, — indeed, a storm of denunciation began.

"Notes on Poems and Reviews," 1866.

Friends and partisans rushed to his defence; and at last the poet spoke for himself, with no doubtful force of satire and scorn, in reply both to the reviewers and to an able but covert attack made against him by a rival singer. So fierce a literary antagonism has not been known since the contests of Byron and the Lake school. Of course it gave the book a wide reading, followed by a marked influence upon the style of fledgling poets. The lyrics were reprinted in America, with the new title of "Laus Veneris," —

A literary antagonism.

taken from the opening poem, another presentment of the Tannhäuser legend that has bewitched so many of the recent French and English minstrels. The author's reputation, hitherto confined to the admirers of "Atalanta," now extended to the masses who read from curiosity. Some were content to reprehend, or smack their lips over the questionable portions of the new book; but many, while perceiving the crudeness of the ruder strains, rejoiced in the lyrical splendor that broke out here and there, and welcomed the poet's unique additions to the metric and stanzaic forms of English verse.

That Swinburne fairly provoked censure he must himself have been aware, if he cared enough about the matter to reflect at all. I have no doubt he was astonished at its vehemence, and in truth the outcry of the moralists may have been overloud. People did not see, what now is clear enough, that these poems and ballads represented the primal stages of the poet's growth. Good or bad, they were brought together and frankly given to the public. Doubtless, were the author now to make up a library edition of his works, there are several of these pieces he would prefer to omit. Of what writer may there not as much be said, unless, like Rossetti, he has lived beyond the years of Byron before publishing at all? It chances, however, that certain lyrics which we well could spare on account of their unpleasant suggestions are among the most beautiful in language and form. Others, against which no ethical objections can lie, are weakened by the author's feeblest affectations. All young poets have sins to answer for: to Swinburne men could say, as Arthur to Guenevere, "And in the flesh thou hast sinned!" so morbid and absurd are some of the phrases in this collection. Certainly there was an offence against good taste and discretion, and, if some of the poems were open to the interpretation given them, an offence of a more serious nature, for all indecency is outlawed of art. The young poet, under a combination of influences, seems to have had a marked attack of that green-sickness which the excited and untrained imagination, mistaking its own fancies for experience, undergoes before gaining strength through the vigor of healthy passion, mature and self-contained. Still, there are those who can more easily forgive the worst of Swinburne's youthful antics than those unconscious sins of commonplace, plagiarism, turgidity, — the hun-

Censure fairly provoked, but too vehement.

The volume an outgrowth of the poet's formative period.

dred weak offences that are pardoned in the early verse of men who make their mark as poets.

After all, " Poems and Ballads " *was* a first book, though printed later than " Atalanta." The juvenile pieces which it contained, written during college life, are now announced for removal into a volume of acknowledged " Early Poems," including also the dramas of " Rosamond" and " The Queen Mother." But the original volume is of great interest, because it exhibits the germs of everything for which the author has become distinguished. Its spirit is that of unbounded freedom, of resistance to an established ideal,

— for Swinburne, with Shelley and kindred poets, has seen that finer ideals will take the place of those that are set aside. Meantime, in advance of a new revelation, he devoted himself to the expression of sensuous, even riotous beauty. Unequal as they are, these lyrics led up to work like " Atalanta," " Songs before Sunrise," and " Bothwell." They were the ferment of the heated fancy, and, though murky and unsettled, to be followed by clarity, sweetness, and strength. The fault of the book is excess. This poet, extravagant in spiritual or political revolt, in disdain, in dramatic outbursts, was no less so in his treatment of sensuous themes. He could not be otherwise, except when restrained by his artistic conscience in work modelled upon accepted forms.

Among the earlier lyrics are to be numbered, I imagine, those mediæval studies near the close of the volume which belong to the same class with much of Rossetti's and Morris's verse, yet never could be thought to come from any hand but Swinburne's own. Such are " The Masque of Queen Bersabe " (a miracle play), "A Christmas Carol," "St. Dorothy,"

and various ballads, — besides the " Laus Veneris," to
which I already have referred. In other pieces we
discover the influence which French art and literature had exerted upon the author. His acquaintance
with the round of French minstrelsy made it natural *French,*
for him to produce a kind of work that at first would
not be relished by the British taste and ear. The
richness of the foreign qualities brought into English
verse by Swinburne has made amends for a passing
phase of Gallic sensualism. What now crosses the
Channel is of a different breed from the stilted formalism of Boileau. With the rise of Hugo and the
new Romantic school came freedom, lyrical melody,
and dramatic fire. Elsewhere in this volume we note
the still more potential Hebraic influence. " Aholi- *Hebraic,*
bah " is closely imitated from Hebrew prophecy, and
" A Ballad of Burdens " is imbued with a similar
spirit, reading like the middle choruses in " Atalanta."
More classical studies, " Phædra " and " At Eleusis,"
approach the grade of Landor's " Hellenics." The
" Hymn to Proserpine " is a beautiful and noble
poem, dramatically reviving the emotion of a pagan
who chooses to die with his gods, and musical with
cadences which this poet has made distinctly his own.
" Anactoria " and " Dolores," two pieces against which *and classical*
special objection has been made, exhibit great beauty *influences.*
of treatment, and a mystical though abnormal feeling,
and are quite too fine to lose. The author holds
them to be dramatic studies, written for men and not
for babes, and connects them with " The Garden of
Proserpine " and " Hesperia," in order to illustrate
the transition from passion to satiety, and thence to
wisdom and repose. The little sonnet, " A Cameo,"
suggests the rationale of this conception, and the

17 *

latter, I may add, is practically illustrated by a review of Swinburne's own productions, from the " Poems
and Ballads " up to " Bothwell."

*Very fine
poetry.*

The value of the book consists in its fine poetry,
and especially in the structure of that poetry, so full
of lyrical revelations, of harmonies unknown before.
Take any stanza of an apostrophe to the sea, in
" The Triumph of Time " : —

> " O fair green-girdled mother of mine,
>   Sea, that art clothed with the sun and the rain,
> Thy sweet hard kisses are strong like wine,
>   Thy large embraces are keen like pain.
> Save me and hide me with all thy waves,
> Find me one grave of thy thousand graves,
> Those pure cold populous graves of thine,
>   Wrought without hand in a world without stain."

Or take any couplet from " Anactoria," that musical
and fervent poem, whose imagination and expression
are so welded together, and wherein the English
heroic verse is long sustained at a height to which
it rarely has ventured to aspire : —

> " Yea, thou shalt be forgotten like spilt wine,
> Except these kisses of my lips on thine
> Brand them with immortality ; but me —
> Men shall not see bright fire nor hear the sea,
> Nor mix their hearts with music, nor behold
> Cast forth of heaven with feet of awful gold
> And plumeless wings that make the bright air blind,
> Lightning, with thunder for a hound behind
> Hunting through fields unfurrowed and unsown, —
> But in the light and laughter, in the moan
> And music, and in grasp of lip and hand
> And shudder of water that makes felt on land
> The immeasurable tremor of all the sea,
> Memories shall mix and metaphors of me."

A certain amount of such writing is bold and fine.

The public knows, however, that it was carried by Swinburne to excess; that in erotic verse a confection of luscious and cloying epithets was presented again and again. At times there was an extravagance which would have been absent if this poet, who has abundant wit and satire, had also then had a hearty sense of humor, and which he himself must smile at now. But go further, and observe his original handling of metres, as in the "Hymn to Proserpine":— *Unwholesome and fantastic extravagance,*

"Wilt thou yet take all, Galilean? but these thou shalt not take,
  The laurel, the palms, and the pæan, the breasts of the nymphs
    in the brake";

and in "Hesperia":—

"Out of the golden remote wild west where the sea without
    shore is,
  Full of the sunset, and sad, if at all, with the fulness of joy,
As a wind sets in with the autumn that blows from the region
    of stories,
  Blows with a perfume of songs and of memories beloved from
    a boy." *for which we are compensated by novel and beautiful effects of rhythm.*

Examine, too, the remarkable group of songs, set to melodies so fresh and novel: among others, "Dedication," "The Garden of Proserpine," "Madonna Mia," "Rococo," and "Before Dawn." If these have their faults, what wrinkle can any Sybarite find in such a rose-leaf as the lyric called "A Match":—

         "If love were what the rose is,
           And I were like the leaf,
         Our lives would grow together
         In sad or singing weather,
         Blown fields or flowerful closes,
           Green pleasure or gray grief;
         If love were what the rose is,
           And I were like the leaf."

The tender and pious stanzas in memory of Landor are included among these lyrics. The collection, after we have noted its weaknesses, extravagance, lack of technical and moral restraint, still remains the most striking, the most suggestive volume of miscellaneous poems that has been offered by any poet of the younger schools. And it must be confessed that since its appearance, and after the period of growth which it represents, not a note has been uttered by its author to which the most rigid of moralists can honestly object.

"Ave atque Vale": a lofty elegiac ode.

The full bloom of his lyrical genius appears not only in the choruses of "Atalanta," but in that large-moulded ode, "Ave atque Vale," composed in memory of Charles Baudelaire. It is founded on the model of famous English prototypes, to wit, the "Epitaph of Bion." If unequal to "Lycidas" in idyllic feeling, or to "Adonais" in lofty scorn and sorrow, it is more imaginative than the former, and surpasses either in continuity of tone and the absolute melody of elaborate verse. Arnold's "Thyrsis" is a wise and manly poem, closely adjusted to the classic phrase; but here is an ethereal strain of the highest elegiac order, fashioned in a severe yet flexible spirit of lyric art. In stanzaic beauty it ranks, with Keats's odes, among our rarest examples. Critics who have sat at the feet of Wordsworth should remember that Swinburne, in youth, was powerfully affected by the poetry of the wild and gifted author of "Les Fleurs du Mal." This threnody comes as directly from the heart as those of Shelley or Arnold lamenting Keats or Clough.

Baudelaire.

Baudelaire and his group constituted what might be termed the Franco-Sapphic school. Their spirit pervades many of the "Poems and Ballads"; but Swinburne, more fortunate than his teacher, has lived to outlive this phase, and is nearing his visioned "Hesperia" of strength and luminous calm. The "Ave atque Vale" is a perfect example of the metrical affluence that renders his verse a marvel. It is found in the opening lines:—

Metrical affluence.

> "Shall I strew on thee rose, or rue, or laurel,
>   Brother, on this that was the veil of thee?"—

The second stanza, recalling the dead poet's favorite ideal, is highly characteristic:—

> "For always thee the fervid, languid glories
>   Allured of heavier suns in mightier skies;
>   Thine ears knew all the wandering watery sighs
> Where the sea sobs round Lesbian promontories,
>   The barren kiss of piteous wave to wave,
>   That knows not where is that Leucadian grave
> Which hides too deep the supreme head of song."

An imagination like that of "Hyperion" is found in other stanzas:—

> "Now all strange hours and all strange loves are over,
>   Dreams and desires and sombre songs and sweet,
>   Hast thou found place at the great knees and feet
> Of some pale Titan-woman like a lover,
>   Such as thy vision here solicited,
>   Under the shadow of her fair vast head,
> The deep division of prodigious breasts,
>   The solemn slope of mighty limbs asleep,
>   The weight of awful tresses that still keep
> The savor and shade of old-world pine-forests
>   Where the wet hill-winds weep?"—

In one sense the motive thought is below the technical grandeur of the poem. Its ideals are Sappho, Proserpine, Apollo, and the Venus of Baudelaire,— not the Cytherean, but the Gothic Venus "of the hollow hill." The round of Baudelaire's conceptions is thus pursued, after the antique fashion, with exquisite and solemn power. The tone is not one of high laudation, but of a minstrel who recalls the dead as he was, — a chant of sorrow and. appreciation, not of hope. What extravagance there may be is in the passion and poetry lavished upon the theme. It is an ode written for persons of delicate culture ; no one else can grasp the allusions, though who so dull as not to be captivated by the sound ! But the same may be said of " Adonais " or " Hylas " ; and here again recurs the question asked concerning Landor, Shall not the wise, as well as the witless, have their poets ?

Tribute to the memory of Gautier. 1872.

The "Memorial Verses on the Death of Théophile Gautier" are also beautiful. They are composed in a grave form of quatrain resembling, though with a difference, FitzGerald's version of the "Rubáiyát of Omar Khayyám." The elegy is the longest of our author's contributions to a volume in which eighty poets of France, Italy, and England united to lay upon the tomb of Gautier a wreath more profuse with laurels than any other which has been recorded in the history of elegiac song. Swinburne's portion of this remarkable tribute includes, also, an English sonnet, a son-

Swinburne's gift of tongues.

net and an ode in French, and Greek and Latin verses such as, I think, no other of the chanting multitude could have composed. A word in respect to his talent for this kind of work. Possibly Landor was a more ready Latinist, but no Englishman has written Greek elegiac to equal either the dedication of " Atalanta " or the Gautier " inscriptions " contained in this memorial volume. Having spoken of

See page 62.

the uselessness of Landor's classical exploits, I would

here add that their uselessness relates to the audience, and not to the poet. The effect of such practice upon himself and Swinburne would of itself argue for this amendment. The younger poet's own language is so modest and suggestive, that in repeating what was privately uttered I simply do him justice by stating his position better than it can otherwise be stated. "The value of modern Latin or Greek verse," he says, "depends, I think, upon the execution. Good verse, at any time, is a good thing, and a change of instrument now and then is good practice for the performer's hand. . . . . I confess that I take delight in the metrical forms of any language of which I know anything whatever, simply for the metrè's sake, as a new musical instrument ; and, as soon as I can, I am tempted to try my hand or my voice at a new mode of verse, like a child trying to sing before it can speak plain." In short, to a poet like Swinburne diversions of this kind have a practical value, even though they seem to be those of a knight tilting at a wayside tournament as he rides on his votive quest.

We have dwelt so long upon the lyrics as to have little space for examination of more recent and important works. My object has been to observe the development of the poet's genius, and thence derive an estimate of his present career. From 1867 to 1871 he gave his ardent sympathy to the cause of European freedom, exerting himself in laudation, almost in apotheosis, of the republican heroes and martyrs. Possibly his radical tendency was strengthened in youth by association with a sturdy grandsire, the late Sir John Swinburne, who was a personal friend of Mirabeau, and to the last of his ninety-

eight years an ultra-liberal of the French revolu-
tionary school. The democratic poets of this century
— men like Landor, Shelley, Hugo, Swinburne — often
are to be found among those of patrician birth and
culture. Swinburne, as if tired of art followed for its
own sake, threw his soul into the struggle of the

*"A Song of
Italy,"* 1867.

French and Italian patriots. *A Song of Italy* is
marked by sonorous eloquence, and carries us buoy-
antly along ; yet, despite its splendid apostrophes to
Mazzini and Garibaldi, it was not a poem to be
widely received and to stir the common heart. It
appeals to the lover of high poetry rather than to

*"Ode on the
French
Republic,"*
1870.

votaries of the cause. The *Ode on the French Republic*
was less worthy of the author, and not equal to its
occasion. It bears the stamp of work composed for
a special event as plainly as some of Southey's or
Wordsworth's laureate odes. We may apply to it a
portion of Swinburne's own censure of a far nobler
poem, Lowell's " Commemoration Ode," of which
many an isolated line is worth more to a great nation
than the whole French ode can ever be to them that

*"Songs be-
fore Sun-
rise,"* 1871.

love France. *Songs before Sunrise* may be taken as
the crowning effort of the author during the period
just named. It is a series of lofty and imposing odes,
exhibiting Swinburne's varied lyrical powers and his
most earnest traits of character. The conflict of day
with night before the sunrise of freedom is rehearsed
in twoscore pieces, which chant the democratic uprising of Continental Europe and the outbreak in
Crete. Grouped together, the effect is that of a strong
symphonic movement ; yet much of it is tumultuous
and ineffective. The prolonged earnestness fags the
reader, and helps a cause less than might some popular lyric or soldier's hymn. A trace of the spas-

modic manner injures much of Swinburne's revolu-
tionary verse. Yet here are powerful single poems :
"The Watch in the Night," "Hertha," the "Hymn
of Man," and "Perinde ac Cadaver." "Hertha" rates
high among the author's pieces, having so much lyric
force and music united with condensed and clarified
thought. "The Eve of Revolution" is like the sound
of a trumpet, and charged with fiery imagination, a
fit companion-piece to Coleridge's finest ode.

In Swinburne's poems we do not perceive the love *No marked*
of nature which was so passionate an element in the *passion for nature.*
spirit and writings of Shelley, that exile from the
hearts and households of his fellow-men. Were he
compelled to follow art as a means of subsistence
and to suit his work to the market, it would be more
condensed and practical, yet would, I think, lose something of its essential flavor. After all, he has been
an industrious man of letters, devoted to literature
as a matter of love and religion. The exhaustive
essays upon Blake and Chapman, his various pref- *Critical and other prose essays.*
aces and annotations, and his criticisms of Arnold,
Morris, and Hugo, among other professional labors,
are fresh in mind. The prose, like the poetry, is
unflagging and impetuous beyond that of other men.
No modern writer, save De Quincey, has sustained
himself so easily and with such cumulative force
through passages which strain the reader's mental
power. His organ of expression is so developed that
no exercise of it seems to produce brain-weariness,
and he does not realize that others are subject to that
kind of fatigue.

He rarely takes up the critical pen unless to pay
honor to a work he admires, or to confront some foe
with dangerous satire and wrath. His language is so

z

A brilliant and original, but not always judicial mind.

enthusiastic that it does not always convince ; in fact, his rhetoric and generous partisanship lessen his judicial authority. His writings often are too learned. Scholarship is a second nature with him ; he is not obscure, like Browning, but his allusions are so familiar to himself that he cannot bring them to the level of popular comprehension. Nor can he, however laudatory of the masters he affected in youth, look upon other modern poets except with the complacency felt by one who listens to a stranger's rude handling of the native tongue. His command of verse is so beyond that of any other Briton, that poets of different grades must seem to him pretty much alike, and their relative gifts scarcely worth distinguishing. By the law of attractions I should expect to see him interested in verse of the most bald and primeval form. Many excel him in humor, simplicity, range of inventive power. But contend with him in rhythm, and, though you are Thor himself, you are trying to drain the horn of which one end is open to the sea.

While recognizing his thorough honesty, I do not assent to his judgment of American poets. In *Under the Microscope* he pays a tribute to Poe, and has a just understanding of the merits and defects of Whitman. His denunciation of all the rest, as either mocking-birds in their adherence to models, or corn-crakes in the harshness and worthlessness of their original song, results, it is plain, not from prejudice, but from ignorance of the atmosphere which pervades American life. A poet must sing for his own people. Whitman, for instance, well and boldly avows himself the mouthpiece of our democratic nationality. Aside from the unconscious formalism that injures his poems, and which Swinburne has pointed out, he has

"Under the Microscope," 1872.

Thoughtless estimate of American poets.

done what he could, and we acknowledge the justice shown to one, at least, of our representative men. But to cite other examples, — and a few are enough for this digression, — if Swinburne thoroughly understood the deep religious sentiment, the patriotism, the tender aspiration, of the best American homes, he would perceive that our revered Whittier had fairly expressed these emotions ; would comprehend the national affection which discerns quality even in his faults, and originality and music in his fervent strains. And if he could feel the mighty presence of American woods and waters, he would see how simply and grandly the author of " Thanatopsis," " A Forest Hymn," and " The Night Journey of a River," had communed with nature, and acknowledge the Doric strength and purity of his imaginative verse. Our figure-school is but lately founded ; landscape-art and sentiment have had to precede it ; but, again, cannot even a foreign critic find in poems like Lowell's " The Courtin'" an idyllic truth that Theocritus might rejoice in, all that can be made of the New England dialect, and pictures full of sweetness and feeling? Of this much I am confident, and this much will serve. America is not all frontier, and her riper thought and life are reflected in her literature. Our poets may avail themselves of " the glory that was Greece " with as much justice and originality as any British minstrel. The artist claims all subjects, times, and places for his own. Bryant, Emerson, Whittier, Lowell, Longfellow, — to cite no lesser or younger names, — are esteemed by a host of their countrymen who can read between the lines ; their poems are the music of a land to which British authors now must look for the largest and ever-growing portion of their own constituency.　Each one of these poets as truly represents his country as any of their comrades who secure foreign attention by claiming a special prerogative in this office.

IV.

To return to *Chastelard*, which appeared close after " Atalanta," but in order of composition, as I have said, is known to have preceded the classical drama. The latter poem seemed flooded with moonlight, but " Chastelard " is warm-blooded and modern, charged with lurid passion and romance.　As a historical tragedy it was a direct test of the dramatic powers of the author, and it is as a dramatic poet that he must be chiefly regarded.　In this play we see the ripening of the genius that in youth produced " The Queen Mother," and to me it has far more interest than Swinburne's political lyrics.　Mary Stuart and her " four Maries " are the women of the piece ;
Chastelard, her minstrel-lover, and Darnley, the leading men ; Knox, who is to figure so grandly in another and greater work, drifts as a gloomy and portentous shadow across the scene.　The poem opens with an exquisitely light French song of the period.　A fine romantic flavor, smacking of the " dance and Provençal song," pervades the interludes of the tragedy. The interest centres in the charm wrought by Mary upon Chastelard, although he knows the cruelty of one who toys with him while her ambition suffers him to be put to death.　The dungeon-scene, in which he foregoes the Queen's pardon, is very powerful.
Swinburne may almost be said to have *discovered* Mary Stuart.　Upon his conception of her character

he lavishes his strength; she becomes the historic parallel of the Gothic Venus, loving love rather than her lover, full of passion, full of softness and beauty, full of caprice, vengeance, and deceit. She says of herself: —

> " Nay, dear, I have
> No tears in me; I never shall weep much,
> I think, in all my life; I have wept for wrath
> Sometimes, and for mere pain, but for love's pity
> I cannot weep at all. I would to God
> You loved me less; I give you all I can
> For all this love of yours, and yet I am sure
> I shall live out the sorrow of your death
> And be glad afterwards."

Yet this royal Lamia, when with a lover (and she never is without one), is so much passion's slave as to invite risks which certainly will be the death of her favorite, and possibly her own ruin. In depicting her as she moves through the historic changes of her life Swinburne has fortunately chosen a theme well suited to him. Mary Beaton, who in secret adores Chastelard, serves as a foil to the Queen, and is an equally resolute character. The execution scene is strongly managed, with thrilling dialogue between this Mary and Mary Carmichael; at the end room is made for my lord of Bothwell, next the Queen. Though alive with poetry and passion, this play, like " Atalanta," is restrained within artistic bounds. It has less mannerism than we find in most of the author's early style. The chief personages are drawn strongly and distinctly, and the language of the Scottish citizens, burgesses, courtiers, etc., is true to the matter and the time. The whole play is intensely emotional, the scenes and dialogue are vigorously conceived, and it must be owned that " Chastelard "

Choice of theme.

was a remarkable essay for a poet of Swinburne's age at the date of its production.

"*Bothwell,*"
1874.

Nevertheless, youth is the time to feel, and therefore for a poet to illustrate, the extreme abandonment of delirious but unselfish passion. The second and greater portion of the Stuart trilogy required a man to write it. Now that almost a decade of creative and somewhat tempestuous experience has strengthened, calmed, and otherwise perfected Swinburne's faculties, he completes the grand historical poem of *Bothwell;* a prodigious work in every way, — possibly the longest five-act drama ever written, and, at least, longer than any whose power and interest have not

The author in the front rank of modern dramatic poets.

given out before the close. The time has not yet come to determine its place in English literature. But I agree with them who declare that Swinburne, by this massive and heroic composition, has placed himself in the front line of our poets; that no one can be thought his superior in true dramatic power. The work not only is large, but written in a large manner. It seems deficient in contrasts, especially needing the relief which humor, song and by-play afford to a tragic plot. But it is a great historical poem, cast in a dramatic rather than epic form, for the sake of stronger analysis and dialogue. Considered as a dramatic epic, it has no parallel, and is replete with proofs of laborious study and faithful use of the rich materials afforded by the theme. Artistically speaking, this painstaking has checked the movement; even so free and ardent a genius is hampered by scholarship, on which Jonson prided himself, though imagination served Shakespeare's turn.

"Bothwell," an epic in dramatic form.

On the other hand, "Bothwell" is a genuine contribution to history. The subject has grown upon the poet. This section of the trilogy is many times the length of "Chastelard." "Things, now, that bear a weighty and a serious brow" are set before the reader. Great affairs of state hang at poise; Rizzio, Darnley, Murray, Gordon, Knox, Bothwell, and the Queen are made to live or die in our presence, and the most of them are tangled in a red and desperate coil. Mary's character has hardened; she has grown more reckless, fuller of evil passion, and now is not only a murderess by implication, but, outraged by the slaughter of Rizzio, becomes a murderess in fact. The sum of her iniquities is recounted by Knox in his preachment to the citizens of Edinburgh. That wonderful harangue seems to me the most sustained and characteristic passage in modern verse; but even this Mary Stuart, who "washed her feet" in the blood of her lovers, — even she has found her tamer in the brutal and ruthless Bothwell, who towers like a black demon throughout the play. Nevertheless, *The Queen of Scots.* amid her cruelties and crimes, we discover, from her very self-abandonment to the first really strong man she has met, that her falseness has been the reaction of a fine nature warped and degraded by the feeble creatures hitherto imposed upon her. Such love as she had for the beautiful was given to her poet and her musician, to Chastelard and Rizzio; but only the virile and heroic can fully satisfy her own nature and master it for good or evil. Under certain auspices, from her youth up, she might have been a paragon of love, sovereignty, and womanhood.

Among the various notable passages in this drama *Notable passages and scenes.* are: the death of Rizzio, the scenes before and after the murder of Darnley, the interviews between Bothwell and Mary in Hermitage Castle and elsewhere,

the populace harangued by Knox ; finally, the closing speech of the Queen to Mary Beaton, whose
sinister avowal,

> "But I will never leave you till you die!"

connects the entire plot with that ominous future,
whose story, ever deepening in gloom, has yet to
make the trilogy complete. "Bothwell" exhibits no
excess but that of length, and no mannerism; on the
contrary, a superb manner, and a ripe, pure, and majestic style. To show the strength, richness, and
dramatic variety of Swinburne's mature language, let
us take a few extracts from the dialogue of this
historical play, with its threescore personages and as
many shifting scenes. The first portrays the soldier,

Bothwell. Bothwell : —

> "*Queen.* Does your wound pain you?
> *Bothwell.*   What, I have a wound?
> *Queen.* How should one love enough, though she gave all,
> Who had your like to love? I pray you tell me,
> How did you fight?
> *Bothwell.*   Why, what were this to tell?
> I caught this riever, by some chance of God,
> That put his death into mine hand, alone,
> And charged him; foot to foot we fought some space,
> And he fought well; a gallant knave, God wot,
> And worth a sword for better soldier's work
> Than these thieves' brawls; I would have given him life
> To ride among mine own men here and serve,
> But he would nought; so being sore hurt i' the thigh,
> I pushed upon him suddenly, and clove
> His crown through to the chin."

Mary.
   The second is from the lips of Mary, shut up in
Lochleven Castle : —

> "*Queen.* Ay, we were fools, we Maries twain, and thought
> To be into the summer back again

And see the broom blow in the golden world,
The gentle broom on hill. For all men's talk
And all things come and gone yet, yet I find
I am not tired of that I see not here,
The sun, and the large air, and the sweet earth,
And the hours that hum like fire-flies on the hills
As they burn out and die, and the bowed heaven,
And the small clouds that swim and swoon i' the sun,
And the small flowers."

Lastly, a few powerful lines from Knox's terrific *John Knox.*
indictment of the Queen : —

"*John Knox.* . . . . Then shall one say,
Seeing these men also smitten, as ye now
Seeing them that bled before to do her good,
God is not mocked; and ye shall surely know
What men were these and what man he that spake
The things I speak now prophesying, and said
That if ye spare to shed her blood for shame,
For fear or pity of her great name or face,
God shall require of you the innocent blood
Shed for her fair face' sake, and from your hands
Wring the price forth of her blood-guiltiness."

. . . . "Her reign and end
Shall be like Athaliah's, as her birth
Was from the womb of Jezebel, that slew
The prophets, and made foul with blood and fire
The same land's face that now her seed makes foul
With whoredoms and with witchcrafts; yet they say
Peace, where is no peace, while the adulterous blood
Feeds yet with life and sin the murderous heart
That hath brought forth a wonder to the world
And to all time a terror; and this blood
The hands are clean that shed, and they that spare
In God's just sight spotted as foul as Cain's."

The exceptions taken against poems of Swinburne's
youth will not hold in respect to this fine production.
The most serious charge that can be brought is that

18

Length of this poem.

of its undue length, and as to this the judgments of different readers will be as various as their temperaments. " Bothwell " is a work for vigorous minds, and to such it must always seem the bloom of beauty and power. I think it would be fortunate if some new outlet of expression could be made for the dramatic spirit of our time. Men like Browning and Swinburne do not readily become playwrights; the stage now requires of a drama that it shall be written in sparkling prose or the lightest of verse, and, of the author, cleverness and ingenuity rather than poetic greatness. It would not injure this writer to shape

Restraint an element of perfect art.

his work for a direct hearing, to be restricted by the limits of an arbitrary system ; but might have upon these historical tragedies a gracious effect like that which resulted from the antique method applied to his " Atalanta." Ritualism, the bane of less prolific natures, is what such a man need not fear. Ease of circumstances has not made an amateur of this artist and enthusiast ; nevertheless, in his case, the benefits of professional independence are nearly balanced by the ills.

V.

See page 1.

TAINE brings a great cloud of examples to show that each period shapes the work and fortunes of its authors, but it is equally true that men of genius create new modes, and often determine the nature of periods yet to come. Swinburne may live to see the time and himself in correspondence. To me he seems the foremost of the younger school of British poets. The fact that a man is not yet haloed with the light that comes only when, in death or in hoary age, he recalls to us the past, need not debar him from full recognition. A critic must be quick to estimate the present. For some years, as I have observed the successive efforts of this poet, a feeling of his genius has grown upon me, derived not only from his promise, but from what he actually has done. If he were to write no more, and his past works should be collected in a single volume, — although, as in the remains of Shelley, we might find little narrative-verse, what a world of melody, and what a wealth of imaginative song! It is true that his well-known manner would pervade the book ; we should find no great variety of mood, few studies of visible objects, a meagre reflection of English life as it exists to-day. Yet a subtile observer would perceive how truly he represents his own time, and to a poet this compendium would become a lyrical hand-book, a treasured exposition of creative and beautiful design.

Amount and richness of the work already accomplished by this poet.

Acknowledging the presence of true genius, minor objections are of small account. A poet may hold himself apart, or from caprice may do things unworthy of his noblest self, but we think of him always as at his best. The gift is not so common ; let us value it while it is here. Let us also do justice to the world, — to the world that, remembering its past errors, no longer demands of great wits that they should wholly forego madness. Fifty years ago, and Swinburne, for his eccentricities and disdain, might have been an exile like Byron and Shelley, or, for his republicanism, imprisoned like Leigh Hunt. We have learned that poets gather from strange experiences what they teach in song. If rank unwholesome flowers spring from too rich a soil, in the end a single fruitful blossoming will compensate us

Genius to be measured at its best.

for the sterile *fleurs du mal* of youth.   Lastly, Swinburne has been said to lack application, but ten years of profuse and consecutive labors refute the charge. Works like his are not produced without energy and long industrious hours.   If done at a heat, the slow hidden fire has never ceased its burning.   Who shall dictate to a poet his modes and tenses, or his choice of work ?   But all this matters nothing ; the entire host of traditional follies need not abash us if, with their coming, we have a revival of the olden passion and the olden power.

Retrospective summary.

The Georgian era: 1790 - 1824.

DURING the Georgian era a romantic sentimentalism, exalted to passion in the utterance of Byron, was the dominating spirit of British verse.   The more subtile but slowly maturing influence of the Lake school, and that of the idealists Shelley and Keats, did not lay firm hold upon the immediate generation.   Their effect was not wholly apparent until the beginning of our own time.   Nevertheless, a few poets, among whom Hunt and Procter were notable, extended it over a

A transition period.

transition period, and finally saw it become a general and potent force.   The reader now has observed the technical finish, the worship of pure beauty, and the revival of classical taste, discernible, before the work of Keats, in the artistic method of Landor, — a poet who so recently ended his career.   These constituents, more fully developed by the exquisite genius of Keats, were to mark the outward features of English metri-

Victorian poets.

cal literature during the refined era whose poets have been included under this review ; whose spirit, moreover, suggested that contemplative method which rose to imagination in the high discourse of Wordsworth, and too often sinks to didacticism in the perplexed and timorous strains of his disciples.

After passion, — reflection, taste, repose ; and such have been the qualities displayed by numbers of the Victorian poets in the contemplation of beauty and knowledge, and in the production of their composite verse. At last a Neo-Romantic school, of which Browning and Rossetti have been leaders, is engaged in a nervous effort to reunite beauty and passion in rhythmical art. Swinburne, beyond the rest, having carried expression to its farthest extreme, obeys a healthful impulse, seeking to renew the true dramatic vigor and thus begin another cycle of creative song. Even Tennyson, in the mellow ripeness of his fame, perceives that the mission of the idyllist is ended, and extends to the latest movement his adherence and practical aid. Going outside his special genius and lifelong wont, he now — through sheer intellectual force, and the skill made perfect by fifty years of practice — has composed, with deliberate forethought and consummate art, a drama that does not belie the name. Without much imaginative splendor, it is at least objective and adapted to the fitness of things, and thus essentially different from Browning's essays toward a revival of the dramatic mould. On the other hand, it also differs from the work of the Elizabethan dramatists, in that it is the result of a forced effort, while the models after which it is shaped were in their day an intuitive form of expression, — the natural outgrowth of a thoroughly dramatic age. The very effort, however, is alike honorable to England's Laureate and significant of the present need. Wisdom, beauty, and passion — a blended trinity — constitute the poetic strength of every imaginative era, and memorably that of Shake-

The present situation and outlook.

Tennyson's drama: "Queen Mary," 1875.

See page 191.

The constituents of great dramatic verse.

speare's time.   So long as the true critic's faith, hope, and charity abide (and the greatest of these is charity), he will justify every well-timed, masterly effort to recall the triune spirit of Britain's noblest and most enduring song.

[END OF THE ORIGINAL TEXT.]

TWELVE YEARS LATER.

A SUPPLEMENTARY REVIEW.

1887.

W ITH respect to the poetry of Great Britain, the fancy may be indulged that this year's festivals not only celebrate the rounding of a brilliant and distinct period, but stand for a kind of Secular Games as well. It is just a century since Burns and Coleridge and Wordsworth were ` in the joy of that new dawn, when

"To be young was very heaven";

and no other land than theirs, meanwhile, has shown a more unbroken procession of imaginative poets. There was a brief nooning between the early and later rehearsals, but the music of great voices has never wholly stopped. This still is heard, though more than a decade of years ago it seemed, and rightly, as if the typical Victorian era were complete. But in the summer of the North the last hours of a day whose wings of light come near to touching its successor's, — although the winds fall and the chief workers mostly go to rest, — have a lustre of their own. The survival of influences that long since became historic is a chance coincidence with the prolongation of a fortunate reign, and due to veteran leaders whose strength has been more than equal to their day.

Limits of the typical Victorian Period.

Survival of its leaders.

Tennyson and Browning, although two generations of younger men pay homage to them, have been, with the exception of Swinburne, the most unflagging poets of the recent interval. Moreover, — and maugre the flings of wits who judge them by trifles and failures, and who neither care for nor comprehend their important work, — they have given us much that is up to the standard of their prime. In no respect have they been superannuated or piping out of date, — little as they have had to do with the jest and prettiness, the vivacious experiments, with which youth busies itself ere an hour comes for serious attention to the conduct of a new movement.

Its specific characteristics.

Yet if literary eras, like those of Elizabeth and Anne, are characterized by a special style or spirit, that for which the Victorian is already historic, on its poetic side, results from certain idyllic and reflective tendencies, with their interblendings and outgrowths. It ceased to be dominant before 1875, going off, as I pointed out, into æsthetic neo-Romanticism on the one hand, and a sub-dramatic or psychological method on the other. If life may be judged by its mature and most prolonged activities, the Victorian school will be recognized as we have recognized it. It is beyond ordinary precedent that its two chief poets are still in voice, and still preeminent. Of Browning it may be said that he has bided his time, and now is the master of an enthusiastic following. But even Tennyson has charged his later idyls with passion, and succeeded in making at least his lyrics dramatic. On the technical side, recent craftsmen take their cue from the forms, melody, color, of Swinburne and Rossetti. What differs and is strictly novel, though much in vogue, seldom aspires to the higher range in which these elder leaders have moved almost alone.

The conjectural length of a poet's life doubtless is not yet reckoned in the tables of insurance actuaries. But the longevity of modern poets really seems to have been governed by their mental cast. The romancers, and the lyrists of great sensibility or intense experience, quicken their heart-beats and often have died young. Many poets of "self-reverence, self-knowledge, self-control," whose intellect is the regulator of well-ordered lives, have lived long: such men as Emerson and Longfellow in America — as Wordsworth, Tennyson, and Browning in England. The recent drift — and they have strengthened it — has been toward the rule of intellect over passion, and the brain-power of such masters has maintained them in wonderful vitality and productiveness to an advanced age. *The poet's horoscope.*

However this may be, the most suggestive portion of the record now before us is that concerned with the last-named poets. England alone can now boast of two so equal in years and fame, yet so distinct in genius, and still producing works unsurpassed by the efforts of their juniors. Like two brave galleys they still head the fleet, and with all sails spread, though the mists of an unknown sea are straight before them. As for the Laureate, all England knows him by heart. Successive ranks of generous and cultured youths have doted on his works, so that his gradual age is watched and understood, somewhat as in a family the bodily and mental changes of its revered master are observed by the household. At times his verse, and oftener than that of his more dramatic compeer's, has sprung from sudden *Two noble kinsmen.*

outbursts of feeling, and never more so than in the
fine heat and choler of his later years. New readers may not comprehend these moods, but they are
intelligible to those who have owed him so much in
the past, and do not affect our judgment of his long
career.

I.

Tennyson.
Cp. Chaps.
V., VI.

A good deal of force has been expended by the
Laureate to disprove the claim that he would not
greatly excel as a dramatist for either the closet or
the stage. His mental and constructive gifts are
such that, if he had begun as a "writer of plays," he
doubtless would have been successful, — but never,
I believe, could have reached his present eminence.

His dra-
matic
efforts.
Cp. pp.
191, 413.

His first drama, "Queen Mary," seemed to confirm
an early prediction that he might yet produce a tolerable work of that kind, though only by a *tour de
force.* Since then, through strong will and persistency,
he has composed a succession of dramas, historical
and romantic; but neither will nor judgment, nor
the ambition to prove his mastery of the highest
and most inclusive form of literature, has enabled
him in the afternoon of life to triumph as a dramatist. The first actor of England, with matchless resources for theatrical presentation, was able more
than once to make the performance of a play by
Tennyson a notable and picturesque event, but nothing more; nor have those produced with equal care
by others become any part of the stage repertory.

Minor
Plays.

There are charmingly poetic qualities in the minor
pieces, and one of them, "The Cup," is not without
effects, — but even this will not hold the stage, —
while "The Falcon" and "The Promise of May" are

plainly amateurish. They contain lovely songs and trifles, but when a great master merges the poet in the playwright he must be judged accordingly. *Harold* and *Becket* are of a more imposing cast, and have significance as examples of what may — and of what may not — be effected by a strong artist in a department to which he is not led by compulsive instinct. Their ancestral themes are in every way worthy of an English poet. " Harold," in style and language, is much like the Idyls of the King, nor does it greatly surpass them in dramatic quality, though a work cast in the standard five-act mould. There is a strong scene where the last of the Saxon kings is forced to swear allegiance to William of Normandy. As a whole, the work is conventional, its battle-scenes reminiscent of Shakespeare and Scott, and the diction tinged with the author's old mannerisms. " Becket," seven years later, is his nearest approach to a dramatic masterpiece, and at a different time might have ranged itself in stage-literature. It is quite superior, as such, to pieces by Talfourd, Knowles, etc., that are still revived ; but this is poor praise indeed for one of Tennyson's fame, and assuredly not worth trying for. It must be admitted that years of self-abstraction, of intimacy with books and nature, are not likely to develop the gift of even a born novelist or dramatic poet. Human life is his. proper study : his task the expression of its struggle, passion, mirth and sorrow, virtue and crime, — and these must be transcribed by one that has been whirled in their eddies or who observes them very closely from the shore.

In striking contrast, Tennyson's recent lyrical poetry is the afterglow of a still radiant genius. Here

Tragedies.

" Harold," 1876.

" Becket," 1884.

Lyrical Verse.

we see undimmed the fire and beauty of his natural gift, and wisdom increased with age. What a collection, short as it is, forms the volume of *Ballads* issued in his seventy-first year! It opens with the thoroughly English story of "The First Quarrel," with its tragic culmination, —

> "And the boat went down that night, — the boat went down that night ! "

Country life is what he has observed, and he reflects it with truth of action and dialect. "The Northern Cobbler" and "The Village Wife" could be written only by the idyllist whose Yorkshire ballads delighted us in 1866. But here are greater things, two or three at his highest mark. The passion and lyrical might of "Rizpah" never have been exceeded by the author, nor, I think, by any other poet of his day. "The Revenge" and "Lucknow" are magnificent ballads. "Sir John Oldcastle" and "Columbus" are not what Browning would have made of them; but, again, "The Voyage of Maeldune" is a weird and vocal fantasy, unequally poetic, with the well-known touch in every number. Five years later another book of purely Tennysonian ballads appeared. Its title-piece, *Tiresias*, may be classed with "Lucretius" and "Tithonus," yet scarcely equals the one as a study, or the other for indefinable poetic charm. "The Wreck" and "Despair" are full of power, and there are two more of the unique dialect-pieces, "To-morrow" and "The Spinster's Sweet-'arts." A final Arthurian idyl, "Balin and Balan," is below the level of the work whose bulk it enlarges. "The Charge of the Heavy Brigade," much inferior to the Balaklavan lyric, shows that will cannot supply the heat excited by a thrilling and instant occasion.

A poem in this volume, "The Ancient Sage," consists of speculations on the Nameless, — and on the universal question which presents itself ever more strenuously as life's shadows lengthen.   In this sense, it is of kin to Browning's " Ferishtah " and " Jochannan Hakkadosh."   Still more noteworthy is the impetuous elegiac " Vastness," written in 1885, and as yet not placed in a collection.   The persiflage bestowed upon this, and afterward, in various quarters, upon the second *Locksley Hall*, proclaimed the rise of a generation not wonted to the poet's habit of speech ; more, it revealed one out of patience with its creeds, and consoling itself by avoiding resolute thought upon what confronts and challenges our mortality.   Tennyson, smitten by the death of a friend, reflects that not here alone dear faces steadily vanish, — but

" Many a planet by many a sun may roll with the dust of a vanish'd race."

In the knowledge of this, what are all our politics, turmoil, love, ambition, but "a trouble of ants in the gleam of a million million of suns"?   What is it all, forsooth, if at last we end,

" Swallowed in Vastness, lost in Silence, drown'd in the deeps of a meaningless Past "?

As was natural, the sequel to " Locksley Hall " was received with more than curiosity — with a certain philosophical interest.   I do not see that it is out of temper with that fervid chant which, forty-five years before, seized upon all young hearts and caught the ear of the world.   Here is the same protest against

" Locksley Hall Sixty Years After," 1886.

conditions : in youth, a revolt from convention and class-tyranny; in age, a protest against lawlessness and irreverence. The poet now as then resists the main grievance — but with an old man's increased petulance of speech. His after-song does not wreak itself upon the master passions of love and ambition, and hence fastens less strongly on the thoughts of the young; nor does it come with the unused rhythm, the fresh and novel cadence, that stamped the now hackneyed measure with a lyric's name. Yet, as to its art and imagery, the same effects are there, differing only in a more vigorous method, an intentional roughness, from the individual early verse. The new burthen is termed pessimistic, but for all its impatient summary of ills, it ends with a cry of faith. And so ends " Vastness " : —

The poet's youth and age.

> " Peace, let it be ! for I loved him, and love him forever : the dead are not dead but alive."

If Browning is more intelligibly an optimist, it is because he studies mankind from a scientific point of view, keeping his own temper and spirits withal. He has a more abiding and " saving faith " in the immanence of a beneficent ruling power. Both these poets have deepened and widened their outlook : the one listens to the roll of the ages, and marks the courses of the stars ; the other pierces the soul, to find the secret of a universe in the microcosm, man. Tennyson is the more impressed by that science which observes the astronomic and cosmic whole of nature, while biology and psychology are anticipated by Browning and subjected to his usufruct.

When the laureate was raised to the peerage — a station which he twice declined in middle life — he gained some attention from the satirists, and his acceptance of rank no doubt was honestly bemoaned by many sturdy radicals. It is difficult, nevertheless, to find any violation of principle or taste in the receipt by England's favorite and official poet of such an honor, bestowed at the climax of his years and fame. Republicans should bear in mind that the republic of letters is the only one to which Alfred Tennyson owed allegiance ; that he was the "first citizen" of an ancient monarchy, which honored letters by gratefully conferring upon him its high traditional award. It would be truckling for an American, loyal to his own form of government, to receive an aristocratic title from some foreign potentate. Longfellow, for example, promptly declined an order tendered him by the king of Italy. But a sense of fitness, and even patriotism, should make it easy for an Englishman, faithful to a constitutional monarchy, to accept any well-earned dignity under that system. In every country it is thought worth while for one to be the founder of his family; and in Great Britain no able man could do more for descendants, to whom he is not sure of bequeathing his talents, than by handing down a class-privilege, even though it confers no additional glory upon the original winner. Extreme British democrats, who openly or covertly wish to change the form of government, and even communists, are aware that Tennyson does not belong to their ranks. He has been, as I long since wrote, a liberal conservative : liberal in humanity and progressive thought, strictly conservative in allegiance to the national system. As for that, touch but the territory, imperil the institutions, of Great Britain, and Swinburne himself — the pupil of Landor, Maz-

Created Baron Tennyson of Aldworth, Surrey, and Farringford, Freshwater, Isle of Wight, Jan. 24, 1884.

zini, and Hugo — betrays the blood in his veins. Tennyson, a liberal of the Maurice group, has been cleverly styled by Whitman a "poet of feudalism "; he is a celebrator of the past, of sovereignty and knighthood ; he is no lost leader, "just for a ribbon " leaving some gallant cause forsworn or any song unsung. In all fairness, his acceptance of rank savors less of inconsistency than does the logic of those who rail at the world for neglect of genius, and then upbraid them both for coming to an understanding.

" This laurel greener."

As a final word about Lord Tennyson, a laureate of thirty-seven years' service, it may be said that no predecessor has filled his office with fewer lapses from the quality of a poet. Southey's patriotic rubbish was no better, and not much worse, than his verse at large. Wordsworth, during the few years of his incumbency, wrote little official verse. Tennyson has freshened the greenness of the laurel ; a vivid series of national odes and ballads is the result of his journey as its wearer. That some of his perfunctory salutations and pæans have been failures, notably the Jubilee ode of the current year, is evidence that genius does not always obey orders. The Wellington ode, " The Charge of the Light Brigade," the dedications of " In Memoriam " and the " Idyls," and such noble ballads as those of " Grenville," " The Revenge," " Lucknow " — these are his vouchers for the wreath, and, whether inspired by it or not, are henceforth a secure portion of his country's song.

II.

Browning. Cp. Chap. IX.

OLD lovers of Tennyson feel that he is best understood by those who grew up with his poems, and profited by his advance to the mature art and power of " In Memoriam " and the four chief " Idyls." Browning began and continued in quite another way. A neophyte might as well get hold of his middle-life work, and thence read backward and forward. If one prefers to gain an introduction to the author of *The Inn Album* from a sustained poem, rather than from his lyrics, nothing better could be chosen than that nervous, coherent work, the first in date of his productions during the time we are considering. I recall its effect upon one or two of my younger friends, who ascribe to it their first sense of those profound emotions which set the spirit free. Seldom is there a work more inwrought with characterization,ʼ fateful gathering, intense human passion, tragic action to which the realistic scene and manners serve as heightening foils, than this thrilling epic of men and women whose destinies are compressed within a single day. The tragedy ends with the death of two sinners, whose souls are first laid bare. No one of Browning's works is better proportioned, or less sophisticated in diction, — the latter, in truth, being never suffered to divert attention from the movement and interest of this electric novel in verse. It was quickly followed by a various little book, *Pacchiarotto*. The poet now turns upon his critics, with countering satire and a defense of his hardy methods ; but he welcomes, in title-piece and epilogue, "friends who are sound " to his Thirty-Four Port, promising " nettlebroth " galore to the feeble and maudlin. Of the shorter efforts, " A Forgiveness " displays to the full his dramatic and psychological mastery. Its verse is modeled with the strong right hand that painted " My Last Duchess," to which it is in all respects a vigorous companion-piece.

" The Inn Album," 1875.

" Pacchiarotto, and How He worked in Distemper," 1876.

A third translation from the Greek drama, the *Agamemnon* of Æschylus, is marked by fidelity to the text, gained through a free disregard of English idiom, but scarcely has the sweetness and grace of " Balaustion " and " Aristophanes' Apology."

The volume entitled *La Saisiaz: The Two Poets of Croisic,* like "The Inn Album," commends itself to lay readers, being direct and forcible, with abundant food for thought. The opening poem, in the " Locksley Hall " measure, bravely considers the problem of mortal and immortal life. Its successor reeks with humorous wisdom, irony, knowledge of the world. An ideal lyric supplements them, inscribed to the woman whose aid to the writer's song is symbolized by the cricket's note that helped out a minstrel's tune when his lyre had broken a string. But the finest and richest display of Browning's triune lyrical, narrative, and analytical vigor, which he has given us since the memorable " Dramatic Lyrics " and " Men and Women," is found in the

series of *Dramatic Idyls.* These silence critical complaint of the neglect or dilution of Browning's original genius. The most impressive of the metrical tales are " Martin Ralph," "Clive " — a marvelous evocation, and "Ned Bratts " — a Holbeinish conjecture of the effect on a dull brutish hind of Bunyan's teachings. " Pheidippides," a figure of the Athenian runner with news from Marathon, is superb, and " Doctor —— " quite unapproachable for jest and satire. The story of " Muyléykeh " and his Arab steed is already a classic. Always throughout these vivid impersonations, as in " Ivan Ivanovitch " and " Pietro of Albano," the magician's supreme intent is to reveal

> " What's under lock and key —
> Man's soul ! "

Jocoseria, made up of brief and sturdy poems, illus- *"Jocose-ria,"* 1883.
trates again the author's habit of exploration through
all literatures for his texts and themes. After the
grim, pathetic ballad of " Donald " and the grimmer
" Christina and Monaldeschi," we have in " Jochannan Hakkadosh" the vital lessons of the book.
The Rabbi and the pupils, who find his sayings hard
indeed, are no inapt types of our modern poet and
his circle. As in " Paracelsus," Browning's favorite
theorem continues to be the soul's real victory
achieved in the apparent failures of earthly life.
His latter years are given more and more to the
consideration of eternal rather than temporal questions. Under the guise of a Dervish he proffers,
in *Ferishtah's Fancies*, a sum of hopeful wisdom as *" Ferish-tah's Fan-cies,"* 1884.
to the meaning of existence, the goodness of the
Creator. The thought, like all great thought, is simple, yet put so subtle-wise as to make it well that
our latter-day Solomon has the fame that tempts a
world to study the riddling homilies of his old age.
To those who balk thereat no comfort is vouchsafed
except such as they find in " Pambo " of the preceding volume, — for he still merrily "offends with his
tongue," though clearly an interpreter of the purest
theistic spirit of our time. My brief references to
Browning's plenteous aftermath close with his *Par-* *" Parley-ings,"* etc., 1887.
leyings with Certain People of Importance in Their
Day. His intellect disports itself more than ever in
these half dozen citations of far-away personages
whom he raises from the dead at will. The work is
capricious enough, but he does not forget, in the
most rugged and obscure passages, to give us inter-

ludes that prove his voice still unimpaired. "Gerard de Lareise" is smooth and delicate enough for a fastidious ear, with rare bits of song included, and music itself receives expert attention in "Charles Avison." The prologue and epilogue of this book are not its least essential matters. All in all, however, it is not so ultimate and satisfactory as one could desire. At whatever worth he may rate the clubs of quidnuncs associated to study him, he does not disdain to make riddles for them, as in the Prelude, and to choose remote, obscure topics for their discussion — somewhat as the wizard Michael Scott, compelled to supply tasks for his familiar, succeeded at last by ordering him to make ropes out of seasand. He is right in affording them no special clews, for that which, written in verse, can be conveyed as well by a paraphrase certainly is not poetry.

Browning's use of rhyme: Most of the foregoing work, so varied and affluent, is in rhymed verse. Great respect is paid to the observance of the rhyme, even though meaning and measure halt for it. Whitman's Hebraic chant, often vibrating with rhythmical harmony, is the outcome of a belief that rhymes are hackneyed and trivial; and as Browning's rhymes are not seldom forced and artificial to a degree reached by no other master, the question is asked why he should rhyme at all, why he does not confine himself to his typical blank-verse and other free-hand measures.

— Its cause and effect. To this it might be replied that he was born a poet, with the English lyrical ear and accentual instinct; that he rhymes by nature, and exquisitely, as we see from all his simpler melodies, and that he is not the man to slight an intuitive note of expres-

sion. With all his headlong tyranny over restraints of form, an adherence to rhyme, as in the case of Swinburne, is "a brake upon his speech"; otherwise his fluency, although the result of endlessly changeful thought, would quite outleap the effective limits of art. That the brakes creak and groan is a proof they are doing their work. But what of his involved and parenthetical style? A rule concerning language is that it has power to formulate not only problems of absolute geometry, but those of imaginative thought; and clearness of style has been a grace of the first poets and thinkers. When Browning's tangled syntax is involuntary, it may denote a struggling process of thought, for the style is the man. But, in defense of such of these "hard readings" as seem voluntary and of aforethought, we call to mind the oriental feeling that truth is most oracular when couched in emblems and deep phrases. Nature arms her sweetest kernels with a prickly and resistful exterior, so that they are procured by toil which gives them worth. This poet surrounds his treasures with labyrinths and thorn-hedges that stimulate the reader's onset. The habit is defensible when the treasures are so genuine. To experts and thinkers, who do not need a lure to make them value the quest, such things are an irritation and open to the disfavor shown by many who yield to none in respect for Browning's creative power.

Yet it is plain that both the style and matter of his work, after years of self-respecting adherence to his own ways, have at last given occasion for the most royal warrant of fame and appreciation ever granted to poet or sage while still in the flesh. To be sure there never was a time when such a result

An apotheosis.

could more reasonably be expected. Our period exceeds all others, even the Alexandrian, in literary bustle and research. What organized phalanxes for the study and annotation of our classics, — of course, and as is fitting, with the Shakespeare societies at their head! How rude the capture of Shelley, the avatar of our ideality and lyrical feeling! Old and young, even the " little hordes " of Fourier's socialistic dream, divide the ethereal raiment of the poet's poet, that each may bear away some shred of its gossamer. Shelley's lifelong and reverent lovers, who yield themselves silently to the imponderable, divine beauty of his numbers, and who would as soon make an autopsy of Lycidas himself as to approach his verse with hook and scalpel, look with equal wonder at the tribes which now claim their poet as if by right of discovery and the select few who burden his music with their notes and scholia. To its transformation into a "cult" they apply the stricture of a famous preacher who was concerned at the multiplication of cheap Bibles. The evangelical bodies, he declared, by placing Holy Writ in every lobby and corridor, have dispelled the sacred awe in which it was held, and in fact have made it " as common as a pack of cards." Feeling, taste, instinct, — all are against making a text-book of Shelley's poetry, almost the last reliquary guarded, with some right of distant kinship, by those who claim a humble inheritance of song. The sudden uprising of many Browning clubs is the latest symptom of the rage for elucidation. The like of it has not been witnessed since the days of the neo-Platonists and grammarians ; nor were there a thousand printing-presses at the command of the Alexandrian scholi-

Poets and Pedants.

The Browning Societies.

asts. Not only more than one University quadrangle, but every mercantile town, from London where the poet dwells to the farthest outpost of the western continent, has its central Browning Society, from which dependants radiate like the little spiders that spin their tiny strands near the maternal web. Emerson was a seer; Browning is a virile poet and scholar; but it has been the same with the followers of both — a Browning student of the first order can do much for us, — while one of the third or fourth remove, whose degree is expressed algebraically as $B^{\frac{1}{n}}$ or $\sqrt[n]{B}$, may be and often is as prosaic a claimant to special illumination as one is apt to' meet. The "study" of Browning takes strong hold upon theorists, analysts, didacticians, who care little for poetry in itself, and who, like Chinese artists, pay more respect to the facial dimensions of his Muse than to her essential beauty and the divine light of her eyes. The master himself may well view with distrust certain phases of a movement originating with his more-favored disciples; nor is poetry that requires annotation in its own time surer, on that account, of supremacy in the future. Perhaps the best that can be said of this matter is that something out of the common is needed to direct attention to a great original genius, and to secure for a poet, after his long experience of neglect, some practical return for the fruits of his imagination.

A contrast between the objective, or classical, *Dramatic psychology.* dramatic mode and that of Browning is not derogatory to the resources of either. In the former, the author's thinking is done outside of the work; the work itself, the product of thought, stands as a creation, with the details of its moulding unexplained. The other exhibits the play of the constructor's thought. The result, as affecting the imagination, justifies the conventional aim — to make us see, as in real life, the outside of persons and events, concerning ourselves rather with actual speech and movement than with a search for hidden influences, esoteric laws. To read one of Browning's psychical analyses is like consulting a watch that has a transparent glass, instead of a cap of gold, surmounting the interior. We forget the beauty and proportions of the jeweled timepiece, even its office as a chronicler of time, and are absorbed by the intricate and dexterous, rather than artistic, display of the works within. Here is movement, here is curious and exact machinery — here is the very soul of the thing, no doubt; but a watch of the kind that marks the time as if by some will and guerdon of its own is even more suggestive and often as satisfying to its possessor. All the more, Browning represents the introspective science of the new age. Regard one of his men or women: you detect not only the striking figure, the impassioned human speech and conduct, but as if from some electric coil so intense a light is shot beyond that every organ and integument are revealed. You see the blood in its secretest channels, the convolutions and gyrations of the molecular brain, all the mechanism that obeys the impulse of the resultant personage. Attention is diverted from the entire creation to the functions of its parts. Events become of import chiefly for the currents which promote them, or which they initiate. Browning's genius has made this under-world a tributary of its domain. As a mind-reader, then, he is

the most dramatic of poets. The fact that, after
scrutinizing his personages, he translates the thoughts
of all into his own tongue, may lessen their objective value, but those wonted to the language find
nothing better suited to their taste.

His judicial acceptance of things as they are is
largely a matter of temperament, and does not imply *Tennyson and Browning.*
that he is more devout and theistic, or a sounder op-
timist, than his chief compeer. The broadening effect of experience as a man of the world also has
much to do with it. Both Tennyson and Browning
are highly intellectual. The former's instinct for art
and beauty is supreme, and mental analytics yield to
them in his work. To Browning poetic effects, of
which he has proved himself a master, often are nothing but impedimenta, to be discarded when fairly in
pursuit of psychological discovery.

A conclusion with respect to Tennyson, in my re-
view of his career from a much earlier point of time, *Their differing relations to the Period.*
was that he would be regarded long hereafter as,
"all in all, the fullest representative" of the "refined
and complex Victorian age." To this I added that
he had carried his idyllic mode "to such perfection
that its cycle seems already near an end" and "a
new generation is calling for work of a different
order, for more vital passion and dramatic force."
After many years, he still seems to me the exponent
of the typical Victorian period — that in which the
sentiment poetized in the "Idyls" and "In Memoriam" was at its height. It is equally true that
Browning was in reserve as the leader-elect of the
present succeeding time. The Queen is still on her
throne, but her reign outlasts the schools to which
her name belongs. New movements are initiated, and

Browning is their interpreter so far as poetic insight is concerned. To this we only have to add that he is an eminent example of the justice of our exception to Taine's dogma of the invariable subjection of an artist to his accidental conditions. He has proved that his genius is of the kind that creates its own environment and makes for itself a new atmosphere, whether of heaven or of earth.

III.

Swin-burne. Cp. Chap. XI.

SWINBURNE also has been a leader, particularly on the side of form and expression, and through his brilliant command of effects which novices are just as sure to copy as young musicians are to adopt the "methods" of a Chopin or a Liszt. Obvious tendencies of the new school reveal the influence of Browning, modified structurally by Swinburne's lyrical abandonment and feats of diction and rhythm.

As he reaches middle life, the volume of his productions becomes remarkable, putting to confusion those who doubted his vitality and staying-power.

"Erecth-eus," 1876.

His second classical drama, *Erectheus*, is severely antique in mould, with strong text and choruses. But it is relatively frigid, apart from common interest, and lacks something of the fire and melody of "Atalanta."

Recent lyr-ical vol-umes:

The author's compulsive lyrical faculty, however, has not ceased its exercise — the resulting odes, songs, and manifold brief poems having been collected chiefly

"Poems and Bal-lads," 2d Series, 1878.

in the second series of *Poems and Ballads* and in "Songs of the Springtides," "Studies in Song," "A Century of Roundels," and "A Midsummer Holiday." Their variety and splendor sustain the minstrel's early promise ; — any one of the collections would make a reputation. If they have been greeted with less than our old wonder and relish, it is due to the unforgetable novelty of those first impressions, and to the profusion of this poet's exhaustless outgiving. Masterpieces of their kind among the new songs and ballads are the " Ave atque Vale," of which I wrote in a former essay, and " A Forsaken Garden." The translations from Villon charm the ear with a witching sense possibly unfelt by the vagabond balladist's contemporaries. Swinburne is still at the head of British elegiac and memorial poets. Witness the twin odes in honor of Landor and Hugo, covering the entire progress of their achievements, and the second ode to Hugo, the lines to Mazzini, and other compositions in the highest mood of tributary song. A pervasive element of these books is that relating to the sea, of which their author is a familiar and votary. One of them (as also the poem " By the North Sea") is inscribed to his " best friend, Theodore Watts," the poet and critic to whom Mr. Swinburne is indebted for loyal companionship and devotion. The *Songs of the Springtides* are surcharged with endless harmony of ocean winds and surges. " Thalassius," " On the Cliffs," " The Garden of Cymodoce," full of alliterative and billowy cadence, are fashioned in a classical and nobly swelling mould. The unique poem of Sappho, " On the Cliffs," was suggested by the fancy that the nightingales still repeat fragments of her Lesbian song. *A Midsummer Holiday* takes us again by the sea and through the 'longshore lanes of England ; its refrain — " Our father Chaucer, here we praise thy name " — recalls the enduring freshness of a poet to whom still the avowal can be made that

" Studies in Song," 1880.

" Songs of the Springtides," 1880.

" A Midsummer Holiday," 1884.

> " Each year that England clothes herself with May
> She takes thy likeness on her."

" A Century of Roundels," 1883.

Elaborate and refined as all these pieces are, they exhale a purely English atmosphere. *A Century of Roundels* is the most simple and distinctive of the lyrical collections. Among the noteworthy roundels are several discoursing with Death, and those on Autumn and Winter; best of all, the clear-cut series on " A Baby's Death." In the latter, as in the cradle-songs and other notes of infancy and childhood, he is winning and tender — in all his poems on age, reverent and eulogistic. The artistic motive of his political outbursts, at various crises, is quite subordinate to their writer's impulsive views; their satire and invective possibly act as safety-valves and are of interest to curious students of the poetic temperament in its extremes.

"Tristram of Lyonesse," 1882.

Not a few consider *Tristram of Lyonesse* to be his most attractive and ideal narrative poem. The conception of the Arthurian legend is distinct from that of either Tennyson or Arnold, and the verse is rich with desire, foreboding, and pathetic beauty. The opening phrase, " The Sailing of the Swallow," is enchanting; the description of Iseult of Ireland is a wonder, and the whole coil of burning love and piteous mischance was never before so marvelously woven.

New Dramas: " *Mary Stuart,*" 1881.

Of Swinburne's recent dramas, *Mary Stuart* completes the most imposing Trilogy in modern literature, and is, while less romantic than " Chastelard " and less eloquent than " Bothwell," a fit successor to the two. Its vigor is condensed and joined with a gravity becoming the firm hand of maturer years as it depicts the culmination of this historic tragedy — the

taking-off of a picturesque, impassioned, superbly self-
ish type of royalty and womanhood. The author's
consistent ideal of Mary Stuart is formed by intuition and critical study, and is reasonably set forth in
his prose essay. The future will accept his conception as justly interpreting the secret of her career.
In the Trilogy her fate, through the agency of Mary
Beaton, is made the predestined outcome of early and
heartless misdeeds, and dramatically ends the steady
process of the work.

Marino Faliero, postdating by sixty-five years Byron's drama of that name, following the same chronicle and with the same personages, is a direct challenge to comparison. Both are fairly representative
of their authors. Neither is a stage-play: Byron's
was tested against his own judgment, and he found
no fault with the critics who thought his genius un-
dramatic. There is no talk of love in either play,
except the innocent passion which Swinburne creates
between Bertuccio and the Duchess. Both poets make
the Doge's part o'ertop all others, but Byron light-
ens Faliero's monologues with stage business, etc.,
and pays serious attention to the action of the piece.
Swinburne uses the higher poetic strain throughout ;
his language is heroic, the verse and diction are always imposing, but proportion, background, and the
question of relative values obtain too little of his attention. All know the slovenly and unstudied character of Byron's blank-verse. Swinburne adheres to
the type, equally finished and prodigal, to which he
has wonted us. In every sense he is a better workman. But the directness and simplicity of Byron's
drama are to be considered. The death-speech which
he puts in Faliero's mouth, theatrical as it is, will

"*Marino Faliero: A Tragedy*," 1885.

Contrasted with Byron's drama.

continue memorable as a fine instance of Byronic power. In the modern play the Doge's speech extends to fifteen pages (with the chanting interludes), and this directly after a trial-scene in which he has done most of the talking. Half this rhythmical eloquence would be more impressive than the whole.

Swinburne's later prose.

In spite of Swinburne's deprecation of Lord Byron, and his own more direct inheritance from Shelley, he has several of the former's traits : the scorn of dullness and commonplace, faith in his own conclusions, and the swift and bold mastery of a forcible theme. Continuing the habit of prose-writing, as is the custom of the times, he has displayed his scholarship and versatility in new critical essays. The value of some of these — such, for example, as

" Victor Hugo," 1886.

the prose dithyrambic on Hugo — lies not so much in their judicial quality as in those felicitous critical epigrams which take the reader by their sudden insight and originality. " A Note on Charlotte Bronte "

" Charlotte Bronte," 1877.

is admirable in this way, for all its tendency to extremes. The volume of *Miscellanies* contains, on

" Miscellanies," 1886.

the whole, his soundest and most varied prose-writing, much of it as well considered as one could desire, and expressing, brilliantly of course, the judgment of a poetic scholar in his dispassionate mood. It is interesting to see how easily and royally Mr. Swinburne keeps up his domination over an active class of writers. His scholarship, indisputable talent, and Napoleonic method of judgment and warfare render him a kind of autocrat whom few of his craft care to encounter openly, though specialists in matters of research and criticism occasionally venture on rebellion. Whatever ground he loses is lost in consequence of a law already pointed out, which

operates in the case of a vein too rich and produc-
tive. The torrent of his rhythm, beautiful and imaginative as it is, satiates the public — even animals
fed on too nutritious food will turn to bran and
husks for a relief. And the workings of his genius,
from its very force and individuality, are such as he
cannot be expected to vary or suspend.

IV.

DEATH has summoned with his impartial touch
young and old alike from the cycle of poets considered in our original review. None was more deplored than Rossetti, the child of astral light, founder
of a conjoint school of art and minstrelsy, — the
most unworldly and nervously exalted of modern
poets. No one has made a more definite, though
specific and limited, impression in his time. His
work was pursued for its own sake, yet the expression of as rare a personality as the fire of Italy and
training of England could develop. A collection of
his lyrics, piously made by fitting hands, and the
critical mementos by Sharp and Hall Caine, render
it needful for me to add but little more. Among
the rhymes not in former collections, the finely wrought
mediæval poem of " Rose-Mary " and the strong ballad of " The King's Tragedy " are prominent. There
are also a few characteristic minor songs and lyrics,
and at last the full series of quatorzains comprising
The House of Life, — that wondrous rosary of impassioned sonnets of life, love, and death, — so distinct
from Mrs. Browning's yet henceforth to be named
with hers as no less inspired and memorable. Another poetic soul, that of the old minstrel Horne,

Stilled Voices.

Rossetti, d. 1882.

Horne, d. 1884.

has passed away in its due season of years, and therewith a bold and various dramatic bard, typically English in his restless, independent nature. *Laura Dibalzo*, a fruit of his ripe old age, though not so equable and compact a work as " Cosmo de' Medici," is a tragedy befitting the hand of a friend of Landor

O'Shaugh-nessy, d. 1881.

and Browning. Arthur O'Shaughnessy was cut off in the midst of an active but scarcely brightening career. *Songs of a Worker*, the posthumous volume of this young member of the Neo-Romantic group, shows him in his graver and more humane moods, but contains little better than the striking translations from modern French poets with whom he was thoroughly in rapport. Appreciative tributes to his

P. B. Marston, d. 1887.

late brother-in-law are still appearing. Philip Marston's life and early death were very pathetic. There is a touching sincerity in his poems, and their finish, considering his blindness, was noteworthy from the first. He had a sensitive and vibratory but courageous nature. Nor was the life of this suffering writer, fostered always by choice and sympathetic associates, without its compensations. Depth of feeling is evident throughout *Wind-Voices*, his last vol-

Lord Houghton, etc. See Chapters VII., VIII.

ume. He wrote of it in one of his letters : " I can at least say of these poems that they have come from the heart." Among others who have joined the silent majority, and whose later works call for no fresh remarks, are Lord Houghton, George Eliot, Turner, FitzGerald, Thornbury, Calverley, and the Dorsetshire

Robert Stephen Hawker: 1803-75.

idyllist, William Barnes. Hawker, the sturdy Vicar of Morwenstow, left the record of a unique character, a few vigorous ballads, and the " Song of the West-

Menella Bute Smedley: 1825-75.

ern Men." Miss Smedley was a delicate, thoughtful poet, of the Tennysonian school, whose refined lyrics were marked by feeling and quiet beauty. A collection was recently made for the first time of Laman Blanchard's verse. He was the long-ago friend of Bulwer, Procter, and Browning, a journalist-poet and humorist of the old type, who wrote some good sonnets and miscellaneous pieces of variable worth. A book of selections, made last year by Percy Cotton, from the poetical works of the late Mortimer Collins, receives its warrant through their merit. Collins was a genuine poet within his range. " A Greek Idyll," written years ago, is second only to Dobson's " Autonoë." " The Ivory Gate " has captivating original melody, — a lyric that poets learn by heart. One remembers kindly the natural and even careless singers, such as Collins, who utter their song without pretence or affectation, having sweet voices, and because they can thus express fleeting and spontaneous moods, and in no other way.

The reproduction, after half a century and in the author's old age, of Wells's *Joseph and his Brethren*, was a new example of the fact that both gods and men conspire to preserve a work of genius. Rossetti and Morley among others took part in this ante-mortem recognition of a poet neglected by his own generation, who certainly had no ground for Cato's protest against the arbitrament of the people of a time different from that in which one has lived. His poem, heralded by Swinburne's introduction with tempered praise, — though long, diffuse, with various prosaic interludes, and curiously revealing Wells's absolute lack of the sense of humor, — is still an imposing and dramatic narration, lavish with color and notable for an old-English quality of diction and verse. Its author had drunk so impartially at the

Laman Blanchard: 1804–45.

Mortimer Collins: 1827–76.

Charles Jeremiah Wells: 1800–79.

A restored masterpiece.

springs of Marlowe, Shakespeare, and Milton, that it
wants evenness of tone.   But it was well worth reviving, and has excited enthusiasm even in this age
of research and discovery.

V.

THE new poems of several authors discussed in the
body of this work introduce few notes that suggest
much comment or a reversal of early opinion.   Professor Arnold has given us too little verse of late,

but his authority as a critic of modern tendencies
has steadily widened.   Traversing my first notice of
him, and as in the case of Browning, I think it right
to set down a few qualifications.   I feel that the regret and unrest which pervade some of his lyrical

verse, and which I thought opposed to the healthy
impulses of song, were in their own way as truly the
expression of Youth as the romanticism of Childe
Harold or Locksley Hall.   That Arnold was the representative in his poetry, as he has been a leader
through his prose, of the questioning progress of the
day — of a day whose perturbation of itself declares
a forward-looking spirit — is now more plain to me.
Like Emerson in America, he was a teacher and
stimulator of many now conspicuous in fields of mental activity.   A tribute is due, no less, to his most
ideal trait, — the subtilty with which he responds to,
and almost expresses, the inexpressible — the haunting suggestions, the yearnings, of man and nature —
the notes of starlight and shadow, the evasive mystery of what we are and " all that we behold."

The most objective of these poets, William Morris,
to whom I applied Hawthorne's phrase — the Artist

of the Beautiful, now devotes himself rather zealously
to the work of social reform, as if content no longer
to be " the idle singer of an empty day." Yet his
rapid production of verse has scarcely lagged. A
translation of the Aeneids of Virgil, in the sounding
measure of Chapman's " Iliads," while not verbally
archaic, does not fully translate — in the sense of
making modern — an epic that was thoroughly modern in its own time. Morris, with his prodigious
facility, has completed a similar version of the Iliads,
now just published. *The Story of Sigurd the Volsung*
is perhaps his chief sustained work : a timely epic
in this reign of Wagner, built up from the German
Lied and surely with imposing effect :

" There was a dwelling of Kings, ere the world was waxen old;
　Dukes were the door-wards there, and the roofs were thatched
　　with gold."

A wonderful achievement, to fashion this monumental
work, after re-creating for us the classical and mediæval tales of Southern Europe and the Sagas of the
icy North. Of women poets, Miss Rossetti still finds *Miss Rossetti.*
none beside her on the heights of spiritual vision.
The fanciful Masque of the Months, in *A Pageant
and Other Poems*, strengthens belief that her genius is
less visible through such constructions than in brief,
impassioned lyrics, — stanzas like " Passing and
Glassing," — and her sonnets, of which the series
entitled " Later Life " is a complement to that on
Love in an early volume. Of Mrs. Webster's new *Mrs. Webster*
dramas *In a Day*, a terse Greek tragedy, is the
most effective. The lyrics and pastoral romance of
Disguises are its best features. *A Book of Rhyme* adds
to the impression that, with all her uncommon gifts,
she is too versatile and facile: most of her poetry

*Miss
Ingelow.*
is good, but she has yet to write a poem or drama
of the highest class.   Jean Ingelow's *Poems of the
Old Days and the New*, a little graver than those of
her springtime, still have many skylark notes.   Her
ambitious pieces, with the exception of "The World-
Martyr," owe their chief value to the songs which
they include.   It is pleasant to find a general collec-
*Alling-
ham.*
tion of *Songs, Ballads and Stories*, by Allingham, another natural singer.   He justly says that "these little songs, found here and there," are not the product
of the goose-wing or inkstand; —

> " — they came without search, —
> Were found as by chance."

Many will long retain their liking for the modest
poet of "The Fairies" and "Lovely Mary Donnelly."
Some genuine harbor-ballads, in a conjuring legen-
*Richard
Garnett:*
1835–
dary vein, have been written by Dr. Garnett, whose
earlier work should have been noted in my original
text.   Among the Wordsworthians, Aubrey de Vere
De Vere.
is the busiest survivor.   His *Legends of the Saxon
Saints* and *Foray of Queen Meave* exhibit no change
of characteristics.   A diffuse closet-drama, *St. Thomas
of Canterbury*, written from the church point of view,
did not preclude Tennyson from entering the same
Palgrave.
field.   Palgrave's *Visions of England* transcribes many
of the Gesta Romanorum in a great variety of
forms.   "England Once More," at the close, is a
vigorous strain.   It is odd at this late day to find a
critic, who compiled the Golden Treasury, burdening
his own poetry with notes, and in a long, collegiate
preface defending very simple forms of English
Hake.
metre.   Dr. Hake's *Legends of the Morrow* and
Maiden Ecstasy show him as the same quaint with-
drawn maker of symbolic verse; a little more vari-

ous than of old, yet scarcely to be read at a stretch.
In a stray poem of his, " Farewell to Nature," the
"pathetic fallacy" of the soliloquists receives the
best treatment which any writer has given it.

In these days it is probably a mistake to compose
a tragedy upon the scale of *The Soldier of Fortune*
(1876), by J. Leicester Warren, the author of " Phi-   *Warren.*
loctetes." In length it approaches " Bothwell," and   *Cp. p. 283.*
Warren certainly betrays an admiration of Swin-
burne's verse. But this drama is written throughout
with care and vigor, and often with high eloquence,
and the lover of true poetry will find much to reward him in its scenes. *Pygmalion* and *Silenus*, by   *Woolner.*
Woolner, have no more absolute poetic motive than
his early pieces : cold as the marble of his sculpture,
they would be didactic but for the nature of their
themes. John Payne, at the date of his last collec-   *Payne.*
tion, was still a Neo-Romantic extremist. Neither
in the powerful and uncanny *Lautrec*, nor in his *New
Poems*, is there any more trace of realism or mod-
ernness than appears in old tapestry or a vellum
book of lays. He is a lyrical Ruskin as concerns
latter-day innovations. His scholarship and gift for
translation into English verse and prose have been
memorably utilized for his renderings of Villon, The
Thousand Nights and One Night, etc. My early
remarks on Domett apply to the well-named collec-   *Domett.*
tion of his *Flotsam and Jetsam*, which includes " A
Christmas Hymn, New Style," and " Cripplegate " —
a poem concerning Milton. Robert Buchanan also   *Buchanan.*
has made no new departure. His volume of 1882
confirms our respect for him as a balladist, and he
has done few better things than " The Lights of
Leith." Of late he has been scornful of the Muse

and her Arcadian haunts and minstrels, but has extended with success his efforts as a playwright, — for which a melodramatic tendency, that does not improve his novels, has given him undoubted qualifications.

Marked advances.

Definite advances have been scored, however, by a few of these our old acquaintances. *A Poet's Harvest Home*, by the veteran artist Bell Scott, is a century of precious gems in verse, not one of which is without beauty. The quaintness that would be affectation in younger men is his by nature, and withal a taste and intellect resembling Landor's. It is rare that so poetic a little book appears. Coventry Patmore's strain, in the new portions of his *Florilegium Amantis*, is "of a higher mood" than his early realism of the grass-plot and drawing-room. The odes first published as "The Unknown Eros," in irregular but stately measures, have a fine reserved power — visible also in the striking apostrophes to England. His poem to "My Little Son" is exquisitely touching. *The Renewal of Youth*, by Frederick Myers, bears out the promise of his early prime. He is of the school that regards song as a means of expression, and depends on thought and feeling to animate the simplest forms. The "Stanzas on Mr. Watts's Collected Works" are akin to Parsons's lines on Dante — high praise indeed ; and there is a nobility of tone even in his meditative pieces which reveals an unusual character. Roden Noel is another of whom good words may be honestly said — not so much for his more labored volumes, *The Red Flag*, and *The House of Ravensburg* — a semi-drama ; but the utterances found in *A Little Child's Monument* spring from the inmost depths of

Scott.

Patmore.

F. Myers.

Noel.

a poet's heart, whose impulsive feeling always must constitute its strongest appeal. The most suggestive verse latterly put forth by writers named in this section is that of Meredith, whose touch never yet lacked individuality. He is another of those novelists, such as Kingsley and Thackeray, quite at home on the poet's own ground. His lyrics *Of the Joy of Earth* (to which a complemental series is announced) have a purpose that reveals itself to one willing to ponder on their often involved, always thought-hoarding lines. He is, with a difference, the Emerson of English poets : "The Woods of Westermain" and "The Lark Ascending" are in veritable harmony with our Concord "Woodnotes." Meredith's talent for melody and structure is sufficient. Even his sonnets are welcome, and whether aptly or carelessly put together; for in each there is some deep or majestic thought, while in fluent measures he runs too much at large. "Lucifer in Starlight" and "The Spirit of Shakespeare" add to our list of important sonnets, and come from one who, in his own phrase, has "never stood at Fortune's beck."

George Meredith.

VI.

Of the poets whose books have appeared mainly since the date of our earlier review, a few are conspicuous for the extent of their work, and demand attention in any notice of the time. What are their respective claims to the favor awarded leaders whom they rival in productiveness ?

Prolific writers.

Symonds is fairly typical of the best results of the English university training. He is an exemplar of taste ; this, and liberal culture, joined with fine per-

John Addington Symonds: 1840–

ceptive faculties, endow a writer who has the respect of lovers of the beautiful for his service as a guide to its history and masterpieces. A wealth of language and material sustains his prose explorations in the renaissance, his Grecian and Italian sketches, his charming discourse of the Greek poets and of the Italian·and other literatures. He has given us complete and almost ideal translations of the sonnets of Angelo and Campanella. Coming to his original verse, we again see what taste and sympathy can do for a receptive nature ; all, in fact, that they can do toward the making of a poet born, not with genius, but with a facile and persistent bent for art. The division between friendship and love is no more absolute, as not of degree but of kind, than that between the connoisseur and the most careless but impassioned poet. Symonds recognizes this in a thoroughbred preface to *Many Moods*, a book covering the verses of fifteen years. He proffers attractive work, good handling of the slow metres, and an Italian modification of the antique feeling. There is some lyrical quality in his " Spring Songs." Almost the same remarks apply to a later volume, *New and Old*. Its atmosphere, landscape, and notes of sympathy therewith are so unEnglish that one must possess the author's latinesque training to feel them adequately. We have sequences of polished sonnets in the *Animi Figura* and its interpreter, *Vagabundi Libellus*. These studies of a " beauty-loving and impulsive, but at the same time self-tormenting and conscientious mind " are his most satisfactory efforts in verse ; but if their emotions are, as he avows, " imagined," he reasons too curiously for a poet. " Stella " has a right to complain of his hero, and it is no wonder she went mad.

An exemplar of Taste.

His poetical works.

His poems are suggestive to careful students only, in spite of their exquisite word-painting and the merit of sonnets like those on "The Thought of Death." Admiring the finish of them all, we try in vain to recall the one abiding piece or stanza. Here is scholar's work of the first order, the outcome of knowledge and a sense of beauty. Perhaps the author would have succeeded as well as a painter, sculptor, or architect, for in any direction taste would be his mainstay. Nothing can be happier than his rendering, with comments, of the mediæval Latin Students' Songs, neatly entitled *Wine, Woman and Song;* and in the prose "Italian By-ways" his critical touch is so light and rare that we are thankful for his companionship.

Those who wish to make more than a ripple on the stream may profit by the example of Edwin Arnold. During the latest quarter of a busy life he has gained a respectful hearing in his own country and something like fame in America. He is not a creative poet, yet the success of his Asiatic legends is due to more than an attractive dressing-up of the commonplace. He has zest, learning, industry, and an instinct for color and picturesqueness strengthened through absorption of the Oriental poetry, by turns fanciful and sublime. Above all, he shows the advantage of new ground, or of ground newly surveyed, and an interest in his subject which is contagious. There is a man behind his cantos, and a man clever enough to move in the latest direction of our unsettled taste and thought. A distinct theme and motive, skilfully followed, are the next best things to inventive power. The *Light of Asia* was not an ordinary production. With *The Indian Song of Songs*

Edwin Arnold: 1832–

Causes of his popularity.

Cp. " Poets of Amer- ica," p. 465.

and *Pearls of the Faith* it formed a triune exposition, on the poetic side, of the Hindoo and Arabian theologies. Probably Arnold's ideals of Buddhism, even of Islamism, insensibly spring from a western conception, but he conveys them with sensuous warmth and much artistic skill. In these books and the translations from the Mahâbhârata, he works an old vein in a new way. Both the accuracy and ethics of his Oriental pieces have been lauded and attacked with equal vehemence. They have received great attention in that section of the United States where discussion is most " advanced " and speculative, and where Buddhism and theosophy are just now indiscriminately a fashion, and likely to pass away as have many fashions that led up to them. Arnold's longer works may soon be laid aside, but such a lyric as " After Death in Arabia," whether original or a paraphrase, will be treasured for its genuine beauty and serene pledges to human faith and hope.

Alfred Austin: 1835–

Racy criti- cal Essays.

Alfred Austin's essays on " The Poetry of the Period " justly attracted notice. They were epigrammatic, conceived in a logical if disciplinary spirit, and almost the first severe criticism to which our " chief musicians " have been subjected. Here was one who dared to lay his hand on the sacred images. He bore down mercilessly upon " the feminine, narrow, domesticated, timorous " verse of the day, calling Tennyson feminine, Browning studious, Whitman noisy and chaotic, Swinburne and Morris not great because the times are bad, but only less tedious than the rest. While an iconoclast, his effort was constructive in its demand for the movement and passion that have animated more virile eras. When so lusty a critic himself came out as a poet, it fairly might have been expected that he would at least, whatever his demerits, avoid the tameness thus deplored. But movement and the divine fire are precisely what are lacking in Mr. Austin's respectable and somewhat labored books of verse. *The Human Tragedy*, a work by which he doubtless would wish to be judged, includes an early printed section, "Madonna's Child," which is a key to the poem. The whole requires ten thousand lines, cast in *ottava rima* and other standard forms. The Georgian measures are here, but not their force and glow. The movement is of the slowest, the philosophy prudish, and the story hard to follow : lovers are kept from marriage by religious zeal ; they don the Red Cross, travel and talk interminably, and finally are shot, and die in each other's arms to the great comfort of the reader. " Savonarola " is a better work, — a studious tragedy, but not relieved by humor and realism, and with few touches that are imaginative. The title - piece of *At the Gate of the Convent* is artistic and interesting, and is followed by a good deal of contemplative verse, mostly lyrical in form, with the lofty ode not slighted. What we miss is the incense of divine poesy. The author's satirical interludes have point, and I have seen graceful lyrics from his pen ; but his ambitious verse, on whatever principle composed, is not of the class that reaches the popular heart, nor likely, on the other hand, to capture a select group of votaries like those so loyal from the outset to Rossetti and Browning.

In every generation there is some maker of books who, without being a great writer, figures as such in his own and other minds. His thorough belief in his function and his hold upon a faithful constituency are things which men of better parts may not envy

" The Human Tragedy," 1876.

Lewis Morris: 1834-

him, yet find beyond their reach. Lewis Morris with his *Epic of Hades, Gwen, Songs of Two Worlds,* and other works of many editions, seems to be a writer whose fluent verse satisfies the popular need for rhythmical diet. Certain observances usually are noted in poetry of this kind. Its author handles a pretentious theme, and at much length, thus giving his effort an air of importance. He falls into the manner of popular models, and with great facility. He has a story to tell, or some lesson to teach, in all cases trite enough to an expert, but more impressive to the multitude than the expert suspects. Finally, he has zeal and measureless industry, and takes himself more seriously than if he were a sensitive and less robust

Ambitious facility. personage. It would be wrong to say that Mr. Morris's verse is no better than that of Pollok, Tupper, and Bickersteth. But he bears to this, the most refined of periods, very nearly the same relation which they bore respectively to their own. "The Epic of Hades " is written in diluted Tennysonian verse, its merit lying in simplicity and avoidance of affectations. It is, however, only a metrical restatement of the Greek mythology according to Lempriere, and without that magic transmutation which alone justifies a resmelting of the antique. "Gwen " is a drama in monologue — an English love-story, and, as far as "Maud " is dramatic, an attenuated Maud, without novelty of form or incident. In few of Morris's poems is there the radiant spirit which floods a word, a line, a passage, with essential meaning. In "The Ode of Life " he girds himself for a Pindaric effort, and strives with much grandiloquence to display the entire panorama of existence. His truest poetry, though neither he nor his admirers may so regard it, is found among the " Songs of Two Worlds " and *Songs Un-sung*, and chiefly in simple pieces like "The Organ Boy." A longer poem, " Clytemnestra in Paris," should be mentioned for its originality and interest ; it is based on the trial reports of a recent murder, and shows the worth of a vivid subject and a conception due solely to the poet. Morris also is forcible, though prolix, in some of his speculative theses, but leaves an impression of infallibility and that there are few subjects he would hesitate to preëmpt.

A survey of these energetic writers leads to the inference that the more ambitious recent efforts do not acquaint us with the new poets who possess the greatest delicacy of hand and vision, and are subject to the most spiritual moods. Barlow's many volumes, *George Barlow:* 18– and the successive books of Walter Smith, — author of *Olrig Grange, Hilda, Kildrostan*, etc., — only strengthen *Walter C. Smith:* 18– this inference. The vogue of Dr. Smith's productions with a certain class is due to the fact, that, like Mrs. ("Violet Fane") Singleton's very feminine *Mrs. Singleton:* 18– poem of *Denzil Place*, each is what she honestly calls the latter — a story in verse. They are metrical novelettes, with the excess of interest and liveliness in favor of the lady, who gives zest to her romance by a warmth of realism, upon which the Scotch idyllist would doubtless blush to venture. His *North Country Folk* contains some good short pieces. Mrs. Singleton's *Queen of the Fairies* is a tender story, purely and simply told. Her drama, *Anthony Babington*, is very creditable, above the common range of woman's work, which scarcely can be said of her miscellaneous lyrics. Her love-poetry is of all grades, and not always in the best taste. Mrs. Pfeiffer has been an *Emily Pfeiffer:* 18– untiring producer of verse of a different cast. Her early *Poems* embraced, besides a good ode " To the Teuton Woman," one or two striking ballads which indicated her natural bent, since developed in " The Fight at Rorke's Drift," and other spirited pieces. *Under the Aspens* is perhaps her most enjoyable collection. Her sonnets are thoughtful and intelligible, in this wise differing from the work of many sonnet-mongers, and those on Shelley and George Eliot are well worth preservation. In her more arduous flights she often fails, but there is an air of refinement and sincerity in much that comes from her pen.

Harriet E. Hamilton King: 1840–

Mrs. Hamilton King's long poem, *The Disciples*, has been widely read. Four disciples of Mazzini narrate, chiefly in blank-verse and rhymed heroics, the story of Garibaldi. The influence of the two Brownings is visible in Mrs. King's style. Her chief poem, the story of Fra Ugo Bassi, though too long, has strong passages, and effective pictures of Italian and Sicilian scenery. Her defects are a lack of condensed vigor and imagination.

Arthur Joseph Munby: 1828–

There are one or two marked exceptions to the inference just now drawn. When Mr. Munby's *Dorothy* appeared, sound-minded readers had a sense of refreshment. It was a novel pleasure to light upon a complete and wholesome poem, faithfully and winningly going at its purpose, that of depicting pastoral English scenes and extolling health and strength as

" Dorothy," 1880.

elements of beauty in woman. The heroine of this unique " country story in elegiac verse " is genuine as one of Millet's peasant-girls or Winslow Homer's

A charming idyl.

fisher-maidens. Seldom, nowadays, do we find such pictures of farm-life, bucolic work and sports, outside of Hardy's and Blackmore's novels. The ploughing-scene is a subject for a painter, and he could find, indeed, a score of charming themes in this one poem. Dorothy's sweet face and noble bearing require, it is true, the device of an aristocratic fatherhood, and there is possibly an implication of the benefits of cross-breeding. Munby equals Millet in honest candor, but I think he goes beyond nature in the one blemish of his idyl; there is an over-coarseness in giving even a plough-girl hands that would disgust a navvy or pitman. As might be expected of the poet who wrote "Doris," that lovely pastoral, he is an artist, and has achieved a difficult feat in popularizing his elegiac distiches.

A second exception is that of a man to whom a long chapter might be devoted, and whose life and writings, I doubt not, will be subjects of recurring interest during years to come. For it may almost be said of the late James Thomson, author of *The City of Dreadful Night*, that he was the English Poe. Not only in his command of measures, his weird imaginings, intellectual power and gloom, but with respect to his errant yet earnest temper, his isolation, and divergence from the ways of society as now constituted, — and very strangely also in the successive chances of his life so poor and proud, in his final decline through unfortunate habits and infirmities, even to the sad coincidence of his death in a hospital, — do the man, his genius, and career afford an almost startling parallel to what we know of our poet of "the grotesque and arabesque." Shelley, Heine, Leopardi, Schopenhauer, — such were the writers whom Thomson valued most, and whose influence is visible in his poetry. Yet the production already mentioned, and many others, have traits which are not found elsewhere in prose or verse. So much

James Thomson: 1834–82.

Cp. " Poets of America," pp. 230–239.

A sombre and powerful genius

" The City of Dread- ful Night," 1874.

might be said of Thomson's work that I scarcely ought to touch upon it here. But "The City of Dreadful Night" may be characterized as a sombre, darkly wrought composition toned to a minor key from which it never varies. It is a mystical allegory, the outgrowth of broodings on hopelessness and spiritual desolation. The legend of Dürer's Melancholia is marvelously transcribed, and the isometric interlude, "As I came through the Desert thus it was," is only surpassed by Browning's "Childe Roland." The cup of pessimism, with all its conjuring bitterness, is drunk to the dregs in this enshrouded, and again lurid, but always remarkable poem. We have Omar Khayyám's bewilderment, without his epicurean compensations.

" Vane's Story," 1864.

Vane's Story, the title-piece of another volume, is similarly impressive, and minor lyrics are worth study for their intenseness and frequent strange beauty. "Vane's Story," though melodramatic, and curiously outspoken in its notion of life and death, its opposition to ordinary views, is not easily forgotten. On the side of artistic poetry we have the Arabic love-tale of "Weddah," and "Two Lovers" — a beautiful legend in quatrains. No one can read these, or the passionate "Mater Tenebrarum," or such a rhapsody as "He heard Her Sing," surcharged with melody and fire, without feeling that here was a true and foreordained poet. More profuse than Poe, less careful of his art, often purposely and effectively coarse, he holds a place of his own. He was a natural come-outer, and declared for all sorts and conditions of men, independently of rank or record. At times he proved, by such verses as "Sunday at Hampstead" and "Sunday on the River," that a blither nature underlay his gloom, and that happy experiences would have made his song less pessimistic. But if ever a poet learned in suffering, it was he, and if the cup had passed from him we should have lost some powerful and distinctive verse. The posthumous volume, *A Voice from the Nile*, contains, with a friendly memoir by Bertram Dobell, the fugitive productions of Thomson's early and later years.

"A Voice from the Nile," 1884.

What may be termed the poetry of conviction is not yet without a few representatives. Of these Call, the author of *Reverberations* and *Golden Histories*, is the most facile and poetic. Transcendentalism and positivism are curiously blended in his utterance, and he was one of the first after Emerson to recognize the scientific movement on its imaginative side. He has written, also, verse of an ideal kind, including some winning lyrics. One of the latter, " In Summer when the Days were long," is to be found in anthologies, and usually without the author's name. Miss Bevington's *Poems, Lyrics, and Sonnets* largely consist of earnest, but troubled, speculative verse. Miss Blind is another altruistic writer whose work, in *The Prophecy of Saint Olan*, has feeling, but is a trifle monotonous. Her later volume, *The Heather on Fire*, shows a decided gain in vigor and the art of picturesque wordpainting. The radical and rebellious lyrics of Clarke, the young author of *Storm-Drift*, evince talent, but his well-told "Story of Salerno" betrays a willingness to take risks in an ultimately profitless direction.

The Poetry of Conviction.

Wathen Mark Wilks Call: 1817–

Louisa S. Bevington (Mrs. Güggenberger): 18–

Mathilde Blind: 1850–

Herbert E. Clarke: 18–

VII.

THE poetry of many recent authors is still to be considered. They scarcely can be said to initiate a new school, or to divide themselves into groups like those formed by the minor poets of a slightly earlier time. Listening to various masters, and feeling the absence just now of any special tone or drift, more than one new aspirant essays some note of his own. Their very lack of assumption, and failure to claim by bold efforts a share of the attention secured by the novelists, imply a tacit acknowledgment that poetry cannot maintain at the moment its former dominance in the English world of letters. This is an unpromising attitude ; but if they do not exhibit the ardent, full-throated confidence that begets leadership, there still are not a few who devote themselves to ideal beauty, and sing, in spite of discouragements, because the song is in them. They bear in one respect a mutual likeness. Though not given to the technical freaks of the recent art-extremists, the work of all displays a finish unknown at the outset of the Victorian period. The art of dexterous verse-making is so established that the neophyte has it at command. As with the technics of modern instrumental music, it is within common reach and not a subject for much remark.

Gosse, whom the public first knew as a poet, and who has become prominent as a literary scholar and critic, has not suffered general authorship to hinder his more ideal efforts for any length of time. That he is an attractive and competent master of English prose the leading journals and magazines bear constant witness, no less than his " Studies in Northern

Literature," his edition of Gray, lectures on poetry, and other essays, biographies, and contributions to works that are richer for his aid. All this prose matter has been refined and bettered by his poetic sensibility. And as a poet, the title of the first book for which he was sole sponsor, *On Viol and Flute*, hints of his early quality. Though plainly alive to the renaissance movement, it was full of young blood and tuneful impulse; its contents appertaining to music, art, love, and the Norse legendary so familiar to him. His *New Poems*, six years later in date, are simpler, more restrained and meditative. They are deftly finished, pure and cool, a degree too cool for current taste. His classical sonnets — from the first he has been a good sonneteer — exhibit all these traits. He has a strong and logical sense of form, while his color is keyed to the tranquil and secondary, rather than the sensuous primitive tones. A grace in which he has few equals is the fidelity to nature of his pastorals and lyrics. There is true and sweet landscape, the very spirit of the English coppices, rivers, and moors, in his quiet pieces. Successful with the French forms which he did much to introduce, he uses them sparingly; in fact, he seldom or never plays the tricks of the extreme decorationists, but trusts to the force of his thoughts and impressions. The contents of the volume, *Firdausi in Exile*, may be taken, I suppose, as his most mature and varied work, for the early drama of " King Erik," though creditably done and on a theme quite native to him, does not show his bent to be strongly dramatic. Reviewing his verse, one finds a genuine feeling for nature, and subtile ideality, in " Sunshine before Sunrise," " The Whitethroat,"

" On Viol and Flute," 1873.

" New Poems," 1879.

" Firdausi in Exile," 1885.

*Wilfrid
Scawen
Blunt :*
1840-

*Eric
Mackay :*
18-

"Lying in the Grass," "The Shepherd of the Thames," "Obermann Yet Again." His "Theocritus" has delicious melody and charm. There is a return in his longer poems, "Firdausi" and "The Island of the Blest," to the Italian method of Hunt and Keats. Gosse is an example of the latter-day poet who does so well and learnedly in prose as scarcely to obtain full credit for his natural poetic gift. His verse, like that of Arnold, with whom its spirit is allied, grows on one by acquaintance. It is not often of a swift and lyrical character; yet that he can be both resonant and picturesque is evident from a vigorous ballad, "The Cruise of the Rover," which will bear reading with the sea-ballads of Tennyson and Kingsley, and of itself bestows upon its author the name of poet.

Blunt's *Love Sonnets of Proteus* are interesting as the artistic and sole utterance of their composer — the record, whether personal or not, of a man's successive love-experiences. This series of sonnets comes from one guided by the foremost English master, yet they are idiosyncratic and do not betray a weak or inexpert hand. Their savor of artificiality disappears when the writer ceases to be introspective, as in the fresh and wholesome sonnet on Gibraltar at the close. While the composition of these Protean verses seems to have been, as a man's love is said to be, an episode, it is plain that *The Love Letters of a Violinist and Other Poems* (1885), by Eric Mackay, are the handiwork of a brilliant metrical artist and poet born. It requires an effort to acknowledge this, after reading the preposterous "Introductory Notice" with which the author permits some absurd friend to preface the "Canterbury" edition of his book. Despite, however, the flaunting bush displayed at the portal, the wine within is rich and brimming, and of an exhilarating flavor. The series of Love Letters in six-line stanzas, while confessedly of the ecstatic virtuoso-type, is a beautiful and passionate work : its beauty that of construction, language, imagery, — its passion characteristic of the artistic nature, and while intensely human, free from any taint of vulgar coarseness. The poem is quite original, its manner Elizabethan, freshened by a resort to the Italian fountain from which the clearest streams of English song so often have flowed. Mackay's poetic ability is of varied range. The appended studies and lyrics, though conspicuously uneven, all have *quality*. He is a natural lyrist, with a singing faculty, a novel metrical turn, such as few recent lyrists have at command. In some of his pieces we come suddenly upon a prosaic, almost grotesque, fault of expression ; but there is a fine impulsive spirit animating all. With the very striking poem of "Mary Arden" we at last have, to apply Lowell's phrase, something new said of Shakespeare, and it is said sweetly and imaginatively. It is a pity that there was any clap-trap in the early heralding of these poems, for they do not stand in need of it.

A claim to regard was at once established by "Michael Field," through her first volume, embracing the dramas of *Callirhoë* and *Fair Rosamond.* It seemed a reoccupation of Swinburne's early ground, but this was only true with respect to the choice of themes. "Callirhoë" is classical merely in subject and time, and is treated in a modern way, the characters being living men and women with a language compact of beauty and imagination. "Fair Rosa-

" Michael Field" : 18–

mond " is brief, strong; the culminating act of a tragic scheme that has beguiled great artists to its handling. The dramas in this writer's second book, *The Father's Tragedy*, etc., reveal the same vigorous touch, but are diffuse and lack contrasting lights and shades; there is no humor, — speech and action are always at concert-pitch. Their diction, however, is very original. Often an epithet carries force, and is used in an entirely fresh way. This dramatist lacks proportion; her manner betokens close study of the Elizabethans, but of the minor ones rather than the greatest. Her work is notable for its freedom, even audacity, and contrasts in all respects with that of Tennyson — so correct of style and proportion, yet without natural dramatic fire. Her advance in *Brutus Ultor* is not of the right kind. It seems as if she hunted history for plots and themes. This is a Roman tragedy, compressed and over-virile — even coarse at times, as if the effort to speak as a man were a forced one. " Michael Field " is ambitious and has warrant for it. Her motto should be " strength and beauty," and not strength alone. The *Nero* of Robert Bridges, an historical tragedy of the emperor's early reign, with narrower extremes of passion, is to my mind a more essentially virile work. There is a nobler severity in dialogue, which merits the name of Roman. The diction and blank-verse are restrained but impressive. The characters of Nero, Poppæa, Seneca, Agrippina, are distinctly drawn. While in a sense conventional, " Nero " shows the mark of a selfpoised, confident hand. A few of the lyrics in Bridges' eclectic and privately printed volume of 1884 strengthen my opinion that he is a very ideal and artistic poet. The elegy " I

Robert Bridges: 18—

have loved flowers that fade" is matchless in its
way, apparently old in feeling yet perfectly original;
and some of his songs rival it in their brief melody.

Canon Dixon's early work betrayed the close affinity between the new ecclesiasticism and the methods
of Rossetti. His *Odes and Eclogues*, on the other
hand, are the most extreme type of Anglo-classic
verse, — that peculiar grafting of modern thought
upon the Grecian stock in which Arnold was a leading expert, and which is so fascinating to a scholar-
poet. His latest lyrics have a peculiar wandering
beauty. All his work is finished to a notable degree. Dixon and Bridges at this distance appear to
be the chief lights of a quaintly esoteric Oxford
School.

Miss Robinson's verse is a delicate spray, engendered by influences which began with Ruskin
and the pre-Raphaelites, and in the end supplied
the motive of British taste in plastic and decorative
art, in letters, and in all the refinements of social
life. She shows the effect of culture upon an im-
pressible feminine nature, placed among devotees
of the beautiful, and breathing its atmosphere from
her childhood. Her classical studies were like those
of Mrs. Browning, with an æsthetic training superadded that was not obtainable in Mrs. Browning's
time. Her first little book, *A Handful of Honey-
suckle*, bears the obvious impress of Rossetti, — a
shoot from his garden, but with new and fragrant
blossoms of its own. The lyrics appended to her
next work — a praiseworthy translation of *The
Crowned Hippolytus* — were of a maturer cast. Afterward, applying her gift to humane transcripts of
real life, she wrote *The New Arcadia*, a group of

*Richard
Watson
Dixon:*
1833–

*Agnes
Mary
Frances
Robinson:*
1857–

ballads in behalf of suffering womanhood and England's poor. Doubtless this was too grave an experimental task, for in turning at last to Italy, and its *rispetti* and *stornelli*, she seems thoroughly at home. Her book of songs, *An Italian Garden*, is the most essentially poetic of her works thus far. It breathes the Anglo-Italian spirit which is in fact her own. The *rispetti* forming her wreath of Tuscan cypress, with their beauty and sadness, are in every way characteristic of this poet, and in her most suggestive vein. Meanwhile her acquirements enable her to take an active part in the critical and biographical industries which the inevitable book-purveyor now opens for every rising author. Of her sister poets not yet mentioned, Mrs. Liddell and Miss Nesbit deserve notice. The former's "Songs in Minor Keys" are suffused with deep religious feeling, always expressed in good taste. Miss Nesbit's "Lays and Legends" suggest immature but promising individuality. She is capable of strong emotion, which is most effective in her shorter lays.

Watts, the scholarly critic of poetry and romantic art, and a frequent contributor of verse to the literary journals, has thus far made no public collection of his poems. My knowledge of them is confined to some very perfect sonnets — a form of verse in which he is a natural and acknowledged master — and a few lyrics of an elevated type. His ode to a Caged Petrel shows an eloquent method and a perception of Nature's grander aspects. He apparently seeks to revive the broad feeling of the Georgian leaders; at all events, his touch is quite independent of any bias derived from the eminent poets with whom his life has been closely associated. Among

Catherine Christina (Fraser-Tytler) Liddell: 1848–

E. Nesbit: 18–

Theodore Watts: 1836–

the many writers of good sonnets I may mention Caine — Rossetti's young friend and memorialist. Professor Dowden, whose critical work is always of a high order, has published a volume of poems, from which two or three imaginative examples of the same class have met my eye.

Watson, judging from *The Prince's Quest*, is a disciple of Morris and a good one — a poet of slow movement, from whom we have also careful sonnets and Landorian quatrains. Lee-Hamilton's varied *Poems and Transcripts*, with the studies in *Apollo and Marsyas*, remind one of the sculptor-poet Story by their reflection of Browning's manner ; yet where he is Browningesque or Rossettian it is usually because the subject cannot be so well treated in another way. He has a taste for the psychologically-dramatic, and usually interests the reader. "The Bride of Porphyrion" and "The Wonder of the World" are far from commonplace, and his sonnets are exceptionally fine. Dawson is quite possessed by Rossetti, but has resources of fancy, rhythm, decoration. If he contrives to outgrow his pupilage, something of worth may be expected from him. There is much simplicity and grace in the *Poems* of Ernest Myers, largely suggested by study and travel, and they belong to the composite art school. The contents of Wyville Home's volumes are too diffuse, and there is nothing in his *Lay Canticles* superior to a few sonnets in the earlier *Songs of a Wayfarer*. His failures, however, are those of one who aims high and in time may reach his mark.

Many of the young writers devote themselves to cabinet-picture making, whether their dainty verse is properly idyllic or dramatic. The scenic tendency

T. Hall Caine :
18-

Edward Dowden :
1843-

William Watson :
1858-

Eugene James Lee-Hamilton :
1845-

William James Dawson :
1854-

Ernest Myers :
1844-

J. Wyville Home :
18-

Crayon-Verse.

increases, just as it has grown, with an Irving to foster it, upon the stage. New poets strive, through affecting the mind's eye, to outdo the painter's appeal to the bodily vision. This invasion of a neighboring domain is a failure to utilize their own, and an undervaluation of the noblest of arts. Very pretty things of the kind, however, are often produced in this way.

Edward Cracroft Lefroy: 1855–

A graceful scholar-poet is Lefroy, whose *Echoes* introduce us to old friends in a new guise. His open method is to compress into a single sonnet the tenor of some well-known poem. Gautier's " L'Art," already paraphrased by Dobson, thus appears in sonnet-form, and many idyls of Theocritus are treated similarly. But these are supplemented by pleasing sonnets of English cloister and outdoor life. Pollock's *Songs and Rhymes*, with a prelude by Lang, make up a little book of neat and polished verse à-la-mode, which doubtless scarcely represents the mature or serious purpose of its author. Raffalovich's *Cyril and Lionel* contains well-turned verse of a motive which, although it is not imitative, I find difficult to understand. By his name this writer would seem to be more justified than others in eking out his book with lyrics in other tongues than the English. Since the date of " Chastelard " this practice has been more or less affected by the new men. Swinburne put French songs into a play where they rightly belong, as an *obligato* to the action and discourse. Now every lutanist splits his tongue, like a parrot's, to sing strange words, — but there are capabilities still left in our native English. If such linguistic feats must be essayed, why not compose in the universal Volapük, — or more mellifluously in the late Mr. Pearl Andrews's " Alwato " ?

Walter Herries Pollock: 1850–

Mark André Raffalovich: 18–

A phase of the æsthetic crusade in defense of poetry as an utterance of the beautiful solely, — a movement having almost perfect development at its start with Keats so long ago, — has appeared in the outgivings of some of Ruskin's disciples, and avowedly in the verse of Oscar Wilde. His *Poems*, with all their conceits, are the fruit of no mean talent. The opening group, under the head " Eleutheria," are the strongest. A lyric to England, " Ave Imperatrix," is manly verse, — a poetic and eloquent invocation. " The Garden of Eros," " Burden of Itys," " Charmides," are examples of the sensuous pseudo - classicism. There is a good deal of Keats, and something of Swinburne, in Wilde's pages, but his best master is Milton, whom he has studied, as did Keats, to good effect. His scholarship and cleverness are evident, as well as a native poetic gift. The latter indeed might prove his highest gift, if tended a little more seriously, and possibly he could be on better terms with himself in his heart of hearts if he would forego his fancies in behalf of his imagination — as there is still time for him to do. It is fair to accept the statement of his own ground, in his preface to the decorative verse of his friend Rennell Rodd, — though one doubts whether Gautier would not have dubbed the twain *jeunes brodeurs*, rather than *jeunes guerriers, du drapeau romantique.* The apostles of our Lord were filled, like them, with a " passionate ambition to go forth into far and fair lands with some message for the nations and some mission for the world." But not until many centuries had passed were their texts illuminated to the extent displayed by Mr. Rodd and his printer, with their resources of India - paper, apple-green tissue,

Oscar Wilde: 1856-

Rennell Rodd: 1858-

vellum, and all the rarities desired by those who die of a rose in aromatic pain. Yet the verse of *Rose Leaf and Apple Leaf* is not so effeminate as one would suppose. The minstrel's greensickness is now well over, judging from his *Feda and other Poems;* and in throwing it off he gives a token of the vigor needful for a decisive mark.

Robert Louis Balfour Stevenson: 1850–

Now, as a minor but genuine example of poetic art, not alone for art's sake, but for dear nature's sake, — in the light of whose maternal smile all art must thrive and blossom if at all, — take *A Child's Garden of Verses* by Stevenson. This is a real addition to the lore for children, and to that for man, to whom the child is father. The flowers of this little garden spring from the surplusage of a genius that creates nothing void of charm and originality. Thanks, then, for the fresh, pure touch, for the revelation of childhood with its vision of the lands of Nod and Counterpane, and of those next-door Foreign Lands spied from cherry-tree top, and beyond the trellised wall.

VIII.

William Sharp: 18–

THERE is promise in *Earth's Voices*, by Sharp, who celebrates Nature, not in a Wordsworthian vein — but somewhat after the manner of Heine and the Germans. The trouble with a long series of studies, like "Earth's Voices" or the *rispetti* entitled "Transcripts from Nature," is that much of it is mere word-painting, and only a few numbers are apt to be spontaneous. "Sospitra" is his strongest effort. Possibly Sharp — whose critical biography of Rossetti is of value — should not be named with the Australian contingent of writers, though some of his

Colonial and Provincial Verse.

sketches and ballads are by one familiar with the South Sea Continent. But there is no questioning the local flavor of Gordon's " Bush Ballads," or the ringing, spirited effectiveness of his lyrics of the field, the turf, and the campaign. Receiving from Melbourne the posthumous collection of his *Poems*, I was at once taken by the dash and verve of this ex-cadet and Australian refugee, — a sheep-farmer, sportsman, amateur steeple-chase rider, and author of " How We Beat the Favorite," the best racing ballad in the language. Gordon's tragic and untimely death may, or may not, have involved a loss to poetry : he was one of the headstrong adventurous spirits whose talent is unquestionable, but whose restless nature and lack of fixed purpose hinder its full development, and from whom their mates are always expecting more than is achieved. Gordon was all by turns and nothing long. There are plentiful traces of Byron, Browning, Swinburne, in his careless style ; but when most himself he bears to Australia the relation of Harte to California, as a poet. What originality marks *A Poetry of Exiles* and *Australian Sketches*, by Sladen, is mainly the effect upon one reared in England of a novel atmosphere and sky. Otherwise, *Cœlum non animum mutant* may be said of many colonial poets, and certainly of this scholar of Trinity, Oxford. His key-note is that love of motherland, not yet stifled even among Americans, and which the home-keeping Briton does not fully comprehend. Of a few rising British Canadian poets Roberts, the author of *In Divers Tones*, seems to be foremost. His verse is thoughtful and finished, and conveys a hopeful expression of the native sentiment now perceptible in a land so long only " the child of nations." Toru

Adam Lindsay Gordon: 18–

Douglas B. W. Sladen: 18–

Charles George Douglas Roberts: 1860–

Dutt's *Ballads and Legends of Hindustan*, edited by Gosse, are the pressed leaves of a tropic flower that, striving to adapt itself to an atmosphere not its own, exhaled some fragrance ere it died. Her verse was curiously western, while narrating legends of a faith which this " pure Hindu, full of the typical qualities of her race and blood," had learned not to believe. It has touches of lyrical melody, and an aspiration that might in time have strengthened into fulfilment. The list of colonial aspirants in Australia, Tasmania, India, and elsewhere, is growing, and after a ' season more than one of these imperial outposts will give voice to a language of its own. Among local and

provincial verse - makers, Anderson, " the surface-man," may be mentioned as one of the best. His dialect-pieces, and poems "of the rail," are welcome, but when he ventures toward the high precincts of Keats and Shelley he leaves his proper ground.

Song,
Sentiment,
and Fancy.

Hamilton
Aïde, 18-

Marzials.

The song-writers and makers of popular verse are relatively fewer than of old. Many of Aïde's *Songs without Music* are excellent, — the work of a connoisseur. He preserves for us a little of that spring-time sentiment, without which the world were colder. The later songs of Marzials, who is both composer and balladist, are far more enjoyable than his early rococo-verse which served as a text for a comment in Chapter VIII. As I have said elsewhere, a poet is to be envied who can hear, wherever he goes, his

own words and music. In Clement Scott's *Lays of a Londoner* there are some effective, sympathetic lyrics, — " A Prisoner of War," the " Story of a Stowaway," " The Midshipmite," — and apt memorial poems. His lighter verse also marks him as a successor to the London group of Hood, Jerrold, Thackeray, etc. *The Lazy Minstrel* is Ashby-Sterry's latest collection of old-style ditties, and warranted by the favor bestowed upon "Boudoir Ballads." Most of his work is more strictly society - verse than much which goes under that name. A queer but popular field is that laid out and occupied by Dodgson, who, as "Lewis Carroll," has proffered a merry antidote to the hyper-æsthetic and other fads of the day. His *Rhyme and Reason* contains "Phantasmagoria" and "The Hunting of the Snark" — bright audacities in which the fancy that created "Alice in Wonderland" plays without tether, and affords delight to the healthy and fun-loving mind. Courthope, also, has a clever vein of his own. His *Ludibriæ Lunæ*, a light satire on "woman's rights," and *The Paradise of Birds*, an Aristophanic extravaganza, are enlivened by an easy command of measures, scholarly humor, and abundant fancy.

The few who are bold enough to write poetry for the dramatic stage lead a forlorn hope, and at least deserve consideration. But first a word of tribute is due to Dr. Marston, of whose works a general collection was made in 1876. Some of his dramas were well suited to their purpose, and scenes of true poetry and emotion are not wanting in "Strathmore" and other plays. Merivale is the most elevated of the dramatists not hitherto mentioned, and success as an artistic playwright is of marked advantage to a dramatic poet. *The White Pilgrim* is a good poetic drama, with weirdly imaginative scenes. *Florien*, a later tragedy, is scarcely a literary advance ; but it displays the author's skill in historic reproduction, is consistently English, and of decided interest. Merivale's songs — the "Venetian Boat-Song," for example —

Joseph Ashby-Sterry: 1838–

Charles Lutwidge Dodgson : about 1833–

William John Courthope: 1842–

The Poetic Drama.

Westland Marston: 1819–

Herman Charles Merivale: 1839–

"Ross Neil," 18–

are especially good, as those of a dramatist should be. " Ross Neil " has been a fertile composer of metrical dramas and plays. Of the many contained in five books published since 1872, I have seen only those grouped with *Andrea the Painter.* They are creditable for incident, situation, language, and construction, but the writer seldom gains a height com-

William Gorman Wills: 1828–

mensurate with her poetic aim. Wills's *Melchior*, a long romantic art-poem, which I mention as the work of an active playwright, will not increase the reputation of the author of " The Man o' Airlie " and " Clau-dian." Plainly the shield has been touched with most lightness and precision by the bearer of Mercury's

William Schwenck Gilbert: 1836–

caduceus, — that wit and singular genius, Gilbert, whose *Original Plays*, delightful with humor and pathos, have captured the airiest spirit of our time and added to "the gayety of nations." " Pygmalion and Galatea," " The Wicked World," — and that little poem so charming in scene and dialogue, so pure and original as a piece of fancy, " Broken Hearts," — may not be cast in the noblest moulds of imaginative art; but for ideality, truth to nature, and thorough adaptation of means to ends, they have not recently been surpassed in English dramatic literature.

Transla-tions.

The field of translation is less persistently tilled than at the date of my former review. The British scholar no longer deems it his bounden duty to produce a fresh metrical version of Horace. There have been a few more translations of Homer, — the most noteworthy being Cayley's Iliad, and the prose texts by Lang and his associates. Kegan Paul's literal and lineal " Faust " appeared in 1872, and five years later Miss Swanwick published her translation of the same drama. Attention has been paid to the Italian and

Spanish masterpieces, and to minor reproductions from the Turkish, Russian, and other modern anthologies.

IX.

FINALLY we observe what has been, all in all, the most specific phase of British minstrelsy since 1875. This is seen in the profusion of lyrical elegantiæ, the varied grave and gay ditties, idyls, metrical cameos and intaglios, polished epistles and satires, classed as Society Verse, the Court Verse of older times. Perceiving signs of its revival, I could not foresee that it would flourish as it has, and really constitute the main thing upon which a lyrical interval would plume itself. Its popularity is curious and significant. The pioneer in verse of a movement already evident in society and household art was Austin Dobson. This favorite poet, by turns the Horace, Suckling, Prior, of his day, allying a debonair spirit with the learning and precision of Queen Anne's witty fabulists, has well advanced a career which began with "Vignettes in Rhyme." Enjoying the quality of that book, I felt that its poet, to hold his listeners, must change his song from time to time. Of this he has proved himself fully capable. His second volume, *Proverbs in Porcelain*, gave us a series of little "proverbs" in dialogue, exquisite bits of "Louis Quinze," and perfectly unique in English verse. Nothing can excel the beauty and pathos of "Good-Night, Babette," with the Angelus song low-blended in its dying fall. The lines "To a Greek Girl," in the same collection, and the paraphrase of Gautier, "Ars Victrix," superadd a grace even beyond that of Dobson's early lyrics. Who has not read the "Idyl of

Garde-Joyeuse. Cp. "Poets of America, pp. 275, 448.

Dobson. Cp. p. 273.

the Carp," and the racy ballad of "Beau Brocade"?
Here, too, are his little marvels in the shape of the
rondel, rondeau, villanelle, triolet, — those French
forms which he has handled with an ease almost inimitable, yet so wantonly provoking imitation.

*His many
followers.* Perhaps Dobson more than others has shaped the
temper of our youngest poets. A first selection from
his works appeared in the United States in 1880, its
welcome justifying a second in 1885. Meanwhile the
choice editions de luxe, *Old World Idyls* and *At the
Sign of the Lyre*, represent the greater portion of his
verse. Any author might point to such a record
with pride ; there is scarcely a stanza in these volumes wanting in extreme refinement, and this without marring its freshness and originality. In his
place one should never yield — as there are stray
omens that he sometimes is yielding — to any popular or journalistic temptation that would add a line
to these fortunate pieces, except under the impulse
of an artistic and spirited mood.

*An École
Intermé-
diaire.* The influence of Dobson and his associates has
been a characteristic — a symptomatic — expression
of the interval between the close of the true Victorian period and the beginning of some new and, let
us hope, inspiring poetic era. It has created, in
fact, a sort of *école intermédiaire*, of which the gay
and buoyant minstrelsy is doubtless preferable to
those affected heroics that bore every one save the
egotist who gives vent to them. For real poetry,
though but a careless song, light as thistle-down and
floating far from view, will find some lodgment for
its seed even on distant shores and after long time.
The roundelays of Villon, of Du Bellay and his
Pléiade, waited centuries for a fit English welcome

and interpretation. Lang's *Ballads and Lyrics of old France*, in 1872, captured the spirit of early French romantic song. Nine years afterward, his *Ballades in Blue China* chimed in with the temper of our new-fangled minstrel times. Such craftsmanship as the villanelle on Theocritus, the ballade to the same poet, and the ballades "Of Sleep" and "Of the Book-Hunter," came from a sympathetic hand. In the later "Ballades and Verses Vain" are new translations, etc., and a few striking addenda, memorably the resonant sonnet on the Odyssey. A "Ballade of his Choice of a Sepulchre" is Lang's highest mark as a lyrist, and perhaps the freest vein of his *Rhymes à la Mode* is in the long poems that do not fall under that designation, such as "The Fortunate Islands." He has almost preëmpted the "Ballade," but his later specimens of it are scarcely up to his own standard. "Cameos" and "Sonnets from the Antique" are at the head of their class, and naturally, for no other Oxonian is at once so variously equipped a scholar and so much of a poet. The fidelity, diction, and style of his prose translations of Homer and Theocritus are equally distinguished. Thus far his most serious contribution to poetry is *Helen of Troy,* — a poem taking, as one would expect, the minority view of its legend, and depicting the fair cause of Troy's downfall as a victim to the plots of the gods. It is written felicitously in eight-line stanzas of a novel type, and, while not strong in special phrases and epithets, has much tranquil beauty. On his working-day side, readers never wait long for something bright from this versatile, inventive feuilletonist, — a master of persiflage, whose learned humor and audacity, when he is most insular, are perhaps the most entertaining.

Andrew Lang: 1844–

X.

IF imitation be flattery, Dobson and Lang have breathed sufficient of its incense. Their "forms" have haunted a multitude of young singers, and proved as taking and infectious as the airs of Sullivan's operettas. They have crossed the seas and multiplied in America more rapidly than the English sparrows which preceded them, — so that, as in the case of their feathered compatriots, the question is whether a check can be put to the breed. As I have said, this elegant rhyming, however light and delicate, is in fact a special feature of the latest Victorian literature, and, with its pretty notes tingling on the ear, is a text for some last words in discussion of what has gone before.

First, let me say that it is but shallow reasoning to worry over the outbreak of any fancy or fashion in art. Let a good thing — a much better thing than any form in verse — be overdone, and people will signify their weariness of it so decisively that the quickness of its exit will be as surprising as its temporary vogue.

What conclusions, then, are derivable from our summary of the British poetic movement of the last dozen years? We have paid tribute to the noble chants of a few masters who still teach us that Poetry is the child of the soul and the imagination. But one looks to the general drift of the younger poets, who initiate currents to the future, for an answer to the question, — What next? The direct influences of Keats, Wordsworth, and Shelley are no longer servilely displayed; few echo even Tennyson; Browning, Rossetti, and Swinburne are more widely favored; but ancestral and paternal strains are as much confused and blended in the verse of the newest aspirants as in genealogy. Their work is more composite than ever, judging from the poets selected as fairly representative. Only two of its divisions are sufficiently pronounced for even a fanciful classification. One is the Stained-Glass poetry, if I may so term it, that dates from " The Blessed Damozel " and cognate models by Rossetti and his group; the other, that Debonair Verse, whose composers apply themselves by turns to imitation of the French minstrelsy and forms, and to the æsthetic embroidery of Kensington-stitch rhyme, — for in each of these pleasant devices the same practitioners excel. Now the class first named, and the first division of the second, are of alien origin: they are exotics — their renaissance is of the chivalry, romance, mysticism, and balladry of foreign literatures. Only that witty, gallant verse which takes its cue from the courtly British models of the seventeenth and eighteenth centuries is an exception, — and that, whatever its cleverness and popularity, can hardly be termed inventive.

Stained-Glass poetry.

The Debonair Poets.

The next thing to be noted is the finical nicety to which, as we see, the technique of poetry has advanced. Never were there so many capable of polishing measures quite unexceptionable as to form and structure, never fewer whose efforts have lifted them above what is, to be sure, an unprecedented level — but still a level. The cult of beauty and art, delightfully revived so long ago by Hunt and Keats, has brought us at last to this. Concerning inspiration and the creative impulse, we have seen first: that recent verse-makers who are most ambitious and prolific have not given much proof of exceptional

Artisanship.

Two kinds of limitation.

genius. Their productions have the form and dimension of masterpieces, and little more. Secondly: those who appear to be real poets, shrinking from the effort to do great things in an uncongenial time, reveal their quality by lovely minor work — sometimes rising to an heroic and passionate but briefly uttered strain. And it is better to do small things well than to essay bolder ventures without heart or seriousness. Still, I think they must now and then doubt the importance of thus increasing, without specific increase of beauty and novelty, the mass of England's rich anthology. Looking back, years from now, it will be seen that one noble song on a compulsive theme has survived whole volumes of elaborate, soulless artisanship by even the natural poets.

The epoch. What is it, then, that chills the "heart and seriousness" of those most artistic and ideal? The rise of conditions adverse to the imaginative exercise of their powers has been acknowledged from the first in these essays. It is clear that instinct has become measurably dulled, as concerns the relative value of efforts; so that poets do not magnify their calling as of old. There is less bounce, and, unfortunately, still less aspiration. Nor has the modern spirit, now freed from sentimental illusions, as yet brought its *True Realism.* wits to a thorough understanding of what true Realism is — viz., that which is just as faithful to the ideal and to the soul of things as to obvious and external matters of artistic treatment. Here again the law of reaction will in the end prevail. Its operation is already visible in the demand for more inventive and wholesomely romantic works of fiction; and this is but the forerunner of a corresponding impulse by which the poet — the maker — the creative idealist — whose office it is to perceive and illumine *all* realities, both material and spiritual, will have his place again.

For a time, however, the revival of creative prose-fiction may occupy more than one poetic mind. Novel-writing is more vigorously pursued than ever, by fresh hands. Journalism opens new and broader courts tempting for their influence, sense of power, and the subsistence yielded. Criticism, book-making, book-editing, are flourishing industries. Scholar's work is steadily pursued, and carried even to analysis of living authors. Our poetry itself is too scholarly. A recent happy statement concerning Byron, that he "did not know enough," does not apply to the typical latter-day poet. He has too much learning withal, of a technical, linguistic, treasure-hunting sort. The over-intellectuality and scholarship of many lyrists absorb them in curious studies, and deaden their impulse toward original and glowing efforts. They revive and translate, and borrow far too much the hoardings of all time. Even in their judgments they set an undue relative value upon the learning or philosophy of a master under discussion. Moreover, their literary skill and acquirements make the brightest of them serviceable aids to the publishers. No sooner are their names in public favor than the great houses smooth their way along the lucrative paths of book-making. Great and small houses have multiplied, and printing is easy and universal. To all this we indeed owe attractive series of critico-biographical volumes, anthologies catholic and select, encyclopædias, translations, and texts without end. Good and welcome as much of this work is, my present question must be : Does it not

Cp. " Poets of America," pp. 26, 27, 437, 463.

Learning vs. Imagination.

Book-making.

chasten and absorb the poet's faculties? Has he
not, at last, too good a literary market? The common-sense reply is, that, after all, he must live, —
and the belief is antiquated that poets, like caged
birds, sing better for starving. Yet if you chance of
late upon a unique and terribly earnest bard, — a
man like Thomson, — you find that he was out of
the literary " swim " and usually out of pocket;
while his well-to-do brother more often is the man
of letters, corresponding to Southey and Wilson
rather than to their fiery contemporaries. If the poetic drama, for example, were now more frequently
calling for elevated work, imagination and subsistence
would both be subserved. The stage does make
welcome beautiful and witty verse of a light order,
but what it regularly supports is the facile playwright; and its operettas and scenic plays are logi-
cally adapted to the zest for amusement and the
ruling decorative frenzy.

*Lack of a
national
style.*
The desire of the critic and the public alike, and
first of all, is for something new and additional.
But that which is new is of higher worth when it
contributes to the furtherance of a true national
style. What is Spanish, French, German, we at once
recognize as such, however different from previous
works of like origin; but how seldom the later Victorian minstrelsy is essentially English! A recent
article by W. P. P. Longfellow criticises existing
tendencies of architecture in Great Britain. He records the progress of a style which advanced to its
culmination with the design for the new Law Courts,
and until the " Victorian Gothic was everywhere."
He writes that —

" Success was due, not so much to the style chosen as

to the fact, that, having found a style which suited them, the English followed it unitedly and persistently. Here seemed to be a national movement, strong, deep, and promising to endure. . . . Then, suddenly, at the signal of two or three restless and clever young men, whose eyes had caught something else, the English architects with one accord threw the whole thing away; as a boy, after working the morning through at some plaything, with a sudden weariness drops his unfinished toy to run after the first butterfly. . . . They have seemed to show us that their progress was at the impulse of whim rather than conviction, ruled rather by fashion than tradition. It is the mobile Frenchman who in this century has set us an example of steadiness. If his work, like all the rest in our day, lacks some of the higher qualities of older and greater styles, it has, more than any other modern work, the coherency and firmness that are at the bottom of all style." *See " The New Princeton Review," March, 1887.*

The point thus made has a bearing upon more arts than one. A style of architecture, it is true, is the outcome of centuries. Literary style has a readier formation and is quickly affected by individual leadership. Yet a national manner has distinguished the most subtile and inclusive of literary forms in every important era. This is not sustained by curious devices and imitations, however choice and attractive, but by harmonizing personal quality with the national note of expression. I think there is a lack of recognizable and pervasive style in our English poetry of the period ; that, with the exception of the portion which confessedly revives the manners of Queen Anne's time and the Georgian, it is chiefly English in its intense desire to escape from Anglicism.

What does this imply, — style being a visible emblem of spiritual traits, — other than a want, so far *A deduction.*

as poetry can indicate it, of individual and national
purpose? Breadth, passion, and imagination seem to
be the elements least conspicuous in much of the recent song. The new men withdraw themselves from
the movement of their time and country, forgetting
it all in dreamland — in no-man's-land. They compose sonnets and ballads as inexpressive of the reso-
lution of an imperial and stalwart people as are the
figures upon certain modern canvases — the dis-
traught, unearthly youths and maidens that wander
along shadowy meads by nameless streams, with their
eyes fixed on some hand we "cannot see, which
beckons" them away.

*Post
nubila
Phœbus.*

It may be that before we can hope for a return
of poetic vigor some heroic crisis must be endured,
some experience undergone, of more import than the
mock-campaigns in weak and barbarous provinces,
whereby Great Britain preserves her military and col-
onizing traditions, and avoids the stagnation of utter
repose. The grand old realm bids fair to have her
awakening. There are clouds enough to bode sterner
issues and nearer conflicts than she has faced since
Cromwell's time. Ireland is filling men's ears with
her threats and appeals. In a season of jubilee socialists crowd St. Paul's, their banners inscribed with
"Justice and Liberty, or Death"; the Marseillaise
is chorused in London thoroughfares, and London
poets sing — triolets. The wise are not swift to pronounce this troubadour insouciance a mark of ef-
feminacy and declining genius. A great dramatist
makes Combeferre, Jean Prouvaire, and their comrades within the fated barricade, heroes all, while
casting bullets and waiting for the struggle at dawn,
sing — not battle-odes but love-songs. England's

heroism and imagination are not to be judged by her verse at this moment. Whether the Mother of Nations is to be like Niobe, or long with loyal children to rise up and call her blessed, her poets in fit succession will enrich the noblest imaginative literature of any race or tongue, though, peradventure, "after some time be past."

INDEX.

INDEX.

THE END.